Kiss the Boys Goodbye

How the United States Betrayed
Its Own POWs in Vietnam

Monika Jensen-Stevenson and
William Stevenson

With Material from
Captain Eugene "Red" McDaniel
(United States Navy, Retired)

M&S

Canadian Cataloguing in Publication Data

Jensen-Stevenson, Monika
  Kiss the boys goodbye

Includes bibliographical references.
ISBN 0-7710-8326-2

1. Vietnamese Conflict, 1961-1975 – Prisoners and
prisons.   2. Prisoners of war – United States.
3. United States – Politics and government – 1945-
4. Corruption (in politics) – United States.
I. Stevenson, William, 1925-   .   II. McDaniel,
Eugene B.   III. Title.

DS559.4.J46 1990   959.704'37   C90-093292-9

Every effort has been made to contact the copyright holders of material in this book. Any oversights will be corrected in subsequent editions.

Printed and bound in the United States

McClelland & Stewart Inc.
The Canadian Publishers
481 University Avenue
Toronto, Ontario
M5G 2E9

CONTENTS

ACKNOWLEDGMENTS

It is impossible to thank everyone who helped us. Some requested anonymity but in the end decided they would risk their official positions to be identified, since we were all motivated in part by a deep concern that failures in secret intelligence have been too readily hushed by the simple expedient of concealing details for reasons of security. These brave souls now emerge in the text, as do most of our informants. We can only hope this inadequate acknowledgment of their assistance will be seen as much more than a polite thanks.

Among those many good Canadians and Americans who fought in Vietnam, or lost menfolk in the wars of Southeast Asia, and who went to endless trouble to hunt down information, we owe much to Mike Quinn of the Canadian Vietnam Veterans, to Mark Smith, and to members of The Telephone Tree: to Mike Van Atta, Jim Badey, John Brown, Earl Hopper, Jerry Mooney, and to the wives, mothers, and daughters whose integrity and hard work shame the bureaucrats. Congressman Billy Hendon took us through the labyrinths of Capitol Hill procedure. The BBC's David Taylor shared, in the best of old-fashioned journalistic traditions, his extensive files and tapes. Hugh Taylor, a former U.S. Navy fighter pilot who remembered old alliances, gave generously from his own Site 85 research.

General Eugene Tighe, the former director of the U.S. Defense Intelligence Agency, is the heroic figure who remained loyal to the highest principles. He belongs, along with Ross Perot, General "Robbie" Risner, and lawyer Mark Waple, in the ranks of men who made America great. Each in his own way had to gamble a great deal upon our own integrity during a three-year period when none of us was quite sure who else to trust.

American politicians gave us encouragement as well as assistance, even if it meant (as it did for Congressman Hendon) considerable political risk. Senator Charles Grassley and Senator Jesse Helms provided pillars of strength and also research staff whose ability and openness came as a relief: notably Kris Kolesnik and Dan Perrin, who went where ordinary mortals could not go.

Elvus Sasseen of Oklahoma proved that the heart of America is still to be found in the heart of America, and not necessarily presiding over the big news organizations. His energy kept the investigations alive among small town newspapers and radio stations, many of whose editors freely gave us their help and advice.

John Kelly, from the BBC office in Washington, D.C., readily forwarded volumes of research, carefully checked and supported by official documents. Nelly Duncan Lide, at the time an associate producer with *60 Minutes*, in the Washington office, confirmed conversations and lent moral support of immeasurable value. Our professional colleagues could not have been more ready to assist our inquiries.

Perhaps this book will help repay those who spent so many hours of their own time at computers, running down the irregularities and concealment in official papers. Patty Aloot, daughter of a missing American, symbolizes their incredible devotion.

We are indebted to Pat Kennedy, the Canadian editor who worked so hard to lick our manuscript into shape; and to publisher Avie Bennett for having had faith in us. Eugene Scheiman, the New York lawyer, courageously fought our cause; and John Downing bravely gave editorial support in a time when the media has been under every pressure to ignore this story.

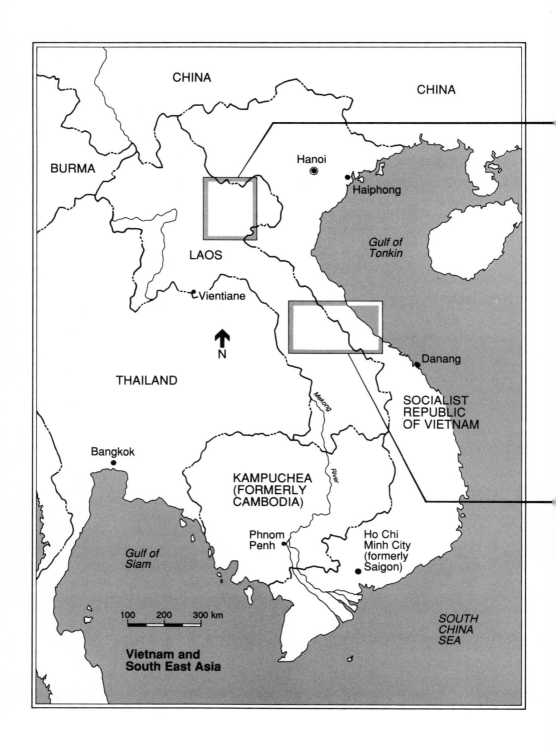

CHINA

CHINA

BURMA

Hanoi

Haiphong

LAOS

Gulf of Tonkin

Vientiane

THAILAND

N

Danang

SOCIALIST
REPUBLIC
OF VIETNAM

Mekong

Bangkok

KAMPUCHEA
(FORMERLY
CAMBODIA)

River

Phnom
Penh

Ho Chi
Minh City
(formerly
Saigon)

*Gulf of
Siam*

100   200   300 km

**Vietnam and
South East Asia**

*SOUTH
CHINA
SEA*

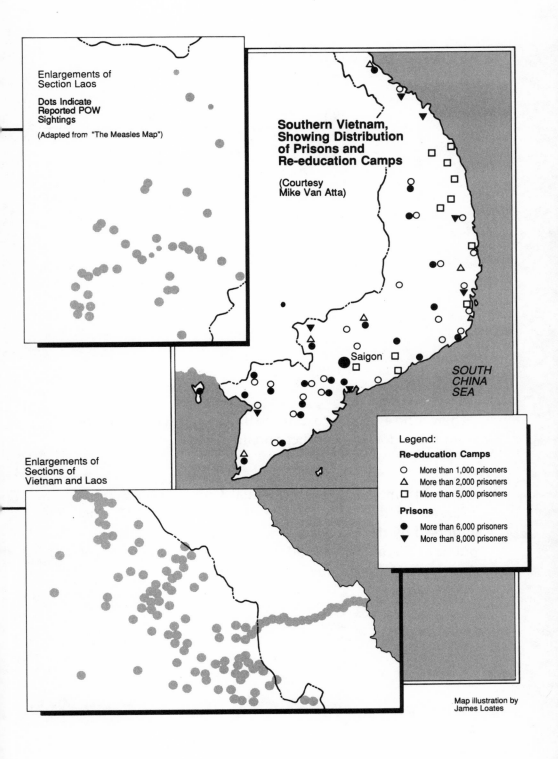

Enlargements of
Section Laos

Dots Indicate
Reported POW
Sightings

(Adapted from "The Measles Map")

**Southern Vietnam,
Showing Distribution
of Prisons and
Re-education Camps**

(Courtesy
Mike Van Atta)

Saigon

SOUTH
CHINA
SEA

Legend:

Re-education Camps

○ More than 1,000 prisoners
△ More than 2,000 prisoners
□ More than 5,000 prisoners

Prisons

● More than 6,000 prisoners
▼ More than 8,000 prisoners

Enlargements of
Sections of
Vietnam and Laos

Map illustration by
James Loates

"There is no evidence to indicate that any American POWs from the Indochina conflict remain alive. . . . "

Quoted from the U.S. Presidential Commission Report, released by the White House on March 23, 1977, and endorsed by the Ministry of Foreign Affairs, Socialist Republic of Vietnam, in a 1980 study entitled: *The Question of Americans Missing in the Vietnam War.*

THE STORY

I was pregnant with my first child when this story began with an episode I produced for CBS TV News's *60 Minutes*. Soon my daughter will be six years old. I am aghast at how she has gone through so many stages since I produced that segment about men who might be dead or alive. For Americans who are among the missing, though, whole lifetimes have passed. Their children are fully grown.

My *60 Minutes* report, aired during the Christmas season of 1985, looked at the possibility that U.S. government spokesmen were not telling the whole truth about men and women of the armed forces being left behind in Vietnam when they said that there was no credible proof that prisoners had been kept by the enemy. President Richard Nixon had promised, on January 23, 1973, that with a ceasefire imminent "all American prisoners-of-war [POWs] throughout Indochina will be released" with "the fullest possible accounting for all those who are missing-in-action [MIAs]." MIAs are American servicemen who were involved in specific battles with the enemy, but who were not acknowledged officially to have been either killed in action (KIA) or taken

1

prisoner by them. In many cases, I found later, their capture and imprisonment was monitored by U.S. intelligence.

I had stirred up a hornets' nest. From all over the United States, and later from abroad, came letters and telephone calls from Vietnam veterans, families of the missing, and serving officers who said they were relieved that finally a powerful news outlet had the courage to deal with a great national scandal.

The last thing I had in mind while preparing the television news-magazine segment was to expose an American scandal. I was so innocent that when I got calls from a National Security Council colonel in the White House to drop the story, weeks before I had completed the necessary interviews, I failed to take his threats seriously. My knowledge of Vietnam was limited to what I had read in the newspapers at the time (much of it forgotten) and to wearing a POW bracelet while I was a student at the University of Wisconsin. The emotional impact went no further than my distress over the disappearance of my friend Lance Sijan, a Phantom pilot who behaved with incredible heroism after he was shot down near Hanoi. For me, "the longest war in American history" had no clearly defined beginning or end.

However, when I began to research the story, I found that much of the background of the POW/MIA issue was already on the record. There were said to be 2,497 unaccounted for by the 1980s, but the figure fluctuated. I quickly learned that President Nixon's promise had not been kept. When prisoners were officially released in the early months of 1973 the enemy gave virtually no accounting of the missing in action. The North Vietnamese released 591 men – far less than anyone expected.

Among those unaccounted for were prisoners lost during the secret war in Laos. It had been a long though un-acknowledged war. When French rule ended in 1954, the enemy had used terrorism and treachery. He routinely ex-ploited neutral territories in Laos and Cambodia to smuggle weapons into South Vietnam – against international agreements. But the U.S. had responded in kind since 1958, six years before Congress passed the 1964 Tonkin Gulf Resolution that formalized U.S. entry into Vietnam. The secret "war" in Laos continued throughout the Vietnam conflict.

In January of 1973, just before the Vietnam peace accords were signed, the Pentagon books carried the names of 317 men missing in Laos. At the same time U.S. government spokesmen were quoted as saying they believed the number was much higher. The Communist Pathet Lao spokesman, Soth Petrasy, told reporters that the Pathet Lao had a detailed accounting of prisoners and where they were being held. He insisted that they would be released only if there was a separate truce agreement between Laos and the United States. Some headlines of the day tell the story: "Pathet Lao says no truce, no American POWs," "Fate of U.S. POWs still a mystery," and "U.S. demands list of POWs in Laos." But the Pathet Lao, were not part of the negotiations for the release of prisoners.

Secretary of State Henry Kissinger insisted to the public that prisoners in Laos would be returned by Hanoi. He maintained this stance despite the fact that Bui Tin, chief spokesman for the North Vietnamese, also insisted the United States must deal for prisoners held in Laos with the Pathet Lao. Tin said, "We clearly reiterate our position that the question of persons captured in Laos is within the sovereign power of Laos and beyond the competence of the four part joint military commission." Despite evidence to the contrary, Kissinger said he had been told there were no POWs in Cambodia.*

Just before the release of the last group of prisoners from Hanoi after peace terms in March of 1973, the Pathet Lao, in a statement laced with undertones of malice, agreed to the

---

* On March 17, 1976, three years after Kissinger had proclaimed there were no prisoners in Cambodia, Lt. Gen. Vernon Walters said, "In Cambodia, several personnel known to have been captured prior to April 1975 have never been accounted for."

release of nine Americans captured by the Vietcong in Laos. Their agreement was redundant. All nine had been captured by, and were in the hands of, the North Vietnamese. No single prisoner captured by the Pathet Lao was ever released. On April 14 Roger Shields, the Pentagon's Prisoner of War Task Force chief, said "there were probably no more live American soldiers loose anywhere in Indochina." Families of the missing claim it was a statement he would later say had been forced on him. Shields said, further, that there was no evidence that any POWs (with three exceptions) had been executed during the war years. So where were the 371 and possibly more men known by the U.S. government to have been captured by the Pathet Lao? There was no answer from any of the governments involved.

The families of these men had become alarmed when, on June 8, 1973, a North Vietnamese defector named Nguyen Thanh Son surfaced. He told AP, UPI, and NBC correspondents that he had seen six prisoners. He believed they were Americans who had not yet been released. An American officer present at the interview requested that news services play down the details. Soon after I began questioning families of MIAs about this press conference, I received a copy of a State Department declassified telegram which persuaded me that the National Security Council move to stop my story was not the first time attempts had been made to silence the media. The telegram, sent from the U.S. embassy in Saigon to Washington, said, "In follow on [defector Nguyen Thanh Son] . . . AP mention was consistent with embargo request, while UPI and NBC after talk with embassy press officer omitted item entirely from their stories."

Missing from the group of men who were returned by the North Vietnamese were over fifty men known by the U.S. government to have been captured and held prisoner at one time or another. Beyond that there was a large number of men suspected of having been captured by the North Vietnamese. Many returning prisoners had seen such men being taken captive or displayed to Vietnamese villagers, but they had never been seen in the prison system. I would learn later that the U.S. government had a list of over one thousand such men – a list that included detailed knowledge of their capture, physical condition, and whereabouts until 1975, when Saigon fell. The United States was able to obtain such information on its prisoners through electronic eavesdropping and its extensive network of Vietnamese agents.

Other prisoners who were not acknowledged were all those whose existence had not been verified by returning prisoners. According to some intelligence analysts who tracked prisoners, the U.S. government knew that many were kept in remote prison camps, although it listed such men in the MIA category. Some of those prisons and camps were especially geared for technical talents – highly skilled American servicemen who had expertise in fields like electronic warfare, about which the North Vietnamese and their Soviet and Chinese allies needed information. Some of those special talents were put to work in highly secret North Vietnamese war projects; others were farmed out to the Soviet Union or China. Amputees, the emotionally disturbed, and other seriously maimed prisoners were kept in special camps from which not one prisoner returned. Most astounding, some prisoners were actually hidden in the main prison compounds in Hanoi. One such man, Air Force Colonel Norman Gaddis, who was shot down on May 12, 1967, did appear on the 1973 list of returnees – unexpectedly. He had never been accounted for by the Vietnamese. Yet for almost four and a half years he was kept in a section of the prison known as "Heartbreak Hotel". In all that time no other American prisoner had seen him. If he had not finally been spotted by other prisoners after the Vietnamese moved POWs and consolidated them in several key locations because of the attempted Son Tay raid to rescue prisoners on November 21, 1970, Gaddis would probably have ended up an MIA.

I learned of another group who never came home. Hearing of *60 Minutes'* plan for a segment on MIAs, a few families contacted me about a subject they had held close to their hearts for twelve years. Their men had been sent on missions, primarily in Laos and Cambodia, after the peace accords were signed on January 27, 1973. Some of these men had voiced their objections to base commanders, because they feared that if they were caught by the enemy in contravention of the Geneva Agreements, they would be charged as war criminals. The families who came to me had excellent intelligence information that their men had not been killed in action but had been captured.

After the ceasefire, the U.S. had demanded from the Vietnamese and the Laotians lists of all prisoners on their records. It was made clear that the Vietnamese were expected to return all prisoners captured by their allies. I was shocked when I was told that some of those prisoners, captured in Laos after the ceasefire and known by the U.S. negotiating team, through the efforts of U.S. intelligence eavesdroppers, to be alive and in captivity, were first pencilled in on the list of prisoners that were demanded from the Vietnamese and then crossed off. To acknowledge them would have meant acknowledging the continuing involvement of the United States in covert wars in Laos and Cambodia. I was told by the families that some Department of Defense officials were so disturbed by this that they registered their objections in writing. Those documents, I was told, were classified.

It was easy for me to understand why the Pathet Lao would continue to hold prisoners who had not been negotiated for by the U.S. government or who were caught in contravention of the peace agreements. It was harder to understand why the Vietnamese would hold on to prisoners after the peace was signed. Then I learned this was not the first time the Vietnamese Communist government had kept prisoners long after a conflict ended. French POWs were sold for many years after the French-Indochina war, for cash and other concessions. They were called "pearls."

A former foreign service officer in Vietnam, considered to be one of the foremost experts on the French POW/MIA experience, testified before a 1976 House Select Committee that two hundred French POWs were released by the Vietnamese some eleven to fourteen years after the war. The Socialist Republic of Vietnam had never admitted holding them. She suggested to the Committee that American government representatives speak to the Vietnamese not about prisoners, but about deserters, or better yet "war criminals," since the Vietnamese had categories for such men, but none for prisoners. The French had paid an unrevealed but supposedly large sum for French remains and the maintenance of French graves and cemeteries in Vietnam, she said.

It seemed that the U.S. government had expected to bargain for prisoners, but somewhere along the road, abandoned the idea. Article 20 of the Peace Agreement stated:

> The United States anticipates that this agreement will usher in an era of reconciliation with the Democratic Republic of Vietnam as with all the peoples of Indo-China. In pursuance of its traditional policy, the U.S. will contribute to healing the wounds of war and to post war reconstruction. . . .*

President Nixon reinforced that pledge with a secret promise of four and one-half billion aid dollars in a letter to Prime Minister Pham Van Dong on February 1, 1973. That letter was not released until four years later. The promise of reconstruction aid was never kept, largely because Congress, an-

---

* On February 21, 1973, a peace agreement between the Laotian Provisional National Union government and the Pathet Lao was signed. The agreement also took note of a promise of aid from the U.S. government. Article 1, Sect. c. read: "The two parties take note of the declaration of the U.S. Government that it will contribute to healing the wounds of the war and to post-war reconstruction in Indo-China. The Provisional National Union Government will hold discussions with the U.S. Government in connexion with such a contribution regarding Laos."

gered by reports from returning prisoners of war of torture and mistreatment by Hanoi, would never grant such aid. Because of Watergate and his attendant resignation, Nixon lost all possibility of arranging fund transfers from other programs. The promises that were not kept rankled the Vietnamese Communists. Time and again they were to hint during negotiations that the prisoner issue was tied to the promised reconstruction aid.

Over the next twelve years, scores of Vietnamese refugees told stories of prisoners who were held back as "pearls," but who were never bargained for by the U.S. government. There were stories that the Vietnamese aired statements made by U.S. government officials who claimed there were no more prisoners in Southeast Asia, in order to humiliate and torture prisoners who had been left behind.

The fact that prisoner returns were intimately connected to payment of reconstruction funds was clearly understood by the 1976 House Select Committee on Missing Persons in Southeast Asia. On December 13 of that year the members concluded their report, *Americans Missing in Southeast Asia,* with the following statement:

> That the Socialist Republic of Vietnam has called for selective implementation of the Paris Peace Agreement specifically article 21 dealing with American reconstruction aid to Vietnam in exchange for POW/MIA information under article 8b. (p. 239).

Over the years that knowledge received little attention from committees on Capitol Hill. Perhaps lawmakers were too busy, but it seemed to some families as if a war of attrition was being waged against the men who had been left behind. No matter how much solid intelligence was obtained that men were alive and imprisoned in Vietnam, some government official or committee would find a way to negate it — even when those intelligence chiefs in charge of the issue declared that they too believed men to be alive and imprisoned in Indochina.

What started as possibly an error of judgment, or an act of political expediency, grew with the passing years into a conviction that national security would be hurt by the disclosure that U.S. intelligence capabilities, which were formidable, had failed to serve the men who fight.

Hundreds of refugees reported seeing American prisoners in all parts of Communist Southeast Asia in the early postwar years. Some of those refugees had spent time in prison with Americans. A few of them took their responsibility to report what they had seen seriously enough to testify under oath before congressional committees. Analysts at the Pentagon's Defense Intelligence Agency (DIA), often took seriously one part of a witness's testimony only to debunk that part having to do with live men. For example, in the early eighties a former Vietnamese colonel of Chinese descent testified in disguise before a congressional committee about a warehouse of remains of over four hundred Americans in the heart of Hanoi. He explained the Vietnamese would cold-heartedly pull out some of those remains and return them to the United States when diplomatic concessions were required. The colonel, known as "The Mortician," passed lie-detector tests, and his story about the remains became part of DIA formal history. Yet a retired DIA official told me that The Mortician had been just as truthful about live prisoners. He had testified that he personally saw groups of prisoners on numerous occasions before he fled Vietnam in 1979. That part of his testimony, even though he had passed all interrogations and lie-detector tests with flying colours, was determined to be a fabrication.

There was an effort to steer anyone with an interest away from the subject of living men. It took me a long time to see that the issue was larger than the roughly 2,500 MIAs admitted to by the U.S. government.

My real education began after the *60 Minutes* broadcast. The show had presented two sides of an argument. One was that there was no credible evidence that anybody had been left behind from among loyal, serving Americans. This was the government case, but officials covered themselves by adding, "If any are still there, getting them back is a priority – unless they're deserters and traitors." The opposing view was that our intelligence on prisoners was voluminous but never put to use: two highly qualified Special Forces men said the intelligence was suppressed.

My husband had many friends in the military and intelligence. So did I. He also had a great deal of experience in Southeast Asia. He could assess the growing complaints reaching my office that secret intelligence was not serving those it was meant to serve. Vietnam marked the blossoming of covert warfare. If the men who fight these wars cannot depend on the intelligence services, they have justification for asking awkward questions.

Those who contacted me were driven by anger and concern for the defense of their country. Their misgivings had crystallized around the POW/MIA issue because many proffered detailed knowledge of how American intelligence on prisoners had never been acted upon. I might have dismissed their allegations if I had not received those curious NSC threats; and if, after *60 Minutes* ran my segment on prisoners, a Pentagon publication had not appeared, exclusively devoted to branding as liars all those who had appeared on the program to state their belief that, based on the best possible current intelligence, prisoners were still being held by the Vietnamese and their allies.

Kinfolk of the missing, and the doubting vets, lacked the resources of a national broadcast-news network. I could call upon such resources, but I was to experience a milder and briefer version of the nightmare of frustration experienced by these Americans. Intelligence documents were declassified, then hastily reclassified when the critics pointed out discrepancies and demanded answers. Some vets with experience in electronic intelligence in Southeast Asia had started to build complex information networks. By 1989 these networks were described by one former intelligence officer, Colonel Earl Hopper, Sr., as "better than the intelligence resources at

DIA" – even though the Defense Intelligence Agency had the task of coordinating all intelligence on the missing. Colonel Hopper's son, also a colonel, was still among the missing.

The DIA director, through the toughest war years and long afterwards, was Lt. Gen. Eugene Tighe, who told me flatly that he had seen the best possible evidence of Americans still alive. For speaking out, he was publicly humiliated.

He was not alone among senior officers whose audacity was punished when they failed to toe the official line. Yet they had to confide to somebody. They peeled away my innocence. First I learned never to ask direct questions when mysterious references were made to outfits like ISA, MACV, SOG, CCN, or SLAM.* Bit by bit, I discovered these were units with roots in a special secret service created in 1958, nominally under the South Vietnamese president, and supported and financed by the Central Intelligence Agency.

I found that intelligence on prisoners had been efficiently collected; so much so that today, more than fourteen years after the U.S. evacuation of Saigon, all Vietnam is laced with grapevines of human intelligence on prison camps – on who is in them, and on who runs them. Yet despite the intelligence and despite the existence of a special unit designed to rescue them, no American military prisoner was ever officially brought out. POWs and MIAs seemed to be getting lost in what many military men considered an ever-increasing isolation of intelligence agencies.

A friend of my husband, with intelligence experience going back to World War II, suddenly resigned from the CIA. He had quarreled with the Director, Bill Casey, the year before Casey died in 1987. Casey, he said, tampered with intelligence reports, and slanted them to suit White House thinking. It wasn't in the spirit of the words at the entrance to CIA headquarters in Langley, Virginia, which quoted the biblical promise that "ye shall know the Truth, and the Truth shall make you free."

---

*   For further details on these units see pp. 181-2 and the glossary.

My husband's friend had held one of the most sensitive posts. Now he was discarded, implying serious problems in the agency. This was a difficult conclusion for my husband to reach. He had liked Casey as CIA director.

A new director, Judge William Webster, appeared before Senate Intelligence Committee hearings on April 8, 1987. The committee, judging Webster's fitness for the new task, asked him what his philosophy on intelligence might be. Webster said he could add nothing to what my husband had written in his book *A Man Called Intrepid*: "Among the increasingly intricate arsenals across the world, intelligence is an essential weapon, perhaps the most dangerous. Safeguards against its abuse must be devised, revised, and rigidly applied. . . . The character and wisdom of those to whom it is entrusted will be decisive. . . . "

Americans really have little opportunity to know if they have abdicated a small part of their freedom to people they *should* trust. They dutifully refrain from poking their noses into national secrets, confident that those who guard them are doing the best possible job with the greatest integrity. The armed services, in turn, need the best possible intelligence to carry out their duties. They deserve first consideration. If an American is taken prisoner, he should know that he will get the full and non-political attention of his country's formidable intelligence resources. Admiral William Crowe said at his retirement as Chairman of the Joint Chiefs of Staff in the autumn of 1989, "We need first and foremost the best possible intelligence." He should have added, "And the integrity to act upon it for the good of all the people." Without integrity, secrecy can become a license for opportunists to distort and corrupt the system. It suddenly struck me that, for once, ordinary Americans could get a sense of how effective these intelligence services were from the way the POW/MIA issue had been handled.

My husband knew something about such things. He had extracted a Canadian fighter pilot from China, where Communist officials swore they knew nothing of the flier's existence. He had talked to French prisoners in Communist Vietnam, long after Hanoi and Paris jointly agreed that none existed.

What we could not understand, as we went along, was the intelligence bureaucrats' fear of re-examining their own performance. Were there deep reasons for hoping the issue would die in time, just as death in time must release all Americans left behind? Or was it merely a military *morale* problem?

One ordinary American who felt she could break the usual conventions of secrecy was Ann Holland. Her husband, Melvin, had vanished at a super-secret base in Laos. He was not in uniform, and technically there wasn't a war there. Ann had obeyed all the demands made upon her by the U.S. Air Force officials to stay silent. Then she discovered that nothing at all was being done for her husband; and she would not be jeopardizing any rescue operations, which she thought were in progress, if she made waves. She was like a growing number of Americans who gladly surrendered a part of their independence in the interests of "national security," but who decided that, on this issue, they had every right to ask questions in public and demand replies from public institutions.

She wrote me after seeing the *60 Minutes* segment: "The pain the families have had to live with. . . . The nights, the sleepless nights . . . I would find my youngest child wandering through the house looking for something. Looking in closets, cupboards . . . and when I asked what he was looking for, he didn't know. . . . "

Her children have grown up with a ghost for a father. Ann would write me again: "Two of my sons now serve in the Air Force. If I quit asking questions now, who will be there for them if their time comes? This is *our* country and if the people running it aren't doing their very best, then they need to be reminded of what this country stands for. We do *not* leave men behind who gave all they had to give when they were asked, believing we would give all we had to give to get them back."

Not all my sources put things down on paper. I taped many conversations and to give a sense of just a few of the stories of courageous Americans like Ann, they are quoted to illuminate both the issue of POWs and the abuses of secrecy. Some of our sources were afraid to be identified. In the end, however, most decided to risk their careers or harassment, and agreed to let me use their names.

I am not by nature secretive, or cautious. But since that seemingly innocent entry into a secretive world five years ago, I have learned not to take things at face value. One of my tutors was Ross Perot, who is much more than a Texan entrepreneur. He displayed a grim resolve to get to the bottom of the POW/MIA issue from the moment he realized the numbers of prisoners returned in 1973 were inexplicably small.

I called him one day about an inquiry from a "federal government investigator." The man wanted to question me about possible crimes involving U.S. officials in Southeast Asia. He gave me his office phone numbers and his official designation. Perot used his resources to probe. He called me back. "If there's such a government department, I'll buy you the biggest steak in Texas," he said.

Perot had to pay up. We discovered there was an investigative service buried within the General Accounting Office in Washington, D.C. It had no authority, though, to dispatch agents to find out what I might know. I rejected the man, who had asked me to cooperate in "a matter of national security." He then showed his true colors. "You'd better be sure to tell the truth in your book," he said. I had never told him I was writing a book.

So many of our sources had similar stories to tell. Calls in the night. Veiled warnings. I didn't believe them. Not in the beginning. In the end, I kept going for the same reason that motivated Ross Perot. It was "the right thing to do."

It seemed the right thing to do because so many of the POW/MIA families and the veterans of the war had never had the opportunity to tell their side of the story. Since 1981, the government, including the official organization designed to deal with the issue, had said that the issue of POWS and MIAs had the highest priority, but that there had been no credible evidence of men left alive in captivity that was strong enough to act on. They had many outlets for telling their side of the story and they had the advantage, because so much of the material on POW/MIAs remains classified.

The secrecy that cloaks the issue has led many people to conclude that there are some in the government who don't want the truth to come out. The natural question that arises is "Why?"

There are undoubtedly many reasons behind the reluctance of officials to look seriously at the allegations of those most directly involved in the issue. Some of those responsible have been caught up in bureaucratic inertia, some have acted on directives that they thought were legal and appropriate, others have acted from a moral and professional belief that the POW/MIA issue could be resolved properly only if national-security concerns were paramount, and some have seemed motivated primarily by a desire to defeat Vietnam and its allies in Cambodia, and have tied the POW/MIA issue to the resolution of that situation. Some have possibly believed that activists might compromise government efforts to get men back – either through rescue missions or relocation. Some have engaged in Iran-Contra-like activities, demonstrating the same confusion of motives that were revealed during those hearings. Just as with Iran-Contra, it is almost impossible to say which bureaucrats and which government departments were responsible for specific actions.

However, pinpointing motives and pointing the finger at individuals was never the object of this book. That is the job of the appropriate government agencies. We wanted to give voice to those Americans who had not been heard and who seemed to have good cause to criticize and to demand an overhaul of a system that stalled whenever they asked for a proper accounting of their friends and loved ones lost in Southeast Asia.

CHAPTER 1

TRAITOR

In 1985 I had been a producer at the CBS TV news-magazine *60 Minutes* for five years. Home was in the Georgetown area of Washington, D.C., and I often walked to my office at 20th and M streets, even after learning I was pregnant. My husband, William Stevenson, seemed happy to live wherever he could write his books undisturbed. Sometimes I wondered if there was anywhere he had *not* lived both as a fighter pilot in the British navy during World War II and as a foreign correspondent. He had reported from inside most of the Communist countries from Poland to Ho Chi Minh's Vietnam and had spent fifteen years in Asia as a foreign and war correspondent. He had written a number of books about national movements and counter-terrorism, such as *Ninety Minutes at Entebbe* and *A Man Called Intrepid*. If I could not reach someone by going through *60 Minutes'* files, I generally could by going through his contact book.

One morning, as I entered my office and checked for messages, I found a scribbled card from Angie Prijic, my classmate at college. She was writing to say that someone in

16

Indochina had found an Air Force Academy ring belonging to Lance Sijan, a Phantom pilot we had known when we were at school. Why, she was wondering, would his ring show up eighteen years after he disappeared in Vietnam? She had heard conflicting reports on rescue missions.

It was an intriguing question, but a busy day loomed ahead. I turned to a more immediate matter: Lucille Ball. Her press agent had called to confirm an interview if we still wanted to do it. Fred Astaire's press agent also had a good idea for a segment. It would be fun to produce a show biz item for once.

However, Don Hewitt, our executive producer at *60 Minutes*, phoned from the New York center to say he couldn't go for a profile on Lucille Ball. She had been part of the CBS stable of talent, but she didn't fit *60 Minutes'* criteria – not enough of a legend. Fred Astaire? There was a star Hewitt loved, and whose name was already in the history books. "Go for Astaire!" he said. "Forget Lucille Ball."

Hewitt had an uncanny instinct for what kept fifty million viewers watching our show each Sunday night. He combined street smarts with years of television and journalistic experience. He might seem to fly by the seat of his pants, but his one hour of prime time generated a quarter of the CBS network's profits, said his admirers. He had held only one meeting since he started at *60 Minutes* some twenty years earlier. Conferences took the form of ideas barked on the run, strangled shouts in the screening room, yelps of the wounded when Hewitt and the lawyers, the brass, the producers, and the correspondents battled over weekly segments that were usually around fourteen minutes in length. It always amazed me how much drama Hewitt could compress into so short a span of air time, or within such narrow corridors. He was as disdainful of routine as only a $2-million-a-year man could afford to be, as *Vanity Fair* once observed with undisguised envy.

I reached for Astaire's file and, on my way through the A's, prepared to put away Angie's card under A for Angie. I had opened her file a few months before, in late 1984, after she told me Lance Sijan had been awarded a posthumous Medal of Honor.

I felt a surge of pride. Angie and I wore prisoner-of-war bracelets with Lance's name on them at the University of Wisconsin. He was twenty-five in 1967 when he dragged his way for forty-six days and nights through the Vietnamese jungle with a smashed leg and broken hands.

"No one's ever told his story," Angie had said.

The medal was for the way he resisted torture and mental thuggee. Prisoners who did come home described his resistance as awesome. It was a great story. But for *60 Minutes*? Ed Bradley, the correspondent I had been assigned to work with, was amused. Profile a dead Medal of Honor winner from the Vietnam War? Not in 1985.

However, something about Lance Sijan's story bothered me. And now here was Angie with rumors of a rescue mission and retrieval of Lance's ring. Funny that nothing official was ever said. Trust Angie to ferret out awkward facts. She'd become a psychologist, working among down-and-outs in city slums, and although she was the busy mother of three children, she remained the kind of person who would look unflinchingly at things others preferred not to see.

My husband, Bill, did not get involved in my work. As a writer, he found my stories could be a terrible distraction. However, when I told him about it, the mystery of Lance Sijan's ring intrigued him as well. He was going to Thailand on a writing assignment. Could he inquire into the rumors Angie had passed along? It was said that U.S. rescue missions had been launched from Thailand into the Communist territories.

"I'll drop by Lucy's Tiger Den in Bangkok," he offered. He generally knew what watering hole to visit in a foreign place. He had spent part of his life rubbing shoulders with intelligence spooks. His father had worked in Nazi-occupied France with the Resistance networks. Bill had worked in strife-torn Malaysia while wars raged in neighboring Indochina. I felt I could reasonably draw upon his experience just this one time.

Before he got within ten thousand miles of Lucy's Tiger Den, though, a letter came to Ed Bradley from Bill Davison and Kyle R. Eddings in Pennsylvania. *"60 Minutes* continues to be concerned about human rights in every country except the United States," it said. "Why can't – or why won't – *60 Minutes* cover Americans missing in Southeast Asia? 2,483 are still there. . . . "

The letter was routinely investigated by a *60 Minutes* researcher who told me, "The government says it's nonsense. *There are no Americans left alive and held against their will."* Usually a researcher's report satisfied me, but I found this issue was nagging at my mind.

I decided to follow up Angie's lead with a few questions for the Pentagon. I was particularly curious about a Green Beret colonel, Bo Gritz, who was reported to have led a mission in 1981 to recover American servicemen left behind in Southeast Asia. His service record made him sound like a resourceful, highly decorated commando type who had carried out daring behind-the-lines operations in the Vietnam War. General William C. Westmoreland, after commanding U.S. forces in Vietnam, singled out Gritz as the quintessential American soldier hero in his memoirs.* But now one of my contacts sent me a *Soldier of Fortune* magazine with the cover headline: "Bo Gritz: Hero or Huckster?" Inside was a savage attack on Gritz, claiming that the rescue mission was a Gritz fantasy, typical of the barroom tales in Lucy's Tiger Den.

It was not uncommon for me to be casually interested in a potential story and then find myself tripping over relevant bits of information wherever I turned. Most reporters know the feeling. Either a significant bit of luck or a meaningless string of coincidences is at work.

One night I was at an informal dinner given by a highly respected former CIA official who had become a good friend. Among the guests were a number of journalists, a former CIA station chief, a Soviet expert, a counter-intelligence specialist,

---

* Westmoreland devoted a chapter to Gritz in *A Soldier Reports* (Garden City, N.Y., Doubleday 1976).

and Cord Meyer, such an old hand in diplomacy and intelligence that the *New York Times* had profiled him on January 7, 1973, as a man who had made a long journey from idealistic hopes for world unity to "the Department of Dirty Tricks." Newspapers had quoted Meyer as talking openly about his success in carrying out a CIA assignment to discredit a book alleging CIA involvement in the illegal drug trade.*

Later, one of the guests came to me. "Bo Gritz is an unmitigated liar," he said.

I felt a stab of unease. Maybe Bill should avoid Lucy's Tiger Den. He was going up-country to research a book. Why get him tangled up with Bo Gritz, rescue missions, and a ring?

"It's such a nice project you're starting," I said to him when he telephoned later that night. "Forget Lucy's."

"If you keep to nice assignments."

He did not want a pregnant wife producing more of what Hewitt called "the dirty-face stories." One, about a notorious killer, had won me an Emmy. Frothy subjects would be welcome now. Why make something of what was probably just coincidence? It was silly to think the government was out to make Gritz seem loony to me just because someone had sent me that critical article about him in *Soldier of Fortune* magazine and a former intelligence man had appeared to make a particular point of calling him an unmitigated liar.

A few days later, working on a segment about the Shoreham nuclear plant on Long Island and the mob's involvement in faulty construction, I pulled an old memo from my research files in the New York office. "A Marine keeps trying to talk about Americans we abandoned in Vietnam," I had written. "The Marine came out of Communist hands

---

* *The Politics of Heroin in Southeast Asia* by Alfred W. McCoy (New York, Harper and Row, 1972) was condemned by CIA sources as pro-Communist propaganda. It was selling very well, in a Singapore edition, throughout Southeast Asia in 1990.

belonged to U.S. servicemen. I couldn't understand why the Pentagon was so vehement.

I soon discovered that it wasn't just Garwood or Asians who said Americans were left behind. It was being said publicly by sober citizens like Ross Perot, the Texan billionaire who was a member of President Reagan's Foreign Intelligence Advisory Board. He was also rumored to have privately financed missions to rescue prisoners in Asia. Perot denied this when I spoke to him, but he remained adamant that there was current intelligence on live American POWs.

I started to ask around Washington about rescue missions. Nobody would officially admit there had been any. I could understand that public statements might jeopardize ongoing secret operations, but another U.S. Army colonel, Nick Rowe, of special intelligence operations, soon told me all rescue efforts had been stopped years ago. He gave me details of a Delta raid that was aborted in 1981 after top-level intervention. "We had precise intelligence on the camp, we had our men ready to strike from an Asian base, we knew how to pluck out the Americans in captivity. And we were ordered to stand down. . . . " When I asked why, Colonel Rowe stared at me for a long time before framing a single word: "Conspiracy." He would not elaborate.

Confirmation of the information Rowe gave me also came from Larry O'Daniel, a former army intelligence officer in Vietnam, who had written a book, *Missing in Action: Trail of Deceit*. He told me that, in 1981, a former intelligence chief, who had advised Reagan in the transition period between his election and inauguration, had told him they had positive proof that seven prisoners were alive and were planning a rescue effort.

I was expecting my baby in March. At the end of February, the doctor forbade further travel. The Garwood story seemed to fit my domestic plans. The bluesheet had been approved. It could be researched in Washington.

I began by reading through transcripts of the Garwood court martial. The trial *had* been unfair, the judge, Colonel Switzer, agreed when I spoke again with him. The CIA's original lie-detector expert confided that he thought Garwood a victim of "a far-reaching conspiracy."

Now I had to find Garwood. The Marine Corps still kept him on the books, but no base would have him. Was there any address where I could find him? The Corps shrugged its collective shoulders. No.

Surely his pay must be mailed somewhere? No. The Marines were holding it back, together with all medical benefits.

I finally discovered him pumping gas in rural Virginia. This black-market job was his only way of keeping body and soul together. He hadn't been released by the Marines – but they weren't paying him either. His wages at the garage were low, but he was in no position to bargain; it was a no-win situation. He seemed scarcely able to talk in English. He'd been sent to Vietnam in his teens and came back fourteen years later in early middle age. Even if the Marines had let him off the hook, he was virtually unemployable on the basis of his Marine medical report: it recounted a formidable list of disabilities as the result of his years among jungle Communists. Military physicians, with no ax to grind, declared him to be suffering *more* than the usual list of ills after long confinement in tropical jungles. Wouldn't a collaborator be in better shape?

His manner toward me was hostile. There seemed small prospect of a *60 Minutes* interview. He had already turned down Morley Safer, who I assumed had approached him through his lawyer. I realized Garwood was guided by combat veterans of the Vietnam War, since they provided a constant bodyguard when he talked to strangers. That seemed odd. A so-called traitor, protected by fellow soldiers? And what were they protecting him against?

On March 22, four days before the baby's birth, I walked over to the National Press Club, where Garwood's supporters had called a press conference. The club was practically within shouting distance of the White House, which was about as close as these vets felt the disgraced Marine would ever get to the chief occupant. The bureaucrats in the Pentagon had blocked all other channels, they said. They hoped the media would carry Bobby's message about POWs left behind in Vietnam to the President.

Garwood was easily intimidated by the newsmen and still had his eerie Vietnamese accent. They wanted to know why he'd waited so long to speak. One of his supporters said, "Bobby's still a prisoner. The Marines haven't paid him in twenty-one years, but they keep him on a leash."

"At least they haven't executed him for what he did," sneered a reporter.

Garwood said he had personal knowledge of live POWs, but would give details only to appropriate officials of the U.S. government – if the information would lead to their being rescued. He did not want to make any more information public, fearing the Vietnamese would kill any prisoners he identified. It was an unfortunate stance to take with the reporters. As I watched, I was intrigued yet again by the fact that he held the loyalty of the ex-soldiers and provoked the dislike of civilians who had no battlefield experience. That was an odd turnabout. A soldier accused of joining the enemy is usually shunned by former comrades.

One of Garwood's protectors joined me on the sidewalk outside the press club. A March wind blustered down 14th Street. He said, "Why doesn't *60 Minutes* do the Bobby Garwood story?" Then he added, "Aw, the government'd make you back off."

"Nobody makes us back off!"

"I'll give you a chance to prove that," said the ex-soldier.

His name was Mike Van Atta – one of the most unlikely characters to have rallied to Garwood's side. A reporter at the press conference told me that Colonel Richard Childress, a National Security man in the White House, had called Van Atta "a royal pain in the butt – he wants to fight the Vietnam War all over again – with U.S. bureaucrats as the enemy." As an army ranger, he had carried out deep-penetration jungle missions, and the judgment among his peers was that "Mike's pure gold – the bravest of the brave." He now ran his own energy and construction business near the federal capital. Like other vets, and with a young and growing family, he had to scramble to make up for the lost years. In addition, he paid a heavy price in time and effort for his involvement in a newsletter he published, *The Insider*. It specialized in helping the families of missing men understand how to read the obfuscations of intelligence bureaucrats, and extract information on prisoners from "secret" files. The National Vietnam Veterans' Coalition had put up the money for Garwood's unsuccessful press conference, but it seemed Van Atta was the man who could best help to arrange an effective one-on-one interview. He said Garwood's poor performance before the reporters was a result of being degraded by the enemy first, and then by his own countrymen. Van Atta promised to get back to me.

While waiting to hear from Van Atta about a Garwood interview, I found an authority whose word opened up a whole new range of possibilities. This was General Eugene Tighe, former Director of the Pentagon's U.S. Defense Intelligence Agency. Among its heavy global responsibilities, DIA was also required "to pursue and analyze all intelligence pertaining to the POW/MIA issue." The man who had directed this effort in the key years now told me that he was convinced Garwood was right. "There *are* other live Americans over there," said Tighe, one of the handful of men in the world who had peered into secrets of the enemy's mind and weaponry. "When I look at satellite pictures of Soviet silos," he added, "I don't have to see the missiles to know they are there."

I had my baby: a girl, Alexandra, on March 26, 1985. A week later I returned to the office to find a letter from a former "Raven." He explained that Ravens were U.S. aviators who flew in covert operations in Asia. He'd heard about my interest in Garwood and recommended I see what he considered a Communist propaganda film that would show "how the poor guy was brainwashed."

The film had never been shown in America, so I called the London office of an East German film outfit for a copy and renewed contact with Garwood through an elaborate system of phone calls set up by his champions. He had isolated himself again. His voice on the phone was that of a severely depressed man. The Vietnamese accent was stronger than before. But he'd heard about the baby, and this seemed to be what broke through his defenses. The quality of his voice changed as soon as he questioned me about it. I learned later that the one thing he had desperately wanted was a child of his own.

He finally agreed to see me again, provided he was accompanied by the vets. He did not want to be seen talking to a journalist alone. He would come to my home with the vets; and if anyone else wanted to know why, it was to visit the baby.

While I was waiting to see Garwood, the film from East Germany arrived. It consisted of short clips from a longer documentary movie that seemed to suggest that Garwood was a well-treated friend and collaborator of the Communist Vietnamese. He appeared as a whey-faced, stooped native. He stumbled through Hanoi markets, talking to the peasants in Vietnamese, and showed off a ramshackle "apartment," luxurious by Vietnamese standards, that was supposedly his own, though later he claimed to me that he saw it for the first time when the film was made. He responded like a robot in stilted English to questions asked by what sounded like an American.

I determined to ask Garwood about the film at our meeting. However, when he arrived a few nights later, and I saw his almost frightened demeanor, I decided to postpone my questions. The vets charged into my house, bundling him along with them. He seemed passive, responding only to their prodding. I explained how *60 Minutes* worked, and that this was just a preliminary discussion, for background.

Over the next three hours Garwood rambled about his fourteen years in Communist hands. He had been in Vietnam almost half his life, a proportion that was difficult for me to imagine. He spoke mainly about how he had made his way in Vietnam, since his success had been used against him at his trial. He swallowed words as if he feared they might betray him. Yet, despite the ramblings, he made it clear that when the war was long over, he had learned to survive in the camps by his wits, and by exploiting an enormous black-market operation run by Communist backsliders. Garwood's skills as a mechanic were used by the Vietnamese to repair vehicles left behind by the U.S. armed forces. To carry out these missions he was allowed out of detention. Because of his uncanny ability with the language, he was able to make his way in Vietnamese society.

However, Bobby had never given up hope of finding a chance to escape. He said, "The Communists now trusted me – but also, they didn't. They always had guards on me when I was allowed out. I'd be taken to wherever a vehicle broke down, so I could repair it on the spot to save fuel. I'd accomplished what I set out to do, which was getting out of camp. But the guards were over me like hawks. Security was tighter outside than in the camps. I had to create a circumstance."

His circumstance became Hanoi's black market. After 1975, he'd learned through the gossip of army drivers that China, Russia, and Eastern Europe had reduced aid. Hanoi regularly hosted foreign diplomats from neutral countries. A black market flourished there, trading in smuggled goods and whatever the foreign diplomats wanted to buy or sell. Vietnamese Communists would try to earn hard Western currencies by supplying Russian vodka, for instance. With the currency they got from diplomats, they bought black-market Vietnamese currency, or *dongs*, making quite handsome profits.

"I found the Vietnamese were no different to drivers in our army. These guys smuggled all kinds of stuff – tires, gas tanks, watches. . . . My mind started working. But I didn't know that much about Hanoi."

Later, during this long evening at my house, Garwood became agitated. He was talking about his first attempt to escape after twelve years in captivity. Border conflicts with China created another "possibility of a circumstance". The Vietnamese were rounding up Chinese as potential traitors and shipped some to Yen Bai, then Garwood's camp. He became friends with Nana, a nineteen-year-old Chinese girl who had run a coffee shop in central Hanoi. Talking with her, he realized she knew which hotels were used by foreigners – Swedes, Cubans, Algerians, Russians . . . He had a glimpse of hope. If he got a message for help into neutral hands, he was sure his government would come to fetch him, somehow.

By advising Garwood, and introducing him to her contacts, Nana made it possible for him to smuggle a note to one of the Hanoi hotels. Soon after, Garwood was suddenly frog-marched to the parade ground for "an execution." Was it to be his own? Prisoners were never sure. It was one of the many methods used by his captors to keep prisoners off balance. He found himself staring at Nana, roped to the execution tree. "Six men emptied their AK-47s into her while I watched," he said. "I hadn't had the courage even to acknowledge her. I just stood, paralyzed. She never realized the significance of what she'd done. I had used her. They accused her of being a CIA operative." He began to shake, and got up abruptly.

I followed him out onto the street. At that hour, on O Street between 30th and 31st, there were few passersby. From the porch, I saw a man under a street light. Mike Van Atta, who had come with Garwood, joined me and said, "He's shadow-ing Bobby." Then Van Atta laughed self-consciously. "You'll think I'm paranoid."

I said no, I didn't. But I did walk over to get a better look at the watcher. He stared insolently back. I was about to speak to him when he turned and walked abruptly away. Another figure broke from the shadow of the house once owned by Senator John F. Kennedy. The first watcher joined him and together they stood at the corner of 31st, waiting.

"Is anyone trying to unnerve you?" I asked Garwood. He shrugged and went inside. I felt foolish. He'd spent most of his adult life under close, incessant, and hostile scrutiny. He was used to it.

Later, after they left, I outlined this meeting very carefully in a memo for Ed Bradley. It raised real questions about Garwood's status in Vietnam. Despite pressure from other MIA families, no one at the court martial had questioned the government view that he was *not* a returned prisoner but a deserter. I was convinced he was one of those American prisoners who had been unaccounted for and abandoned in 1973. If he had collaborated, it took place after 1973. He really might have won his freedom by the use of considerable ingenuity. There was a good possibility he was telling the truth about other prisoners.

Garwood's escape must have embarrassed Washington and Hanoi. Hanoi had declared to two U.S. presidential commissions that *no* Americans were left in Vietnam – and Washington had accepted it. When I queried them the State Department had denied all knowledge of Garwood's first appeal for help in 1977. State seemed anxious to save face for the Vietnamese, as well as to serve the U.S. line after the release of less than six hundred prisoners in the spring of 1973. That line said that no Americans were left behind *against their will*.

I reviewed my notes of the meeting. Garwood had had more success in smuggling out another cry for help a year later, in 1978. After Nana's execution, and in the time leading up to his "escape," he had begun to be sent on extensive runs to repair vehicles as far away as the area north of Hanoi. The lieutenant who regularly rode with him as a guard had a family in Hanoi.

One day, close to the Tet holidays, the Vietnamese New Year, the guard was dropped off at his family's home while

Garwood was driven on to fix a jeep near the Victory Hotel. Technically, the lieutenant was guilty of desertion, even though he was to be picked up by the driver on the way back. In the meantime, Garwood played up to the Vietnamese driver. While he worked on the jeep, he made suggestions: "You know," he said, "it wouldn't be a problem for me to go get some cigarettes, booze, candy, all you want – I'd be in and out of there in five minutes. It's only a couple days to Tet." Garwood, because he was Caucasian and could pass as a foreign guest, could enter the stores, whereas his Vietnamese driver could not. The driver finally said yes, and gave Garwood flip-flops and North Vietnamese Army (NVA) trousers and a white shirt, because Garwood's own prison pajamas would have given him away. Garwood walked in, found a snack bar, bought what his driver wanted, and walked out. He handed over the purchases, but kept the tiny bits of paper that served as receipts. He thought, *This guy is my prisoner now*. But he said nothing at this point.

Instead, he said to the driver, "Look, I'm going to be in Vietnam for the rest of my life. Is it wrong to want to get things like beer, cigarettes, when I can get access to them and I don't harm anyone? You can make some money, you can get stuff to your family, and I'm asking very little in return." When the driver said no, Garwood pulled out the receipts to indicate his power to blackmail. The driver got angry and threatened to shoot Garwood. Then he began to see the possibilities. He asked what Garwood wanted. Garwood explained, "Just create a circumstance where I can go into hotels, buy stuff for you, and you sell it on the black market, because all I want is cigarettes once in a while and maybe a beer." He explained how "circumstances" could be created: "The truck can break down every time we go out – pull off the battery cable or something." Garwood had the driver hooked, and was closer to contact with foreign visitors – and a means to escape.

Soon he had two guards implicated. Within a year he was the front man for a lively black-market operation in Hanoi. But there was only one thing he really wanted – access to a "foreign guest" from a neutral country whom he thought he could trust to get his message out. Garwood had seen that all foreign guests were provided with drivers and jeeps like his own. His driver and lieutenant validated him in the eyes of those who did not know he was under guard. Foreigners who were allies of the Vietnamese would see him get into the jeep and tell the driver, "*Go*," which told them he was okay. They relied on Vietnamese drivers and transport too.

A year after the first effort with Nana, Garwood smuggled out another cry for help. He had worked it out that she had been shot because she had been overheard discussing "state secrets" with him – details of her old life in Hanoi. The Communists had apparently not known that she had provided his courier.

This time he did not involve anyone else and made the contact personally with a World Bank diplomat from Finland, Ossi J. Rahkonen, who got the message to the British Broadcasting Corporation. After the BBC aired a report on the smuggled note, Hanoi was obliged to produce Garwood like a rabbit out of a hat. However, before his release in 1979, his captors subjected him to four weeks of suspense, interrogation, and intimidation. The film I had seen was shot during this time, showing him stumbling around Hanoi. A high-ranking Vietnamese security man warned him, "We can find you anywhere. We'll know if you identify prisoners we hold, and we'll kill them. We'll punish you right inside America if you say anything that hurts us." The moment he was delivered into U.S. hands, he was again instructed to say nothing. This time he was going to be court-martialled and maybe shot by his own side.

For the moment, he thought there must be some mistake. *Both* sides of the war surely could not want to gag him!

I puzzled about the attitude of Van Atta and the other vets. They believed that Garwood would have been killed *by his own side* while still a prisoner?

The ringing of the telephone made me jump. The caller was a Los Angeles police lieutenant who had carried out search-and-destroy missions in Vietnam. He was on the anti-drug beat now, and he had once helped me with a story on credit-card fraud. I had developed a deep respect for him.

"Some of the guys are worried," he now said. "There's a lot of evil out there. We hear you're digging into a relationship between the cover-up and the stuff I'm dealing with."

"No," I said automatically. He was talking in riddles.

"Well. . ." He sounded disappointed, and also relieved. "Remember, I can rustle up plenty of muscle if you get into any difficulty."

My husband was overseas, but this was the first time I had felt uncomfortable in the emptiness of the big house. I sat for a long time afterwards, staring at the phone. The police lieutenant had been afraid of wire-tappers. Who on earth would want to bug my phone? I got a grip on myself. "Nobody. That's who."

I thought about that call, on and off, in the days that followed. What was "the stuff I'm dealing with"? Drugs? And what did he mean about a cover-up?

Word of my interest in the Garwood case spread through The Telephone Tree. This was a network of Vietnamese vets and families of missing men. They kept tabs on anything to do with Americans whose fate in Vietnam was uncertain. They put out reports like Van Atta's *Insider*. Some called themselves "Forget-Me-Nots" and circulated newsletters like *Task Force Omega, The Bamboo Connection, Homecoming-II, Skyhook,* and smudgy sheets that seemed the equivalent of the Russian underground *samizdat*. I had been plugged into The Telephone Tree without any effort on my part.

I was visited in my office soon after the Los Angeles cop's call by a lean, youthful-looking commercial hunter and fisherman from Alaska who had fought as a combat infantryman. He was so convinced that something was seriously wrong that he made shameless use of his wife's top-level family connections in society, in academe, in the military, and in the State Department to push his way into the private counsels of the high and mighty and ask irritating questions. He gave me a signed statement: "It is those we served, not us the soldiers, who abandoned our comrades into enemy captivity, and who subsequently covered up this fact with official secrecy and who have now told us in witnessed meetings that these were *'acceptable casualties'* and that they and we *'cannot afford to be emotional about the POWs left behind,'* or that we *'do not understand the complexities of the situation as it relates to our enemies or to our Asian allies.'* "

His name was John Brown. The word along The Telephone Tree was that I was puzzled about the motives behind all this agitation, and he had come to answer my question.

"That's what motivates us," said John Brown, plunking down his statement. He was Chairman of the National Vietnam Veterans' Coalition Committee on Prisoners and Missing Men. His disillusionment had driven him, in the postwar years, to raise his family in the backwoods, as far from bitter memories as he could get. But no matter how much he tried to work off his rage in hard physical labor, in trapping and fishing, in lumberjacking and guiding big-game hunters, he was always driven back to battle with the mandarins in Washington, D.C.

There were others like John Brown. They had gone to fight a difficult war, feeling little support from home. They did their duty. Some became uneasy when they were directed into covert operations in areas of Laos and Cambodia where their countrymen at home thought there were no wars at all. They had known comrades who were caught without uniform because they were on covert assignment. That, of course, meant the enemy could execute them as spies if the mission failed.

Those who came home were often made to feel ashamed for having gone to Vietnam in the first place. They had to run to catch up with others of their generation who had never gone to war. In their middle years, they finally found the time to face the possibility that some of their comrades-in-arms were deliberately cast adrift. They could not get on with their lives until they discharged an obligation to the dead and missing, by forcing the reluctant bureaucracies to disinter their secrets. They were soldiers waking from a long sleep.

I listened to these callers, but initially I set aside anything that did not directly impinge upon Garwood. I was accustomed to hearing odd stories, because *60 Minutes* had become a sort of ombudsman to investigate citizens' complaints. Victims would seek our involvement if they knew that even the hint of a CBS investigation often rectified a bad situation. The so-called POW/MIA issue seemed to fall into this category.

By late spring 1985, Bill was resisting my growing curiosity about Vietnam. He had seen the country first when he shuttled between the French colonial war and the conflict in Korea as a correspondent. He assumed my interest was the sign of a producer being conscientious, but he also warned me not to get stuck in the quagmire of obsession with Vietnam. He had seen it happen to others.

One night I said to him, "If Garwood was just an unimportant little turncoat, why do so many important people want to sit on him?"

Bill groaned. "Don't you have any other assignments?"

"Yes, of course. I'd still like to clear this thing up, though. Do you think Garwood unwittingly got involved in our secret wars out there – ?"

"There were so many," he said sharply. "Does any of it matter now?"

His tone told me to expect more opposition from him on this. He was tired of Asia's back-alley politics. But, like my father, he had the fighter pilot's personality: impatient, opinionated, hostile to bureaucracy . . . This last prejudice gave me an idea. "It matters to the bureaucrats," I said.

"A *political* decision," he interrupted, "closed the door on prisoners."

"Not necessarily," I argued back. "A Republican president sat on policy. Democrats continued it."

Bill got the point. "When a policy survives both political parties," he said, "the policy is set by bureaucracy."

I recognized a gleam in his eye. Maybe that hostility to authority would work in my favor for once. He asked if I'd got other bluesheets approved on the issue.

"Not yet."

"And I'll bet not ever!" he warned me. "Missing men are political dynamite. They give bureaucrats fainting spells. Don't go beyond the tale of a Marine who got lost. If you want peace of mind, just stick to Garwood's story!" Bill spoke with feeling. "I'd hate to see you sacrifice your career by chasing the dragon."

CHAPTER 2

"ROADBLOCKS" IN THE NAME OF NATIONAL SECURITY

I had not pressed Bobby Garwood to give us the formal *60 Minutes* interview because I was not sure he had enough self-control to deliver a concise and coherent account of things. In mid-May 1985 I was busy with other stories. Suddenly Garwood called. He wanted to see me. Alone.

There was a new confidence in his voice. I took him to dinner at Chez Grand Mère on M Street and did what I was now sure the intelligence experts had never done. I let him just talk.

In the Communist prison camps he was, he said, "broken down to the lowest form of animal." Towards the beginning of his captivity, he was in solitary when another American was brought in. "Ike," Garwood called him. "Captain, Special Forces . . . said I should learn the enemy's language, to stay one step ahead. Ike taught me a Vietnamese word a day. Said it would keep me going. Said, if I survived, that was a victory. He showed me how to stay alive on bugs, lizards, plants. . . . "

The Indiana high-school dropout who had joined the Marines at seventeen thus got his first solid dose of real education in a jungle hooch. These were some of the survival skills that were later held against Garwood.

"One night," he said, "Ike picked a star and said it was ours. We'd watch it and pretend our folks back home were watching it too. It kept me going after Ike died a year later."

Who was this Ike? Garwood hedged. "I'm going to see his daughter in a few days. I know where her dad's buried. I buried him myself."

Why had he taken all this time since his release to face the daughter? I kept the question to myself. A wrong move now would make Garwood withdraw again.

Much later Garwood was in a punishment cell "when I heard Henry Kissinger over the 'Liars' Box.' That's the loudspeaker the Vietnamese used to communicate with U.S. prisoners. He said the release of prisoners had been concluded. 'There are no more live POWs in Vietnam.'

"Other Americans were in hooches across the river. The Communists rebroadcast Kissinger.* He'd said we no longer existed. . . . The Communists said they could do what they pleased with us. They said why would we resist when our own government deserted us?"

The Kissinger broadcast had dealt the prisoners a devastating blow. They concentrated on just staying alive after that. It was after this that Garwood got involved in the black market.

---

*   Kissinger was sensitive to charges that the 1973 Paris Agreement on Ending the War with Vietnam was a face-saving device to get America out of the war before the inevitable collapse. "We were determined," he told ABC's Barbara Walters, "that our withdrawal from Vietnam occur not as a collapse but as an American strategy." When pressed on the POW/MIA question by Tom Jerrold of ABC's 20/20, Kissinger grew angry and hurled a book at the wall, according to one witness. He had heard 20/20 was reviewing the record, and frequently asked Barbara Walters "if that piece is going to appear." It finally did appear in the late spring of 1986.

He had many encounters with other American prisoners. It never left him, he said, that he had fellow countrymen in that God-forsaken place. And when he had finally passed a message to the Finn, Rahkonen, he had emphasized in it that there were other Americans like himself.

Leaving Vietnam had been surreal. Originally Garwood was to be picked up by a U.S. military plane, but the Vietnamese and the U.S. concurred that was not a good idea. Garwood now speculated that if the U.S. had picked him up, as it had other POWs in 1973, that would have validated he was a POW. Instead, the impression was given that he was indeed a collaborator who had always been free to come and go. He was put on an Air France plane, whose crew turned him into an instant hero with champagne and caviar all the way to Thailand. It was his one moment of glory. In Bangkok he listened in stunned disbelief while a Marine gunnery sergeant read him his rights, then put him aboard a military aircraft with legal counsel. Why, Garwood wondered, am I being read my rights? But a military officer just kept repeating, "Don't say anything. Shut up. Don't say anything to anybody about anything." Garwood says he tried to tell him about other American prisoners but claims that all he said was, "You want to get *killed*?"

Garwood told me, "The one time anyone talked to me about what it had been like, being a prisoner, it was just after I got out. I tried then to discuss other Americans left behind – but they kept cutting me short."

This seemed true. Copies of an interview by the Marine Corps on March 29, 1979, and a one-page defense-intelligence "evaluation" said that Garwood "did not provide any new or potentially useful information."

There was a Moroccan waiter at the restaurant. Garwood spoke to him in Arabic. The waiter, who knew me, said, "It's a pleasure to hear my native tongue well spoken."

I looked at Garwood. He seemed unaware of what had just happened. This was a man who had had little formal education when he went to Vietnam. "Where'd you learn Arabic?" I asked him.

"In hospital. Men from the Palestine Liberation Organization were there. . . . " It was an explanation I had to accept. I found out later that in 1976, working in the motor pool of Prison Camp #5 close to the China border, Garwood suddenly became very ill. His captors took him to a hospital that seemed to him to be filled with Vietnam's allies – Cubans, Russians, and Palestinians. He did not know why he received such good treatment. He thought perhaps they did not want to lose his skill in fixing and maintaining the equipment the Americans had left behind.

His face lit up with renewed interest as I told him about a conversation I'd had with Walter Cronkite at CBS. Cronkite had asked Henry Kissinger, in 1973, to write to Hanoi and ask for information on twenty-one American journalists missing in Vietnam and Laos. Kissinger agreed, but inserted a curious sort of apology in the letter. He assured the Communists he had no basis for believing the missing were alive.

I had asked Cronkite to confirm the accuracy of all this. He assured me there was no doubt about the record. He later tried to find out why Kissinger took such a defeatist attitude. Cronkite said, "Every time I'd see Kissinger at any social gathering, I'd ask him this. But I never got a satisfactory answer."

"You mean Kissinger would ignore a man like Walter Cronkite?" Garwood asked in an awed voice.

We left the restaurant. A man who was lounging outside stirred, and began to follow. We stopped, forcing him to pass, and I recognized the same man I had confronted outside my house. He was joined by another man at the corner of M and Wisconsin and they both disappeared around the corner. There was something deliberate in the way they showed themselves to Garwood, but I said nothing and neither did he.

Garwood walked me to the corner of M and 30th and said goodbye. I pressed him once more to commit himself to a film interview by the end of June, and unexpectedly, he said yes. I headed up 30th before he could change his mind.

At home, I described the evening to Bill. "There he was, in the heart of our enemies. He spoke their language, he must have passed right through their military and prison system. It was like we had a spy all those years in the enemy camp. And we never asked him about it. Isn't that weird?"

Bill wanted to know more details about how Garwood himself made contact with a foreign diplomat. Was it set up? I didn't know. I had not been in a position to cross-examine him. I would find out later, I said, feeling a trifle cross with myself and with my husband.

"Garwood said live Americans are highly prized – they call them 'pearls,' because they may be valuable in any future bargaining."

Bill nodded and explained that French prisoners were "pearls" too, useful to sell one by one to Paris, for money, technical aid, even diplomatic recognition. When he was with the truce commission after the Battle of Dienbienphu in 1955 and 1956, the North Vietnamese showed Bill two French prisoners deep in the jungle. The Communists were proud of them as showpieces, and pretended they were not prisoners but converts. They were proof that Ho Chi Minh's ideology was correct because they "voluntarily defected." The Frenchmen hadn't seen another Caucasian in years. They were from Paris. Bill thought they'd jump at the chance to ask questions, pass messages. . . . But all they did was recite propaganda. They were terrified to say one word out of place. At one point two jars of drinking water were placed between them. One prisoner's hand shot out, then hesitated. His eyes shifted over Bill's shoulder to a Chinese in a straw helmet who gave him a sharp nod. The hand finished its movement. They were prisoners, though the war with France had ended – and although the Communists called them converts.

"Hanoi never reported those two men were alive," Bill said after a pause. "I got the information to the French government. Twenty thousand of their soldiers were known to be still on the POW rolls. Hanoi would pass along a name and fix the price for the man's release whenever the fancy took them. Paris has paid out a fortune, quietly getting some back. . . . "*

During June 1985 I read through thousands of pages of testimony from Garwood's court martial and spoke with many who were involved in the trial. There were no direct eyewitness descriptions of clearly disloyal behavior on his part.

How was it possible for the Marine Corps to court martial Garwood and to find witnesses willing to testify against him? The answer lay in his unique talent for learning languages and the skills of survival that "Ike" Eisenbraun had taught him. Although those talents helped him to survive in an elemental way, they made his captors suspect he might be a provocateur sent to stir up resistance among the other prisoners. So from camp to camp they progressively isolated him from the other Americans. Eventually he was forced to live with his Vietnamese captors. He was devastated by the move, but the other POWs in that camp thought he was getting special treatment and special food and they would testify against him more than ten years later. The Vietnamese made him translate their orders and interrogations of his fellow POWs with the threat that both he and they would suffer if he disobeyed. Worst of all, they took him on working trips to outlying fields and made him carry their weapons just before they arrived at camp so that the other POWs would think he had taken up arms against his own countrymen – though no one ever saw him use the guns. This kind of trickery was well known to others who had been imprisoned by the Communists in Korea and China. Some American prisoners in one camp grew to despise him. One prisoner

---

* A total of 36,979 French POWs were captured in Vietnam. Only 10,754 were repatriated. (See *Hell in a Very Small Place*, by Dr. Bernard B. Fall, published by J.B. Lippincott, New York, 1967.)

who knew better was Russ Grisset, who had been with Bobby and Ike Eisenbraun in the first camp after his capture. Then Grisset was beaten to death in front of the other prisoners in Bobby's absence. When Bobby found out, he committed the act that would lead to a guilty finding at his court martial seven years later. Emotionally distraught at losing his only friend in the camp, he pushed fellow prisoner David Harker aside.

The prosecution at his court martial described that action as "striking a fellow prisoner," something considered by the military to be the most heinous crime an American prisoner can perpetrate on another. The truth was, as Harker readily admitted to me when I questioned him, that Garwood had indeed only pushed him. Harker said he had been uncomfortable with the emphasis the prosecution placed on this one incident, but he was still convinced Garwood was a traitor. Why else would he have lived with the Vietnamese guards and presumably gotten better treatment than his fellow countrymen? Harker was also convinced that when Bobby was moved from the camp the following year it was because he volunteered to throw in his lot with the Vietnamese. That impression was reinforced when he did not return with the other prisoners in 1973.

Garwood had no interest in defending himself by telling tales on the prisoners who testified against him, but he now wanted to talk about other prisoners who had been left behind in 1973.

Judge Switzer, the Marine colonel who presided over the court martial, told me that Garwood was never given a chance to disclose what he knew about any other prisoners. He was never debriefed in the same way as other prisoners. Usually the DIA or the CIA did that. All the other prisoners who came out in 1973 had talked with intelligence officers from the armed forces or the agencies.

The military psychiatrist on the case said that Garwood, despite the pressures, insisted he had information on other American prisoners. "He was held in maximum security at the time, and so he felt he need not fear leaks reaching Hanoi to hurt other Americans there. He couldn't understand why he was never questioned on what he knew."

Psychologist Edna Hunter, who had directed the POW center for the Department of Defense from 1971 to 1978, said she'd interviewed almost every prisoner who had returned in 1973. "And I interviewed the prosecution witnesses. None really wanted to testify against Garwood." She concluded that lots of Americans were abandoned. "I knew reports about them had been suppressed. That's why the prosecution stopped me testifying at the court martial." She also told me, "There is no doubt that Garwood, like so many others, was set up by the Vietnamese. They deliberately kept him apart and spread the rumor that this prisoner was getting special treatment, that he had crossed over. Our government knew it. We all knew it."

The judge had not been shown photographs of Garwood in Vietnam, hands tied behind his back and under guard. "At least not until the court martial was over," he told me. Was he surprised? "Well, it's not the way I would have defended Garwood," he said.

I asked Roger Shields, who had directed the Defense Department Task Force on POWs in 1973, just what constituted collaboration for a prisoner. He said he didn't know. I asked him if rumors were true that men captured after the ceasefire had been crossed off the list of prisoners for the 1973 homecoming. He said I should ask Kissinger why there had been such haste to run a line through the names of remaining prisoners. Kissinger never answered my calls, but he later conveyed a message through Diane Sawyer that it was all nonsense – there were no American prisoners.

I asked the State Department if any action was taken on behalf of the other American prisoners after Garwood's first communication with a diplomat in Hanoi.

"We know of no 'first communication.' "

"Well, the second time."

"Garwood never mentioned other Americans."

"Did we take action then only because a friendly foreign government knew about Garwood?"

"State does not comment on the confidential actions of friendly foreign governments."

"If there had not been a third government involved, would we have left Garwood to rot?"

"No third government informed the U.S. government."

"Then why did Mr. Ossi J. Rahkonen tell me, yes, he was the Finn who transmitted the information?"

Silence.

"You can find him now at the World Bank," I added. "Right here, in Washington." I got no response.

I went back to the Finn to ask if Garwood had indeed spoken of other American prisoners while in Hanoi.

Rahkonen said the matter was "very complex." Was I sure I wanted to get into such a touchy subject?

"All I want to know," I said, "is, did Garwood, in his message to you, refer to other American prisoners?" I supposed the Finn would say, "No." It would mean Garwood really had invented this part of his story.

The stuttered reply shook me. "Y-yes," said Rahkonen.

Why had State lied? Was it a simple matter of bureaucratic ineptitude or a concerted effort? A friend in State's own Bureau of Intelligence and Research said there were internal memos concerning Garwood prior to his escape. One was a memo from the files of the National Security Council. "It says, 'A live American defector has been sighted in Hanoi who claims he knows of other Americans alive in Vietnam,' " said my friend from the bureau. I wondered how they knew about Garwood. How did they know he was a defector?

"State says it never heard about live Americans," I challenged.

"Yes – well, what most people don't know are the details of the secret negotiations behind our leaving Vietnam. Nixon wanted to get the Paris peace agreement signed in 1973 before Watergate engulfed him, so he secretly promised more than four billion dollars' worth of economic aid to Hanoi and took whatever prisoners they said they had. When the government reneged on the four-billion-dollar promise, Hanoi hung onto the remaining prisoners in retaliation, and as a means later of trying to get the money," he said.

My State Department friend claimed that, in the days following the 1973 official homecoming of prisoners, intelligence on those left behind was constant. The prisoners were known as "Brightlights" in intelligence code. "We wanted to just forget Vietnam and cut and run. No one wanted to hear about Garwood, and certainly nobody wanted him to come home and spill the beans about other American prisoners." He spoke in anger. He had been a Marine in Vietnam. He was torn between loyalty to the department and a deep sense of injustice committed against his comrades in war. He guided me to the internal memos that bore out what he said: that Garwood had been gagged.

A prosecution witness who talked to Garwood as part of the pre-trial procedure prior to the court martial deposed that Garwood had quoted the Communist security chief in Hanoi as saying to him on the day before his release: "We'll let the rest of the prisoners go only when the U.S. pays those four billion dollars promised by President Nixon. We're not so stupid as to turn over more prisoners for a promise and a bit of paper." This testimony was disallowed at the trial as "irrelevant" and never appeared in court papers.

An Assistant Director for Collection Management at the Defense Intelligence Agency, Commodore Thomas A. Brooks, told a Congressional inquiry, "Investigation of Garwood's information has unproductively absorbed a great amount of our analytical resources." In fact, DIA still had never debriefed him.

Had the Central Intelligence Agency questioned Garwood? I tackled Johnny Shaheen, a New York oil man who was a close friend and former business partner of Bill Casey, at that time director of the CIA. Shaheen had carried out swashbuckling covert operations in World War II when Casey was in the London end of OSS (Office of Special

Services), father of the CIA. At a midnight reception given by Shaheen, he passed me over to Casey, whom I already knew through my husband. "We left live casualties behind," Casey said, "and I certainly would never pass up the chance to get them back." He asked me to be patient: he would look into what I told him about Garwood. Casey never did give me a precise answer. The CIA had never reviewed Garwood's years in Vietnam because, said Casey, the DIA was supposed to have done that already.

No matter how I tried to limit inquiries to Garwood, I kept running into wider issues. I was puzzled by former POW Task Force head Roger Shields's suggestion that Kissinger could tell me about claims that some men's names had been crossed off the official list of POWs to be returned in 1973. Surely, I thought, he could not have meant names were crossed off by U.S. government officials. The Telephone Tree put me in touch with Florida police detective Bob Cressman, brother of Air Force Sergeant Peter R. Cressman, and the story he told was that this is exactly what happened.

Sergeant Cressman was a Morse systems operator assigned to an EC-47Q "Flying Pueblo" reconnaissance (eavesdropping) aircraft. On February 5, 1973, while he was flying a mission on the Vietnam-Laos border, the EC-47Q was shot down. The shoot-down occurred nine days after the Paris peace accords were signed. Cressman had read the terms of the Paris Agreement and had realized that he and his colleagues were flagrantly violating the peace in a neutral country. He worried about the possibility of becoming involved in and responsible for war crimes. He visited the base legal office to find out what his rights and obligations were regarding the orders he was being given. He was told that he had no right to do anything but obey orders, even if they were illegal. The consequences of disobeying were so severe, he left the legal office feeling that disobedience was impossible.

Sergeant Cressman's family would never have known about their son's mental anguish in the days before his shoot-down if he had not written several drafts of a letter, addressed to a public official, outlining his dilemma and asking for help. If he ever completed an official letter, there was no public record of it. Instead, the draft letters were returned to his family with his belongings. Evelyn Cressman was certain that someone in her son's unit wanted his family to know the truth, and that this was how the draft letters escaped the notice of military censors.

After the crash, it seemed unlikely there would be survivors. Air Force sources later told the Cressmans there was little chance of skilled specialists like their son being taken prisoner. Because of the sophisticated electronic equipment on board, arrangements existed for the immolation and destruction of the aircraft before it could fall into enemy hands. The electronic equipment was packed in so tightly that it was almost impossible for the men to bail out.

The unlikely occurred. Shortly after the shoot-down, another U.S. reconnaissance aircraft intercepted enemy communications and ascertained that at least four members of the EC-47Q had survived and been captured. This information was conveyed to U.S. officials almost immediately after the crash. A few days later, a U.S. search party found more evidence that some crew members were taken captive. On February 17, four members of the EC-47Q crew were seen and identified about twenty-five kilometers from the crash site, in apparent good health and under the guard of their captors. U.S. officials were again made immediately aware of this information.

The Cressmans and other families of the EC-47Q flight crew were not told that some of the crew had survived, were known to be prisoners, and were in good health, even though Air Force directives ordered that families of such men be given the most complete information possible. On February 22, 1973, seventeen days after the shoot-down, while information on some crew members' survival was still being with-held, the Air Force declared all of the men dead.

Long after the war was over, Mrs. Cressman and Mary Matejov, the mother of Sgt. Joseph M. Matejov, one of Sgt. Cressman's fellow crew members, went to see POW Task Force Director Roger Shields. He told them, they said, that their sons' names had initially been placed in the U.S. list of POWs to be returned in 1973 (i.e., those for whom the United States insisted on an accounting based on its own intelligence that they were alive). The mothers reported that Shields told them the names had then been crossed off the list. Shields wanted them to know, he said, that he himself had not made that decision. Congressman Billy Hendon (Rep. N. Carolina) would later tell the Cressmans that he personally saw their son's name pencilled in the official Operation Homecoming Bluebook. The name was crossed through and marked over with "Killed in Action."

To Congressman Hendon, it seemed that the government was indicating to the former enemy that the United States was abandoning the men and the Communists could there-fore treat them as badly as they wanted. The Cressmans, like many other families, vowed to find out what really hap-pened.

It took them years to find out that two months after the shoot-down, the four captives were sighted again, still in apparent good health, about sixty-five kilometers from the crash site. Again, such information was known immediately by U.S. officials but withheld from the families.

The Cressmans also found there were persons in the De-partment of Defense who strongly objected to what was done, but to no avail. When the dissenters were unable to prevent the continuing abandonment of the EC-47Q crew and others, they succeeded in having a written memorandum of their protest included in official files. Those files remain classified. When I first spoke to Evelyn Cressman, she told me, "Some of those dissenters told me privately what happened. They say they can't go public because it will hurt the country. It will damage national security. Whose security? The security of boys like my son, Peter?"

She sent me a voluminous file on her son. It included clearly stated "live sighting" intelligence reports on her son and a lengthy correspondence with government officials. The Cressmans explored every avenue in an attempt to get their government to take some action to bring back its own men. The best answer they ever got was an evasive admission that information indicating that some of the crew might have survived the shoot-down had been received and withheld by the government. The information was not, however, enough to warrant a reconsideration of the determination of death.

Evelyn directed me to a letter written by attorney Dermot Foley, the brother of an MIA who acted for the Cressmans in a legal attempt to pry more information from the government. "Foley," she said, "put what happened to my son in a nutshell." He had written:

> Despite protests and objections, the crew of the EC-47Q was coerced aboard an aircraft that was designed to be a death trap and was compelled to commit war crimes. When their aircraft was shot down it became known to U.S. officials that the death-trap was only a partial success and that some of the men survived and were captured by an enemy known to be harsh and brutal in its treatment of American prisoners. The response of the government which placed these men in such a situation was to lie to their families and to abandon the men by issuing determinations of death which were known to be corrupt and fraudulent. . . .
>
> The determinations of death in this matter cannot be defended . . . there is not a shred of evidence that they are not alive today – many POWs survived far longer in captivity. . . . These men, as opposed to earlier POWs, actually have been abandoned by their government; [they face] the additional punishment [meted out to] war

criminals. These elements can only tend to erode any restraint a hateful enemy might be inclined to feel.

Foley had written the letter to the Cressmans seven years earlier, in December of 1978, a few months before Bobby Garwood came out of Vietnam.

The Telephone Tree also introduced me to Diane Van Renselaar, whose twenty-two-year-old husband, Lars "Larry" Van Renselaar, had been shot down in 1968 while he was still the youngest Navy pilot then in combat. Diane had been young, beautiful, and very much in love.

Long after she was notified of his death in action, she learned accidentally that U.S. intelligence always knew Larry had been captured alive. Such information was kept classified. Diane saw the records only because she became involved in a bureaucratic tussle with the Navy when they mistakenly sent her husband's pension payments to his parents instead of to her. When her lawyer demanded to see all relevant documents, he was given papers Diane had never been shown. "Those official papers said the government knew Larry Van Renselaar had been taken prisoner," the lawyer told her. "I was heartsick at the thought of all those years lost, when I could have been trying to get Larry out," Diane said.

"They classified everything on POWs to keep secrets from falling in the hands of the enemy, '*to protect our national security*,' " she said. "But in this case the secret wasn't kept from the enemy. The enemy knew he was their prisoner; his own family did not. Does national security require keeping such 'secrets' from our own people? I'm unravelling new stuff every day."

"Send it to me," I said.

"I will," promised Diane. "If only as a precaution."

"Against what?"

"It hasn't happened to me yet, but I know others who've been told if they don't shut up, their benefits will be stopped. I'd feel happier if I knew *60 Minutes* had the records."

What national security was endangered by the presumed widows and orphans, or the parents, of the missing? I requested intelligence documents on alleged live sightings of lost Americans. I was told they were classified.

Diane found that some lists of prisoners, on which her husband appeared, had been declassified, as documents routinely are after sufficient time has passed. They were placed in various parts of the National Archives – only to disappear after POW activists asked embarrassing questions about the material contained in them. When families asked for copies, they were told the documents had been reclassified. Intelligence on POW/MIAs had become a national secret all over again, long after the only obvious reason for such secrecy – the war – was over. Who reclassified them? On what grounds? Whatever the answer was, the ploy failed. Some activists had made copies during the time they were declassified.

I decided to ignore my husband's warning and began to dig through congressional records. I was taken aback to find this kind of secrecy had been used against Representative Douglas Applegate, a Democrat from Ohio. He had told Congress in August 1984 that he'd finally obtained – he did not say how – "some very disturbing information . . . a listing of 97 CIA reports of live American prisoners in Laos. . . . I also have a listing of 300 CIA reports of that agency tracing live Americans as late as 1979. . . . I am outraged to think that our government knew of these live Americans, up to and past the end of the Vietnamese conflict, and yet knowingly left them in captivity and did nothing about it."

Applegate spoke for the record. Nonetheless, one of his staff members told me that his words had been edited by the Defense Intelligence Agency before publication. The official explanation was that Applegate referred to satellite photographs of Laos, showing prison camps with Caucasian inmates. They were taken by the National Reconnaissance Office. The DIA censor had stepped in "because NRO, which is part of the Department of Defense, does not officially exist," Applegate was told.

Applegate had known of other reports that he told Congress he could not investigate "because I have run into roadblocks in the name of national security. . . . At what point does national security override bringing back known POW/MIAs' bodies or securing the release of live Americans held captive?"

Applegate turned shy when I asked if he'd ever received an answer. "The Congressman got badly burned," an aide said bitterly. "He is not likely to speak on the issue again." He had been accused by CIA Director Bill Casey of hurting national security. That rang alarm bells. Had Casey been playing games in his earlier conversation with me when he said he would never pass up the chance to get back the live prisoners he was certain we had left behind?

"Casey gives this a very low priority," said a sympathetic but powerless Johnny Shaheen.

"Then he's a fool," I told Casey's old partner. Couldn't Casey see that the top priority was morale? "That won't be very high, if servicemen think we send them off to war, then abandon them when they become political hot potatoes."

"Not just *political* hot potatoes," said Shaheen. "The CIA's hotshots in Asia were openly contemptuous of the military. When the Vietnam War ended officially, the CIA continued with its own secret wars all over Southeast Asia, including the Resistance in Vietnam." Shaheen didn't think the agency would risk those interests for a bunch of captured fly-boys and grunts.

I was well out of my depth. Shaheen advised me to "drop it." He was a brave and audacious man, as I knew from the declassified reports he had entrusted to Bill in connection with World War II operations. When he said I was sailing into dangerous waters, I had to believe it.

Then a congressman opened his office safe one day and shocked me with the photograph of a prison camp, taken, he said, from a remote-controlled, pilotless spy plane over Vietnam. He seemed unafraid of being charged with breaking security, but he was destined to be more badly burned than Applegate. He was Billy Hendon, a Republican from North Carolina.

I first met him early in the summer in his congressional office. One of Applegate's aides had suggested I might want to talk to him. He had his laid-back Carolina folksiness down to a fine art. On Capitol Hill, everyone seemed to know him. Messengers in the corridors cracked jokes with him; aides responded warmly to his cheerful face. Walking with him was like strolling down Main Street with a popular mayor. However, his easy manner concealed a shrewd brain. His rough-and-ready political style had provided excellent cover for secret missions into Southeast Asia, sponsored by, of all people, the CIA's Bill Casey.

The missions had been political intelligence probes, to search out factions in Indochina with whom America could work in the early eighties. After losing the 1982 election for Congress, he had been given a deliberately low-profile job inside the Pentagon's Defense Intelligence Agency. He thought Casey, who then appeared hot on the issue, wanted him to find evidence of American prisoners. He found that evidence by going through voluminous intelligence messages giving details of current prisoners. He made several journeys to Southeast Asia, won a measure of cooperation from Communist officials, and then Casey went cold on the POW/MIA issue, leaving him dangling. "It's not," Casey told him, "politically sexy."

That was a change in heart from the days when Casey had met with Reagan's Intelligence Advisory Transition Team to plan the rescue of six prisoners who he was certain were still being held in Laos. Those plans had been based on the very best intelligence. A former intelligence chief, who had advised Reagan, only made this clear much later.

Hendon's disillusion came late, but it brought with it a deep and burning anger. "The U.S. government knows absolutely that Garwood's telling the truth about prisoners," Billy said. "All information about POW sightings has been suddenly labelled 'confidential,' but the talk about national security is horse shit! It's job security."

He speculated that, because POWs were pronounced officially dead ten years before, the careers of certain intelligence and military officers rode on this. They served politicians who were in such a hurry to get out of the war that they glossed over the large number of POWs thought to be alive but not returned. The politicians had staked their reputations on the supposed fact that they brought *all* the prisoners back. Politicians of both parties shared responsibility for the cover-ups of successive governments. They could not now admit the errors. And they certainly would not want to have to mount a rescue operation. If it went wrong, the fallout would be worse than the failure to get hostages out of Teheran. *"That's* what finished President Carter!" declared Hendon.

I objected that when Reagan took office, he had declared the missing men a priority and had given the all-clear on any efforts to return any who remained.

Congressman Hendon shook his head in disbelief at my naïveté. "You've a lot to learn."

It made sense, though, I argued, to have the clandestine services do the job of penetrating hostile territory to recover captive Americans. Hendon replied, "In this town, it also makes sense to use the recovery of MIAs as cover for unofficial covert operations. You don't have to admit they're there. Just say what the administration is saying: that you're going on the assumption, but that there has never been any real evidence."

"We're talking about American lives!" I protested.

Billy nodded heavily. "I can't quarrel with you there," he said.

We went to a restaurant to continue talking. He had in all his pockets bits of paper, scraps of information, hand-drawn maps, old envelopes covered in squiggles: a trove of aide-mémoire that amounted to a personal archive. I asked questions and Billy patted his shirt pocket and hunted inside his jacket. Finally he pulled out a paper napkin from a back pocket and, consulting it, sketched for me on the tablecloth a map of Indochina and where Americans were kept: "Here! Here! And here. . . . " He cross-hatched large areas, allowed me a glimpse, and then carefully blacked out the map and said the information was officially classified.

Around us sat politicians, lobbyists, journalists, and gurus from government departments, all tucking into lunch, absorbed in controversies that seemed burning then and would be forgotten the next day . . . I had a sudden vision of men in bamboo cages. If they could *see* how their world had moved on to other things, what would they feel? Forgotten. That was the kindest word.

"You should see the 'Measles Map,' " Billy cut in.

Another bit of notepaper fluttered from a pocket, and I said, "D'you keep all your files in there?"

"Only on this issue." Billy sat back and stuck out his long legs. "Bulky stuff I keep in a safe."

Whose thievery was he protecting himself against? Clearly he never let the basic papers out of his sight, but he was bursting to talk about the Measles Map. It was based on many years of intelligence analysis, he said. To a map of Vietnam were added clear plastic geographic outlines, pinpointing new intelligence on prisoners as it came up. Then the whole was photographed. The data came from secret intelligence on the most credible reports of American prisoners. It correlated reports on where lost Americans were concentrated. The individual reports, supplied by agents working for U.S. agencies, as well as by refugees who escaped from Vietnam, dovetailed. Some had to be accurate. Many prisoners had probably died since, but the map dramatized the reality of men abandoned. It made the general map of Indochina look like the chart of a measles outbreak. Hendon wanted to place it before Congress, but Casey was forcefully advising him to drop it.

Congressman Hendon was not to be bullied. After we talked, he let his intention be known that he would produce the

Measles Map at an upcoming meeting of the House Subcommittee on Asian and Pacific Affairs. The subcommittee was in charge of the POW issue. He didn't anticipate that he was to meet formidable opposition, armed in advance by his advertised intentions. Garwood was also scheduled to appear. So was General Eugene Tighe, the former chief of the Defense Intelligence Agency, who had recently been quoted in the *Wall Street Journal* as saying that prisoners were indeed still being held.

The *60 Minutes* story was at the stage where background interviews overlapped the filming of "cover shots," the short clips that illustrate sections of the script. The day of the House Subcommittee meeting, we filmed what we could of the proceedings for such cover shots. Hendon promised to make good television. Garwood's testimony would be secret, so it could not be filmed, but there was nothing to prevent his repeating it at some later date in a formal interview with Ed Bradley.

When we arrived with the crew, Garwood, impressive in his Marine uniform, stood in the corridor waiting. He told me that he planned to be careful in what he said, because Hanoi's Communists had been quite clear in their threats to kill American prisoners if he gave specific locations. Yes, the threats were now more than five years old, but he believed every word uttered here would be known in Hanoi by nightfall. That was why he was upset at only being able to give testimony in secret. He had asked to speak in open session, since he felt that Hanoi, always sensitive to American opinion, would then not act hastily to punish prisoners – or even kill them – as they promised to do if he ever revealed what he knew about them. He had already written, "It is my understanding, from other POWs as well, that we received better treatment when it was publicly known that we were important to the American public."* The committee had no intention, though, of letting him use this as another platform.

---

* See Appendix 1 for Garwood's letter to the Committee.

I would have dismissed his apparent fear of Hanoi's long reach if my husband and Colonel Nick Rowe had not described clinically the methods used to brainwash prisoners. I had also read French accounts of indoctrination in the camps, notably books by Bernard Fall, who made a close study of Communist techniques of ruling by fear. Fall was eventually killed in Vietnam. But I remembered something he had said to Bill after Dienbienphu, and which he had later repeated: "Nobody who has not been there can understand. . . . " It was very possible Bobby's fear was genuine.

Cries of "Traitor!" from some congressmen met Garwood as he walked stiffly to the door of the committee room. His face turned white. He turned to me and said, "It doesn't matter. . . . " Then the doors closed behind him.

Congressman Hendon, in his turn, was barely allowed to speak in open session. Many families felt that Stephen Solarz, the committee chairperson, had shown an overall hostility to the issue in all previous hearings, an opinion that seemed to be supported by the official congressional records I had now read. Hendon's attempts to interject his points were frustrated until near the end, when the room was emptying fast. Because the time allowed him was too short, the Measles Map never saw the light of day.

General Eugene Tighe did manage to say in open session that he was now, and always had been, convinced there were Americans still held in Indochina. This was a bold position for him to take. It soon became apparent Tighe had been too bold.

The CBS crew recorded the sounds of the session – "wild sound," to use as background noise placed behind the narration that would be read over film. When I later saw the printed record of Tighe's statement, it seemed a watered-down version of what I remembered having heard in the session. I checked these audio tapes and found I had been correct. Someone had altered the views of the former intelligence chief.

This was too striking to ignore. There was another story

here. The defense agencies could censor, if it appeared that testimony unwittingly endangered the country. However, as far as I could judge, there was nothing in what General Tighe had said during the open hearing that was remotely injurious to national security, unless a bureaucrat produced some serpentine argument claiming that if the ex-DIA chief said anything about anything, it would somehow help our enemies.

I approached General Tighe. He was staunchly loyal to the system. It was inconceivable to him that anyone would abuse the power that is conferred upon the practitioners of secret intelligence. He felt that it was a common and necessary practice to edit the record where required for national security. However, he held to his assertion that prisoners were still alive. What he knew from intelligence reports squared with Garwood's statements to me about numbers of Americans he had seen between the fall of 1973 and his release in 1979: a score in a camp at Bat Bat; six loading a truck at a warehouse at Gia Lam; about thirty getting off a train at Yen Bai, near Lake Thac Bai; more than twenty in an island prison camp, Tac Ba; fifteen in Hanoi. Garwood had compiled another list of actual names of prisoners he believed were alive at these times, but he did not wish it made public because of Hanoi's threats of retribution.

I spoke with a Defense Department spokesman, who said, "We doubt if the camps mentioned were in existence after the prisoner release of 1973. The only consistency is that before 1973 we knew about those camps." But Tighe had spoken of prisoners held during his term as head of DIA long after 1973.

"Who are you to contradict Tighe?" I asked.

"I speak for the Department."

I wondered how a spokesman, reading from a handout, could dismiss a great American in the name of the U.S. government? Tighe's experience had won him worldwide respect. A NATO intelligence chief called him one of history's great masters of the craft. An Israeli Air Force chief regarded him as "having covered the gathering of intelligence in all its manifestations, from ground and human reportage to the most sophisticated aerial and space methods."*

I suggested a second *60 Minutes* segment, to follow Garwood's story, on Tighe and the prisoner issue. Don Hewitt thought it was a great idea. I gave it the working title "Unwanted – Dead or Alive."

If Hewitt was hot for the story, and the correspondent was hot too, all the producer had to do was come up with the goods: good interviews, good script, good proof. In our routine, there was no interference while the producer developed the story, and it was usually one of several the producer had in hand. The correspondent, also dealing with several stories at the same time, would play his role at the appropriate moment. Changes were made at the preliminary screening. This was the one time when there was anything like a formal meeting. Hewitt had a flair for bringing out the drama in a story and, if I argued with him, I rarely quarreled with the way he adjusted the style of the piece. He gave it the *60 Minutes* touch.

Research on the POW piece started well, but the first hint of trouble was a phone call I received late at night. "Do you know what you're getting into?" a voice asked.

"Who is this?"

"Just a friend who doesn't want to see you get hurt."

"Would you like to repeat that on national television, on *60 Minutes*?"

Dial tone.

Bill said, "It's just the babbling of some nut."

A few days later, another man's voice told me not to be fooled by General Tighe. "He's senile," said the caller, hanging up.

---

*   This highly professional assessment of General Tighe was made by Issar Harel, the former chief of Mossad, the Israeli Secret Intelligence Service. Harel, an old friend of Bill's, told him this during a conversation that took place during the summer of 1989.

I did not tell Hewitt. He was interested in results, not in peripheral inconveniences. Besides, what could he do? And what were these calls worth, really? There were not direct threats. They were just cranks. Scary cranks.

The Telephone Tree knew my name and my unlisted number. I asked John Brown if somehow The Tree might have leaked the information that I was researching Tighe and POWs.

"Anything's possible," was his surprising reply. "I've had direct threats from a guy who was CIA in Asia. He says I should stop stirring up trouble over men who never came back, or else take out ten million dollars' worth of life insurance for my wife and kids."

Then a prominent Washington lawyer called me. "I heard what's been happening," he said. "I'm a fan of your husband's books. I think maybe you should know I've had direct and explicit threats from inside government. I mean, they even used that ridiculous phrase I thought appeared only in spy novels, about 'terminating me with extreme prejudice' if I kept on with my investigations – "

"Into *what*?" I asked.

"Stuff related to what you're doing. Some very important people just don't want the public to know they used American prisoners to cover dirty tricks that filled their own pockets."

The lawyer was willing to disclose documents on condition that, for the time being, Bill could use them in fiction form only. That material had come into his hands accidentally while he investigated international commercial dealings for a powerful client. The evidence of wrongdoing was such that he'd seen it as his civic duty to go to the appropriate authorities. What he said boggled my mind, but I couldn't accept his conditions. If I hadn't known the lawyer's reputation for integrity, I might have suspected a political motive for discrediting some members of government. I showed Bill my notes. The lawyer was convinced that a group took advantage of insider information on the wars in Indochina to develop billion-dollar enterprises.

The lawyer said he did nothing more after he was warned not to intrude. Instead, he said, he began to get lucrative federal-government contracts. The lawyer was satisfied that he'd accidentally trespassed onto national security turf. "You can't *buy* justice," he claimed.

CHAPTER 3

TAKING ON THE GOVERNMENT

One May night, Alexandra's cries woke me. Later, in the kitchen, getting myself a glass of milk, I thought I smelled gas. I quickly opened windows and called an emergency repairman. He showed me the outside turncock. It had been closed and then reopened. He said, "Must have been men working on your furnace. Turned the gas back on but forgot to relight the pilots."

I had not had men working on the furnace.

I called the Washington Gas Light Company. Was it dangerous when gas leaked from unlit pilots? The blunt response: "Haven't you heard of houses blowing up?"

"Could gas leak if the outside gas line was turned off, and then turned on again?"

"Only authorized persons can turn it off or on, and none of our people were working in your area last night."

Later, I mentioned the gas leak to a Vietnam vet in the heating business. He said the gas would leak from bathroom and kitchen heating fixtures – "Maybe from the furnace too, if it was old. Was it?" It was. He came over, installed a safety valve, refused payment, and said he could get me vets for bodyguards any time.

That did make me sit up.

The vet was on The Telephone Tree. The Tree was beginning to work like a private nationwide security agency. It always knew somebody who was still on active service or had access to records or could locate another source. It reached into every walk of life. Another Vietnam vet in the D.C. police department called to say that if I had more frights, my house could be put under police protection.

Bill had been away. When I told him about the gas leaks, he laughed: "Don't let the vets panic you."

I shrank from bothering Hewitt with what might seem like postnatal hysteria. I talked instead with Jim Badey, a former Marine sergeant in Vietnam, who was now a detective working on Vietnamese crime rings in the Pentagon area. He had written a valuable textbook on Vietnamese crime that was used by police departments wherever in North America there were illegal-drug problems – which was just about everywhere. After twenty years as a police officer, he did not pussyfoot around. "Some in the Pentagon hate Garwood and anyone who stirs up questions about POWs and MIAs," he said. "We are investigating. Our casework keeps getting stopped at higher levels."

I looked at his police-intelligence reports and compromising photographs of one man. They suggested, at the very least, that there was a substantial security risk in the Pentagon.

Badey said, "Maybe you're too nice to get into this." He had testified before the recent presidential crime commission on the Pentagon situation, then found nothing of what he said in the final report. "Someone struck it out on grounds of national security," he said. His own career, said colleagues, was jeopardized because he couldn't "take a hint."

The Telephone Tree assured me that because I took Badey seriously, it didn't mean I was paranoid. I sensed families and vets closing protectively around me. Many came into Washington to walk quietly beside The Wall. They spoke with me of sad postwar encounters with obstructive bureaucrats. Politicians saw them as troublemakers. They seemed relieved that their experience was shared by an outsider, by someone in the media. They felt that American editors turned their backs on the men after the war was lost.

"The women have been treated with the same contempt," said John Brown, talking about Betty Foley. The missing colonel's wife had been reduced to the pathetic stratagem of feeling for President Reagan's hand and slipping him a written appeal at a White House reception. She believed from experience her story would never reach him by any other means. President Reagan's hand had closed swiftly over Betty Foley's note. He had said nothing. Later, he wrote to her, *"Poor security during a secret mission to rescue POWs made other missions difficult"* (italics mine).

What secret mission? What other missions?

The colonel's wife was offended by the clumsy contradictions. Reagan's letter had disclosed what was always denied: there were American POWs still alive in enemy hands. When she tried to learn more, she was warned by Pentagon officials that her constant prying could cost her husband his life. "By their own statements, it can't cost him his life," she said. "They've already announced he's dead. Or do they know he's alive? Did they slip up?" She wondered if some group could be making a policy which had the effect of insulating *all* presidents from certain facts that the bureaucracy wished to suppress.

"When I made direct contact with President Reagan," she said, "I couldn't be stopped any more."

"Who did you talk to before?" I asked.

"Colonel Richard Childress at the White House."

I tried to contact this Childress, a new name. No answer. The only background the White House would give: "He's with the National Security Council." I then called Richard Armitage, who was said to "run" POW/MIA affairs in the

Pentagon. I was told he also "ran" U.S. covert-warfare operations.

"Neither Childress nor Armitage know anything about a presidential letter such as you describe," said a spokesman.

Then I received copies of a letter to President Reagan, to which he did not reply. It was from General Lam Van Phat, a Vietnamese resistance leader who had been military commander of the Saigon area until the 1975 collapse. After getting out of Communist captivity, he had written to Reagan, "As a prisoner of the Communists myself, I can confirm Marine Garwood was held prisoner and was not a deserter." Van Phat was held for seven years, together with other South Vietnam generals. "Seeing Garwood every week over a long period, we know him well and can clearly recognize the face. . . . I feel an obligation to testify that Garwood was not a deserter."

I called Childress and Armitage again, this time for a statement on the Van Phat letter. Neither would speak to me. I was told nothing was known about Van Phat or his letter. However, I was sent a defense-intelligence (DIA) evaluation report on Van Phat, ridiculing the Vietnamese general's "pretensions" to lead an anti-Communist resistance movement. Later I directly questioned the Pentagon's new defense-intelligence director, General Lenny Perroots. He denied knowing anything about Van Phat.

I hoped to enlist Bill's help by recounting these denials. They should stir up his dislike of bureaucrats, especially if they made ready use of secrecy. Instead, he said, "If these bureaucrats are intelligence officers, their job would be to stop presidents from blurting indiscretions about secret missions."

"You're not much help," I said.

"If nosy women quizzed the secret armies fighting Nazism, Hitler would never have lost."

"Bobby Garwood's not part of any war."

"Perhaps he is," said Bill, "without knowing it."

One war was between the Defense Intelligence Agency and its former chief, General Eugene Tighe. DIA said it had definitely debriefed Garwood. Tighe, who was director at the time, said the Marine Corps had prevented DIA from conducting a proper debriefing.

I got hold of a "DIA Evaluation of U.S. POW/MIA Information Provided by Pfc. Robert L. Garwood" and thought defense-intelligence had debriefed him after all. But the document recorded only some halting dialogue between Garwood and an officer assigned by the Marine Corps that took place on March 19, 1979, the week after Garwood ended his fourteen-year captivity. The DIA "evaluation" summary of this so-called interrogation covered one side of a single sheet of paper. A normal debriefing can take hundreds of hours. An American who had been so long inside the enemy camp should have been questioned back and forth many times over, most especially if it was seriously believed that he had enjoyed considerable freedom of movement.

Garwood, having trouble with his English immediately after such a long and total immersion in Vietnamese, had said "it was common speaking" among Vietnamese peasants that Americans were still held prisoner. His words were recorded: "And why, why can I have this knowledge and how could I get it? Because I made it a point to be able to survive under that Communist government, to know these people, and especially their language . . . I was able to make messages with them. . . . There are many things the people don't know about, and as curious as any, if somebody doesn't know about something or they even have, what you say, a breeze, they try to find out about it." He then tried to explain the location of prison camps. "I know the hell they [the prisoners] are going through. It is your military duty [inaudible] I know better than you [inaudible]. And you study, you study how I got out of it."

The report was made available by DIA to congressional investigators. It showed his Marine Corps legal counsel saying: "I believe we will be debriefing at greater length and in considerable detail."

There had never been another debriefing, although General Tighe tried. After he retired in 1981, DIA and the Marine Corps joined in publicly stating that the brief discussion between Garwood and the Marine captain represented a full debriefing.

Men like General Tighe, bound by secrecy laws, had a hard time speaking their minds in public on this issue. In this case, the Garwood transcript had been reclassified, making it impossible for any patriotic critic to raise publicly a concern that Garwood had not been sufficiently interrogated. My copy came through a Capitol Hill researcher.

This devotion to secrecy had to explain the caution of Roger Shields, the Pentagon man in charge of POW/MIA affairs during the key years of 1971 to 1976. I let him know that I had seen confidential documents since we had spoken the first time. Would he be more forthcoming?

He was. He said, "We negotiated the prisoners away."

Would Shields repeat that on camera?

"I'm in a sensitive position," he said.

What did he mean? He had left government employ to go into private business. Couldn't he afford to say publicly what he had just told me?

No, said Shields. These were government secrets.

I was being swept along by events. Hewitt had said, "Keep going!" This always, in the past, meant full freedom to explore. He understood when his producers went after bigger fish, and trusted them to make shrewd use of time and resources. I was tugging away at the threads of two stories. One I now labelled "Garwood/Hero or Traitor?" The other was "Unwanted – Dead or Alive." I began to see that the threads belonged in a larger tapestry.

During long investigations, the producer does not report on a daily basis. This allows initiative full rein. But there is none of the satisfaction of the print reporter, who sees his running story appear as it unfolds. The producer is left alone to work out the disposition of the film crews, to direct researchers, and to make the best use of the correspondent's time once the final interviews and script have been roughed out. Because there is all this time to prepare, it can happen that the producer ends up knowing more about the relatively simple story she is producing than she can ever use.

Bits of information kept coming in. The *Dallas Times-Herald* of October 28, 1984, had reported an organizer's claim that Richard Childress on the National Security Council had tried to thwart plans for a parade of Vietnam veterans drawing attention to the MIA issue. After the newspaper published the story, Bill Bennett, a Washington lawyer who had taken up Garwood's cause for the vets, wrote to Congressman Solarz as chairman of the congressional subcommittee on Asian and Pacific Affairs: "This is not the ranting of some crazed 'Rambo' freak, but the sober conclusion of a major metropolitan newspaper. . . . If there are no live POWs, it seems odd that activists claiming their existence would be harassed. . . . It is highly unusual for the National Security Council to be engaged in political activity. . . . [It] would lend further credence to coverup accusations."

I needed someone like General Tighe, a recognized authority, to back up on camera the claim that there was evidence of live POWs before I could present it as a reasonable possibility. General Tighe would be hard to challenge. Forty years in the profession of intelligence had taught him to conceal his feelings, so that when he did express a forceful opinion, it made people jump. The disinformation about his "senility" was cruel. He happened just now to be dealing with grave health problems, affecting both his eyesight and his hearing. However, his mind was razor sharp. I asked if he would voice his unconventional opinions on camera.

Tighe thought about it. "A man has to follow his conscience," he said after a moment. "Yes, I'll do it."

One of Tighe's congressional opponents was Solarz. A self-confident man, Solarz had gone from noisy anti-war protester, during the period when his peers were going to war in Vietnam, to strong government supporter as Democratic chairman of the POW/MIA subcommittee. He had become a team player, even in a Republican era, and his low opinion of General Tighe for breaking ranks was more carefully disguised than his scorn for Bobby Garwood's "treachery." When Solarz protested against Garwood's testifying in public, in a July speech before family members in the National League of Families, he said: "We have the spectacle of someone who betrayed his nation, somebody who worked for the enemy, somebody who deserted the institution he was pledged to support . . . refuses to take polygraph tests, refuses to cooperate with the Defense Intelligence Agency. He only came forward with this alleged information years after he returned to the United States. . . ."*

Lawyer Bill Bennett nailed Solarz on each inaccuracy in his extremely inappropriate speech. Garwood had never refused a polygraph test. The desertion charge had been dismissed. And Garwood had not refused to cooperate with DIA – it would be fairer to say that the Defense Intelligence Agency had refused to cooperate with Garwood.

"Solarz speaks for the inter-agency group using Garwood to squash the demand for disclosure of POW/MIA intelligence," alleged Mike Van Atta when I spoke to him. "He led protests against the war we were fighting when he was at an age to fight. Now, at forty, he wants to prove his patriotism by doing what he's told."

When Solarz chose to denounce Garwood to the National League of Families, its former president, Marian Shelton, told me, "The League was started by wives to force a wartime

---

*   My researcher, Nellie Duncan, took notes during the speech.

administration to act on behalf of their men held in prison camps. Now it's run by the government as a front to kill open discussion." Marian Shelton was the wife of the only missing American who was still carried officially on the prisoner-of-war lists. She would suffer later for her bluntness. She said, "Thanks to Solarz's speech and the League, the American people don't have a chance to decide the truth. My heart goes out to Bobby Garwood. . . . Other families feel the same. Any of our men might have been forced to make decisions Garwood made."

Her husband had been one of the most dedicated American fliers in Indochina. He had tried repeatedly to escape from captivity. The CIA reported he had killed his jailers in one such attempt. It made his wife's support for Garwood, allegedly a traitor, all the more striking, and Solarz's attacks that much more difficult for the families to understand.

Late in June, Garwood finally talked to *60 Minutes* on film, face to face with Ed Bradley in a suite at the Madison Hotel in Washington. He filled in the picture he had given me of "Ike," Special Forces Captain William F. Eisenbraun, who had been in captivity twice as long as Garwood when he was transferred, almost naked in a cold jungle rain, to where the Marine was in solitary. Ike was shocked, said Garwood, by the private's ignorance about survival in prison. He explained to the young man that the rules the Marines had taught him about the behavior expected of an American prisoner had changed. It was no longer necessary to give just your name, rank, and serial number, no matter how badly you were tortured. "You can let out anything that's public knowledge. You do it bit by bit, to win a respite, so you can bounce back," Ike told him.

It also now became clear why Garwood delayed seeing

Ike's daughter after his return. He said he'd been ordered to keep away from her by the Marine Corps when he left Vietnam.

Shortly after the interview, Bradley went on vacation. The film remained in the New York cutting room, where the film editor voted it the most troubling and dramatic footage seen in a long time. When Bradley returned, he declared that Garwood "was just not good television."

Soon after, Congressman Billy Hendon called me to say the country would soon see incontrovertible proof of a deliberate cover-up of intelligence on prisoners. Representatives of the government and the U.S. military had sabotaged – that was his word, *sabotaged* – a rescue effort.

I was wary. "What evidence is there? Who's willing to go on camera?"

"Well," said Billy, "I guess you'd say these people are pretty impressive. The most highly decorated American alive . . . a colonel who's won the Medal of Honor . . . a major from the really dirty part of the jungle war in Vietnam, wounded twenty to thirty times, then a prisoner, then did Special Forces work behind the lines in Asia. A former U.S. Air Force intelligence officer who holds the Distinguished Flying Cross and says the biggest obstacle to collecting information on downed airmen was not the enemy but the CIA. . . . "

We seemed to be getting into never-never land, but it was too late to pull out. I scribbled down a name at Billy's dictation: Mark Waple of Fayetteville, North Carolina.

Shortly after, I visited Waple in his office in the law firm of Hutchens and Waple. The office bore the stamp of military tidiness from the lawyer's days as a paratrooper. A handsome West Point graduate, who walked with a certain poker-backed stride, he came, like his wife, Elizabeth ("Buff"), from a military family. Their fathers were colonels who between them had fought in five wars. Their combined families had been represented in every conflict involving U.S. honor in this century. Mark and Buff had travelled the world with the Army. Now they lived, with their children, in the heart of Special Forces country, where elite units prepared to move in quick reaction to emergencies abroad. There was nothing the least bit flaky about the Waples.

Mark told me how, in the spring of 1985, a man in military camouflage had come to ask if he minded having his office swept for electronic bugs.

"I have two friends," said the visitor, "who wish to discuss a very sensitive subject with you."

Waple assumed his prospective clients were in trouble with Army rules and regulations. He was building a reputation for defending enlisted men who fell afoul of Army justice. He sat back, slightly bemused, while his visitor brought in military electronic debugging specialists ("rat-catchers"), who tore his office apart. "They lifted the carpets, looked behind pictures, pulled away wall panels," said Waple. "It made a frightful mess. And of course they found nothing – we don't go in for hidden microphones at Hutchens and Waple."

The "rat-catchers" left, and a tough-looking soldier entered. Waple stared at him for a long time and then, gesturing at the disarranged office, said, "The men who were just here – they said they had two friends needing help."

"That's right," said the soldier. "Me – Major Smith – and Sergeant McIntire." He indicated the man behind him.

Smith beat around the bush for a couple of hours. Major Mark Smith, it turned out, was a highly decorated Green Beret. In one week-long battle in Vietnam, he was finally captured after collapsing from a succession of wounds. He had been given the singular honor of being first to disembark from an Operation Homecoming aircraft that brought back prisoners after the Vietnam ceasefire. Smith became commander of Special Forces Detachment, Korea (SFD-K), which, among other duties gathered intelligence in Southeast Asia and ran covert missions. He was so good at secret and gruelling assignments that his commendations rose steadily and spectacularly. Then out of nowhere came a barrage of adverse reports about his personal and professional failings. The source was inside the White House.

Waple listened patiently, hiding his growing perplexity. Smith seemed to be sounding him out. He now supposed, after all, that Smith was leading up to some extremely delicate matter of national security. When the major finally centered on an investigation the Army was conducting into alleged cross-border violations in Southeast Asia, the "plausibly deniable" operations sounded to Waple like something in a spy thriller. Smith and his companion had been brought back from Asia to face charges of breaking international laws. The government denied authorizing their operations.

"What do you want me to do?" Waple asked.

"You've got to find some legal way to force the Army to send us back," replied Smith. Clearing his name seemed secondary to what he felt he still had to do in Southeast Asia.

The whole story tumbled out. Major Smith and Sergeant First Class Melvin McIntire, also SFD-K, believed one of their tasks was to locate and, if possible, to rescue American prisoners-of-war. They claimed that in April of 1984 Smith received word from a high-ranking officer in Thailand that there would be three American POWs available to be taken out of Laos in May. Smith passed that information on to Army Major General Kenneth C. Leuer, along with a briefing paper containing two years of intelligence on POWs that had been collected by a team he had set up in 1982. According to Smith, Leuer read the two cover letters to the report and responded, "This is too hot for me to handle, big guy." Smith said the general then told him that, if he were smart, he'd shred the report and forget the whole thing. Smith told Waple that after the meeting with the general, not only did their government stop their operations, it scuttled the POW rescue – and its agents sabotaged them in Thailand.

"What about this criminal investigation?" Waple asked.

"We're innocent," said Smith. "But I'd like you to be present while we're interrogated."

Smith and McIntire, who had worked as a team on this issue since Korea, had crashed down on the lawyer like a ton of bricks. They tested his sense of order, but Waple had a shrewd perception of the qualities that make for good soldiers, and in his opinion these two had them. There was also a deep stubbornness in Lawyer Waple: the kind that makes a man hold position in combat when all his comrades have fallen and expediency urges him to get out. Waple suspected a large number of combat soldiers also knew a great wrong was being done, because Smith and McIntire had been able to bring the military "rat-catchers" into play. Possibly they had Special Forces behind them, or at least those in covert operations who realized that what happened to the major and the sergeant might also happen to them. Once the government denied them, soldiers in covert action were vulnerable to being discredited or even charged with illegal activities. He said yes, and thereby sentenced himself to years of heartbreak.

In late spring, Tracy Usry, an agent from the U.S. Army Criminal Investigation Command (CIDC – formerly CID) examined the two soldiers for five days in the offices of Hutchens and Waple. At the end, Usry said he found all the allegations against them to be unfounded and unsubstantiated. This did not prevent their enemies from perpetuating a myth that the men were found guilty.*

Finally, on September 4, 1985, the two Green Berets, with Waple as their attorney, filed suit against the President of the United States and virtually every current and former government official involved in making decisions on POWs on

---

* The Army CIDC report clearing Smith and McIntire was classified "secret." It was not to be until September of 1989 that Senator Charles Grassley (Rep. Iowa) would personally walk into the Department of Defense's office of Congressional Legislative Liaison and insist on seeing the copy. By that time Major Smith had been smeared to such effect that the general public thought he was no longer credible.

behalf of all living American prisoners-of-war still held in Southeast Asia. The plaintiffs presented the case that the U.S. government had, since 1973, failed to act on the best possible intelligence and try to bring the men home.

The decision by the two Green Berets was greeted by the media as eccentric. Part of the problem was that most of the information being gathered for the lawsuit fell into a category that could be labelled top secret. I knew from long talks with Waple that he felt fiercely engaged in a battle that went to the very heart of American values. The nature of the fight, though, would require him to respect the classification of documents as highly confidential when he knew they contained secrets of value only to government agents seeking to suppress the truth. The very safety of the U.S. Delta forces – highly trained in special operations such as hostage rescues – and other special combat units based all around his home was, he believed, jeopardized by this unwillingness to utilize "secret intelligence." Such unwillingness increased the risk to men in war if they were taken prisoner. He seemed like an old-time sheriff fighting for justice on a lawless frontier, but the bad guys behaved as if they were the ones who carried warrants for his arrest.

It was a good story for *60 Minutes*. It would go beyond "Unwanted – Dead or Alive." Perhaps a better title was suggested by the label on Waple's lawsuit: *"Smith vs. The President."*

CHAPTER 4

THE WHITE HOUSE COLONEL

The story was shaping itself in my head – two certified heroes who separately confirmed the claims of Bobby Garwood and POW families that there was evidence of live POWs. There was also a new twist, and a new character. These Green Berets, attacking a Republican president, were whisked to Dallas by the Republican who played a major role in putting Reagan into the White House: H. Ross Perot.

What did Perot have to say to them? Why was he interested?

The billionaire had popped up throughout our investigations. The Telephone Tree used his name generously. Vets regarded him as the one powerful champion of their cause. Congress considered making him head of a commission investigating missing Americans.

Perot called me one day at home, and got Bill instead. Bill listened to the Texan's explosive recounting of the dastardly way intelligence on U.S. prisoners had been wasted. When

Perot paused for breath, Bill said innocently, "Maybe you should talk to the CIA about this." A clap of verbal thunder rumbled down the line. Perot's language left little to the imagination. "I gather," Bill said to me later, "he doesn't think much of the CIA."

Was that why Perot had flown Major Smith and Sergeant McIntire to Dallas all of a sudden? Was he planning another rescue operation – free from blunderings of the CIA? It wouldn't be surprising. During the Iranian revolution, he and his employees had improvised and executed a daring commando raid to get two of his employees out of Iran. At Perot's invitation, novelist Ken Follett wrote a bestseller about the events, *On Wings of Eagles*, which was later turned into a five-hour television mini-series. A new Perot rescue plan would explain why I kept running across his tracks. My own military and intelligence sources were the kind he'd need in preparation for a mission. He was always going out the back door as I came in through the front.

I decided to call at his own front door. Perot was then still boss of Electronic Data Systems, so the front door of his corporate headquarters was not modest. It stood on the far side of what had been the biggest golf course in Texas, flanked by flags of all nations. Driving into his corporate grounds was like visiting an alternative United Nations, except that the grass was greener, the architecture less assertive. Joggers humanized the flawless acreage, and distracted the eye from security fencing hidden behind crew-cut shrubbery.

When I left the elevator at the seventh floor I was brought to a dead halt by the portrait of a young man in an anti-gravity suit and jungle boots, a flying helmet tucked under one arm. It was Lance Sijan, the boy who once whirled me across the dance floor of the old Saratoga at 16th and Muskego in Milwaukee, the place well known to students, sometimes as The Irish Club, sometimes as The Balkan Hang-Out. Perot, I was to learn, was fascinated by heroes, and Lance was now a Medal of Honor winner.

I stood there, time forgotten. Fresh in my mind were words spoken at the Air Force Academy when a building was dedicated to his memory. "At 2039 Hanoi time on 9 November 1967 he was shot down . . . so badly hurt that when a Jolly Green rescue helicopter dropped a jungle penetrator to hoist him home, he could not crawl the twenty feet. When the rescue pilot radioed that a parajumper was coming down to help, he called back: 'Negative, Jolly! There's *bad* guys down here, real close.' " He refused to let fellow Americans risk their lives, knowing the enemy was all around. Yet, despite this and his many injuries, he tried to escape once, and defied his captors until he died." If his death had not been witnessed by other American POWs who made it back, the story might never have been told.

He'd be in his early forties, the same age as Chairman Solarz.

I said nothing to Perot about the portrait. Seeing it, right here, had shocked me, but if Perot was like other men of immense wealth, he would regard any display of feeling as an attempt to get under his guard. Yet the way he decorated his offices with drawings, sculptures, and photographs of other aviators made me feel I had come to the right place. I counted a score of Remington statues. Just like the painting of Lance, each image of a cowboy on horseback was in its way a tribute to the human spirit. There was a large painting of an American prisoner, beside a glass sculpture of a sailboat running free: the two works of art reinforced each other. There were Norman Rockwell paintings of fathers with sons, and the sons all reminded me of Perot, who was now ushering me to the rear of his barn-sized office. When he was swallowed up in his rocking chair, he looked like a pugnacious schoolboy.

He was a trim five feet six, and his restless bouncing belied his fifty-four years. His style reminded me of the inventor and businessman who became a spymaster, Sir William Stephenson, known as Intrepid. The two men had a lot in common: pride in their plain-folks roots, a refusal to put on airs, a belief in the individual. Stephenson had been a bantam-weight boxer. Perot's nose had been smashed breaking in horses. Perot was said to poke fun at his own ugliness. I would have called his features blunt. He had a disarming way of sticking his face up into the light, forcing you to look at ears jutting like a small boy's, and a nose that was lumpy and broken. I had heard the unadorned accent often enough on the telephone. Put together with the rest of him, it said: What you see and hear is what you get.

Perot would say nothing about Smith and McIntire. Instead, he was full of questions. Did I think there was a conspiracy of silence about Americans lost in Indochina? Just about every newspaper and broadcasting outlet had sent journalists to interview him at great length. They always asked him if there was anything left he wanted to do. Yes, he would say, he wanted to win freedom for the men still left behind in Southeast Asia, because any country that abandoned its men on the battlefield was in dire need of rearming itself morally.

And none of the journalists' reports, he told me, had noted this one thing he wanted to accomplish.

I did not think it was possible to censor the media in America, I replied. They were too competitive. What could sometimes happen was that a climate of opinion developed quickly in this age of soap-opera news coverage. A fixed idea spread fast like an infection. Maybe the fixed idea on MIAs was that they weren't hot television any more. I said, "TV sets the standards these days."

Perot gave me a sharp, searching look.

I wanted to seize the initiative and be the one who asked the questions. He was clearly not ready for that. He wasn't exactly falling over himself to dish out information, but he was a natural horse-trader. I said enough to let him see I had sources that he did not, and I volunteered a few details – just enough to prick his curiosity. I was sure he'd deal when the right moment came.

Later, I told my husband about the similarities between Intrepid and the Texan. "And Perot's got this infatuation with flying, like Sir William. There's a terrific trophy on one of Perot's shelves, cast in bronze. It's of General Robinson Risner, the fighter ace shot down in Vietnam." The trophy was awarded to outstanding aviators, and Perot sponsored the award and thus honored General Risner.

"Now there's someone you really should see," Bill said.

"Why?"

"He's very close to Nancy Reagan." Bill knew that Risner had worked closely with Perot on a successful campaign to purge Texas of illegal drugs. When Reagan became president, he asked him to work with Nancy in her war on drugs. Bill felt that if my inquiries were hurting the country, or jeopardizing lives, General Risner would tell me.

"Don't tell me *you're* starting to take the anonymous calls seriously?" I said.

"No. But suppose Perot *is* getting men out? You could stir up interest at the worst moment – "

I felt crushed. I could handle Bill's disapproval of the pressures put on me because of a particular story, but didn't he understand how decent American patriots had been silenced by such secrecy? This was not just another *60 Minutes* piece.

Early in September, David Taylor, the British Broadcasting Corporation's Washington-based producer – whose office was next to mine in the same building – came to my door. He was furious because I had made Tighe promise not to do any other interviews until my program aired. I wanted the audience to pay full attention.

"Why keep him exclusive from *us*? You don't compete with the BBC!"

"I didn't know you wanted him – "

"You must have known! You talked to Colonel Nick Rowe." He surprised me by naming Rowe. I had been protecting his identity because of his connection with Army covert operations.

"Hold on. . . . " I made Taylor sit down. "Are you working on MIAs?"

Taylor turned cautious. "Among other things."

I said I was sorry. I wanted to keep Tighe from the rest of the American media, not from British viewers. "Anyway," I asked, "what's the connection with Nick Rowe?"

"It's a related story." Taylor groaned. "All these stories are jinxed, anyway."

"You were only fighting against me," I said. "I don't know who it is I'm fighting."

Taylor raised his hands. "Some government outfit tried to scare me off. Even tried to have me arrested as a drug-runner."

"*What*?" This quiet-mannered young Englishman had one of the BBC's plum foreign assignments. He would be the last person to wreck his career in such a stupid way.

"I'd been to see a very interesting fellow who has at various times worked for law enforcement and the CIA. He claims he was on a mission to find missing Americans." Taylor continued, "He claims he was ordered to kill them when he did locate them. . . . "

I froze.

"It seemed so far out, we ran checks on this fellow. He was for real." Taylor met the source in Los Angeles. When he got back to Washington, he was stopped at National airport by two drug-enforcement agents who went through his bags. They said he was under suspicion of trafficking in drugs. It took him a while to react, but he finally got mad when they went through his notebooks. He told them they wouldn't find dope *there*. One of the agents got smart and replied, "No, but we might find the name of a well-known drug dealer." He then dropped the name of the man Taylor had seen in L.A.

Taylor's White House pass had fallen to the floor. One of the agents picked it up and said quickly, "He's a journalist."

That sobered them up. The other agent piled Taylor's things together and said, "Hey, could you be upsetting someone high up?" The first man said, "We had this strong tip from the L.A. police. Guess someone's trying to send you a message. No hard feelings, huh?"

I listened to Taylor with growing discomfort and said, "The silly bastards figured you'd be recalled to London – "

"I grant they're not very efficient. I was terrified the agents would find drugs *planted* in my bags."

"Maybe it was just a message," I said. "Like the ones I've been getting . . . "

As we compared notes, we became almost giddy with relief. We had discovered we were not alone. Thus was formed an informal alliance, from which I got an immediate benefit – the name of the man Taylor saw in L.A.: Scott Barnes.

Barnes was a thirty-one-year-old freelance specialist in covert warfare. Ross Perot later described him as "a mystery box." He was said to be well trained in the black arts of intelligence, from the use of deadly weapons to the smuggling of arms. I had heard rumors of "a CIA man" who spoke of finding American prisoners in Indochina. When I phoned him in California, Barnes admitted he was the "CIA man" referred to. He said he'd gone to ABC *Nightline*, but CIA Director Bill Casey had personally pressured ABC to kill the show – a claim I didn't believe. ABC's news department had too much integrity, too much independence.

Over time, Barnes told me wild stories about being a freelance assassin for the CIA. He talked with seemingly intimate knowledge about secret wars financed through the sale of drugs and arms. When I checked with friends inside the intelligence community, they said many of the technical details could only be known to someone who had worked among them.

I had Barnes investigated by an expert, a man who had at one time worked for the Army's Criminal Investigation Command. The investigator came back with an extraordinary tale.

Barnes said he was on a multi-purpose mission, sanctioned by the CIA, the Drug Enforcement Agency (DEA), and one of the Pentagon's secret-intelligence units, when he saw Americans in a Communist part of Indochina. Barnes concluded that some part of the U.S. government had special reasons for not wanting them out, because, he claims, his team had been ordered to get rid of "the merchandise."

"It's easy for the CIA or whatever to disown him, though," I said to the investigator. "Will any authority speak for him?"

"There's the man who set up the CIA's lie-detector system, Chris Gugas. He's retired now, but he polygraphed Barnes. Says he's telling the truth."

Before I called Gugas, I asked General Tighe for an opinion. "Gugas is the best in his field," said Tighe. "I'd believe *him*."

I phoned Gugas, who said: "Barnes passed every polygraph I gave him. Every psychiatric test showed he told the truth . . . that his team saw the prisoners and was then told 'Liquidate the merchandise,' which Barnes took to mean *kill the Americans*."

"But why?"

"There's a deep and evil conspiracy at work. It all stinks to high heaven."

Gugas, who also supported Bobby Garwood's claims, said he had been warned by someone in the government that, if he persisted with his support for Garwood and Barnes, his son, an Air Force officer, would find his promotion delayed. Gugas did not go public with the threat until his son got the promotion.

Scott Barnes published his own account of secret missions, and then told me about frightening events that caused him to keep changing his story. However, Chris Gugas saw the secret documents that he provided to investigators and believed them to be authentic.

Official National Security Council and Pentagon sources insisted Barnes was a fake. Other military-type sources, however, confirmed Barnes's claim that there had been a secret mission. Pentagon sources told me for the first time about the Army's Intelligence Support Activity (ISA). This must have been the secret-intelligence unit mentioned by Barnes. ISA insiders, angered by CIA efforts to curtail their undertakings, insisted that the CIA's Casey had known about the Barnes mission, originally conceived as a reconnaissance mission to find prisoners for the ISA.

But that mission, Barnes said, was taken over by a secret arm of the CIA known as The Activity.* The Activity sounded like the product of a thriller-writer's imagination. One of its formerly most active members explained that it came about because of concern during the Vietnam War that the politicians could cripple covert operations. Ingenuity created new arms of secret-intelligence activity, deliberately hidden from politicians – some buried inside the armed forces, some grown independently under the direction of CIA "creative loners." These activities were funded by CIA-type "proprietaries." Such front companies grew with the Southeast Asian wars and defeat in Vietnam. Funding for CIA-run wars, after the evacuation from Saigon, would have attracted the hostile curiosity of Congress and, through leaks, the public. One suspected proprietary, the Nugan Hand enterprise, a banking operation based in Australia with offices in Thailand, had collapsed in 1979, the year Bobby Garwood was placed under Marine guard in Bangkok on his arrival from Hanoi. The Australian financial enterprise became the subject of several Australian government inquiries and a royal commission into charges that the enterprise laundered profits from smuggled arms and illegal drugs to pay for the continuation of rogue secret wars in Asia.

"Don't forget there's the official CIA and there's a really deep-cover, privatized CIA," claimed my source, and went on to say that, in his opinion, "the privatized CIA has a hold over Barnes."

---

* The name "The Activity" was also used to describe the Army's Intelligence Support Activity (ISA), which caused some confusion.

Barnes said he had been deeply involved in the fallout from the collapse of another enterprise similar to the Australian one. It was an investment firm named Bishop, Baldwin, Dillingham, Rewald and Wong (BBDRW), based in Honolulu, that provided funds for part of the mission during which Barnes claimed to have seen prisoners.

I had reservations, though, about Barnes's version of events. He reminded me of another young American, Christopher Boyce, who was also very persuasive. In the Boyce case, an introduction to secret intelligence at a very young age had sent him off in an entirely different direction. He had talked to *60 Minutes* in aggrieved terms about abuses by the U.S. government's intelligence agencies of its secret powers. *That* young man had sold highly secret information to the Russians. My *60 Minutes* story on him was simply titled "Traitor."

Throughout the summer of 1985, I juggled between diapers and documentaries. I was caught between kitchen and cradle when I got a call. A man's voice said, "I hear you're looking into men left behind in Vietnam."

I was extra wary by this time. "How did you get this number?" I countered.

"Could we meet?" The caller was equally cautious. "My name's McDaniel. Captain Red McDaniel, U.S. Navy, Retired. I'm President of the American Defense Institute."

I agreed to a meeting far enough away to give me a chance to look into his background. CBS News files showed that McDaniel and the ADI, a non-profit, private organization with strong ties to the military, were above reproach. They worked for a strong national defense policy. The advisory board included the former commander of U.S. Forces in Vietnam, a former Chairman of the Joint Chiefs of Staff, some solid senators and congressmen, and an assortment of distinguished citizens.

McDaniel himself sounded like everything I admired. He held the Navy's top award for bravery and numerous other decorations. Before the Vietnam War he had flown highly secret, practice nuclear-weapons missions against simulated Soviet targets. Shot down over North Vietnam in 1967, he spent six years in Vietnamese captivity. He made sure that, despite endless torture sessions, the enemy never discovered his earlier operations. After Hanoi released him in 1973, Red took command of the aircraft carrier *Lexington* and for several years was director of liaison on Capitol Hill for the Navy and the Marine Corps. His heroism was legendary among vets. One of his combat squadron pilots said, "The guys worship the ground he walks on." McDaniel's credentials were so respectable that I figured his job was to persuade me that Garwood really was a traitor and that all the talk of Americans being still alive in Asia was subversive propaganda.

What I got was devastatingly different.

McDaniel was fifty-three, a tall and immensely dignified man with a crown of graying red hair and the loping walk of an athlete. One of his arms twitched regularly as a consequence of Vietnamese torture. He had the look of someone who has suffered and risked so much that nothing is left to frighten him; who is so secure in his sense of integrity that it would never occur to him to dissemble.

McDaniel started by saying he'd received a disturbing call from Richard Childress in the White House. He characterized Colonel Childress as part of a tight-knit team around the President. He had joined the National Security Council as what was termed a Southeast Asian Political and Military Affairs officer in 1981. He was also responsible for calming the fears of POW/MIA families. Betty Foley remembered him standing between President Reagan and herself. According to the *Dallas Times-Herald*, he had tried to stop the POW/MIA protest parade.

Childress abused McDaniel for defying the official line on prisoners. The phone conversation was heard by Red's wife, Dorothy. Childress called into question Red's patriotism, and nobody knew better than Dorothy what her husband had sacrificed for love of country. He had been on the U.S. Navy's fast track, clearly destined for high rank, when he stepped aside to do what he felt was more important: arouse civilians and politicians to an awareness of defense needs through the American Defense Institute.

McDaniel had logged the call shortly after eleven at night. He said Childress began by trying to revive an old buddy-buddy relationship that had existed between them from the days when Red served on the National League of Families Board, before it became what Red now called "an arm of government to discourage questions about Administration policy on prisoners in Vietnam." Then Childress scolded Red for stubbornly attacking the concealment of intelligence on prisoners in Indochina. Red refused to back off. By midnight, Dorothy said that Childress was shouting at the top of his lungs. McDaniel had offended the White House, according to Childress, who claimed that he briefed the President on POW/MIA matters.

"Do *you* think we have Americans still in captivity in Southeast Asia?" asked Red.

"You're damn right I do."

Red was surprised. Childress seemed to be contradicting his public statements that he knew of no live POWs.

"When can we expect some of them back?"

"In two or three years."

"That's too long," said Red. "We're running out of time."

Childress hung up. Red realized with a pang that if there was not some quick action at higher levels, there would be no prisoners to rescue. The Americans left behind would all be dead.

Early next morning Red got another call that was perhaps more insulting. A woman told him, "Regarding your attitude, you'll be getting a call from Colonel Childress at the White House."

Regarding your attitude? Her tone made Red feel he was back in the country schoolhouse in his native North Carolina. The caller was Ann Mills Griffiths, the salaried Executive Director of the National League of Families. Red's wife, Dorothy, had helped form the League, along with Marian Shelton, to pressure the government during the Vietnam War to act on behalf of prisoners. It had been an up-hill struggle. Now Dorothy, like Red and Marian, was convinced the League was acting for the government in trying to control troublesome relatives who refused to accept there were no more prisoners. If Griffiths was using the threat of White House clout, it must have worked before. "You'll get this call from the President's advisor," Griffiths repeated. Finally Red cut her short. "I already did."

Ann Mills Griffiths was a mournful figure who appeared in official photographs that were taken whenever the U.S. President displayed a periodic concern for missing Americans by attending a League meeting. Many families noted that she usually dressed in black for these occasions. She charged that those who campaigned independently on behalf of live prisoners were "profiteers and charlatans."

Because Griffiths was soon to go to Hanoi as part of a White House team, Red wrote to her after the call: "The disturbing aspect of public statements by U.S. officials, as POW/MIA talks begin in Hanoi, is the lack of mention of live prisoners. ... I am here today because my wife, working closely with U.S. officials during the years that I was missing in action, presented a very convincing case that she knew I was alive."

I contacted Griffiths, who dismissed the letter, and an invitation to take part in the *60 Minutes* MIA segment. "I have made four journeys to Hanoi and held countless meetings in New York with representatives of the Peoples' Republic of Vietnam on this issue," she said. "I cannot comment on speculative assertions. No, I cannot give you any names of families that might be willing to appear on your program."

"What about Major Smith's lawsuit?"

"I don't know what you mean."

"Major Smith, a Green Beret, says his team was stopped from investigating reports of live POWs."

"I know nothing about him," said Griffiths.

The secretary for *60 Minutes* Washington, Alison Curran, mouthed the words "White House" one morning and handed me the telephone.

"Are you doing a piece on POWs?" demanded a bullying man's voice.

"Who is this?" I asked.

"Colonel Childress. National Security Council." My turn had come.

I motioned Alison to stay on the extension and make notes.* I also called in Nellie Duncan, my researcher, who knew I had tried fruitlessly to reach Childress in the past. Now, all of a sudden, *he* was calling *me.*

"Are you including those fanatics Smith and McIntire?"

"Yes," I said.

"You know why Smith is bringing this lawsuit, don't you?" said Childress. "He's mad because he didn't get promoted to colonel. He's a violence-prone bully. A fanatic and a compulsive liar. Beat his wife. You know he's guilty of smuggling gold into Thailand?"

"That's news to me."

"McIntire," said Childress, "is also guilty of smuggling."

"Both men have been completely cleared of the only charges ever brought against them."

"Just take my word for it," said Childress. "They're *bad.*

---

*   This verbatim account of part of that conversation is taken from my notes, confirmed by Alison and Nellie. The notes were also conveyed to Don Hewitt.

Who else are you talking to? I suppose people like McDaniel.
. . . " Childress rattled off the names of other men I had
talked with about prisoners, including a Colonel Robert
Howard. I remained silent as Childress tried to discredit each
of my contacts. He returned to Colonel Howard. "A drunk,"
he said.

I knew Howard was a Medal of Honor winner. He had
sworn out an affidavit in support of Major Smith, and at
present commanded U.S. Army special troops in West Germany.

"As to General Tighe, he isn't too bright," went on Childress. "Why didn't he speak up while he was Director of
Defense Intelligence?"

I said, "Would you come on the program?"

"I can't do that," said Childress. "My advice to you is, drop
the story."

I began to defend my decision, then pulled myself up. I
didn't have to justify *anything* to the government, much less
to a voice on the telephone.

Then Childress said softly, "You could jeopardize the lives
of the prisoners still there."

My God! I thought. He's admitting live people are still
there – not just the bones he always emphasized in his
negotiations with the Vietnamese.

Nellie looked startled when I said, "You're *admitting* men
are still alive over there?"

"You won't be doing yourself any good by producing such
an irresponsible story," Childress said, and hung up.

I called Don Hewitt. I felt I must this time ask for advice. I
was being threatened. What was the National Security Council doing, mucking around in this? Hewitt defended his own
people. I fully expected him to give his famous imitation of a
tiger with a bee under its tail. He listened carefully and made
no comment. Instead I got a call from my correspondent, Ed
Bradley. "We need to give the U.S. government point of
view," he said.

"I couldn't agree more," I replied. "But until now, I haven't been able to get a formal government response."

"You will this time," said Bradley. "Richard Armitage will do it."

Armitage was the man, according to POW families, who knew what really happened to their men and could – if he wanted – do something about it. He was the uniquely powerful covert-activity chief in the Pentagon who also ran policy on the POW/MIA issue. When I had tried to line up Armitage before, I got no response from his office. Now, when I tried again, Armitage immediately agreed to be interviewed.

Then I remembered. Towards the end of my conversation with Childress, he had told me Armitage was the Pentagon man officially controlling the POW/MIA issue and he would give me an interview.

My Bobby Garwood story was now in trouble. The bluesheet had been approved long ago, but Bradley was still cool on the idea after interviewing the disgraced Marine. Executive-producer Hewitt decided the Garwood piece and the story on the lawsuit, *Smith vs. The President*, should be combined as simply "Dead or Alive."

One of the problems with any segment in which interviews and research are spread over many weeks is that everyone comes back to it between dealing with other stories. After too many interruptions over too long a time, the in-depth story that seemed so exciting in the beginning may have grown stale. That seemed the likeliest explanation for dropping Garwood as a separate story and combining him with Smith and McIntire.

CHAPTER 5

THE GOVERNMENT POSITION

Another anonymous caller caught me at home. I told him to convey his message of abuse to Don Hewitt or the president of CBS, along with his accusations against my patriotism. "The Pervs," as I now called them, were making me uncomfortable. They seemed to know my husband was abroad and I was alone with the baby. The one person I could turn to in Bill's absence was Red McDaniel.

"All these appeals to patriotism," I told him, "are so fakey."

"The last refuge of the scoundrel is patriotism," he replied, and described three Medal of Honor winners who took action to free prisoners. "This has jeopardized their careers and even threatened their lives. Anyone who tries to get the prisoners out seems to get in trouble. So don't let anyone preach to you about patriotism."

I flew to Fayetteville, N.C., to film the interviews with Major Smith and Sergeant McIntire in Mark Waple's law office. I already knew now that the two soldiers' stories were corroborated by Lt. Col. Robert Howard, who was a friend of Red McDaniel's.

Howard had said that in 1983 Smith's investigators found evidence that three American prisoners were under the control of a team of non-Communist Laotian resistance fighters. Through a high-ranking Thai military official, who insisted on remaining anonymous, Smith made an agreement with the Laotian team. They would bring the POWs to the Lao-Thai border. He would honor their terms. There would be no exchange of money. But they insisted there be no infringement of Thai sovereignty. Also, because they considered U.S. policy on prisoners ambivalent at best, they specified that the prisoners would be handed over only to officials of the U.S. embassy in Bangkok. The Laotians were often dependent on U.S. good will in obtaining arms and other materials and had no intention of alienating the superpower.

No U.S. officials showed up to meet the Laotian team with the three prisoners, and they turned back. The team reported later that, soon after, one of those prisoners died.

Howard had come to investigate the matter after Smith protested formally that there was an attempt to shut down his entire POW investigation and its rescue efforts. He found that he himself was in danger for now supporting Smith. "The attempt to shut us all down," he told Red, "could have cost my life and that of Smith and McIntire. And our own side was responsible. . . . Those two guys were my best. Later they were put on phony criminal charges to try and stop them that way. They were told to shred their evidence of live Americans, and they refused. . . ." Only later was I to learn the details of the attempt to "shut down" the three men.

As our *60 Minutes* crew set up for the interview with Smith and McIntire, a man lingered on the edge of the proceedings. He was helpful and seemed to belong to Waple's staff. He had donated a thousand dollars to the Smith-McIntire lawsuit fund and was to turn up in other places later: on Ross Perot's doorstep, at meetings of vets, at the trials of men charged with smuggling drugs, arms, and explosives after they became nuisances with their insistence that there were live Americans still in Indochina. I found the stranger spooky, and his name untraceable. Perot once said, "Well, of course, he *is* a spook. He's been planted by the opposition to find out what you're doing."

I was sure my piece on Smith and McIntire would go ahead, because CBS had promised the two Green Berets that their segment would run on the first program of the new season – a night with an almost guaranteed large audience, which included reviewers and critics. *60 Minutes* was fully committed to it. It was because of this promise that Smith and McIntire gave an exclusive interview. Then Hewitt phoned to tell me the two soldiers were "fanatics." He said he had not seen the tape, but that they sounded like "crazies" and "Rambos." I found myself shouting back. Finally I said, "You're worse than Kissinger – "

"What?" Hewitt stopped, nonplussed.

"He said, 'Military men are dumb, stupid animals to be used as pawns for foreign policy.' "*

"I didn't say that!" yelled Hewitt.

"No, according to Woodward and Bernstein, Kissinger did. But you came close." Hewitt rang off.

"Hewitt has a whim of iron," Morley Safer had once said. I decided this was just another whim, and went about getting the confidential service records of the two soldiers to prove Hewitt wrong. I knew an Army general who was outraged by gossip spread against Smith and McIntire. He arranged to get copies of combat reports. "See for yourself what they've gone through," he said. "Start with seven days in April . . . in Vietnam."

Seven days in April 1972 had seen a slaughter. When it ended, Mark Smith was recommended for the Medal of Honor. But he couldn't collect it. After four years of combat in

---

*   Quoted in *The Final Days* by Bob Woodward and Carl Bernstein (Simon and Schuster, 1976).

Vietnam, a record period, he had been captured by the enemy. His rank was then that of captain, and fellow officers called him "Zippo."

A field intelligence report said he'd fought "until bodies were seen by the hundreds" in the base he commanded at Loc Ninh. "With most of his men dead, 'Zippo' Smith directed napalm air strikes into his own operations post, then called in artillery to destroy his position. He made himself the target so that the enemy all around him would also be hit."

In captivity, Smith was kept chained up until he was released ten months later. The first U.S. Army doctor to examine him recorded his thirty-eight wounds in excruciating detail.

McIntire's records showed that he had been "one of an elite team" in covert operations. He had been given the highest professional ratings for "integrity, moral courage and self-discipline." He was highly skilled in "night airfield assaults with the precision of Entebbe."

Both "Zippo" Smith and "Entebbe" McIntire were rated tops by the Army in all areas of professional ability. So where had they gone wrong? McIntire was an Asian linguist, according to his military records; he had built up networks of agents and had "proven ability to win the confidence of senior allied officers in Asia."

I talked with others who had served with the two men in Special Forces Brigade in Korea and Southeast Asia. They argued that Smith and McIntire had trampled over CIA sensitivities. The CIA watchers in Bangkok had spotted the regular soldiers invading CIA "territory" with their POW investigation in neighboring Indochina. When the soldiers threatened to make a public scandal over live Americans still in enemy hands, it was speculated, they had to be silenced. It would seem impossible to smear them. Yet the government – so went the speculation – had set out to do just that.

Hewitt now agreed that men with exemplary records like Smith and McIntire must have deep convictions to take a stand that put them in such jeopardy. The government side must be shown, though – through Richard Armitage, then Pentagon Assistant Secretary of Defense for International Affairs. The families and POW activists wondered why his job as head of covert operations included responsibility for POW/MIAs. They thought he seemed to wield more power than his job description implied.

Armitage was a huge man, who dwarfed even the tall Bradley. His press aide took me aside to make a final attempt to convince me that Smith and McIntire had no authority to go looking for missing Americans. He said again that even to hint that the government was failing to do everything for the POW/MIA issue would damage the morale of the armed forces.

I reminded the aide that one of our *60 Minutes* concerns was General Tighe's reference to live American prisoners, made while he was Defense Intelligence director. The testimony was in the *Congressional Record*. Armitage on camera said Tighe, as DIA chief, never spoke of Americans held against their will. He professed to know little about Smith and McIntire's offer to go back and collect evidence. It was never their job to gather POW intelligence, he claimed. Shown a copy of the order authorizing the collection of POW intelligence, he said, "I'd say it's a collateral duty."

Had information collected by Smith and McIntire on specific Americans been passed to the DIA for investigation, as required by law? "I'm not sure," said Armitage. "I would be under the impression that it was, but – ah – ah, I'll have to find out." Armitage suddenly seemed lost.

During one of the breaks, I pushed Bradley to ask a question not on the list written out for him. How could Armitage refute what was in the *Congressional Record*?

It was, I thought, an important question. Bradley told me, "We've agreed to a time limit." Then, when taping recommenced, he repeated the question Armitage had earlier fumbled. This time, Armitage responded: "I'm informed that it [information on the Americans] was passed on to DIA and investigated." Armitage insisted that there had never been enough credible evidence on POWs for the U.S. government to act. Nevertheless, finding live POWs was the number one priority on the Reagan agenda.

Armitage had greeted Bradley as an old friend from the Vietnam War days, and sat with the correspondent after the interview, chatting privately. When Bradley rejoined us, he announced that the interview with Tighe, set for the next day, should be cancelled. He felt that Tighe's filmed statement in front of a congressional committee could be used instead.

"General Tighe put off a vacation for this," I protested in front of the whole crew. We were gathered on the steps of the Rayburn Building on Capitol Hill. "He's kept himself exclusively for us. It took *months* to organize – " Bradley shook me off and began looking for a taxi.

Nellie Duncan, my researcher, said in an appalled voice, "Ed, we need Tighe to specifically counter Armitage!"

"I'm spending the weekend at my ski place," he shouted, running down the steps. He scrambled into a cab and was gone.

The crew were packing gear when I returned. A sound man said, "What the hell happened?"

That evening I was silent as Bill drove us to a small dinner with Supreme Court Justice Bill Brennan. Brennan was a good friend. I had been bursting to ask him about the legalities underlying both the Garwood and the MIA stories. The incident outside the Rayburn Building, though, had knocked the wind out of me.

"You're very quiet tonight, dear," said Justice Brennan.

I wanted to tell him the truth. But the trust between us was too precious. Once, I had secured for Brennan a rare, written apology from Mike Wallace for something he'd said amiss about the Justice on *60 Minutes*. That was as close as I ever came to mixing business with personal friendship.

My husband made up for my silence, expounding on the

rule of law. He had recently lunched with Brennan and Justice Lewis Powell, just the three of them alone. Powell had been attached in World War II to British "Ultra" decoding headquarters and was later invited to be the first director of the Central Intelligence Agency. At the lunch, my husband, "balancing between the left and the right wings of the Supreme Court," had been impressed to see that it didn't matter what political opinions were held by these upholders of the law; in argument, they let the facts lead them to the final verdict. I was fast coming to the conclusion that this was a rare quality – and not one conspicuous in the POW issue.

On the way home, I said, "All your eloquence at dinner – I was dying to ask about the Hostage Act."

"What's that?" asked Bill.

"It requires the government to act on behalf of men under forcible restraint abroad."

Bill heaved a sigh. "Not MIAs again!"

"It's what those two Green Berets have turned to as a last resort." I told him how Mark Waple had invoked the Act in his lawsuit against the President to try and circumvent government gags. The government position was that secret government documents must remain secret to protect national security. Waple was trying to prove that, by withholding those documents, they were negligent in their duty to do everything short of war to bring prisoners home. The proof had to be examined, he argued, before it could be acted upon. I had just spent the evening next to the most venerable member of the Supreme Court and couldn't talk about a situation that I felt struck at the roots of America's security. I broke my own decision not to talk business, and described to Bill the way the Armitage interview had gone. I explained about General Tighe and said: "He states on the record that the evidence of POWs being alive is overwhelming. Armitage insists that Tighe never said it. And now we've just lost the chance to have Tighe refute him."

There had been pressure on Bradley to finish the MIA story for the new season's opening in September 1985, thus honoring the promise made to Smith and McIntire. The pressure had bothered Bradley, who became less enthusiastic. Still, the "Dead or Alive" story was on the opening night's schedule, and I would have to do the best with what I had.

There was barely time to prepare for the opening show. I wanted to include an interview with Congressman Stephen Solarz, who had chaired the hearing that disallowed Garwood's open testimony and frustrated Bill Hendon's attempt to show his Measles Map. Solarz asked, "Are you planning to sandbag me?" He evidently suspected I had hard evidence on live POWs. As a Democrat, he nevertheless was seen as "a key supporter" of Republican policy in Southeast Asia.

I told him I had no plans to embarrass him. In our filmed interview, he denied there was any evidence of Americans held against their will in Asia. Privately, he modified the assertion, telling me there was nothing to show any Americans had survived.

"Someone in this administration made it clear to me that some men are alive," I said.

Solarz gave me a long, hard look. "Who?"

"My source asked that it be off the record."

Solarz didn't believe me, so I added, "The source is close enough to the President to say, if I went ahead with this story, I could jeopardize the lives of men over there."

Solarz shook his head as if I must have got it wrong.

Two days later, I picked up a message in my Washington office. "URGENT. CALL NATIONAL SECURITY COUNCIL." It was Colonel Childress again.

"What the hell do you mean, telling Solarz I said there are POWs alive in Indochina?" he screamed.

"I never told Solarz about any conversation with you." I get icy calm in a real crisis.

"He says you said – "

I cut in. "This is what I said." I repeated what I had told the congressman. Then I added, "I still don't understand how I can jeopardize the lives of POWs if there are none left to jeopardize."

There was a sudden silence. Finally Childress said, "You misunderstood."

"Oh no. I have a record of the conversation in front of me."

Childress took a deep breath. "You won't do yourself any good. . . . " He refused to explain, and hung up.

The conversation had been heard by Nellie Duncan. She was working that day for Suzanne St. Pierre, another producer, the wife of Eric Sevareid. Nellie put down her files, threw herself onto my office couch, and stared hard but unseeingly at the TV monitor. Nellie was very much aware that Eric Sevareid was a consultant to CBS after his great years as a network correspondent of the old school. "Maybe you could talk to Eric about all this."

I shook my head. "Believe me, it's best to just get the story done and on the air."

"But there's more than a jinx on this. Childress and Solarz must be close as peas in a pod. How else could Childress know what you said? That's why Solarz was afraid you'd sandbag him." Nellie felt that Solarz knew about the rescue mission Reagan mentioned to Betty Foley. As a congressman he would have access to the intelligence that led to the planned attempt. "He's afraid it will all come out, making him seem part of a cover-up."

So I had dinner with Suzanne and Eric Sevareid. They had invited along a man wrongfully jailed for a murder. He had been vindicated in a story Suzanne had produced for *60 Minutes*. The talk turned to life in prison. The freed man spoke of the double jeopardy of sitting in a cell, knowing you have committed no crime, believing that society has turned its back upon you. I observed that American prisoners in Asia must feel abandoned in the same way.

Later, Sevareid questioned me about U.S. policy on war prisoners. He could not believe soldiers would be simply written off. He peppered me with questions. Why? Who stood to gain? Surely such things could not be covered up?

When I gave him the barest glimpse of what I had been told, he looked flabbergasted. His whole career with CBS had been carried out under very high standards of reportage. In war, he had walked the thin line between reportorial independence and the need to avoid comforting the enemy. He had been one of the giants of the broadcast news business, a friend of presidents in a time when integrity was the first and vital requirement. Times were changing.

CHAPTER 6

BETRAYAL

I bumped into the BBC's Charlie Wheeler outside the CBS Washington complex at M and 20th streets the next day. He was another reporter in Sevareid's class, a man who still did his own research, still wrote his own scripts. He was developing an hour-long BBC TV documentary on Americans missing in Asia. As he brought me up to date, he spoke regretfully of "a kind of Gestapo here."

"Isn't Gestapo a bit extreme?"

He shrugged. "I'll suspend judgment if my documentary reaches your TV screens unaltered."

I envied his producer, David Taylor, whose own experience of intimidation, when the Drug Enforcement people met him at the airport to search for drugs, was taken seriously by the BBC. Taylor's inquiries had taken him into an explosive area. He was looking into allegations of drug smuggling under the cover of secret warfare, and the laundering of criminal profits to finance clandestine U.S. military activities. Taylor was drawing on the resources of BBC investigators

105

around the world. He said, "It's an American story, but nobody here seems to care much."

Except for the vets. They still cared. The Telephone Tree put me in touch with a former cop named Liam Atkins* who had worked in Vietnam for the Army's super-secret Command and Control North (CCN). He had been ordered, Atkins said, to kill Garwood in captivity. He knew better than to question the order, but he failed to track down Garwood.

Atkins was whip-like, with sharpshooter eyes and sandy hair. Later, he said, he questioned why Garwood was listed as dead when precise intelligence showed him alive. Was the intelligence false or bad? Were those wartime kill orders based on similarly bad intelligence? He burrowed into Marine Corps records in the Forrestal Building at Arlington, Virginia. There he saw that Garwood's file had been removed and classified. Atkins smelled a rat. He could not draw public attention to the Garwood case without breaking secrecy rules. Still, he tried. If Atkins could show there had been nothing to justify the "kill order," he might at least atone.

He was now running his own business in the Washington, D.C., area. The vets vouched for Atkins, but warned me that he had become embittered. I asked Red McDaniel and his American Defense Institute to look into the Atkins story.

Meanwhile, I went ahead with an interview that would replace General Tighe. This would be with Marian Shelton, whose husband, Colonel Charles Shelton, was the only missing American still listed as a prisoner-of-war. Marian Shelton had struggled to keep him in that category, making use of CIA reports she had obtained through her husband's Air Force friends.

Charles Shelton had taken off from Udorn Air Base in Thailand, piloting an intelligence-gathering aircraft and wearing civilian clothes. Both pilot and aircraft were "sani-

---

* Atkins would later be charged with criminal offenses and sent to jail. He would say it was because he talked too much about the POW/MIA issue.

tized," that is, cleaned of military identification marks, since he would be flying into Laos, where there was no "officially acknowledged" war. At 11:59 a.m., local time, on April 29, 1965, the plane was hit in the Sam Neua region of northern Laos. Air Force officers brought the news to Marian Shelton that he was safe on the ground and a rescue mission was under way to bring him out very shortly.

Then things went wrong. For more than three years, Shelton was hidden in notorious "prisoners' caves" between heroic attempts to escape. Heavily censored CIA files told of his movements, his interrogations, his refusal to cooperate. "Duck Soup, " said Marian Shelton, "was the code name of a secret rescue attempt by Laotians working for the CIA. It got him away from his captors . . . then – " She shivered. "I don't know what happened."

She was told never to reveal that her husband was a prisoner-of-war. "I had to say he was detained," she said. "It sounded like he went to tea and didn't come back."

Marian Shelton, with five children to raise, had no choice but to cooperate. But she began her own quiet search for facts. It took her years to obtain heavily censored CIA documents showing that Shelton and other American fliers had been tracked by U.S. intelligence as they passed through an extensive Communist Pathet Lao prison system.

One CIA report said: "On 10 June 1968 two of four American pilots held prisoner in Tham Sua cave . . . south of Ban Nakay Neua . . . were sent to Hanoi, apparently because one killed three North Vietnamese Army soldiers when they attempted to interrogate him. The pilot refused to answer questions and instructed other pilots not to cooperate." When the North Vietnamese had attempted to chain Shelton to a desk, he had overturned it on his captors and beaten three of them to death with his chains.

Marian Shelton told *60 Minutes*: "The different agencies have a mind set to ignore the intelligence they're getting, and I don't think they're giving it to the President. Maybe in the beginning it was just neglect and wanting the war to be over.

People didn't want to think we'd left men over there, then they got ashamed of themselves, regretted it, and just like any lie, it all got bigger and bigger."

I worked all through the night in the New York editing rooms to get "Dead or Alive" ready for preview. The director of *60 Minutes* operations, Joe Illigash, had been saving news clips about missing Americans for a long time, and he brought me the whole collection. It was an unusual display of emotional involvement, similar to those shown by my film crews and editors.

By lunchtime the following day, I had edited the blocks of film and scripted Bradley's final voice-overs. Then I dashed across West 57th Street for a meeting with Eric Ober, CBS News Vice-President. He had requested to see me on urgent matters. I was dumbfounded when he told me a transfer was in the air – I was to go to the television newsmagazine *West 57th*. I thought at once of the White House warning to drop POW/MIA stories or risk my career.

"Is this transfer connected with the work I'm doing on POWs?" I asked Ober.

"*No!* Of course not!"

"Is it because I'm now a mother?"

"No, not at all. Your work's always excellent," said Ober, shifting around in his chair. "Matter of fact, you've worked twice as hard since the baby. No, your energies would be good for the new show. They need someone like you quickly."

I walked back across the street, and decided I did not want to leave *60 Minutes*. I could not junk Smith, McIntire, the vets, and the families on The Telephone Tree. It was clear to me: if I left the show, the piece could be cut from the schedule without an embarrassing fuss. Also, if I made the transfer out of *60 Minutes*, I would be deserting what I felt to be a moral commitment.

I went to see Mike Wallace, who had first brought me into *60 Minutes*, and told him something had gone wrong. I was being moved out of the show, no matter how the decision was sweetened with the *West 57th* offer. Mike called Hewitt. Within minutes, a group had assembled in the executive producer's office.

"The decision was forced on me," said Hewitt. "I've been *ordered* to make budget cuts. Didn't you tell Bradley, Phil?"

Senior producer Phil Scheffler shook his head uncomfortably.

"Look," I asked Hewitt. "Is this because of the 'Dead or Alive' story?"

"No!" Hewitt answered sharply.

Mike Wallace was irate. "If this was forced on you, Don, let's unforce it." He wanted to head straight over to the administrative officers. "We'll make it clear that she stays with us."

"Okay," said Hewitt. "We'll get the decision reversed." He took off at once with Morley Safer, Mike Wallace, and Ed Bradley in his wake. I had a sick feeling as I watched from the ninth-floor window while they trooped across the street. Then I went back to the editing rooms to finish the rough cut for screening the next day, when CBS executives and lawyers would view the segment and suggest last-minute changes. Even though I was unhappy about not being able to include a General Tighe interview, I had a terrific and explosive story, which had never been told.

I worked through the night, and returned to the Park Plaza Hotel shortly before dawn, tired but happy. The meeting with Ober had receded in my mind during the hours of intensive editing. Now, as I thought about it again, I felt a fresh wave of incredulity. I had walked into Ober's office a confident and successful professional, wondering only what attractive career possibilities lay ahead, because Ober had always championed me. Despite his denials, I had walked out of there feeling I should either apologize for being obstinately loyal to the story, or for being a mother. That I felt obliged to turn to Mike Wallace for help at this stage in my career made me angry.

Nellie Duncan, the researcher, joined me for breakfast. She was upset. "Why aren't they running your piece?"

"Of course they're running it. Why d'you think I've worked right through two nights in a row?"

"Joe Illigash was surprised you had a screening today. Then I heard Morley Safer's secretary say the 'Dead or Alive' piece is in trouble."

"How can it be in trouble if it hasn't been looked at yet?" I asked. As the producer, I would normally be the first to know if a screening was cancelled.

I returned to the editing room to work with Antoinetta, the film editor. Hewitt, who was passing, greeted us.

I went next to Joe Illigash. "What about that screening, Joe?"

"I thought it was cancelled," he said.

"Not by me. And I just saw Hewitt on my way to your office. He didn't give any indication that it was off."

Joe gave me a worried look. "Well, okay, I'll check again."

Then Hewitt called. Without having seen it, he wanted the segment cut to eight minutes and thirty seconds to fit his timing. This was ludicrously short. The average segment ran fourteen minutes. Even if I thought this was the greatest story in the world – and every producer always does – Hewitt did not. Cutting it by a third I considered butchery.

Once the segment was screened, Hewitt denounced Major Smith and Sergeant McIntire as lunatics, their story as pure fabrication. The others in the screening room were shocked into silence. Ed Bradley sank into his seat. Mouth agape, Ober stared at Hewitt. Phil Scheffler, however, interrupted. "I believe them," he said.

I waited for Hewitt to finish, and said coldly, "I've just had those men's story supported by a brigadier general who called me out of the blue. He'd heard from his friends in

Special Forces that attempts have been made to stop the show being taken seriously by the press." I stopped myself. The segment had to be judged on its merits. "He insists that Smith and McIntire are being victimized."

The general was Harry "Heinie" Aderholt, who had been responsible for USAF support behind all CIA operations in Asia during the Vietnam War. Aderholt had been the last serving general out of the region after the Vietnam War ended. He had run the Thai-based operations from which Colonel Shelton never returned. He had overseen Air Force officers working in the "black" for the CIA's secret wars. I was impressed that Heinie Aderholt had been moved to call me. He was taking a big risk. His career was built on covert operations, the sort involving Smith and McIntire. Their victimization infuriated the general. Aderholt swore they were good soldiers.

I offered Hewitt the backup of Aderholt. He shrugged it off. The segment would have to be dropped from the upcoming show. "If we redo it, I want more of Armitage saying that American prisoners are the government's highest priority."

"Armitage?" I remembered my last glimpse of him after the filmed interview, talking with Bradley. Since then, I had learned that CBS News's former acting bureau chief in Southeast Asia, David Hatcher, had been hired by Armitage and put on the government payroll. General Aderholt had told me Hatcher had worked for him. He then became involved in the same issue that was part of Armitage's portfolio – prisoners. Hatcher in his earlier CBS days had been convinced there were Americans still alive, but now that he sat in Armitage's office as head of the Pakistan desk, he was tied to the official government line that no proof was available, but POWs were a priority. I wondered if Hatcher ever really left the intelligence service he worked for during and after the Vietnam War.

I could not explain my suppositions at a screening. They were too involved. I was not going to make it easy for government officials to blow Smith and McIntire off the map, though. I still had Red's friend, Robert Howard. "There's an active-service battle commander who will swear the two men were ordered to shred all intelligence on prisoners," I said.

Nobody in the screening room spoke. I pressed on. "He's a colonel, Medal of Honor, and he was originally sent to Thailand to check out Smith and McIntire. He reported to Washington they were telling the truth. He's a Special Operations man himself. He swears on the *Bible* that he, and the other two men, were deliberately sent on an aerial practice mission that would have dropped them into Communist-held territory – either to get rid of them or to discredit them by charging them with cross-border violations. He swears a major general said the evidence of live Americans must be destroyed because it was 'too hot to handle.'

"Is that," I concluded, "what this story is becoming for *60 Minutes*? Too hot – ?"

Hewitt bridled. "The way the segment now looks, Smith and McIntire are fanatics." He said he could tell by the look in their eyes. "And why didn't we interview General Tighe?" he added.

I looked at Ed Bradley. He had ruined the chance of a Tighe interview. It was up to him to explain. Instead, he sat mute.

"And Marian Shelton!" said Hewitt. "She's a distraught widow. Cut her out. She's unbelievable."

"That's how I felt," said Bradley.

I gathered up my files. I had forced Hewitt to talk about reconstructing the segment. He'd seemed intent, at the start, on canceling it. Maybe I should quit while I was ahead. The important thing was to get this show aired. But the screening had knocked the wind out of me. I had been a producer and reporter for television documentaries and newsmagazine segments since 1977. Before that, I had been a national magazine editor. Unless I had suddenly lost all talent, unless I had suddenly forgotten all my experience, unless, in fact, I had become incompetent overnight, something was very wrong.

I called Mark Waple and broke the devastating news that, despite the promises *60 Minutes* had made to Smith and McIntire, the segment had been bounced from this coming Sunday's program. "It's been taken out of my hands," I told the soldiers' lawyer.

Waple asked to speak with my boss, and I set up a conference call. Hewitt surprised me by asking Waple if he would fly to Germany to persuade Colonel Howard, the Medal of Honor winner, to speak on camera. The issue, said Hewitt, was very much larger than they had anticipated. I was heartened. I must have persuaded him at the screening that the military men in my story were not all crazy.

After what had just happened to the Smith and McIntire segment, however, Lawyer Waple was disinclined to advise another soldier to risk his career with a *60 Minutes* interview. The colonel had been warned by the Pentagon that he must not speak to the press. If he agreed to this interview, he would have only the protection of public knowledge. It would be difficult to smear him or destroy his career once his full record had been publicized. But we had broken our promise to Smith and McIntire. If *60 Minutes* broke its agreement to run the interview, as it had with Smith and McIntire, Howard would risk losing everything.

Waple wrote in his running diary for September 15, 1985: "I offered to fly at once to New York with enough documentation to show Smith and McIntire were not lying. They [*60 Minutes'* executives] agreed there had been a breach of our agreement. They repeated that the story had gotten much bigger than they'd expected."

"Are you with *West 57th* or not?" my husband asked on the phone that night.

"No – " I was back in my room at the Park Plaza. It had been a long twenty-four hours, but my spirits were picking up.

Bill said, "You're wasting your time."

"I can't give up now." As I recounted the day's events, with the radio tuned to a classical-music station, all the annoyances of the day ebbed away. I could even listen patiently to his testy argument against tilting at windmills. "Look," I said, "the story's beginning to grow. I know Hewitt. His bark is worse than his bite. He sees this all might result in a much more effective program later – "

"What?"

I thought to myself that it was after another violent eruption with Hewitt that I had produced a winner, "In the Belly of the Beast." The segment examined the murderous consequences of Norman Mailer's infatuation with a jailed killer. All the way to the finish line, Hewitt opposed it. My final product won an Emmy.

Bill's voice broke into my thoughts. "It used to be known around newsrooms as the Iron Ball," he was saying. "You never saw it coming and you never knew who'd swung it. All you *did* know was that you'd offended somebody very powerful and this was the end of you." He cut himself short. "But I guess you know how your own outfit works, and I don't."

We said goodnight. Bill was right. Nobody outside *60 Minutes* could ever comprehend the way the outfit worked. I had always been fierce in defending the show's integrity. I still believed in it.

In this mood, I called Marian Shelton. "I hate to tell you – the show's been cancelled for Sunday."

"I'm not surprised," Marian said cheerfully. "This isn't the first time I've been asked to tell my story, and had it killed. I have been warned by the government to keep quiet about the issue because national security's at risk."

"It wasn't like that." I stopped. I wanted to explain, but did not want to discuss internal affairs at CBS.

"I suppose they thought I was a 'distraught widow.' " Marian laughed while I tried to conceal my surprise. "It's okay, I've heard it already. It's what the government *always* calls me."

Colonel Howard could not be reached at the West German base where he commanded special troops. His friends phoned me, pleading that I discourage him from making a public statement. "His career is in real jeopardy," a fellow officer told me. "You don't realize the kind of rumors they'll spread about him if he persists. . . . "

They? I asked Mark Waple who "they" might be.

"The same government people who stabbed you in the back," replied the lawyer.

"Nobody's stabbed me – " I was back to being the incurable optimist. I explained that *60 Minutes* doesn't like being pushed around, least of all by government officials. I firmly believed that if Colonel Howard talked to us on camera, and then reprisals were taken, there would be the biggest row imaginable.

"Maybe you'd better come down to Fayetteville and listen to the *whole* story," said Waple. "I don't want to talk on the phone."

Waple's office was part of a dignified, low-profile building complex that I had always admired. I liked the warm sanity of Mark's room and its country-gentleman atmosphere, reinforced by discreetly framed military insignia that evoked America's past. There was a comforting smell of leather, polished walnut, and pipe tobacco. When I walked in, the lawyer said, "My last visitor filled that doorway and left me stymied. . . .

"He was big and square like an icebox." Waple leaned back in his chair. "He was dressed in shorts, T-shirt, and a baseball cap." A day earlier, someone had phoned, telling Waple to call another number. There, a man asked how he could see him without attracting attention. Waple told him how to come in through back stairways. When he burst in, he could have been a truck driver. What he scattered across Waple's desk were the medals and I.D. of a highly decorated three-star general!

Waple met my skeptical eye. "It sounds like fantasy, doesn't it? I'll show you the proof without compromising the general. I call him 'General Icebox.' "

"In shorts and a baseball cap?"

"That's right. He said if anyone ever knew he'd been to see me, it would ruin everything he'd worked for. But he's a very angry man. He talks of cover-up – the cover-up of missing Americans. He's seen the intelligence."

"Why come to you?"

"I guess he wanted me to know there's a lot of powerful support for Smith and McIntire, and if things got really tough, he would speak out. He said, 'I will if I must, but they'll destroy me.' "

"*They* would destroy him?" There was that mysterious *they* again. "Would he see me?"

Waple laughed. "Good try, but obviously – no."

"And Colonel Howard?"

"After what's happened, he doesn't want to talk with *60 Minutes*. He's going to try and bring everything into the open by testifying before Congress – "

"Wow! Can he – ?"

"It gives him some protection against reprisal. It's a serious offense to convey intelligence – that's why the classified POW/MIA files have been *re*classified, so servicemen *can't* discuss them."

Waple sat upright and shuffled papers on his desk. "Colonel Howard says I can give you the whole background. In spite of everything, he trusts you."

There was a brief silence. Then I told him I could understand that he was wondering right now who to trust, but that whatever went wrong with our agreement, *60 Minutes* did not act as an arm of government. There were sins of omission – in the rush of events, stories got bounced around the schedule, memos got lost – but our only concerns were strictly professional.

Waple nodded. Colonel Howard had come to see him, he explained, like others had, because word got around pretty fast about what was being done to Smith and McIntire. The world of special operations was like a small, exclusive men's club. "Guys know each other's reputations," he said. "They've got terrific *esprit de corps.*"

The same description could fit The Telephone Tree, I thought. The Tree had told me about a colonel, one of the big guys in covert warfare. It must be Howard. He'd been posted from Asia to Europe, his orders hardly allowing his feet to touch ground in America.

Waple said, "The only free time he had in America was a Sunday. *And he gave it all to me!* His one Sunday in America. He spent it driving across the country from – I can't even tell you the name of the air base – so he could swear out an affidavit for me. The rest of his Sunday was spent driving back to board the next plane to West Germany."

Waple had warned Howard that, if he joined the lawsuit, it could hurt his career. The colonel brushed the warnings aside. He said, "They're trying to pretend we'll destroy morale among the troops by letting all this stuff come out. I say we'll do more real harm to ourselves as a nation by hushing it up."

That Sunday in Waple's office the colonel swore under oath, that as chief of the Combat Services Coordinating Team (CSCT) – which acted as a liaison with the Korean special forces – he was sent to check out Smith and McIntire's charge that a recent mission to rescue POWs had been compromised by American officials. Howard became convinced by three years' evidence, gathered by Smith and McIntire, that Americans were alive and captive in Laos and Vietnam. He had told his superiors this, and gave Smith and McIntire a clean bill of health. It was then that all three were sent on a training mission. It appeared they were to be parachuted into another part of Thailand.

But the three checked the flight route with the pilot. That was an unforeseen circumstance. On covert operations, mock or real, each group followed its own orders in accordance with clandestine methods, in which units were told only what they needed to know. But the SFD-K team had become uneasy about elements that seemed abnormal. They asked to see the secret flight plan.

This tied in with what Sergeant McIntire had told me, on film, about this mission: "It was gonna be a survival problem. We were to jump into one of the Thai camps and navigate our way back out. But the original aircraft got recalled. The replacement aircraft had its own flight plan, which was unusual because normally the crew made their flight plan when they joined us. Then – we were suddenly left totally alone. Whenever we have an operational training exercise, people from the U.S. embassy, Pacific Command, and so on, just come to watch and observe. This time, all the hangers-on disappeared. And we got chow, radios, weapons, like for a real operation. A senior Thai officer came over and said, 'Listen, if you guys need helicopter support, if you need ammunition, we'll be glad to help you out.' Now, the Thais didn't have those kinds of assets, so this was unusual, to make that offer. Another Thai officer asked me, 'What are all these other aircraft doing? Are they part of this?'

"And the other aircraft were a type nobody had in the Pacific area at this time – they'd come specially from the States. Suddenly I got aircraft that don't belong there, I got the offer of arms and helicopters, I got a C-132 to myself with nobody to control me. And I got a crew that's got a flight plan they don't know about."

Colonel Howard, Major Smith, and Sergeant McIntire went into a huddle with the C-132 captain. If that hadn't happened, the Air Force would have followed *its* orders, and Colonel Howard would have followed *his* orders and jumped with Smith and McIntire into what they'd been told was a Thai training area. In fact it was a few miles the other way – inside Laos, where the CIA fought its secret war, in a region thick with Communist forces.

"I said, 'It's a trick!' " McIntire had told me. "I said, 'We ain't gonna do this!' and I cancelled the flight."

"But they thought we went," Smith had interjected. "All the hangers-on, the usual official observers, had cleared the field before we aborted the flight. To this day there's people think we parachuted into Laos."

It would have been a convenient way to dispose of combat soldiers who defied the official contradiction of their own intelligence reports. And Smith's immediate commander, Colonel Howard, was sure of it.

When Colonel Howard had turned up in Korea, against all expectations, he faced charges of illegal cross-border operations – before it was realized the training mission was never completed. Howard was then posted to Germany. Major Smith was not promoted, and consequently was hit with mandatory retirement when his lawsuit *Smith vs. The President* was filed.

Howard had concluded in his statement, "There are in fact live Americans in captivity, and there is an ongoing effort by the Defense Intelligence Agency to ignore this."

The near-fatal training mission had been designated "secret," making it treasonous for anyone to disclose details. This was why Mark Waple offered to fly to New York to salvage the *60 Minutes* agreement. He could personally verify the claims made by his client. He believed the secrecy classifications were misused, but he did not want to expose others to harsh penalties for disclosure. He had documents that everyone assumed Smith and McIntire had shredded, as ordered. They included details of missions and reports from other intelligence sources of live sightings of Americans in Laos.

Major Smith had said to me, "In America, the soldier just doesn't count any more. . . . The media stars who built million-dollar reputations on the Vietnam War no longer need us."

CHAPTER 7

THE FREELANCE
OPERATIVE

When Hewitt came to me in the New York office, a week or so after the screening, to say, "You're still part of *60 Minutes*. We made a mistake," I told him about a new development. Admiral Jerry Tuttle had just described for me how he briefed men for a covert mission into Laos to rescue Americans. I said, "He was Deputy Director of the Defense Intelligence Agency at the time. He left before he knew the mission's outcome, and he added, 'Thank God.' " His tone implied that he knew the outcome had been an unholy disaster, but he refused to elaborate further.

I added that when I asked ex-DIA Director General Tighe how it could be that Tuttle would not know the outcome of a mission he helped to plan, Tighe explained it was policy in the world of intelligence not to brief retiring chiefs on any covert operations that would continue after they left office.

"Will Tuttle talk, on camera, about the rescue briefing?" asked Hewitt.

"No. He's now Inspector General of the Navy. He can't comment without disclosing information that's just been reclassified."····-

"But you can get Tuttle's ex-boss at the DIA, General Tighe. He's retired. He's free to say the same things, isn't he?"

"We'll see," was all I could promise. Tighe was not a sure thing after the last abrupt cancellation.

However, to my relief, Tighe saved me any embarrassment by agreeing to a rescheduled interview. He renewed his promise to keep it exclusive to *60 Minutes*. "You don't need to explain anything," he told me. "I trust you."

"I'm afraid I've stolen General Tighe again," I told David Taylor as he was entering the BBC's Washington office one morning.

Taylor's inquiries were leading him into the darker worlds of money-laundering, arms deals, and even illegal drugs. My story seemed unrelated to those aspects.

"Remember Scott Barnes?" asked Taylor.

I stopped in the doorway of my own office next to Taylor's. "Sure. The guy who claims his partner on a POW rescue mission may have been murdered." I remembered, too, what had happened to Taylor at the airport after he talked to Barnes.

"The same. I've just filmed him being interviewed under truth drugs. We did it under strict supervision by a doctor well known for his experience in administering these drugs. Mark Waple asked the questions and we interviewed Barnes ourselves before and after Waple. Barnes was desperate to do this so people would finally believe him. He says the CIA hired him to kill a crook named Ronald Rewald, who was also hired by the CIA to run a bank [BBRDW] that laundered drug money. But the crook took the agency for a ride. He's in jail and threatening to tell all. Barnes says he was ordered to silence him. There's a lot of other stuff."

Reluctantly, I went into the BBC screening room. "This is like peeling an onion," I complained. "I'm not sure I want to know – but what's 'the other stuff'?"

"Financial enterprises to make money for covert operations without having to ask Congress for the cash."

I sat down with a sigh. Taylor's last words echoed the rumors I had heard about an alleged CIA proprietary, Nugan Hand, the bank that failed in Australia. Were these proprietaries the bigger story? Were they so much bigger that the prisoners had to be sacrificed "in the national interest" because any real investigation of their situation would automatically reveal illegal covert operations that had continued in Southeast Asia after the war?

Taylor screened the interview for me. In it Barnes talked in detail about the 1981 covert mission into Laos that he had been sent on. He said it had been sanctioned by the Drug Enforcement Agency (DEA) as well as the CIA, although he, personally, had been told to report to one of the Pentagon's most secret covert units, the Intelligence Support Activity (ISA). According to Barnes, the mission had a number of goals, but he was briefed primarily on the portion dealing with a prisoner search. In the tape he graphically described finding the prisoners, and then later being ordered to "get rid of the merchandise."

When the interview was over, I asked, "Was Barnes's mission to locate missing Americans or link up with drug smugglers?"

"Ah, that's the question."

"Is he telling the truth?"

"He asked for the biggest shot of truth serum the doctor dared give. And he said exactly the same things with precisely the same details that he'd told me before."

"Would you mind if an expert saw it?"

"No. It would be good to provide London with some additional backup."

I called the American Defense Institute, and Red McDaniel

came loping over to view the tape. He could barely fit into the BBC's screening room, and stood silent through forty-five minutes of Barnes's questioning. Barnes was most moving when he spoke of Jerry Daniels, said to be the senior CIA man on the mission – the man Barnes claimed was murdered. Barnes talked about the tears in Daniels' eyes and his agonized cry of "Oh my God, we *did* leave them behind!" when the team saw American prisoners in Communist hands.

"Do you believe any of it?" I asked Red later.

"I'm afraid I do," he replied. "Would you be willing to show this tape to someone on the House Armed Services Committee?"

"I'd have to check with David."

Taylor quickly agreed. A few days after the committee saw the film, Congressman Ike Skelton, a Democrat and member of the Armed Services Committee, asked me if I would speak privately with the new Director of the Defense Intelligence Agency, General Leonard H. Perroots, who "wants very much to see you."

On a day in mid-November 1985, I took the Key Bridge route to the Pentagon. It seemed incongruous: one minute breast-feeding my baby, the next dashing off to deal with one of the most powerful men in the world of intelligence.

I was met at the Pentagon by Brig. Gen. James W. Shufelt, then deputy director of Defense Intelligence. He noted my Wisconsin accent as we sat chatting amiably in the anteroom to General Perroots's office.

Perroots proved to be a jovial, outgoing man. He explained he was new on the job and wanted to get a handle on things. Throughout the conversation the same pattern was followed. He would ask a question, I would reply, and then one of his several aides would intervene. They seemed prepared to rebut any information I might have about live prisoners.

They seemed particularly anxious to discount any story told by Scott Barnes.

Red McDaniel had said Lenny Perroots would order an investigation if he knew what I knew, so I reviewed all the events that I thought warranted his attention. He pleaded ignorance on every aspect, saying that he did not know if DIA had received intelligence reports from Smith and McIntire, or if Bobby Garwood had ever been debriefed, or that Hanoi offered to return prisoners if the U.S. government would stick by a "secret pledge" of aid. He said he was not aware of a report that Henry Kissinger told Senate hearings in 1973 that aid was conditional upon North Vietnam giving a better accounting of POWs and MIAs.

The meeting with Perroots was to have lasted an hour, but stretched into late afternoon. Darkness had fallen outside when the Director let me go with a formal request. Could I tell him how to reach Scott Barnes? I said I would check with Barnes. If he okayed it, I would pass along the details.

In the following days, I tried unsuccessfully to track Barnes down. He had gone into hiding, claiming that he was being harassed by government agents for discussing prisoners and secret missions. I passed General Perroots's request to Red McDaniel, who was still absolutely certain that DIA, once it was properly informed, would do the right thing. He finally found Barnes in southern California and encouraged him to go to Washington. Barnes figured if the president of the American Defense Institute said it was okay, then he should certainly talk to DIA's chief.

Barnes went to Washington. Nobody at DIA would see him. General Shufelt said there was no interest in him. General Perroots could not be reached.

David Taylor invited Barnes to stay at his home while he waited for DIA to call, but it became clear that, whatever DIA's purpose had been in asking how to contact him, it was certainly not to have him tell his story first-hand to the agency. The BBC producer called me in Florida, where I was looking into some untoward deaths in a local hospital for another story. "Is there some way DIA could have made a bootleg copy of our BBC tape?" he asked me.

"I can't think of any."

"Because DIA seems to know it intimately and I think Barnes is being victimized for it," said Taylor. He explained that Barnes told him one DIA officer had called him and told him he would personally make him look like a fool for what he had said in the tape.

I told Bill about Scott Barnes's problems. He looked worried. "You've got to be really careful," he said. He was worried about a number of odd incidents that had happened since I'd started working on this story.

A few days after Garwood and the vets came to our home for that first conversation, a man had run through the house. It frightened my mother who was visiting and was alone at the time. The police later found evidence of an intruder and offered to watch the house. Then there was that curious blond man who said he was a former Navy Seal with an interest in POWs. He kept appearing in one way or another every time I filmed something for the POW story. Not only had he contributed the $1,000 to the *Smith vs. The President* lawsuit, and so was conveniently in Mark Waple's Fayetteville office the day we filmed the Smith and McIntire lawsuit, but he showed up again when I filmed Garwood going into the closed hearing of the POW subcommittee. He had also shown up on Ross Perot's Texas doorstep, wanting to talk about POWs. Perot, who had speculated to me that the man was "a spook," had turned him away with a laugh and the question, "Who are you really working for?"

Bill asked, "How does he know just when to show up, and who pays him to travel all over the country monitoring people like Ross Perot and a program like *60 Minutes*?" He went on, "Mind you, it's easy to become too imaginative. I saw Perot the other day on a Bermuda wharf. He was dressed like a gnarled seaman in woolen hat and worn docksiders. I thought, Ah, Perot the Great Detective! But he wasn't looking for clues. He was buying fish."

I watched Bill return to work on some galley proofs. I'd been bending over backwards not to make conspiratorial connections. The result was that I'd probably been gullible! There was the mysterious Navy officer, who came to Congressman Hendon's office, carrying aerial photographs of American prisoners in Laos. "I see confidential cables," said the commander, "and I know Americans are still there. It bothers my conscience." The photographs looked genuine. But the visitor had been identified by Hendon as an alleged government agent who planted false "evidence" and in other ways tried to undermine the credibility of anyone who challenged the government policy. Later, he came to my office to ask what I knew about Bobby Garwood, and I recognized with a shock that he had been at DIA on the afternoon of my meeting with General Lenny Perroots.

Apart from the threats to my job and the anonymous calls, I still led a relatively normal life. I was just a lot wiser now to the strange world of intelligence – what David Martin had called the "Wilderness of Mirrors" in his book of the same name. Barnes's life, though, was becoming a misery. He got telephoned warnings. Articles were planted in his local newspaper, saying he'd been a drug dealer in Indochina. The rumors cost him his job. He found it impossible to get another. He said he kept receiving invitations to go back into covert activities and was being pushed into a corner from which he would never escape unless he returned to what he always called "The Activity." I had by now learned that this was the nickname of the Army's Intelligence Support Activity, as well as of a secret arm of the CIA.

I took a breath and told Bill about my growing worry that I had somehow gotten Barnes in trouble by talking about the truth-drug tape.

That brought his nose out of the proofs. He said, "Well, it's now known to those connected with government policy on missing Americans.*

Still I said, "I have to get to the bottom of this. I couldn't live with myself if I gave up now."

"You'll wake up some day and find all you've done is chase the dragon."

"What *does* that mean?"

"After the Communists took Hanoi, I used to meet old contacts in the one opium den that stayed open. Smoking opium was called 'chasing the dragon.' You search for meaning in the smoke from the opium pipe. When you become addicted, the dragon chases you!"

I shivered. Maybe the dragon *was* chasing me, but I hadn't been caught yet, although I could not deny my addiction.

---

* The film had been shown to approximately fifteen people in one of the congressional screening rooms. I was introduced to representatives of various government bodies, but did not pay any attention to the people who actually handled the tape. I found out later that DIA had representatives there.

CHAPTER 8

THERE BUT FOR THE GRACE OF GOD . . .

The Telephone Tree put me in touch with a former rice-paddy grunt who was now with NBC and who identified the American cameraman who had taken the film of Garwood in Hanoi before he was released. His name was Jon Alpert. He and his wife had specialized in filming inside Communist territories ordinarily regarded as inaccessible. Most of his work got a lot of attention precisely because no one else could get it, but the Garwood film had never been shown anywhere.

I called Alpert at his home and asked if the Garwood film was his.

"Yes, I made the Bobby Garwood film."

"Can I get a copy?"

Alpert hesitated.

I said, "I'm doing a *60 Minutes* piece that will pose a question every congressman is asking, 'Was Garwood held against his will?'"

Alpert said, "He was very well treated when I saw him."

"Will you make the film available so the American public can judge?"

"I sent it from Hanoi," said Alpert. "The CIA intercepted it."

Even if the Agency had intercepted the film, I thought Alpert would have kept a copy, and so would the Vietnamese. How else would the East Germans have gotten hold of the bits I had? I said, "From what I have seen so far, the Vietnamese come out in a very good light. Isn't it worth showing their human side to the American people?"

Someone else spoke in the background. It was Alpert's wife, who had been with him in Hanoi to interview Garwood. I heard snatches of her comments: " . . . Why not?"

"I think maybe we've got a cassette copy," said Alpert.

The Alpert tape astonished me. It proved that, under obvious duress, Garwood's message had remained patriotic. The earlier film clips from East Germany that I had seen were no more than appetizers. This tape must inevitably rekindle the Garwood story. I described the tape to General Eugene Tighe, one of the few U.S. intelligence experts I now fully trusted. He said, "That tape could save what is left of Garwood's life. It'll vindicate him if he gets another day in court. Don't let it out of your sight."

I didn't need to be told that twice.

I also wanted to produce the best possible segment. I asked Garwood to view the tape in my office. The original five hours of film had been shot as a Vietnamese condition of Garwood's release. He had never seen the results. He still only remembered being spruced up and made to wander around Hanoi before the camera. One thing had been made absolutely clear to him: "Say the wrong thing and we'll keep you here forever."

Now, six years after the film was made, he looked back at himself, a stranger under duress, speaking his native language with a noticeable accent, forever cautiously seeking the approval of his handlers. A baggy Russian-style civilian suit cloaks his painfully thin frame. His eyes are sunken, his teeth black with decay. An American is heard prompting him behind the faint Vietnamese of his captors. He is directed to give a message to "the folks back home." The camera is tight on his face. He says he loves America.

There is an abrupt cut. This is not the right message. He should be talking of the good times he has had, in spite of being "a war criminal," of how he has reformed his thinking.

Garwood stares into the camera and says he loves his family. He hopes they'll wait to hear his side of the story.

Fresh murmurs in Vietnamese. It is clear that they are unhappy with what he has said. Doesn't Garwood know he is throwing away his chance of release?

The disembodied American voice is heard again. Garwood ought to try that last bit once more.

Garwood positions himself again in the corner of the Hanoi "residence" he has never seen until that day, nor will see again. His face sometimes shows fear. His eyes show that he knows he must not repeat the earlier mistake; that if he does, the consequences will be fearful. He hesitates. As I watched the tape, I agonized with him. It was without doubt one of the most powerful moments on film I have ever seen. Garwood draws his mouth back in the parody of a smile, half ingratiating and half hopeless. He seems close to tears. I watched in fury at what I expected to see: the complete degradation of a human being brainwashed to obey his masters. There is one more hesitation. Then Garwood pulls himself up slightly. I could not believe what I was seeing. There is just a flicker of defiance as he looks at the people behind the camera. Then he says directly to the camera exactly what he said before: He loves his family in America. He hopes they will wait to hear what he has to say. He begins to say, "My life here has not been easy – " when he is cut off. He has clearly stated twice that he is a true American, has always been one, and loves his country.

As Garwood watched the full production, all these years later, a weight seemed to lift from his shoulders. He'd felt guilty for taking part in a propaganda movie. Now he saw how others viewed it – in the way Ike Eisenbraun had said letters written under duress were viewed, as a means to convey information by a prisoner under threat. Garwood had defied his captors to make a direct appeal through the bars of his invisible cage. It had not been evident to him at the time that he had succeeded.

The silence in my office was heavy. Finally I said to Garwood, "You were like someone from a Russian concentration camp. And your teeth . . . "

He gave me a funny look. "Alpert commented to my guards on the state my teeth were in. So next day they cleaned them up." Garwood's clean white teeth had seemed to former POWs like proof that he had never really been a prisoner. No prisoner who returned in the official homecoming in 1973 returned with healthy teeth.

Garwood's own story now had a new dimension. Whatever purpose there had been behind the film, it unconsciously illustrated the plight of Garwood in Hanoi as a prisoner. I quickly met with Hewitt to suggest how the film could be used in the Garwood segment, which had been put on the schedule once again.

The executive producer's response startled me. He said it might be best to drop the Garwood piece after all. No, he did not want to screen the Alpert footage. No, he did not want to review the BBC videotape of Scott Barnes under truth-drug interrogation.

There was no changing Hewitt's mind. Bradley had also lost interest in Garwoood.

However, word of the Alpert film had apparently spread, and others did want to view the tape. The mysterious "Navy officer," still not admitting his DIA connections, turned up at my office one day and asked to see the film. I asked how he knew I had it. He gave an evasive answer. I told him to go away and not come back until he felt like telling me the truth.

"Can I see this Garwood film?" my husband asked.

"Why not? None of my bosses want to."

He sat through the tape without a word, then jumped up in anger at the finish. "Garwood acts exactly the way those French prisoners of the Vietnamese behaved years ago when I interviewed them," he said. "They had the same lost look in their eyes. It's very clear when you get the detached view of the camera that he's under Communist mind control. What is remarkable is his summoning of courage in spite of such incredible duress."

I had never seen him in such a rage and seized this opportunity to bring him down on my side once and for all. I found a transcript of the Smith-McIntire interview. Bill was returning to Thailand. "Here," I said. "Read this on the flight."

Smith and McIntire knew something about the real collaborators during the Vietnam War. Garwood didn't fit the profile, Smith had said on camera to Ed Bradley. "We had colonels and Navy captains who collaborated with the enemy. They were charged with that – collaboration. They got off with a reprimand. They're drawing retirement pay from the military to this day. Bobby Garwood was a private – don't we expect more from our officers? People are afraid of what Bobby Garwood knows," said Major Smith.

"Garwood's a convicted collaborator. Doesn't his association with you taint your effort?" Smith was asked.

"We don't have any association with him at all," he replied.

"He supports you."

"Wonderful!" interrupted Sergeant McIntire. "He's corroborating what we are saying. And if he says it, if Charles Manson were to say it, if there was a time and place where he was in a position to find out information on missing Americans – "

"Then," finished Major Smith, "it's incumbent on the U.S. government to properly debrief him."

"But aren't these missing Americans not really prisoners any more?" we asked. "Aren't they collaborators?"

"That's a hell of a thing to call them," said Major Smith. "*You* don't know how they fell into the hands of the enemy. Has any American ever talked to them and heard them *say* they *didn't* want to come home?"

"Did Americans *desert* from the cockpits of jets?" demanded Sergeant McIntire. "Did they *jump out* to join the enemy?"

"Yeah," said Major Smith. "We're talking about high-ranking guys who supposedly elected to hoe rice for the rest of their lives!"

Reading this in the skies over Vietnam, in a Thai International jet on its descent to Bangkok, Bill reflected that soldiers who won their spurs in battle almost always showed more compassion than men who never fired a shot in anger.

General Tighe had suggested the delayed *60 Minutes* interview with Ed Bradley should be set for Monday, October 21, at his home in Springfield, Virginia. After that, he would be away for several months. I checked with Bradley, who said he would keep that day free. A film crew was instructed to set up at eight in the morning. I air-expressed a package of background material to Bradley in New York.

The day before the allotted time, Bradley called to say the interview was too early. It meant catching an early morning shuttle from New York.

"So what happens to this interview?" I asked.

"Get him to do it later."

"Not again I can't. This is the only time he's got free."

"Too bad."

"Don't you care about this story?"

"Frankly, no," said Bradley.

I called General Tighe. Once again I had to apologize for the discourtesy. I told him it was my fault, I'd made a muddle of the schedule. Was there any way the interview could take place later? Tighe was polite but sorry. His day really was filled right up. I couldn't argue with a good man who had been stood up twice. Yet without Tighe, the MIA segment was doomed.

I took the baby for a walk while I ruminated on life as a yoyo. It was one of those balmy Indian summer Sundays when the brick-paved streets of Georgetown, bright with flowerbeds and ancient oak trees, could take me back to earlier times. I walked through the gardens of Dumbarton Oaks where Winston Churchill and Franklin D. Roosevelt had seen the first glimmerings of hope for a postwar world. I had a friend nearby who had parachuted into Nazi-occupied France. Old as he was now, he was always standing up in the crowd, shouting some unpopular truth. If I gave up now, I would be breaking faith with such men and those who followed in their footsteps. I owed it to the memory of Lance Sijan not to give up.

I got home and called General Tighe again. "Could we set up the cameras near one of your business appointments? If you could squeeze in forty minutes – "

"Done!" he said. He had a luncheon seminar at the Crystal City Marriott in Arlington. Before dashing off to a three-thirty meeting, he'd squeeze in the interview.

Bradley in New York was less than enthusiastic. "Why didn't you arrange the later appointment the first time?"

I told him he need only fly in and fly out. He'd have a limousine to La Guardia, a limo in D.C. "If I can get Garwood there," I added hurriedly, "maybe you could put a couple more questions to him? Remember, you were feeling ill and didn't press him on collaboration. He's got more to say now. I'd like it, in case we can get the Garwood piece on track as a separate item."

Bradley agreed, rang off, then came back minutes later. "That hotel's under the airport flight path. I can't do it there."

I took a deep breath and asked Nellie Duncan, the researcher, to double-check the hotel's location. Nellie said, "You know he doesn't want to do that interview."

"He will," I snarled. "Or I quit."

The hotel was *not* under the flight path.

Now that Garwood had seen the film of himself in Hanoi, I wanted him to answer a few new points. He was reluctant to take more time away from his unofficial job at the service station. His appeal against the court-martial findings had just been rejected; the Marine Corps had now given him a dishonorable discharge; all his back pay since the date of his capture – some $150,000 – had been confiscated. He could not vote. Even if he'd been able to afford it, he was unable to get private medical insurance because his huge medical file recorded so many maladies to which he'd been exposed in captivity. He had been hit with an income tax bill, retroactive, for $8,000. Someone had reported the money he'd earned to keep himself alive while technically forbidden to work outside the Marine Corps. His brief recovery of self-respect was over.

I told him General Tighe would see him. Garwood overcame his reluctance. The ex-director of defense intelligence and the disgraced Marine were introduced in the hotel suite where Ed Bradley was interviewing them. Garwood drew himself to attention, saluted, and said he was deeply honored. His face and posture betrayed the same awed respect I had seen when Garwood spoke of Ike, his prisoner mentor.

It was a dramatic moment. I knew Tighe was secretly reviewing Garwood's history. I could not help thinking that Tighe should have been allowed to do this when he still had the power of the position of DIA director behind him. He was just about the only professional I could think of with both the professional skills and the integrity to assess whether Garwood's information on other POWs was good. I wondered if the eight Marine Corps lawyers Garwood had been up against recently had brought the same skills to the task. They had conferred with the Secretary of the Navy about the awful consequences if the court-martial decision were reversed or a retrial ordered – Garwood and what they termed "the Rambo Faction" would have a national platform as a result of the publicity.

"General Tighe gives the piece real credibility," Hewitt said at the next screening.

I let it pass. What mattered was that the MIA segment, comprising the Garwood and the Smith and McIntire stories, had been approved at last and was back in the schedule.

Tighe had given answers that contradicted Armitage, the Pentagon's covert-warfare head and a spokesman for the official POW/MIA policy. Armitage had said, for instance, that none of the reports of "live sightings" were current and specific regarding circumstances of captivity, nor could they be verified technically.

Tighe, asked if he had seen reports meeting these requirements, said yes, he had.

Armitage dismissed Tighe's time as Director of the Defense Intelligence Agency, saying the Director had never then spoken of his belief that Americans were being held against their will. I had been upset that Bradley had not refuted this by quoting Tighe's recorded statements from the *Congressional Record*. Now Tighe himself refuted Armitage.

He said he was on record as "repeatedly" stating his belief, while he was Director, that such Americans did exist. "Habitual fatigue sets in among some bureaucrats. Instead of saying 'Let's work out how we get them out of there,' *they discard reports and prevent very valuable intelligence going for evaluation and action* (italics mine)."

Tighe believed to this day there were live Americans held prisoner because of "hundreds of live sighting reports which we filtered and sifted out and cross-checked one against the other, interviewed the sources, polygraphed them, checked their bonafides from every direction and found their reports could not be refuted. . . . Similar but very current reports are on the record today. . . . "

The DIA's ex-Director, though the master of high-tech intelligence tools, still believed nothing was better than human reporting. "What we had of it on Vietnam would've been considered a miracle on Russia. It's very excellent intelligence – very, very high quality, the finest. . . . I'm talking about reports made as a man rides along a road where he can precisely pinpoint the location – a stream, say, crossing a path with woods at a certain distance and angle, and this man describes prisoners, a specific number, how dressed. . . . That's the rather precise reporting I relied on."

"And you saw that on more than one occasion?" asked Bradley.

"Oh, yes, sir. Yes, sir."

"Over and over?"

"Yes, sir. Yes, sir. Might be five prisoners in one sighting, seventeen in another, twenty-six in another, but the quality of reporting after you sort out a lot of extraneous material is high."

"If men are held in Asia in conditions similar to Garwood, is it worth bringing them back just to face a court martial?" asked Bradley.

"If the man broke, we should be first to say, 'There but for the grace of God go I,' and give him a chance," said Tighe. "I'd want him on home ground."

"What about Smith and McIntire?"

Tighe thought carefully: "I can't imagine anyone inventing this," he said.

I could now answer the constant questioning from vets with a firm yes, the show would go on the air and it was called "Dead or Alive." Mike Van Atta wrote me a formal letter listing what he, and other vets, expected *60 Minutes* would accomplish with this one item. From all across the land I got calls thanking me in advance: another demonstration of The Telephone Tree's effectiveness.

"Dead or Alive" ran in a slot just before Christmas week. The audience is usually smaller then, so I was not prepared for the heavy fallout.

First, I received a lengthy rebuttal, wrapped in an imposing white folder embossed with the seal of the President of the United States and bearing the words "The White House." The strange thing was that the package was never sent to the target – me. I got one from a friend. The package was sent to all branches of the armed services; to members of the National League of Families; to other branches of the media. So far as I was able to tell, the White House refutation went out to just about any concerned American (except me) who had ever written to, or called, the White House or the Pentagon with questions about missing men.

The covering letter came from Assistant Secretary of Defense Richard Armitage. Nobody I reached in the White House could, or would, say if any official there had approved distribution of the package. Childress at the National Security Council did not answer my calls. When I asked if President Reagan or Vice President Bush approved the package, I was told they had not been informed about it either before or after publication.

Presumably referring to the transcript of the conversation between a Marine Corps captain and Garwood, and the one-page evaluation of the interview, the rebuttal said Garwood had been debriefed – despite the *60 Minutes* claim. It denied that General Tighe had frequently expressed the opinion that Americans were still alive and captive.

During Christmas week, I received another package, which this time was sent anonymously to my office. It contained an unsigned summary of a divorce action against Major Smith, presenting only his ex-wife's accusations of beatings and drunkenness.

"I got a nice little present too," said David Taylor later. "Same sort of stuff. But there's a way to trace my package by its markings, and I did. It was sent from the Pentagon."

Another strange package arrived in the mail. But this one alleged that Colonel Childress in the White House directed a campaign to discredit Congressman Billy Hendon. It was alleged that Childress had agreed to pay $40,000 and arrange to provide Drug Enforcement Agency credentials to help Skyhook II, a private organization that searched for POWs in Southeast Asia. The DEA credentials would have allowed Skyhook II members to carry weapons and to travel freely in Southeast Asia. But, according to the sworn affidavits that accompanied my package, there was a catch. In exchange for the favors, the head of Skyhook II, former New York Congressman John LeBoutillier, had to defame Billy Hendon before Board Members of the National League of Families by alleging that Hendon had broken national security laws and endangered the lives of POWs. The affidavits stated that it appeared LeBoutillier was under duress. The names and contacts of those who could corroborate this were attached.

I knew LeBoutillier, a member of the Eastern Establishment, who had become a passionate champion of the POW cause. I called him.

"There's a very serious allegation that Richard Childress of the National Security Council staff in the White House asked you to trash Billy Hendon," I said. "In exchange for favors."

"That's right," he said, adding that it was not a money offer that persuaded him. It was the promise of DEA credentials, without which his group could not work in Southeast Asia.

I was startled by the prompt admission, which was corroborated by published interviews LeBoutillier had given. LeBoutillier was financially independent, a member of the Vanderbilt family. He had founded Skyhook II. I had always thought he was honest, but this was honesty *plus*. "You realize what you're saying?"

"Yes," said LeBoutillier. "I was offered false Drug Enforcement Agency I.D. so I could move around Southeast Asia on MIA investigations. I'd get DEA cover and facilities. All I had to do was arrange to go before a League of Families meeting to discredit Billy." The information had been passed to the FBI, which did investigate. Hendon had been getting a lot of publicity after he had recently accused the administration of concealing evidence on POWs.

"But you and Congressman Billy Hendon worked closely together on the POW issue," I protested.

"We did," said LeBoutillier. He explained that he thought Hendon had gone about things the wrong way and probably hindered efforts to get POWs out. Hendon had gone on several goodwill missions to Laos, under the cover of assessing the need for humanitarian goods like medical supplies. He had made good his promises and been instrumental in getting such goods shipped there. Then someone found out and leaked his true objective – to find out about POWs – to the media.

I could understand the difference of opinion. The men were as dissimilar in style as possible – one full of sophisticated urbanity, the other full of backslapping country bonhomie.

LeBoutillier explained further that Childress then told him to write a letter saying he had not acted under duress when he discredited Billy. After he wrote the letter, the White House colonel reneged on the deal. LeBoutillier said, "It's not only important to understand that the National Security Council – because that's who Childress represents – wanted me to trash Hendon. It is more important to realize that the White House agreed to ask the DEA to do something on POWs. It's a tacit admission that there are POWs there from an administration that won't admit it officially, and it's also using the DEA for something they were not supposed to be used for."

"By trashing Billy were you tricked into helping the government cover up the fact that it had evidence on live prisoners?"

"Yes."

I said it was difficult to believe officials would bury missing Americans just to hide their incompetence in getting them back. It was easier to believe the LeBoutillier speculation that they might try to hide incompetence in drug enforcement, or, perhaps worse, the involvement of some of their agents in drug-running activities. "Why were you getting Drug Enforcement Agency cover and facilities? Was DEA running operations in the areas where it's suspected prisoners are being kept? Were the men who search for prisoners interfering with drug-running operations in the areas where it's suspected prisoners are being kept?"

"That could be a powerful reason for wanting to abort investigations in the Indochina region," said LeBoutillier.

The drug trail again? If I wanted to remain with *60 Minutes*, I had to put out of mind any possibility of doing another story even remotely connected to the missing. Otherwise, Hewitt would think I had gone the way of other producers who could not let go of a complex story. But who said I couldn't do a little personal research?

Much later, the St. Petersburg *Times* of March 22, 1987, was to report an FBI investigation into the claims. In it, Childress is quoted as dismissing LeBoutillier's story as "an absolute lie," and Senator Dennis De Concini, who had questioned Childress in a closed Senate committee briefing, said that he believed Childress's denials.

An elderly, wealthy widow, who was one of LeBoutillier's supporters, had seen the *60 Minutes* segment and asked me about it.

"I can't believe the lengths the government will go to to hush up the issue," I said.

"You think it can be discussed openly?"

"What's there to lose?" I asked. "I can't for the life of me see why the government won't sit down with the families and vets to hear them out."

The woman patted my hand. "My dear, Congressman LeBoutillier is accurate. The Drug Enforcement Agency gave him cover. DEA is used to cover off-line secret operations."

The words tripped off the tongue of this distinguished lady with an astonishing cynicism. The woman was among notables who wanted LeBoutillier to be made a special ambassador to represent the missing, and the concerns of their families. She seemed genuine in wanting such a position to get some action. Others joining in her appeal, like then CIA Director, Bill Casey, President Nixon, and General Alexander Haig, seemed to give it lip service only. So maybe this woman was not talking through her hat.

"I'll introduce you to a friend who is deeply concerned," she said. "I'm sure he'd like to talk with you."

I could not refuse. Her friend had retired from the Bureau of Alcohol, Tobacco and Firearms, Department of Treasury, which investigated arms-smuggling. He believed that drugs were often moved by the same people who dealt in illegal or semi-legal arms sales. He told me how profits from a trillion-dollar drug trade could finance covert operations. He said, "They say there's no other way to conduct secret wars against the Communists."

I asked, "Who are *they*?"

He replied, "Covert-war specialists who can conceal their own activities."

"Conceal from whom?" I was honestly bewildered.

"From Congress, I guess. You can't get funds for secret operations without disclosing them, and then they're no longer secret."

Shortly after, in January 1986, I was walking across the Georgetown University playing fields, white with a fresh fall

PFC Robert Garwood, soon after he joined the
Marine Corps in 1963.

Prisoner Bobby Garwood being interviewed in Hanoi shortly before his 1979 release. This still shot, taken from the tape by Jon Alpert, shows Garwood's bad teeth, which were fixed before he reached Bangkok. The film was never shown in the United States.

Sergeant Melvin McIntyre (left) and Major Mark Smith.

Special Forces Captain (later Colonel) Robert L. Howard, Medal of Honor recipient. (Official U.S. Army Photo)

Mark Waple on the day of the lawsuit *Smith vs. The President* was launched. (Jason Brady)

Colonel Richard Childress speaking before a group of veterans in the fall of 1987. Congressman Stephen Solarz, Chairman of the Subcommittee on Asian and Pacific Affairs, is on the left. (José A. Rivera, *New York City Tribune*)

Red McDaniel at the moment of his release, Gia Lam Airport, Hanoi, 1973. (Official U.S. Air Force Photo)

The McDaniel family, 1981: Red and Dorothy (seated), David, Mike, and Leslie (standing left to right).

Ross Perot (right) preparing to give testimony before the House
Foreign Affairs Committee, 1971.

Lieutenant General Eugene Tighe, Director of the Defense Intelligence Agency, June 1977 to September 1981. Between the years 1974 and 1977, he also held the posts of Acting Director and Deputy Director. (Official U.S. Air Force Photo)

of snow, telling my husband about the elderly woman's worldliness.

"She would know all that from an earlier time," Bill said. "The French used opium profits to fight communism in Indochina. I tell you someone else who knew all about it – Clare Boothe Luce. She was very close to General Eugene Tighe and felt a deep concern about how the MIA issue could hurt national morale, but that came long after her husband's stubborn refusal to see the China of Chairman Mao Tse-tung as anything but evil. Henry Luce was right, but I had a big argument with him in Hong Kong once because he also refused to hear any criticism of Mao's Nationalist enemies." Luce, the publisher of *Time*, had been all in favor of Chiang Kai-shek's Nationalist Chinese armies' remaining in the region, where they grew opium to finance military activities next door to the French colonies of Vietnam and Laos. After a time, the CIA's proprietary airline, Air America, had helped freight dope for the Nationalist Chinese. Aigle Azuré and other French freelance airlines lifted the dope for the French government. Bill had seen opium poppies stretching from horizon to horizon all through the high valleys of that area – from Burma, across the top of Thailand to Laos, and into the Chinese province of Yunnan.

Bill's last journey to Thailand was still fresh in his mind. "The King's trying to purge Thailand of illegal drugs. He's got dangerous enemies – dealers in 'foreign mud,' their term for opium. His opponents used to say the drug trade was important to Thailand's national security – "

"It's destroying ours," I said.

"It didn't seem that way when it all started." Bill stood aside. Two young joggers came down a narrow path between the university hospital and Yates Field House Athletic Center. Brightly colored skiers' hats bobbed across the snow. Yates would be crowded with red-cheeked students. Yet, despite these signs of wholesomeness, the frightening truth was that drugs had seeped into every part of society. Even here in Washington.

"As long ago as World War II, the Allies provided opium for jungle guerrilla units fighting the Japs,"* Bill said. "After the Second World War, the French expanded the habit. They organized anti-communist *maquisards* in their colonial territories and paid them in dope."

"And created a terrible problem back home in France?"

"They said that to save France, you had to destroy the human garbage. If the garbage sustained its drug addiction by spending huge amounts of money, and if that money financed the wars in Indochina against communism – well, then you got some benefit from the human garbage!"

---

* *Special Operations Executive in the Far East*, by Charles Cruikshank (Oxford University Press, 1983), describes British behind-the-lines operations and the advisability of carrying opium for local supporters.

CHAPTER 9

LIES IN LAOS

Was there an overwhelming motive for burying all the secrets about missing Americans? Was the American public kept in the dark about prisoners because of intelligence failures? To conceal bureaucratic stupidity? Or was it because some covert enterprises had used profits from the drug trade, and any deep examination of the missing would uncover the truth? Or was it all of the above?

Mel Holland was an American Air Force sergeant with a special talent for electronic intelligence and high-tech warfare who felt trapped in a covert operation in Laos. "They lied to us about this operation," he had written to his wife, Ann. "We'll talk about it on my next leave." But there was no next leave. He was lost soon after in a Communist command strike everyone said was impossible. "They lied to us," he wrote, "real bad."

What did he mean? The question had gnawed at Ann Holland during her long years of struggle to raise five children alone. She was warned by U.S. government officials to drop the issue. When she continued to ask questions, the National Security Council, through the League of Families, described her to journalists as "another overwrought family member" – like Marian Shelton.

Melvin Holland had disappeared in 1968. He had been assigned as a technician to a remote mountain top in Laos: Site 85, one of a chain of bases in the CIA's war in Laos, where, supposedly, no war was going on. Officially, he was based in Thailand. Each time he was flown from Thailand into Laos, he was "sanitized" and turned into a civilian in a secret war. If he had been in uniform, he might have had a fighting chance as a prisoner-of-war. Ann learned through painful investigation that, in his position, he had been "deniable." If he was captured, or if his unit threatened to become a political embarrassment, the U.S. government would deny all knowledge of them.

In March 1968, Ann was told he was missing. She must say nothing, not even to her five small children. Two years later, President Richard Nixon had denied the loss of any Americans in ground combat in Laos. Ann had asked her case-officer, "If my husband wasn't lost in Laos, where was he lost?"

She contacted me after hearing on The Telephone Tree about the "60 Minutes affair." I knew who she was because Site 85 had cropped up in my research for "Dead or Alive." I had even come across a report that at one time the U.S. government had put $6 million in a Hong Kong bank as a ransom payment for six Site 85 technicians. But I could never get a handle on what really happened, because every bit of documentation was classified and most of the family members of men who had disappeared there were afraid to talk because they had signed secrecy oaths. Ann understood my frustration, because, she said, she had struggled for years to learn the truth about what happened to Melvin and slowly realized she was beating her head against a government wall of silence. His story sounded as though it led straight back to the puzzle of Site 85, and Site 85 seemed to have some role in the larger issue.

I felt Ann had a right to find out what happened – the truth might hurt national pride, nothing more. I was also intrigued by Site 85. I told her I'd help, and my education in irregular warfare took a new turn as I looked into her husband's case. I heard, for instance, about "sheep-dipping" – a process for building the secret CIA army. An American serviceman, like Mel Holland, would go through the motions of formal resignation, his records would be transferred to a Top Secret file, and some convincing story would be invented to explain his sudden return to civilian life. In Mel's case, the story was that he was working in his field for Hughes Aircraft. However, he would continue to pursue his military career, though officially "off the books." He was then ready for clandestine activities. Pensions and insurance had to be somehow covered, and the CIA ran its own proprietary companies to deal with such problems. In some cases the families of MIAs who were sheep-dipped in this way still receive two pensions – one from the military and one from the civilian "cover" company. It was thought by some that this was considered a good way to keep the families quiet, since they could be threatened with losing one pension.

I found the man who had been overall commander of the special team at Site 85, Colonel Gerald Clayton. He said, "We had to walk through the dope they were growing to reach Site 85."

Who was growing what dope?

Colonel Clayton did not answer that question. Instead, he said I should ask "Theodore Shackley, the guy in charge of the CIA in Laos." Shackley had appeared before in my investigations. Shackley had been chief of the CIA's vast operations in Vietnam from 1969 until 1972. He had been chief of the CIA station in Miami, Florida, directing the secret war against Castro. His secret war in Laos, carried on during the Vietnam conflict, was a response to the Communist use of sanctuaries adjoining Vietnam.*

Presumably he would be in a position to know what had been going on in "his" area – whether he could talk about it or not.†

In the summer of 1986, Ann came to Washington, D.C., from her home on the Pacific Coast to ask a former helicopter pilot who had flown her husband and other men on and off the peak for rest breaks in Thailand, "Were they captured?"

"That's something I cannot, absolutely cannot, talk about," said the ex-pilot.

She demanded a better answer, and he said, "Ann, those men did not technically exist then. They do not technically exist now. . . . But you're on the right track. Don't give up now."

Ann got a copy of a Top Secret intelligence analysis of the seizure of Site 85 during a brief period when it was declassified. She was incensed by what she read. The report was then reclassified. What she had seen made it clear that her husband and other U.S. airmen were prized by the enemy

---

*   Shackley has always publicly denied any CIA involvement with drugs in Southeast Asia. He told a *Vanity Fair* writer, Ron Rosenbaum, according to the magazine's issue for January 1990, the Laotian warlord who was most closely associated with the CIA–General Vang Pao – was commander of Military Region 2 in northern Laos, and not in the Golden Triangle opium-growing area.

†   A year later, when Ted Shackley's name would be bandied around in connection with the Iran-Contra scandal, Ann would ask for Shackley's help. He would tell her that he remembered nothing about Site 85 or Americans taken prisoner there. Ann wondered aloud if this official ignorance had anything to do with a denial of casualties in the area, read into the Senate record by U. Alexis Johnson in 1971, but Shackley would concede nothing. He was to promise, "I'll get back to you." He never did.

as "Special Talents." In 1968, at Site 85, they ran highly secret equipment to guide American bombers onto targets around Hanoi, 160 miles to the east. The CIA said the enemy could not possibly pierce the heavily fortified, narrow path to the top, or scale the steep 5,600-foot limestone cliffs. Despite such assurances, the enemy took the garrison in a surprise assault, using tactics developed by the Soviet Union's "Spetsznaz" special-operations regiment.

Ann concluded that her husband and other Americans in the garrison had not been growing the opium poppies described by her husband's commanding officer, Colonel Clayton. She was sure the dope belonged to the guerrillas of CIA mercenary General Vang Pao, whose responsibility was to guard the tiny mountain-top fortress and at the same time harvest the opium crop to finance the purchase of more weapons, medicines, and food so they could fight for their American comrades. Ann believed that delivering the opium to market required the help of a Raven-directed U.S. aircraft. Ravens flew whatever cargoes they were ordered to deliver. They also flew dangerous missions behind enemy lines. They were mostly sheep-dipped U.S. aviators directed from the secret city built for this secret war at Long Tieng in Laos. It appeared upon no map and was known to aviators as 20 Alternate, and to a few irreverent observers as Spook Heaven. Did it all begin there?

If Ann's information about the poppy fields around Site 85 was correct, it meant not only that the U.S. government was still anxious to hide the fact that it had engaged in illegal warfare in a neutral country – something everyone knew by now – but that the financing of the effort had also been shady. In an age when the U.S. was fighting a losing war against drugs, huge quantities of which came from Southeast Asia, it would certainly be damaging to have the American people find out that the "illegal" secret war in Laos had been financed, at least in part, by the illegal junk that was destroying so many people in America. If the dope around Site 85 helped maintain the CIA's mercenary forces, it meant that the CIA could be linked to drug cultivation. And if reports about CIA-owned aircraft transporting it for U.S. mercenary allies was true, it meant that the U.S. government had also, however minimally, helped in drug distribution. That could be embarrassing. Ann figured someone must have thought it would be easier to clamp the lid on the whole matter for another twenty years or so. And then, of course, there was the big question. If there had been U.S. involvement with drugs in any sense, just when had such activities ceased?

In the early eighties one of the CIA men who claimed to have once flown in and out of Spook Heaven in Laos regularly had come to see Ann Holland. He took pity on her because he thought she had a right to know what happened at Site 85. He gave her a very cursory briefing – a kind of road map for continuing her search. He said he knew what had occurred when Site 85 fell. He knew men had been betrayed; he knew men had survived; and he knew some had been taken prisoner.

I needed to find him.

At first I knew him only by his voice, having chased him from country to country by phone. He had retired from the Agency in the way most old hands retire, which is to say they never really retire from secrecy obligations. He established solid businesses, but he was still called on often to do contract work for the Agency and for other intelligence units – usually in his old Southeast Asian stomping grounds. He was hard to track down, and harder still to hang on to. Each time he moved, he left no trace. Then quite suddenly he told me that he must see me face-to-face. Somewhere safe, he said, and suggested a casino-hotel.

We met at Maxim's in Las Vegas, where the mindless racket provided protection from eavesdroppers. I had sensed his presence in the elevator. His great talent was that he could always blend with the crowd. Here, he became a tourist, pale and insignificant among the boisterous low-rollers. They had jostled him to my side in their rush to reach the one-armed bandits, and I felt myself nudged toward the coffee shop as his voice, made familiar by the telephone, murmured, "Monika?"

In the coffee shop I was terrified I might scare off the man I filed mentally as "Casino Man." It was very important to hear everything he had to say, but his mumble was artful. Sometimes a word sizzled and spat its way through the clatter of the slot machines. It was like listening to a partially jammed radio signal. He said he had just seen living men who had been declared dead. These were men who had fought for "American values," and who, with others, might have been negotiated away to secure a shameful peace.

Could I trust him? For every answer he gave, he asked two questions of his own. Who were my sources? Where had Bill gotten his information for his books on intelligence?

Suddenly he stood. "Time for a break."

"Good," I said. I needed to escape from the tension and the noise of the casino. In the silence of my room, I called Bill. I told him that I did not know how to communicate with these secret-intelligence and covert-operations people any more. Casino Man had told me a lot, but it was all in a kind of code. He kept saying it was better for my safety if he told me only what he thought I needed to know.

Bill asked, "What is he offering?"

"He's offering to prove that some American prisoners-of-war still survive. That attempts are made to stop them coming back from Southeast Asia because they'll raise questions leading to investigations" – I was careful how I phrased things over an open telephone. "He says one of his friends had his staff brutalized, his offices ransacked in the U.S. and abroad, and his records impounded by foreign agencies after he reported to DIA that he had seen live American POWs – he emphasized they were not defectors. He doesn't want the same thing to happen to him." I tried not to sound melodramatic. "He uses acronyms that I don't recognize. Should I pretend – ?"

"No," Bill said hastily. "Don't pretend. He could be feeding you lies, to test if you *are* pretending."

Bill admitted later he found himself hoping I *would* scare off Casino Man. He was beginning to think it would be a favor to everyone if my contact would just quietly disappear and take with him whatever dirty little secrets still survived the wars in Indochina. Bill thought I should have taken the hint when I first started encountering pointed and worrying resistance. Then he reminded himself that no one had foreseen how my inquiries would lead to a point at which self-respect made it impossible to stop.

I, too, would have settled for a return to normalcy, as I left my room and went downstairs to find Casino Man. He had gone. For a moment I, too, hoped he'd been scared away. But he had only moved to a corner where cocktail waitresses swarmed like honey bees.

He surprised me with a smile. He swung a scuffed satchel up from under his chair. The satchel was made of weather-beaten canvas: the kind of bag I now knew was carried by American aviators on secret sessions after the sanitation crews removed all identifiable insignia. He removed a map: it was folded to an area of Indochina. I could see the contours of the border between Vietnam and Laos, faded and creased. Earlier he had hinted there might be an effort going on right then to bring POWs out of a Communist country, but I had not been able to make out if he meant through negotiation or through rescue. Now he said, "My particular guys are here," before his voice dropped again into that frustrating mumble.

I wondered if his distrust had suddenly overcome his willingness to confide. Or was *I* at fault for being too guarded? Maybe he needed to see in me some small flash of concern, not for him, not for me, but for these "particular guys." But I couldn't fake emotion over what seemed to be something so remote. Then I heard him say, quite clearly, "Look, I'm not going to feed back what you tell me."

So he was afraid I might think he was a sort of stool-pigeon? The thought had occurred to me after he made it clear that he knew the precise details of a meeting I'd had with a Pentagon source. "Are you afraid *I* might report back to someone in Washington what *you* tell me?" I said.

"I'm always afraid." He pulled out a sheet of paper and doodled. I watched, fascinated. He was sketching a series of boxes joined by lines. His fingers were thick and the hands themselves looked capable. He had carpenter's hands. He wrote names in the boxes. Names of government offices and private corporations appeared in another set of boxes. "Commercial deals were made," he said, "after we got officially out of the war in 1973, before the final defeat of South Vietnam in 1975."

I asked what kind of deals were made. Did they include arms and drugs? He did not answer directly, but said, "Some of us who were on the edge of it, we thought it was a way to get even – without interference from Washington. It was the *only* way we thought. Covert operations, financed by 'private enterprise.' " Suddenly he crumpled up the paper and stuffed it in a pocket. I knew there had been a secret and illegal war in Laos, but now Casino Man was alleging that private and highly illegal sources had financed it – sources connected to the government. The vehicle for this, he said, was the Nugan Hand Bank, the company that had collapsed in Australia. He called it by the insider parlance, Yin Han.

According to him, in 1970 and 1971 there was an official decision made by the group of men who had decided to win the war in their own way not to share information on POWs anywhere in Southeast Asia with the military. The CIA kept a watch list of prisoners, and at the time it was tracing over three hundred men. It was felt that to share this information would not facilitate the group's goals and would create complexities in the new game plan. The feeling was that if the situation deteriorated, the military would not protect the CIA. He continued, "They felt no obligation to do anything for a military they did not trust." This group in the CIA had control of the secret unit of Americans placed behind the lines to do rescue work. Most of the military men were not rescued. Casino Man claimed that, "The group got out most of its own men. In 1973 the United States demanded no accounting for the three hundred men on that list."

He opened the satchel and pulled out photographs, which he piled on top of the map. I could see only a crashed military transport plane with the insignia obliterated. The aircraft had come down in one piece. The control cabin had been ripped open. The camera had caught a skeleton in the captain's seat.

"That aircraft," claimed Casino Man, "was officially listed in 1971 as having been destroyed in mid-air by a SAM missile. The crew was officially declared dead. But a ground reconnaissance team found only the pilot died. He made a wheels-up landing because not all the crew had parachutes. Five walked away from the crash. They were captured by Pathet Lao Communist forces. Our government denies this, but I have the intelligence tracking them. . . . If a crash landing is recorded as a mid-air explosion, something is being covered up. The remains of a mid-air explosion look vastly different from a crash landing." He put away the photograph and with it the other pictures, so swiftly that I caught only a glimpse of men in jungle greens.

He gave me nothing a court of inquiry could trace back to him. But he directed me to someone whose reputation ensured I could trust him; a man who would provide me with full documentation that Casino Man was who he said he was.

He looked down at the tiny area of his map that was not folded out of sight. "My particular group . . . I get careless, *they* die. You understand? I don't enjoy mystifications. But they die if *you* talk to the wrong people."

My head was already hurting when he put the map back into his worn satchel and mumbled about being careful. *I* should be careful. There were people, he alleged, who wouldn't want the American people to find out what had really happened to their POWs and why.

I was chasing the dragon, despite my husband's warning. If I stopped now, I could continue to walk to the M Street office from my cozy Georgetown home, watch for the yellow daffodils of spring, and feel life had never been better. In the depths of the winter blahs, the temptation was strong.

But it took an equal amount of time to walk from *60 Minutes* to the wall where Vietnam veterans came every day to look for the names of lost comrades, chiselled into sober black marble. Lance Sijan was among those names.

A Canadian government source had just informed me that in 1981 there had been an offer by Hanoi to *sell* some fifty-seven American prisoners to the U.S. government. Ottawa's ambassador in China had been a go-between, said my source, who explained Washington had requested no publicity. "This is a delicate matter," he said. "It's up to the Americans. We have offered to let any returning prisoners reside first in Canada to save U.S. embarrassment. . . . " The Canadian government denied the claim.

President Reagan had taken part in a discussion, it seemed, at which it was decided to reject the offer, because the administration did not want, ironically, to find itself "paying ransom for hostages." The story was later leaked in a *Wall Street Journal* article by Bill Paul. On August 19, 1986, Paul reported:

> In 1981, just after President Reagan took office, the new administration learned that Vietnam wanted to sell an unspecified number of live POWs still in Southeast Asia for the sum of $4 billion (less than the U.S. had promised Hanoi in post-war rebuilding aid). The proposal was discussed by Mr. Reagan and his advisors at a general meeting on security matters, according to one person who says he was in the room, and whose story is supported by others in attendance. It was decided the offer

was genuine. Then a number of presidential advisors said they opposed paying for POWs . . . it would appear as if the U.S. could be blackmailed. . . . Richard Allen, then the national security advisor, subsequently proposed a reconnaissance mission into Laos which, if successful, would lead to a military rescue of prisoners. The secret mission failed and word of the failure leaked to the press. . . . A new POW policy was concocted [to] maintain that the U.S. can neither confirm nor deny that POWs remain in Southeast Asia but operates on the assumption they are there. Through a turn of phrase, the U.S. government is now able to appear steadfastly committed to getting the men home – without having to take any decisive action.

That policy, of course, had been reiterated to me time and again while I was working on POWs. Indeed, one of the last changes in the *60 Minutes* piece suggested by Don Hewitt was to let Richard Armitage state that very policy, without rebuttal from any of the people we had interviewed.

Vice President George Bush had been at the Roosevelt Room meeting. He had lately spent, Congressman Billy Hendon told me, "nearly two hours on the phone trying to persuade me the offer was for the *remains* of fifty-seven prisoners." However, Billy Hendon claimed he had confirmation from a direct witness who asserted that the conversation was about live men. That same witness confirmed that the offer was about live men to Ross Perot, who was still a member of the President's Advisory Council on Foreign Intelligence.

I asked if anyone on The Telephone Tree knew more. John Brown, the Vietnam vet who had given up his commercial hunting and fishing business in Alaska in the last year and was now a writer, soon reported back to me. With six vets with distinguished records, he had descended upon the former national security advisor, Richard Allen, in his Washington office after the *Wall Street Journal* article appeared.

"Allen seemed shaken when we revealed our detailed knowledge of the White House meeting," Brown had recorded. "He kept writing the number 57 on a piece of paper. He would not deny such a meeting, and asked his secretary to get his notebook for that period. She came back and said she could not locate it, and perhaps the FBI still had it for another investigation then under way.

"This secretary had been with Henry Kissinger in Paris when the peace accord had been drawn up. She had already listened very attentively when, earlier in the meeting, Allen said Kissinger admitted he knew about Americans still in captivity when the Paris peace agreements were signed.

"Allen said, 'I know they're there, and it is my firm belief that live POWs are still being held in Indochina. . . . I authorized one reconnaissance rescue mission after we got pictures of U.S. distress signals in Laos, but the reaction time was so slow that the prisoners had been moved by the time the mission went in.' " This was confirmation of the 1981 Delta mission Betty Foley had found out about.

General Alexander Haig had also been at the Roosevelt Room meeting. Allen told the vets that Haig had just called him after hearing he was going to meet with Brown and the vets, and said, "Look, Dick, I don't think you should see Brown and the other vets. This POW thing is a can of worms. If it's opened up, a lot of people could get hurt."

Among the vets who might have upset the applecart was Colonel William LeGro, who had been the Chief of Intelligence Branch for the Defense Attaché's Office from ceasefire in February 1973 to April 1975. He had a reputation for getting to the bottom of things and for an unimpeachable integrity. LeGro said it was no secret that the then-Chief of Station (CIA), Tom Polgar, held human (as opposed to electronic) intelligence collection on prisoners in low regard, that the very best human intelligence on prisoners was not acted upon.

LeGro's service in Vietnam went back to 1966. He was a combat infantryman by profession and he had endured savage fighting both against the Japanese and later against the Communists in Korea. As a military historian, he had written *Vietnam from Cease-fire to Capitulation* for the Department of the Army. In it he paid tribute to the fighting spirit of South Vietnam's armed forces, meticulously examining the battle-by-battle retreat in the face of overwhelming Communist firepower reinforced by the Soviet Union's equipment and advisors. The South Vietnamese, by contrast, were starved of U.S. equipment equal to the enemy's arms. He viewed the wars of Vietnam through Brown's own rice-paddy grunt's eyes.

LeGro was one of Brown's group, and he corroborated what the shaken Allen had said when they met in the former national-security advisor's office. As I wandered deeper into a tangled jungle of facts and phantoms, Colonel LeGro became increasingly important to me, because of his steadfast faith in moral leadership based on exact information. I understood better that there are fighting colonels who remain so loyal to their men that they haven't the time to play the political game that would advance them to more glorified rank.

CHAPTER 10

TELLING DIRTY SECRETS

"Tell Smith and McIntire to guard their backs." The man who had called me at the office sounded genuinely concerned. "Go to a pay phone and try this number. . . . "

I went outside, found a phone, and dialed. Another man answered and said, "I'm inside The Activity. Tell the two Green Berets they're in danger of their lives if they give evidence before The Committee."

"The Committee" was how Vietnam vets referred to a key Senate hearing coming up early in 1986. Its full name was the Senate Veterans Affairs Committee. They hoped it would publicly air all the allegations made in the Smith-McIntire lawsuit. Smith and McIntire had no intention of letting any threats keep them from making public what they knew about prisoners.

I found The Committee's chairman, Frank Murkowski, a Republican from Alaska, overbearing and self-important. The Telephone Tree had argued that he did not qualify as a member of the Veterans of Foreign Wars (VFW) on the

159

strength of his one year with the U.S. Coast Guard. He resigned from the VFW. He kept his chairmanship of The Committee, but the incident probably did not improve his sour view of activist vets.

His critics held an equally sour view of The Committee. "A government rubber stamp," claimed Colonel Nick Rowe, the Special Force's expert on prison survival techniques, who had told me about the 1981 Delta rescue raid and who had been protective of Bobby Garwood. "It's part of the machinery to make sure the administration doesn't face a political crisis over Americans in hostile hands that could be greater than the Iranian hostage crisis."

"It marks the first congressional POW/MIA hearings with even the appearance of being a good-faith search for truth," commented the Kansas-based newsletter *Homecoming II.* "It's only ten years late. . . . "

Mark Waple, as lawyer for Smith and McIntire, said, "The government cranked up this farce. But I'm going to make them listen to my witnesses."

A struggle for control of The Committee's agenda began. On the Friday before the hearings began at the end of January, the Vietnam veterans' organizations rallying around Smith and McIntire were suddenly told the deadline for written testimony was that day. A sworn affidavit filed by former National Security Agency analyst Jerry Mooney was called "inappropriate" by Murkowski's aide.

Mooney, until 1976, had tracked prisoners like Sergeant Peter Cressman and his crew after their shoot-down and capture. He knew of hundreds of men who, according to the best high-tech and human intelligence of the time were still alive and in captivity after the official homecoming in 1973. He also had precise information on some prisoners who had been executed – another bit of information, he told me, the U.S. government wanted to keep secret.

It was the first time an employee of America's most secret "eavesdropping" intelligence agency would give public testimony that might expose some who lied about prisoners who had been left behind. Not only was the system for tracking prisoners "state-of-the-art," the means of transmitting such information to everyone who needed to know was, according to Mooney, foolproof. Working from a small village in Vietnam, he could transmit precise information via satellite to a U.S. army unit anywhere in the world within sixty seconds. When required, as when the case was one involving a planned execution of a prisoner by the Vietnamese, the information reached the President of the United States in less than five minutes. There were strict rules for the dissemination of information on prisoners. Hundreds of officials in all of the service and intelligence branches should have been informed of prisoners captured. Somewhere along the way that information disappeared.

When Mooney's testimony was suddenly deemed inappropriate the day before he was to appear before The Committee, there was no time left to gather up new testimony.

The night before the first hearing, Lawyer Waple received a warning from the National Security Agency on his answering service: "You were not in when we called, and if you do not return this call, we are having your witness Mooney indicted." The real message was that the NSA didn't want Mooney to give evidence at all. Jerry Mooney had been a specialist lent by NSA to the U.S. Air Force in Vietnam, and according to NSA he knew too much about super-secret procedures to be testifying.

Mooney had an outstanding record of long service in high categories of secret intelligence work. The man was an artist at distilling intelligence from intercepted enemy orders during the Vietnam War. These included Soviet "shopping lists" for captured U.S. technology and technicians. Mooney had studied the case of Sergeant Peter Cressman's EC-47Q "Flying Pueblo," the electronics-intelligence aircraft shot down in February 1973 after the Paris Peace Accords were signed. The Pentagon said nobody survived. But Mooney had electronically tracked not just the four crew members mentioned in intelligence reports but five to seven other survivors as they were moved to Hanoi. "MB," he had written after their names – Moscow Bound.

In the days of his innocence, Mooney had assumed that action followed his reports, that they would as a matter of course be transmitted to the branch of service able to act on them, or to the CIA's special rescue unit that Casino Man had described to me. Whenever he raised questions later, he'd been told anything he might say publicly would jeopardize men's lives, leading him to think secret missions were under way to recover lost Americans. It had been official public denials that there was no evidence of prisoners having been left behind that broke the spell. Mooney now wondered if his reports had been intercepted by people with their own secret agenda, forming a private government answerable to none – people "endangered because an investigation into prisoners would lead to exposure of worse things," he had told me. I did not confide what Casino Man had told me about a small group making its own policy.

Periodically, Mooney received particularly upsetting information. At one point he was told by a former agent inside Vietnam that a blind American POW without legs or arms was the butt of jokes – the village fool in a remote part of Vietnam. During a period of intense soul-searching, Mooney suffered a heart attack. Hospital doctors could find nothing physically wrong. His priest told him, "Jerry, whatever you're bottling up, you'd better let it out or it'll kill you!"

"If I talk publicly for the greater good," replied Mooney, "I'll be accused of breaking secrecy agreements. If I talk to anyone inside the intelligence community, it'll be like shouting into a black hole."

The priest advised him to confide to some congressman he could trust.

Mooney was upset when Richard Armitage appeared on *60 Minutes* saying there was no proof prisoners were alive. He told me, "I know they were alive. The government doesn't want me to talk about the fact that *only five per cent of the hundreds of Americans I documented as being alive and in Communist hands have been returned* (italics mine)."

Mooney swore, in an affidavit for Mark Waple, that he believed there were live Americans left behind in Southeast

Asia "on the basis of exact and precise operational orders drawn from enemy communications." He had compiled a list of more than three hundred U.S. military men he knew to have been captured, and whose movements through the system of Communist prisons he had followed across Indochina. "Twelve days after the 'last prisoners' came home, an order from the U.S. State Department went to the Department of Defense, stating that, as of April 12, 1973, 'There are no more prisoners in Southeast Asia. They are all dead.' I knew that was not true." What Mooney was willing to state publicly was what many I had spoken to in the government admitted (in one way or another) privately.

"Mooney won't get away with this," Colonel Rowe's special-operations friend in the Pentagon confided to me. "If the Pentagon with all of its covert resources says they're dead, they're dead. The institution exercises enormous power and there are many who won't like Jerry Mooney crossing them up." This Pentagon source worked in counter-terrorist planning. The source requested anonymity "for my own safety." Later he volunteered to be identified "if that would help convince people all of this is true." I put him in touch with a congressional investigation when it finally got under way.

As he was getting ready to leave his Montana home for the trip to Washington, Mooney got a call from Senator Murkowski's aide: "The Chairman has to know in advance what you plan to say." Mooney told the aide to consult the affidavit he had given Lawyer Waple. The aide called back to say the affidavit did not go into sufficient detail. "Okay," said Mooney. He added specifics and showed where to go for the supporting documents, which had been classified.

Five hours later, Mooney received an anonymous call. "If you know what's good for you, don't go to Washington." Mooney realized that the call was local. Who could possibly know, in the Montana wilderness, that he was going before The Committee?

Mooney struck me as honest and vulnerable. In the late seventies he had decided that in Vietnam he had won the freedom to work in the backwoods, raise a family, and reflect upon the secret warfare about which his fellow countrymen knew so little. He was no radical. He saw a danger, however, of a passion for secrecy turning his country into a "National Security State."

And so, Mooney came to Washington – despite the threats. Mark Waple put him up at the Pentagon Quality Inn, and stayed himself nearby in Crystal City. At 10 p.m. on their first night in town, Waple got a call from Mooney and later reported to me all the subsequent events.

"I just received three phone calls," said Mooney. "The message each time was the same. 'Better pack your bags and go back home.' I thought it was a prankster the first time."

"You feel your life's in danger?" asked Waple.

"Yes," said Mooney.

Waple leaned against the wall, staring down at the telephone. What was he to do? Major Smith and Sergeant McIntire, who were giving testimony around the same time, had quietly arranged with friends in Special Forces to be given maximum, if unofficial, protection by those who believed they should testify. Now Mooney was being threatened, but in his case Waple could never muster that kind of unofficial help. Still, Mooney was entitled to protection. Waple decided to repeat to the duty-officer for The Committee what Mooney had told him. A short time later, the counsel called Waple: "I hear you need a witness protected."

"That's right," said Waple. "The witness has received three threatening calls to go back home."

"Well?" the counsel paused. "Maybe he should leave?"

Maintaining his control, Waple demanded, and finally got, a bodyguard – a D.C. detective who did his job so well that next morning the National Security Agency men who called on Mooney had a hard time getting past him. They placed in front of Mooney a copy of the secrecy agreement he had signed in 1968 and which he renewed periodically with each new assignment during his years of service. "Break it, and you're for the high jump."

Mooney heaved a sigh. "I have an obligation to my country to go before The Committee."

The Committee had his service records. The National Security Agency director had praised his "wide and diversified skills" and his work as a cryptologist. Mooney had practically written the book on "special methods" in Indochina for getting inside the enemy's mind. It seemed unlikely that this man would have other motives than deep moral conviction.

Mindful of the need for secrecy on technical matters, he asked to explain in secret session how he came to his conclusions on the survival of three hundred specific Americans. He was interrupted by Murkowski: "We're not interested in that kind of information. Have you seen any live American prisoners lately?"

Mooney blinked. In Wolf Point, Montana? "Well, no – "

"If you haven't seen a live prisoner recently, you have no business being here." And that was that.

Mooney stood downcast after The Committee dismissed him. "I know the men of about twenty families are dead, although they are listed as missing and the families still hang on to hope," he said to me. "The government has known they were dead since day one. And there are men still alive whose families think them dead. The government got the details from me long ago." He sighed. "I can't understand why this intelligence is classified and denied the families. It's been handed over to the Communists in Hanoi by U.S. delegates.

"I counted so much on these hearings. I truly believed Congress was the court of last resort. That it would do its duty."

Scott Barnes returned to Washington. He wanted to testify to the Senate Veterans Affairs Committee that he *had* seen live prisoners recently. In open session, he spoke with seeming authority. In October of 1981, approximately five months after the Delta mission was aborted, he had been sent on the multi-purpose mission into a hostile part of Indochina. One objective was to check a specific location for American POWs, as he had explained in the truth-drug interview for the BBC's David Taylor. He was not certain who sponsored the mission. As he had told us earlier, the man in charge had been a CIA officer named Jerry Daniels, at the time using the alias Michael Baldwin. They found two American POWs in a large work gang, he said, and photographed them with highly sophisticated long-range cameras and high-speed infrared film. They also listened to American voices with electronic devices that could pick up sound from over 200 meters away. The emaciated men were in a bamboo-and-wire-enclosed camp with a watchtower. When he returned to Bangkok he was ordered to keep his mouth shut about what he had witnessed. He was told: "It is not in America's interests to have any prisoner come out alive."

"Do you recall who told you that?" asked Murkowski.

"Yes, sir." Barnes straightened up. He named Colonel Paul Mather of JCRC, the Joint Casualty Resolution Center in Bangkok. The Center investigated prisoner intelligence. It was held in low esteem by POW families and concerned veterans because, according to them, it bungled every request from them for information and assistance. The families also asked if Colonel Mather was compromised when Hanoi granted him the special favor of allowing his Vietnamese fiancée to leave the country in 1977.

There was a quick discussion among The Committee members. Senator Dennis DeConcini, a Democrat from Arizona, struggled against the tide. He said, "Well, I want to get the JCRC man here to testify."*

---

* DeConcini was true to his word. He pressed to have Mather testify months later. By then, The Committee was winding down and the JCRC colonel was asked the most perfunctory questions. "He consulted with advisors after each question," reported the BBC's Taylor, "as if he wasn't sure what his job was." In the end, DeConcini said loudly, "I'm still wondering what exactly it is you do." The Joint Casualty Resolution Center had been established

"Jesus H. Christ!" exclaimed one of the National Security Council staffers sitting on the public benches within the hearing of David Taylor. Taylor reported later, "All these guys did was whisper and poke fun at the 'hostile' witnesses until up comes Barnes, this supposed flake. Then out come the notebooks and they start writing down every word of what Barnes says. When the JCRC man is mentioned, they're rattled." This was obviously a sensitive point.

As the congressmen tried to decide what to do, someone tapped Taylor on the shoulder and murmured that he was wanted on the telephone. It was the BBC in London, asking for an immediate feed. The space shuttle *Challenger* had just exploded.

The *Challenger* disaster wiped out whatever interest the media had had in POW/MIA matters. The Committee heard all testimony it considered damaging to national security downstairs in what was known as "The Vault," or sometimes "The Bubble," a tomb-like room for secret sessions in the Hart Building on Capitol Hill. Barnes was invited to complete his testimony in the Vault. He said later that his words down there disappeared into thin air. The public did not hear them; they did not appear in the *Congressional Record*.

Colonel Bob Howard appeared in open session. As he was a war hero, and had won many awards including the Medal of Honor, his presence and strong testimony in support of Smith and McIntire might have seemed to merit journalistic attention. It did not. When he veered toward repeating what he had sworn to – the mysterious military exercise in Thailand which he thought was to get rid of himself, Smith, and McIntire – he was dispatched to the

---

during the Vietnam War to keep track of casualties, and the colonel had held the key post in Asia ever since. "That," Colonel Nick Rowe told me, speaking of Mather's time in that post, "is unique in the U.S. armed services."

Vault. There he was confronted with allegations about drunkenness. Yes, he had at one time gone through an alcohol rehabilitation program, he said quite openly. But the renewed charges of alcoholism after the Smith and McIntire mission in Thailand were, he believed, brought up to discredit his support for Smith and McIntire.

A member of the committee later told Ross Perot that "the Colonel recanted every word in front of Committee members in the Vault. He broke down and cried."

Of course, Perot could not check a written record because there was none. Nevertheless, he found out what had really transpired. Perot repeated to me later what Murkowski had told him about Howard's testimony, adding, "Howard did *not* recant or break down!"

Perot had taken a close interest in the proceedings and could not understand how the democratic processes could be so subverted. He had outflanked The Committee when it announced, on the eve of the hearings, "Colonel Howard cannot attend because he's on maneuvers." Perot had gone to the Joint Chiefs of Staff, using his personal influence to get Howard released. "I spent hours with Colonel Howard," Perot told me. "After the committee member's allegations, I questioned him some more. I believed him when he said that the allegations that he cried and recanted were not true. Someone tried to kill Howard in Laos and now he has to fight to save his reputation."

A professional intelligence man, now retired, added to my growing sense that The Committee hearings were as unlikely to get to the bottom of the issue as the bureaucrats who had thrown away or otherwise ignored intelligence on live prisoners at the end of the Vietnam War.

"We abandoned those men," James L. Shirah told me in Georgia. "I saw firsthand some disgusting examples."

Shirah had spent much of the 1960s as interrogator/analyst/documents examiner for a highly classified Army Intelligence unit in Laos.* He continued operating into the 1970s. "But in 1969 the kind of missions I carried out were stopped, and by 1973, when the war ended, I had quit, emotionally, all other involvement. I'd seen us throw away the best intelligence network our country ever had – " He described a network of Asian agents that had reinforced electronic intelligence on Americans in enemy hands. "When the U.S. ran out of Saigon, the CIA left for the enemy the files on thousands of those agents.

"Call me an anthropologist," said Shirah, referring to his cover. "That's what I still have to tell everyone. Even now, I'd have difficulty going before The Committee because of these unjustified secrecy rules. But I will go on record – we knew everything about every man who was missing. I personally destroyed in acid my copy of the huge file – the number is 5310-03-E. The original's buried in the secret archives at 500th Group, Ford Island, off Hawaii."

Shirah had fought as a member of an intelligence group – "the good side, not the evil part." I did not press him for an explanation until later. He was in a Georgia hospital, in terrible pain, and seemed to want me to have certain information before it was too late. General "Heinie" Aderholt, who had run so many secret air operations from Thailand, vouched for his credentials, saying Shirah shared his own sense of shame.

General Tighe had called the attitude of those who could always find a reason for discounting information from men like Shirah and Howard "a mind-set" – a kind of bu-

---

* Shirah would later confirm to staffers working for Senator Jesse Helms (Rep. N. Carolina) and Senator Charles Grassley (Rep. Iowa) that for a time he was assigned to a project named Blackwatch. In 1975 the Department of State publicly denied the existence of Blackwatch and others like it.

reaucratic malaise that took the issue over. Now I was to find that some in the intelligence bureaucracy were perhaps not so passive; that someone with access to vital intelligence on prisoners had possibly tinkered with evidence to invalidate it. What was even more interesting was that the evidence had corroborated some of Bobby Garwood's information on other American prisoners while he was in Vietnam.

In February I was roused from sleep by a phone call from Red McDaniel. He sounded jubilant. "I just got word from Congressman Hendon in Asia! He says we'll knock The Committee and those government bureaucrats dead."

Hendon had worked out his own smoke-screen mission to Hanoi. Before leaving he had brought the six other congressmen who were making the trip to meet with President Reagan. They covered the floor of the Oval Office with maps and photographs and gave details of why they believed many of the some 2,440 servicemen still unaccounted for in Southeast Asia were alive. There was a compound in Hanoi where Bobby Garwood said he'd seen American prisoners. He had described the compound in detail and given its address. He mentioned particularly a cistern in the compound. DIA officials claimed there was no cistern in the building at that address. Hendon planned to find the compound and prove whether or not Garwood had lied. It was more than fact-finding: it was a mission of vindication.

President Reagan had become interested in the case after a senior Communist official defected and gave an account that supported Garwood's claims about a cistern, which he had seen from a nearby balcony. Reagan was then shown a reconstruction of the compound made by defense-intelligence analysts, in which a water tower replaced the cistern. The analysts argued that the Vietnamese source could not have seen a cistern from the balcony where he said he stood.

Billy Hendon was outraged by this because the mock-up showed a tower, not a cistern, and the tower was located where it would not have been visible to the source. Hendon was sure the mock-up had been made deliberately to discredit Garwood's story. He had Garwood sketch a map from memory. Where the Vietnamese said the cistern was located, Garwood had drawn the same object.

From defense intelligence came a satellite photograph of the compound – without a cistern – and a report that the compound was not a military facility. Hendon believed the cistern was painted out of the photograph.

One night in Hanoi, the U.S. congressman had gone exploring. "I paced the distance from our hotel to the compound," he said. "It was about as far as the Lincoln Memorial is from Red's office near the Capitol. Next day, Congressman Bob Smith, a film cameraman, and I went to the compound."

Hendon towered over the Vietnamese as he shook the tall iron gates. Uniformed guards rushed forward and then stopped, puzzled by Hendon's strange antics. He was, after all, an official visitor, and the Vietnamese did not want any unpleasantness. He attacked a padlock and chain until the gates creaked open. Into his arms he swept up a couple of Vietnamese army officers. What could they do? Hendon was only displaying an excess of goodwill. He was like a small-town politician stumping the countryside. The soldiers fell back with slightly abashed grins. Into view came a cistern, remarkably like Garwood's description. The cameraman recorded it all.

Hendon disengaged and took off, leaving behind about one hundred slightly baffled soldiers in the compound. He had not seen Caucasians, but he had proved the existence of the cistern and a *military* compound – both of which DIA had said were not there.

However, by the time Hendon arrived back in Washington, his thunder had been stolen. The influential *Far East Economic Review* had already reported that Hanoi's officials were annoyed by "wackos and crazies running amok." The *Review* credited the comment to an aide to Frank Murkowski. In the public eye, Murkowski had credibility, because one week before his committee hearings began and before Hendon's visit, he too had returned from Hanoi, a journey he used to give authority to his views. He announced that he had secured a promise from the Communists to give back the bones of prisoners.

The bones, the families of the POWs strongly suspected, came from a location where hundreds of American skeletons, "stacked like cordwood," had been already reported by a Chinese undertaker in Hanoi who later made his way to Hong Kong. Ross Perot had learned about him through his intelligence contacts. The undertaker, a former North Vietnamese colonel, was known in Washington as "The Mortician," the Texan had told me. "The U.S. government didn't want to hear his story about the way Hanoi kept back American remains for future use in negotiation. He said the Hanoi warehouse was a sort of bank from which the Communists planned to withdraw bones for U.S. dollars. . . . There was incredible hostility to him by our own government. I had to retain lawyers and arrange the Mortician's air transport so he could give details to Washington directly. He'd never be heard otherwise."

The Mortician's evidence suggested the Vietnamese were cold-bloodedly wheeling and dealing with the remains of American soldiers, and that Hanoi expected the U.S. government to play along. What he said about remains was accepted as fact by DIA, but his information about live prisoners he had seen was formally discredited. Yet General Tighe told me his information on live POWs was just as sound as the other testimony. "The man," he said, "passed every lie-detector and psychological test." The general feeling amongst Washington insiders was that no administration wished for a crisis requiring action on behalf of live Americans. Whenever public curiosity about the missing in Vietnam reached a dangerous level, some suggested, Hanoi would from now on be requested, by a negotiating team from Washington, to withdraw bones from the bank.

One American skeleton was reported by a French scientist to be standing in the labs of a North Vietnam medical school at Hon Gay City, the bones rewired. The Frenchman recorded details. The anatomical specimen was Lt. Cmdr. Edwin Tucker, shot down in his Navy Crusader over North Vietnam in 1967 and listed as a prisoner until 1973. His family in Baldwinville, Massachusetts, asked for official U.S. government help. It would not be until November 1987 that the family would be handed back his remains – after they and Washington promised not to disclose how and why his bones ended up on exhibition. Tucker was buried with full military honors in Arlington National Cemetery on March 4, 1988. The only official statement was made at Tucker's burial. It described his mission: to draw fire from U.S. bombers attacking rail lines at Hon Gay City. And it was there, in the local medical school, his skeleton had become an exhibit! General Tighe told me, "Reports of how prisoners' bodies were treated were shamefully disregarded. The Mortician reported accurately. We spent a great deal of time and manpower checking it all out. Everything was tossed away."

The story of live POWs told by the Mortician, however, was attacked by DIA's POW/MIA experts. Billy Hendon's account of what he saw with Congressman Bob Smith in Hanoi was explained away: they had wrongly identified a facility, and consequently their film record should be dismissed. As for Bobby Garwood's "continuous public portrayal" of Americans still held captive, this left "a dangerous misconception," stated DIA's then assistant deputy director for collection management, Commodore Thomas Brooks. "The 'proof' being offered consists of a crude sketch of a reported 'detention facility' and a list of a dozen first names and a few common last names. . . . " This was in no way an accurate statement of what Garwood was offering.*

I could see why DIA was unhappy about its former director, General Tighe, who continued to disagree with this line, and who was now delving into Garwood's real story. I ran

---

* See Appendix 1 for Garwood's letter to the Committee.

into Gene Tighe after a breakfast meeting of the American Bar Association around this time. It was the first time I had seen him since the *60 Minutes* piece on MIAs. He took me aside. "You'll be pleased to know you had some effect," he said. "I can't talk about it now. But at last we're getting some action."

In February, the Senate Veterans Affairs Committee reconvened to pay respectful attention to Maj. Gen. Kenneth C. Leuer. Major Smith had handed his report on "Possible American/Allied POWs in Southeast Asia" to Leuer upon its completion in April 1984, hoping for action. Now, almost two years later, General Leuer flatly denied all Smith's assertions. He had never said, "This is too hot for me to handle, big guy." He had never said, "If you're smart, you'll put this through a shredder and forget it." He had never, the month after allegedly telling Smith that the major would jeopardize his Army career if he continued to chase after phantoms, scuttled the delivery of three American prisoners from Laos.

His rejection of Smith's reliability was in startling contrast to his previous assessments of Smith, recorded in the official reports I had obtained: "Remarkable judgement under great stress in a rapidly moving area . . . completely trustworthy . . . completely committed to national goals. . . . "

Soon after Leuer's testimony, I was in North Carolina on another *60 Minutes* story, and since I was passing Fayetteville, I thought I would look for Smith. I had heard he was back from Asia, but I found that all his earthly belongings were stashed in a kit bag locked in a friend's cellar. There was no other trace of his austere life-style.

The man who had backed Smith throughout his confrontation with the U.S. government and who had made sure he was protected during The Committee hearing was Colonel Nick Rowe. He had been increasingly helpful since I had first asked him about Garwood. "Bobby has always been known to our intelligence as a prisoner, not a traitor," he had stated flatly.

If anyone should have known, it was Nick Rowe. He had survived eight prison camps after his capture in 1963 by Vietnamese Communists. After five years' captivity, he escaped on the fifth attempt. He knew the prison system southwest of Saigon in the U-Minh "Forest of Darkness," through which thousands of American prisoners had passed. He had examined intelligence records on U.S. prisoners and concluded they were designed to discourage the public from believing any were left behind. After the 1973 homecoming, he felt so strongly about the fact that not all POWs had returned, he launched a campaign he called Youth Concerned for the 1300 MIAs. Because he was then affiliated with the White House, he made his wife, Jane Rowe, the Executive Director. He never took off a POW bracelet he wore dedicated to the POWs who were left behind.

Because he felt so strongly that the abandonment of one's own prisoners was the very worst of crimes, he talked with me. To protect him, I filed him under the code name Star White One, which was a play on the name of some covert operations in Laos. He was currently commanding the First Special Warfare Training Battalion at Fort Bragg, North Carolina. Later he gave me permission to quote him directly.

"A mythology about 'wackos, crazies and Rambo factions' running amok over MIAs started in 1981," he said. "A whole new disinformation campaign was launched by the government. It followed our near-success with a plan to rescue prisoners. We had first-rate ground intelligence. We knew everything about the camp commanders.

"But we were ordered to cease-and-desist. *Even though we could have gotten the men out.*" Cease and desist? I knew the Delta raid had failed, but who would have called off a mission that had every chance of success?

Rowe explained that the mission had been planned by the Army's Intelligence Support Activity, ISA. This was trespassing on CIA turf in that region, and pressure was put on Secretary of the Army John O. Marsh to stop the Delta force already assembled in the Philippines. "It was the last time the ISA was permitted officially to talk about what we know on living American prisoners," said Nick.

CHAPTER 11

COMPLICATIONS AND CONSPIRACIES

Two film-makers from the Soviet Union got in touch with me a month after the main part of Murkowski's committee hearings were over. One was a member of the Supreme Soviet. The other was a smooth-mannered producer from Moscow's Maxim Gorky Film Studio. They reached me through Dr. Armand Hammer, the American businessman who kept a permanent office and apartment in Moscow and prided himself on knowing all the top leaders. Hammer had discussed with my husband a book project, and now he was making his connections available to the Russian visitors. The Russians wanted to exchange archival film with CBS, and to have Walter Cronkite narrate sections of an ambitious TV series to be called *The Twentieth Century*. Told of this extraordinary proposal – it came before the startling changes introduced by Mikhail Gorbachev – a naturally skeptical Don Hewitt told me to "Give them lunch."

I took them to Sunday brunch at the Four Seasons Hotel near my Georgetown house. What, I asked, could they provide CBS in the way of hitherto unavailable Soviet historical film? The famous show trials ordered by Stalin before World War II? The Stalin period's famines that resulted from forced collectivization? None of my suggestions appeared to upset them. "Got anything on American prisoners in Vietnam after 1973?" I ventured.

"Such film exists," Dmitri Barshevsky of the Gorky Studio replied without hesitation.

I summarized the Russians' proposals for Hewitt. He was intrigued by their prompt response to my question about post-1973 footage of missing men. So was Red McDaniel when I told him. He shot out of his captain's chair with an astonished expression. "The Russians have been after me too!"

He shut the office door. "I was visited by two KGB men. They called themselves journalists, so I treated them as such. They wanted to know what we did here. I said we're a clearinghouse for defense information for Congress and the public . . . and I turned on my tape-recorder."

"Ah!" said Alexander Lutyi of *Tass*. "You brainwash the American people?"

"No," said McDaniel. "We keep them informed."

"To encourage the arms race?" suggested Vitaly Gau of *Pravda*.

"No," said McDaniel, and he described how the American Defense Institute's educational arm "conducts nonpartisan, worldwide military registration drives to encourage military personnel to exercise their right to vote."

"You mean, a soldier must vote capitalist?" asked one of the Russians.

"He's free to vote any way he wants," said McDaniel.

Two weeks later, without warning or explanation, the personal identification card of McDaniel's navigator in Vietnam, Kelly Patterson, was turned over to U.S. officials by Hanoi and was subsequently sent to his parents in California. Kelly had been lost when he and Red were shot down in 1967. The card was the same one Patterson had carried when he bailed out. No explanation came with it. Red felt certain that the visiting Russians had arranged for the I.D. card to be returned. Both he and I, in our separate conversations with the Soviets, had said that as long as prisoners-of-war remained unaccounted for, the American public must always treat Communist overtures with caution.

In his work on the POW/MIA issue, Red was driven by conscience and loyalty to his comrades, but there was also a further motivation that Patterson's I.D. card revealed. "Kelly's always on Red's mind," Dorothy McDaniel told me. "He knows Kelly could very well be one of the ones who's still struggling to survive in a POW camp."

The two men had flown together for eighteen months, a lifetime in terms of aerial combat. Whenever Kelly had some leave, he would seek out his brother, an infantryman, and go on patrol with him in South Vietnam, just so they could be together. "That was a kind of love that didn't come down the street every day," said McDaniel.

Red told top defense-intelligence officials of the sudden and strange stirring of Russian activity in Washington. Had Kelly been handed over by Hanoi to the Russians as part of their barter trade in U.S. Special Talents for arms? "What DIA replied boiled down to this: 'Forget it. Don't make false connections,' " he told me.

"I honestly believe that if the Communists produced Kelly or any other missing men, our government would reject them from fear of the questions they would raise about the reasons for their long incarceration. What I cannot understand is what's so important to conceal that the government doesn't want its own men back. Now the answer is starting to come into focus."

The answer, Red felt, had to do with the sudden admission by the Vietnamese earlier that year that there might be American prisoners in Southeast Asia after all. The Vietnamese had told Billy Hendon and the other congressmen (both Republican and Democrat) who had been on the recent mission to Hanoi, that, while the central Communist government of Vietnam had no American prisoners under its control, "there could be some held in caves and remote mountainous regions." Red, like all those who had experience with the Vietnamese, took this to be a tacit admission that Hanoi positively did know of live prisoners held in Vietnam, Laos, or Cambodia. Red felt the Russian feelers were tied to the Vietnamese move.

What was obvious, however, was that no one in the interagency group that determined POW policy showed active interest in these developments. Red felt that if the U.S. government responded and searched for POWs with the Vietnamese, it would give both governments an out. If they found prisoners, they could say that neither had known about them. However, by late spring it was clear there was no interagency interest in picking up the ball. Although the old lip service was given to live prisoners as the highest priority, the negotiation with our former enemy seemed to revolve around bones.

The BBC had a lot of experience in dealing with the Soviets. A former Moscow correspondent thought the Russians' visits with Red McDaniel and me were not easily dismissed. Maybe the Russians wanted to dissociate themselves from Hanoi's more glaringly inhuman policies.

The BBC staffers in Washington added that their researchers in Asia had put together files on alleged missions like that described by Scott Barnes. They pointed out the growth of KGB interest in drug lord General Khun Sa and the drug-growing Golden Triangle, and how Russian military advisors slipped into the region. I brought up correspondent Charles Wheeler's BBC investigations one night with Bill.

"Charles Wheeler? Did you say *Charles*?" he asked, sitting up.

"Yes. Charlie Wheeler."

"No, no! You said Charles . . . "

"Charles . . . Charlie. What's the difference? It's still Wheeler of the BBC."

"Why on earth didn't you say so?"

"I've been talking about Charlie for months! You don't listen!"

"*Nobody* ever called him *Charlie*! Certainly not when I knew him in India."

"Must be the same. Charlie was BBC bureau chief in New Delhi for some years – "

"Of course he was!" Bill almost shouted. "I shared an office with him. With *Charles*, that is."

"Now he's known as Charlie and he's doing a documentary on missing Americans."

"You mean he believes all that stuff?"

I smiled. "I'll bring him to dinner. You can ask him yourself."

Wheeler was held in great esteem by colleagues. He was later voted Britain's "TV Journalist of the Year." If he had to report the end of the world, he would still insist on three independent witnesses. Bill thought him absolutely *sound.*

Wheeler gave a sober recital at dinner of what he knew or suspected was happening. In his soft-spoken, understated way, he made an outlandish story appear perfectly reasonable.

When he had gone, I asked, "You believe me now?"

"Charles has no ax to grind. Distinguished military background."

I quickly asked, "Now will you see Red McDaniel?"

"Why?"

I took a deep breath. "Apparently you only believe *men* in your own line of business. Charlie's a journalist. Red was a naval aviator."

Bill didn't say yes, but he didn't say no, either.

Shortly after our dinner with Charles Wheeler in late spring, when I was editing film at our West 57th office, three vets of the innocent-sounding Studies and Observations Group (SOG) drove from upstate New York to see me. They wanted to make public, they said, their part in special hit teams operating between the ceasefire of 1973 and the evacuation from Saigon in 1975. They said SOG really stood for Special Operations Group, but disguised its covert action in Vietnam, Laos, and Cambodia under the more academic title. "There were times when we were ordered to kill fellow Americans," one confided to me, little knowing I had heard similar confessions.

As the men huddled in the back of an Irish pub on Third Avenue at 52nd Street, their story came out in a disjointed way. Outlandish though what they said seemed to be, it was reinforced when I spoke to Colonel Nick Rowe later that day. Military Assistance Command Vietnam – Studies and Observations Group (MACV-SOG) was cover for the joint-service high-command warfare task force engaged in highly classified clandestine operations throughout Southeast Asia. The CIA had supported and financed its operations when it began as the "Special Exploitation Service," nominally created in 1958 by the government of South Vietnam. It carried out covert operations until 1973, officially. The CIA, in other words, had started its own clandestine war one year before North Vietnam changed its strategy from "political struggle" to "armed struggle" in 1959 and six years before the Tonkin Gulf Resolution brought the United States into open conflict with Hanoi.

MACV-SOG was assigned elite Special Forces men – never numbering more than 2,000 Americans – and about 8,000 highly trained locals. It had its own Air Force (90th Special Operations Wing). Its strike elements, I now learned, were CCS, CCC, and CCN, for Command and Control/South, Central, and North, names I had heard before. Special units included SLAM (Search-Location-and-Annihilation Mission) companies.* Assassination was listed among their duties in the Pentagon literature on special-warfare units that was classified as top secret for many years.

---

* See glossary for details.

I asked my husband, when we met later that night at my Manhattan hotel, if such men had any justification for their obvious anger at the fact that the CIA had led them into their unusual line of work. They had been soldiers who now felt they should have challenged the morality of their unusual orders.

Bill said, "The Communists used terror to tighten their grip on the countryside. There was always South Vietnamese pressure to hit back, with U.S. help, using similar methods. Of course, there's always a worry about men, highly trained in new intelligence techniques, who might fall into enemy hands. If these men were asked to recover or liquidate men like that, who had been captured by the enemy – it could explain their anger."

My husband had worked in Malaysia during the conflict there that overlapped early U.S. involvement in Vietnam. The Malaysian anti-terrorist campaigns, intermittent from 1946 to 1966, were veiled by the British Official Secrets Act. He still had not talked with Red McDaniel. Once again I urged him to do so.

"I feel I've met him already." He grinned. "I've learned things about him even you mightn't know."

He talked about McDaniel that evening at dinner. "Red's dad died when Red was still a kid in North Carolina. He took charge of the whole family. Got into the Navy by grit and athletics. He was hardly out of school when he flew those solo practise missions before the full deployment of long-range nuclear missiles. He used to fly fourteen hours at a stretch in a single-seater, just above the deck *at fifty feet* to stay under enemy radar, along the perimeter of the Soviet bloc. Red and his fellow pilots *were* the nuclear deterrent. Each man was crammed into a Skyraider cockpit designed as an afterthought. He'd be shot off the carrier's catapult and settle below the level of the flight deck – that was cruising altitude!

"Each pilot was a loner . . . judging the wind by the sea spray under his wings, using mental navigation without being able to break radio silence to get a fix. . . . Landing on a flight deck at sea isn't easy, especially after fourteen hours of total concentration. Pilots would come back with their eyes on stalks."

Later, in Vietnam, Red was shot down and captured. Hanoi had boasted that the toughest prisoners would never be returned. Miraculously, Red, acknowledged by his fellow prisoners to be among the toughest, came back. The Navy took good care of him. In command of *Lexington*, he had swiftly purged the carrier of illegal drugs. "No man," said Admiral Tuttle, "could stand a tongue-lashing from Red." He was one of two POWs who returned from Vietnam who were promoted so far, so fast. He had been on a fast career track, driven to jump that crucial gap of six years stolen from him by Hanoi. Then he had stepped aside.

Why would such a highly motivated Navy man, who some thought could have become Chairman of the Joint Chiefs, voluntarily give up the chance of a top command?

It was this question that still intrigued Bill.

I was developing other ideas for CBS during the summer of 1986 and only kept half an eye on the strange information reaching my office. Sometimes I saw the possibility of a *60 Minutes* story in the material sent by The Telephone Tree. For example, the Nugan Hand.

This Australia-based bank and investment group, which some suspected had been a CIA proprietary, or a rogue equivalent set up by people with ties to the Agency, had pricked our curiosity first when we interviewed former Soviet spy Christopher Boyce, known as The Falcon. Boyce had spoken of the Nugan Hand, and the senior producer of the Australian version of *60 Minutes* had since then kept me informed of new developments. The bank had come up at various points in my research for "Dead or Alive." Casino Man, who called it by the insider term "Yin Han," had alleged that it was formed by American intelligence hands in

Asia in the early seventies as a vehicle to finance the covert war in Southeast Asia they were determined to continue after the 1973 ceasefire.

Then Jim Badey, the Washington detective who specialized in Dich Vu A Dong – Vietnamese for "Oriental Matters" – became curious about Nugan Hand. As a Vietnam vet, he had looked into the possibility of government interference in my POW/MIA story. Badey's investigations had taken him into the Pentagon's haunts around Arlington, Virginia. By the summer of 1986, he was angry and frustrated because the Justice Department had stopped his inquiries, citing reasons of national security. He knew the Vietnamese community around Washington, D.C., intimately, and he was afraid that criminals inside it were protected by intelligence officers who could always claim to be working on secret projects. He continued his investigations, though he was risking official displeasure.

I put some of these details in a CBS memo: "A police inquiry claims there existed a team of specialists in covert warfare who, after we left Saigon, assisted one another with government contracts drawn up in secrecy on the grounds of national security. Their names were associated with Nugan Hand, and also with free-booting CIA agent Ed Wilson, who was later jailed for selling plastic explosives to Muammar Qaddaffi. Wilson implicated high-level officials in the Pentagon and CIA, claiming they were partners in deals carried out by one of his companies, Egyptian American Transport & Services Co. . . . EATSCO reaped millions of dollars in secret overseas deals. The office of the Defense Department's Inspector General established that EATSCO skimmed some $8 million in unearned profits just from weapons sales. Wilson is serving a 52-year sentence for his role."

I had discovered that one EATSCO man had taken an interest in "Dead or Alive." The official had transferred huge quantities of U.S. arms out of Southeast Asia after the evacuation of Saigon. He had worked out of DSAA, the Defense Security Assistance Agency, but resigned while under investigation into another transfer of arms – to the Mideast. I also mentioned that some of the same people who had tried to discredit my *60 Minutes* story on POWs had been involved in some of Wilson's earlier business deals, and that some of those business deals were actually set up as proprietaries for a highly secret naval intelligence unit. One of the declared activities of the CIA's honorable chiefs was, in the 1970s, to search for vast stores of U.S. arms missing in Vietnam.

I wrote, "One Pentagon official who knocked 'Dead or Alive' wrote on official stationery on behalf of a Vietnamese woman. She'd been charged with gambling offenses in the Pentagon neighborhood. . . . Another law-enforcement expert is deeply concerned about the possible influence of subversives. He has given me Playboy-type pictures of the Vietnamese woman who was investigated by the Presidential Crime Commission. She was photographed nude with a picture in the background of herself arm-in-arm with the official."

I did not expect, nor did I get, any response from the New York office. I was facing the fact that this issue could not be handled in the conventional television-news way.

Shortly after I wrote the memo to *60 Minutes*, Bill came back from Thailand saying that disinformation was not limited just to discrediting people in the United States. He had heard about an Air Force intelligence man wandering around Bangkok handing out impressive-looking business cards with his name: General Shinkle.

"Only, he's not a general," Bill added. "He's a retired colonel."

"Shinkle would never go around saying he was a general," I snapped.

"Why not?"

"He swore out an affidavit for the *Smith vs. The President* lawsuit. He gave his correct rank and his entire background and experience in Southeast Asia. He was nine years a professional intelligence officer – and I bet I know where the rumor gained credence, because a government official who tried to dissuade me from doing the POW story, described Shinkle as a fake general, one of the kooks I should stay away from." That had been the first time I heard about "General Shinkle."

Bill nodded again. "That's why I say *guard your back*. Those business cards must have been forged by someone to discredit Shinkle – and anyone else who champions the cause of the missing. Those stories about Shinkle being a lunatic, a wild-man Rambo . . . not true!"

"What do *you* know about him?"

He laughed. "Just thought I'd prove you and Ross Perot are not the only amateur detectives around."

He showed me a report of what Lt. Col. Al Shinkle, U.S. Air Force, told a secret session of the House Subcommittee on Asian and Pacific Affairs when it was chaired by Rep. Lester Wolff (Dem., New York), before the days of Congressman Solarz. Wolff had questioned Shinkle, and the transcript gave his sworn testimony. Shinkle had said that after years of clandestine operations, he developed sources in Laos that made him conclude there were American military personnel held against their will: "The CIA ordered me out of Laos because I got in the way, and because I pinpointed the Communist camps where Americans were then held. . . . "

I looked up. "I don't understand. Was Shinkle in Laos in 1966?"

"From before large-scale U.S. involvement in Vietnam until after the war ended," said Bill. "Laos was a CIA fiefdom from the late 1950s. Shinkle was an Air Force man whose intelligence activities kept interfering with the activities and interests of the CIA. The CIA wasn't interested in Shinkle's continual production of intelligence on Americans taken prisoner."

"We were fighting a war there all that time?"

"Yes, and losing airmen. Shinkle testified that he gathered up detailed reports on captured fliers – he was an aviator himself. He said he even got evidence of twelve POWs from

the French colonial wars. Those prisoners had been held
fifteen years, and then suddenly the Communists let them go.
Shinkle says the CIA prevented U.S. military intelligence
from talking to any one of them about U.S. prisoners. After
he left Laos in 1973, he became upset by the way the secret
war stayed secret. It condemned a lot of good Americans to a
living death. So he's been going back there whenever he can,
asking questions. . . . "

Shinkle had offered proof – reports of first-hand sightings
and electronic data – that almost 500 U.S. fliers were shot
down over Laos, of whom 324 were currently still alive. After
his war service in Laos, he had pleaded with "Heinie"
Aderholt, whom I had come upon earlier when he supported
Smith and McIntire, to take action. General Aderholt had
been twenty-six years in covert operations, and was the last
general officer out of Southeast Asia as commander of MAC-
THAI, the U.S. military advisory group in Thailand, with
duties in Laos and Cambodia. But even Aderholt's hands
were tied, according to Shinkle.

In 1975 he was called in by the CIA Domestic Contact
Service office in Denver, Colorado, and told, "We know what
you're doing, Shinkle. We don't like it. It's counter to U.S.
policy, and if you don't get out of it, you're going to be in a lot
of trouble." This was Shinkle's recollection. Chairman Wolff
told him: "Some people are going to have in their mind, this
fellow looks like he was a competitor to the CIA. . . . "

The committee record showed that Shinkle replied, "If I
stayed on active duty, and we had another brushfire war,
how am I going to motivate young pilots who go out and risk
their lives and may get shot down, if we're not going to come
after them? The CIA does not understand military intelligence in time of combat. Every war the CIA had a finger in,
from Bay of Pigs to Laos, they lost. As an American citizen, I
feel if my country's going to stay strong . . . we can't be all
under one cap called CIA – They do not understand."

Bill let me finish this transcript of the committee proceedings before disclosing the date: July 4th weekend, 1978.

"Eight years ago! How could it be buried all this time?" I asked, stunned.

"By calling it a national secret."

"What's so secret about saying there are 324 American fliers still alive in Laos?"

"That's what I'd like to find out," said Bill.

I felt for the first time that he was prepared to help me; that he didn't regard me as just another of his opium-smokers, chasing the dragon.

In the spring of 1986, my husband finally talked with McDaniel. "This was George Washington's pig farm," Red told him, steering into the driveway of his home in Mount Vernon, Virginia.

The house stood among trees, tranquil and private. "Must have been a pretty posh farm," said Bill.

Once settled in his den, Red continued an earlier conversation. "We tell your wife everything," he said.

"That puts a burden on her," Bill replied.

Red was concerned. "You mean she knows too much for her own safety?"

"I was thinking about her career. . . . If she can't get her story out . . . "

"Well, maybe that's where you come in. You write books."

Bill shuddered. "It would take a lifetime to make it even faintly credible. . . . "

"Nobody wants to believe it," Red said. He pulled out a letter from Rear Admiral James W. Nance, a former National Security Council Chief in the White House. "Strike like a cobra," Nance had advised McDaniel. "Stop public voicing of your theory until you've out-thought and out-planned the opposition. *If you don't, you will continue to be eaten alive.*"

Bill could see that for Red, however, speed meant a difference between life or death. If his back-seater, Kelly Patterson, was still alive, his chances diminished rapidly with each day lost. Others, like Admiral Nance or Ross Perot, thought it best to "outplan the opposition," because there seemed to be no quick solutions. But Red had flown solo against the enemy often in his professional life. He followed his own well-honed instincts.

The man had diverted from a naval career of immense promise to set his own course with the American Defense Institute. He believed America's defense depended on the shepherding of democratic principles. His foundation worked, for example, in voter registration in the military. Why was he so motivated? He had arrived at the place he said had been described by Admiral James Bond Stockdale, who, like Red, survived years of jail in daily danger of blurting out, under torture, secrets of highly sensitive naval operations: "Resolve and commitment and moral leverage are the only glue that ties America's sons to their leaders. Finesse and trickery are not worthy of us," Red quoted Admiral Stockdale.

With Bill, Red for the first time went into detail about the failed 1981 Delta rescue attempt I had been hearing about at intervals. For eight years Red had felt grateful to President Nixon for negotiating him and other prisoners out of Vietnam. Then, as liaison for the Navy and Marines on Capitol Hill in 1981, Red attended an intelligence briefing. Satellite pictures were shown of a prison compound in the Mahoxy region of Northern Laos. The pictures showed standing figures whose shadows indicated they were taller than average Asians.

"The numbers 52 were stamped out in a garden area," he told Bill. "The conclusion I drew was, 'Good ole Yankee ingenuity!' Our pilot-prisoners would know that the figures must show up on satellite cameras. I assumed there was a crew down there from a crashed Arc Light B-52 bomber. Or else that was the number of men in the camp." He went to see his old friend Admiral Jerry Tuttle, then deputy director of the Defense Intelligence Agency under General Tighe. The two men had shared quarters at the Rickover Nuclear Power

School, and a long time later, Tuttle had helped plan the famous Son Tay raid to rescue American prisoners during the Vietnam War. They discussed the photographs. Red knew about the Delta mission being launched by Special Forces. Then he found out that it had been aborted in the course of bitter infighting between bureaucrats. The photographs, the clues from space, were reclassified and in effect buried.

Red could not quote Admiral Tuttle's comments, which were confidential, but he now told Bill, "The first red flag went up for me when news of the spy pictures leaked, and the government discredited them as 'Fort Apache snapshots.' Satellite photographs of the Mahoxy region in Laos were officially denied. Well, the policy is still that there are no prisoners. . . . It seems there is a second government establishing policy. Here's the way I think it works. Its members make their own decisions. These may be shown to the President as if they have full approval. Or they may be kept from the President, but acted upon as if they had the President's authority."

Bill came away from several hours of reading through Red's files and listening to many hours of taped conversations. "I find it all too depressing," he said. He was researching a novel set in prewar Nazi Germany. "At least I'm writing about good guys versus bad guys. . . . "

"There were good Germans – " I protested.

"Not enough to stop Hitler."

"Because they put families and jobs first, and the evil grew until it seemed impossible for one or two people to stop it."

"That's what depresses me. I can't believe these things are happening today without people protesting at the top of their voices. . . . "

"Cheer up," I said. General Tighe had told me the *60 Minutes* show had had an effect when he spoke to me at the breakfast meeting of the American Bar Association. The former defense-intelligence chief had now been brought out of retirement to lead a whole new investigation into the intelligence on lost Americans. At last this seemed like a genuine attempt to meet the rising criticism from vets. Ross Perot had pushed for the Tighe Commission through the men he regarded as old friends: President Reagan and Vice President George Bush.

Perot's high hopes for the commission were moderated by his sense that somehow the American media had been muzzled on the issue. When he had first asked me if there could be a conspiracy of silence, I had replied that I thought the only time the fierce competition within the media could be stopped was when national security was endangered. I had rationalized the performance of CBS in this way when there was no support for me against pressures from the government.

Perot had a different story about NSC behavior. "I went to a guy high in the government Security Council and offered a hundred million dollars to buy back prisoners from Hanoi. Got no response," Perot said. Later, reports came back from Hanoi that such an offer had been made, without letting Perot know just how the offer was put or what the answer was. Perot suspected the man might have offered to buy back remains. "He never informed me. What d'you make of that?" asked Perot.

At the time, he was staring out of his office windows at the flat Texas landscape. "These guys want to give the impression Hanoi will only trade in bones," he said mournfully. "Dead men tell no tales." He said he wanted to focus on "getting our men home alive." The forthcoming Tighe Commission at least promised to shake up the "bloated bureaucrats."

"Can't you find a way to jolt the public?" I asked.

"Like – ?"

"The *truth* about a secret mission funded by the U.S. government, allegedly to search out live Americans. Proof that the American who led it was a senior CIA man named

Jerry Daniels who was more concerned about ongoing covert operations. Show how he rebelled against orders to kill his countrymen who were prisoners. . . . And how he then died under mysterious circumstances."

I had just talked to Scott Barnes again and I told Perot what else had now emerged of Scott Barnes's tale of the mission that failed prisoners in Laos, and the order to "liquidate the merchandise." Perot showed no reaction. Yet I was sure he had heard *everything* about the mission. Its chief, Jerry Daniels, had been shipped home in a sealed lead coffin after he died from gas poisoning. Everyone connected with that mission seemed to have conflicting stories.

Finally Perot nodded. "The name of Jerry Daniels hit raw CIA nerves," he said. "I put it to a gathering at Langley. [CIA headquarters in Virginia.] Said I wanted to know how the man died. Gave his name. And hit the rawest of raw nerves."

I now told Perot some of the new information I had recently put together.

David Taylor had secured court records for the BBC, showing some funds for Jerry Daniels' mission came from another CIA proprietary, Bishop, Baldwin, Rewald, Dillingham & Wong, a successor to the Australian financial group Nugan Hand. In connection with both companies appeared the name of Scott Barnes.

Even General Tighe said an attempt had been made, while he served in Vietnam, to involve him in Nugan Hand. The group was busy in the 1970s loading up with impressive U.S. top-ranking officers – "enough to run a war," said one Australian police report during the subsequent inquiry. Tighe had refused. The promise of a twenty-percent return on his investment did not sound legitimate. He was right. The company failed in 1979, although Casino Man told me branches of it continued until 1981.

A Philadelphia police detective had once tipped me off to some turf squabbles between the Federal Bureau of Alcohol, Tobacco and Firearms (ATF) and the Drug Enforcement Agency (DEA). He believed Washington was ignoring a lot of trade in guns and drugs – trade instigated by government agencies. At the time, the detective's story was curious, but he was obviously a very experienced police officer of great integrity. I got in touch with him again and he sent me a backlog of reports.

The detective's story tied in with fresh research I had received from the BBC's David Taylor. He had tracked down a retired U.S. admiral of great eminence who stated flatly that the Nugan Hand Group had been involved in financing search-and-rescue operations for missing Americans. One of them was the Jerry Daniels mission.

CHAPTER 12

PRISONERS AND POLITICS

Ross Perot wanted to exhume the body of Jerrold Barker Daniels, which had been buried near Daniels' Montana home.

Perot took all the reports on the Daniels mission seriously enough to consider exhumation necessary. Was the body really that of a man known to have worked throughout the secret war in Laos with a CIA army of local tribesmen? If it was, would the body still show evidence of how the man really died? If he had been murdered, it would prove the government had had an interest in covering up the fact, because they would allow no investigation and insisted he died from gas.

Government officials had convinced inquiring reporters that the Daniels mission was a fiction. Yet the active-service officers who met with me in a small Vietnamese restaurant in Arlington, Virginia, insisted otherwise. There had been such a mission, they said, sponsored by the Army's Intelligence

Support Activity ("The Activity"), and terminated by the
Pentagon and the CIA.

Who was telling the truth? I had heard tapes of conversations between Scott Barnes and men who appeared to be his
controllers. Whenever Barnes showed me documents and
provided names, they checked out. They seemed to show
Barnes was a CIA contract agent. Was the Daniels mission
CIA- or ISA-sponsored? Or some rogue operation that used
the rescue of POWs as a cover?

Daniels' body was not the only way to the truth. The
mysterious Nugan Hand provided some answers. The financial group failed in 1979, following the fatal shotgun wound-
ing of one founder, Francis John Nugan. The calling card of a
former CIA director, William Colby, had been found on
Nugan's body where it lay on a deserted Australian country
road. Colby had been involved in Asian operations since
1962 – and the broadening of the secret war in Laos. He was
the CIA liaison to the Phoenix program, which, it was alleged, oversaw the assassination of thousands of civilians in
South Vietnam who were suspected Vietcong collaborators.*
It has been defended as the greatest single success of the U.S.
pacification program that could have won the war, if only the
armed forces had done *their* job properly. CIA officials maintain that their part in Phoenix was entirely removed from the
action. Phoenix ended officially in 1973. Colby then became
CIA Director.† The other founder of the Nugan Hand Group,

---

* See, for instance, John Ranelagh, *The Agency: The Rise and Decline of the CIA* (New York: Simon and Schuster, 1986), pp. 436-41.

† William Egan Colby had made the CIA his career in 1950 after
private practice as a New York attorney. He was Chief, Far East
Division, 1962-67. In 1968, he went to Vietnam for the State
Department with the rank of ambassador. He returned to the
United States in 1971 and became Executive Director of the CIA. He
was CIA Director from September 1973 to January 1976.

Michael Jon Hand, disappeared. He had been highly decorated as a Green Beret with Special Forces in Vietnam before
he was transferred to work amongst the CIA's guerrillas in
Laos – with Jerry Daniels.

Prominent American military and intelligence figures had
been associated with Nugan Hand. The same names were
mentioned to me in connection with the financial institution's successor, the Hawaiian investment firm known as
BBRDW, for Bishop, Baldwin, Rewald, Dillingham and
Wong. "Some people used the POW/MIA issue as cover for
money-making covert operations," I was told by a former
CIA officer of senior rank. "They were initiated by a rogue
group," he claimed. "Any successful search for our missing
men could expose illegal covert activities." I wondered if it
would also expose even more illegal ways to finance them.
My CIA source spoke on condition of anonymity, because "I
feel strongly about the cover-up on prisoners. If we let them
down, then the whole purpose of our intelligence services is
lost."

The Nugan Hand story had been partly laid out by Australian police and agents fighting illegal drugs, who did not
feel qualified to reach conclusions about U.S. intelligence
concerns. Investigations had reached a climax in a royal
commission whose final, voluminous report in 1985 still left a
lot of questions unanswered, since so many findings were
classified Top Secret. The BBRDW story, in turn, also ended
in financial scandal, but the facts had not been as fully aired
as in the case of the Nugan Hand. They leaked out during the
trial of Ronald Rewald, whose name provided the middle
initial of BBRDW. His case arose from an Internal Revenue
tax inquiry, and once the prosecution had gotten into the
system, no appeals in the name of national security would get
it out. Certain evidence was not exhibited in court, all the
same; the Chief District Judge, Harold M. Fong, ruled *"they
relate to the highly emotional issues of the missing-in-action and
prisoners-of-war* (italics mine)."

This extraordinary comment in the court records had escaped attention until David Taylor, going through the puzzling court transcripts, saw its significance. The BBC man had talked frequently to Rewald both in and out of jail. The forty-three-year-old Rewald had no visible qualifications as a banker or financial big-wheeler, which was what had first caught Taylor's interest. It was the collapse of BBRDW, with its fifty affiliates and subsidiaries, that pushed Rewald into the limelight.

"The really fantastic thing was that Rewald's prosecution was led by a former CIA man who left the agency two weeks before Rewald was indicted," Taylor told me. "Then he turned up as Assistant District Attorney on the case. He cut off lines of inquiry that might embarrass the CIA, and one result was that no documents relating to the POW/MIA issue ever got into the public domain in court."

John F. Kelly, a Washington-based writer and researcher, said, "It seemed as if anything on prisoners had disappeared from the face of the earth." But Rewald himself made it possible for Kelly to look at copies of the original BBRDW documents, stashed away before the Agency put a lock on everything in Rewald's office. Some papers referred to funding of a covert mission to seek missing Americans. There were also records of BBRDW funds allotted to the controversial Daniels mission, which became more widely known as BOHICA (for "Bend Over Here It Comes Again") after Scott Barnes talked about it to groups of POW families and finally wrote a book with heavy and apparently authentic documentation.*

The BBRDW records had been sealed at the request of national-security officials, preventing Rewald's lawyers from pursuing as his defense the claim that his actions as part of the BBRDW enterprise were ordered by the CIA. The former small-town businessman had been urged, he insisted, to spend money on a lavish scale and to establish himself on the

---

* See bibliography.

world stage as a financial wizard. Among his clients, as a result of this masquerade, were some of the world's wealthiest anti-Communists, eager to find a way to funnel money into worthy covert enterprises. One was the Sultan of Brunei, worth some $25 billion.

"There's no doubt BBRDW had been a CIA enterprise," said Taylor. The BBC producer had verified this with General Hunter Harris, "a four-star general with the reputation of being the highest-ranking officer ever to serve in War Plans Supreme Command. I asked him straight out, on the record, if he knew Rewald worked for the Agency. Yes, he said. He found that out because, he said, 'the CIA advised me it was well worth investing money in BBRDW. . . . Then I checked with other well-placed friends who tried to find out who ran BBRDW and who were blocked at the very highest level.'

"General Harris told me that *he* had put the Bohica people in touch with Rewald to fund them," Taylor continued.

I remembered denials from DIA Director Lenny Perroots and his aides that they knew anything about the Daniels mission called Bohica, in which Scott Barnes had taken part. Had DIA's files been weeded before Perroots took over? Had something so awful happened on the Bohica mission that the American public could not be allowed to learn about it? General Perroots had earlier told me that he wanted me to call him if I found out more on Bohica. Now when I tried to reach him with questions, he was not available. He asked questions; he didn't answer them.

Rewald was now serving a life sentence, which seemed disproportionate to the simple embezzlement for which he had been finally judged guilty. Taylor interviewed Rewald in his cell on Terminal Island, California. The name had an unfortunate ring. Rewald said he did indeed feel it was here he might be terminated if he said too much. However, he answered Taylor's questions about the Bohica mission. He had never been enthusiastic about it. He was unsure about its real purpose. Rewald added: "The Agency asked me on other occasions to move narcotics money . . . to handle operations once executed by the Nugan Hand Group. The drug profits from Laos alone were enormous. Some were supposed to pay for covert activities that had to be kept hidden from Congress. What happened to the bulk of the drug money, I don't know."

Later, Taylor asked Rewald about reports that some government leaders knew about the drug connection. "If you broadcast that," said Rewald, raising his voice, "your life's in danger. . . . I've got the evidence but I'll use it only if I'm desperate and then I'll bring everybody down." Taylor pointed out that he was already in prison for life. How much more desperate could he get? "I may be in prison," said Rewald, "but my family is safe."

While I had been pursuing the mysterious financial links between the CIA, the Bohica mission, and the POW issue, the Senate Veterans Affairs Committee, from which the vets and their families had hoped to gain so much, was winding down.

Murkowski wanted to wrap up the issue, his staff told me. He was "moving on to other things. No Americans are left alive." The last hearing, in mid-August 1986, was attended by the family of Staff Sergeant James Ray of military intelligence. His stepmother, Jean Ray, had discovered gross inconsistencies in the U.S. government's own statements.

Ray had been captured in Vietnam, according to official records, in March 1968. The family expected him to return with other prisoners released in 1973. Instead, they were told Ray had died in prison on June 11, 1969. A list of alleged witnesses to this death was provided. Ray's family tracked down the first, Michael Kjmoe, who told them he didn't remember Ray dying at all, but said, "He couldn't have died in June because he tried to escape in July." After many more inquiries, the family discovered Ray had been awarded the Silver Star for gallantry in action *the month after he had supposedly died* – by the Army that claimed to hold the record of his death in June. Army records noted as well that he was recaptured in July, wrapped in chains, and deprived of adequate food by the North Vietnamese. "Shortly after this," reads a citation from the President of the United States of America, "he was removed from the camp and never seen again." But if Ray was never seen again, how was it that he was next awarded a Purple Heart for wounds received in action on November 30, 1969, in Cambodia? He had received a Bronze Star "in ground operations against hostile forces" *from April 18 to the end of November 1969!* The Army was obviously severely confused, perhaps not least because there was officially no war in Cambodia.

Staff Sergeant Feliz Neco-Quinones was quoted in all official U.S. government statements as having seen Ray starve himself to death, and having witnessed his body later being removed by Communist guards. Yet Neco-Quinones swore to the family, when they finally traced him to San Juan, Puerto Rico, that he had never known Ray and never made any statement regarding his death.

A similar denial came from Gary J. Guggenberger. The Army stated that he had shared a bunker with Ray, left him one morning for dead, and returned to find the body was gone. Guggenberger wrote emphatically that he never knew a prisoner called Ray and had been in solitary for several months at the time he was alleged to have witnessed Ray's death.

The family presented documents on the case, but felt they were a nuisance to Chairman Murkowski. As proceedings wound down, the Rays concluded they were never going to be treated as anything better than intruders. Murkowski eventually did give an answer of sorts. He said the Rays ought to consider that maybe all these witnesses had not told the truth in order to spare the feelings of Sergeant Ray's loved ones. After all, "if he's dead, he's dead."*

---

*   The old 1973 version of Sergeant Ray's death persisted in official records. It was contained in the DIA "case narrative" handed to Communists in Hanoi by U.S. negotiators in 1988 – long after the family's carefully documented corrections and the denials by witnesses were put before The Committee.

It appeared to me that Jimmy Ray was one of those men who was known to be a prisoner by U.S. intelligence trackers in 1973 when other prisoners came home officially. But he was last heard from in Cambodia, where the United States was not supposed to be engaged in "war activities." That involvement would have turned Jimmy Ray, if he was taken prisoner, into a plausible deniability – a non-person – in Cambodia, at least. At the time, the former Secretary of State, Henry Kissinger, denied that the United States had been involved in a secret war in Cambodia. In the spring of 1973 he said he had been told there were no prisoners in Cambodia, hence no need to negotiate for them with the Cambodians. This policy remained, even though the former deputy head of the CIA, Vernon Walters, stated two years later that Cambodia had held prisoners. The government's official records on Jimmy Ray's activities, like those of all MIAs, remain classified. Had Chairman Murkowski spoken to Jimmy Ray's parents as he had because he had been cautioned to protect the United States' official secrets of the Vietnam War?

I was going to have to make a decision. Cut loose from this story, or find some other way of telling it. Maybe do a book. I mulled all this over during a layover at Miami International Airport on my way to join Bill in Jamaica. Alexandra gurgled away in her stroller as I parked her at one end of a newsstand and browsed. A man came and stood directly between Alexandra and me. I shifted, turning my head to keep Alexandra in view, and put down my briefcase. Another man grabbed it and ran. A car waited with its engine running, one door open. The thief hopped in and was off. It was over in seconds. "They had you marked in Washington," said the Dade County Police investigator, Jim Blackstone. The briefcase held all my notebooks on the POW/MIA issue, and the key to a locked vault full of documents.

"How many more warnings do you need?" asked Bill with notable lack of sympathy.

I left Alexandra with him in Jamaica and flew back to Washington alone to rearrange my source material and make the stolen index worthless. I was in the D.C. Police Headquarters when a man made off with my handbag containing my current contact book. I had gone there to ask how seriously I should pursue the Miami theft, since the Dade County Police had seemed overwhelmed with larger crimes.

I called Bill at the Jamaica house to say I had been robbed again. He said, "*Inside* police headquarters?"

"Don't *you* start," I snapped. I had become so defensive I simply blurted out the names of the D.C. police investigators. "Detectives Ron Carpenter and – ah, Trugman. Call them to find out how something so stupid could happen twice."

The detectives had told me that no crook would have pulled such a stunt. But someone chasing after personal papers might figure that police headquarters was the one place where a person did not guard herself. It had worked on me.

"Suppose there's hard proof that some government agency is silencing people who look too close?" I asked Bill.

"You've got circumstantial evidence," he said reluctantly. "Like your story about Congressman Applegate being censored." I thought that, even if the evidence was circumstantial, there was a pattern. I didn't much like being woven into it.

I remembered that an intelligence officer who had shown a consistent curiosity about the POW/MIA issue had also hampered Tom Ashworth during The Committee hearings. Ashworth was perturbed that a conversation with a senator (who had a security clearance) should have to be monitored.

Ashworth had flown 460 combat missions as a Marine helicopter pilot during the secret war in Laos. He had close ties with followers of General Vang Pao, the CIA "controlled asset" in Laos who had been courted since French colonial days as the toughest of all the warlords. Some of Vang Pao's guerrillas had been growing the opium crop around Site 85, Ann Holland surmised after Commanding Officer Colonel Gerald Clayton had told her the post was surrounded by poppy fields.

And Vang Pao, I found, had directed the proceedings at Jerry Daniels' funeral in Montana. . . .

Ashworth, who speaks Laotian, had helped Vang Pao's people resettle in the United States after the secret Laotian war collapsed. He knew the younger men were still regarded as potential "freedom fighters" in future covert wars. All felt strangers in America, allowed to stay only if they behaved. They talked among themselves about American prisoners still in Laos. They were wary of speaking out publicly. Ashworth tried to explain this to The Committee. When he was told to give the names of prisoners in public testimony, he said he could only do this in closed session for fear of reprisals against them. His request was refused, so Ashworth offered to disclose the names to anyone on The Committee who would meet him outside. Senator DeConcini agreed, but was at once accompanied by an intelligence officer from DIA who had shown a continuing interest in the entire POW/MIA issue. Ashworth did not give away his sources in front of the intelligence officer. By now, he had come to a conclusion similar to that of other vets: evidence disclosed in secret session was taken over by intelligence officers controlling the POW/MIA issue for reasons, they indicated, of national security.* Certainly it never seemed to be used.

The government definitely did *not* seem to want Ashworth to speak openly about what he believed. Like Jimmy Ray's

---

* Ashworth doggedly pursued his suspicions and documented the testimony he gave with after-action reports. He decided to write a book showing the CIA's stake in Laos and the reasons for stopping information from reaching the public.

in Vietnam." The so-called defector was Marine Bobby Garwood!

I was transfixed when I saw the memo. It judged Garwood a defector before the prisoner had been released and before anyone had heard his side. And Garwood had been *accused* by the U.S. government of saying nothing about other prisoners.

Everyone from State to the Marine Corps and intelligence chiefs emphatically denied that Garwood had referred to American POWs in Vietnam. Yet here was a White House memo, written before his release, stating that he had conveyed a message about other Americans alive in Vietnam.

There was also another politically cynical memo from Oksenberg to David Aaron, then Deputy National Security Advisor to President Carter. Oksenberg noted that prior to the defector's appearance in Hanoi, the National Security Council consistently turned down requests from families of missing men to meet the President. "Two reasons now exist for altering our recommendations . . . Garwood and his claims about other captive Americans. It is politically wise perhaps for the President to protect himself by reasserting his continued interest. . . . "

CHAPTER 13

SILENCING THE CRITICS

In the fall of 1986 I left *60 Minutes* to work with my husband on this book. I felt I could not drop an investigation that touched so many lives, and in which I had received so much voluntary help. Some of the finest people I had ever known were risking a great deal. Yet surely they had a democratic right to ask questions, didn't they? It galled me that they were made to look ridiculous, were slandered or harassed for expecting their country to do the right and constitutional thing. I was convinced now that this was not just a story about a bureaucratic boondoggle that had allowed a few missing men to fall through the cracks. A lot of men had been abandoned, and one reason, I felt, was to cover up a secret war that went way past the official end of the Vietnam conflict.

U.S. intelligence agencies had the best proof that men were still alive recently – proof so convincing that in the early months of the Reagan administration the Joint Chiefs of Staff had planned the elaborate rescue mission that I had now heard of from many sources. That effort seemed to have been abandoned, as had follow-up efforts, like Bohica and the Daniels/Barnes mission, to find men and bring them home. Jerry Daniels, who objected to this, died in mysterious circumstances. Even moderate efforts to present the facts to the American people, on the part of honest people who had direct knowledge of the issue, were quashed – in each instance by the government. Bobby Garwood had been a gift of information. He was discredited by his court martial before anyone heard him out on prisoners. Jerry Mooney, who knew exactly how many men had not returned in 1973, which of them were still alive then, and in which prison or camp they had been kept, was turned away from testifying. Casino Man, who saw prisoners in Laos in the early eighties, was harassed and put under surveillance. Major Smith was smeared by rumor and innuendo while the Criminal Investigation Command report that cleared him sat classified and maintained in an office at the United States Army Criminal Investigation Command Crime Records Center, Baltimore, Maryland. It would not be until 1989 that Smith's name would begin to be cleared, and even then it would only be because a senator would make a point of finding out what happened, because there were too many obvious signs of cover-up of Army wrongdoing.

What really made me decide to continue my investigation were the elaborate efforts that were made to question the credibility of anyone who told the truth about existing evidence on POWs and who tried in some way to push the government to bring them home. I had documented these efforts. And I had never forgotten that Colonel Richard Childress of the NSC had told me personally that I would be responsible for the deaths of remaining prisoners in Southeast Asia if I produced a story on their plight for *60 Minutes*. It had been a strange confirmation – but it stuck.

Bill was going systematically through my salvaged files. "Nobody wants to see anything," he said. "That's how every tin-pot dictator gets away with it. They know we'll do anything to preserve the peace, hang on to security for the family. . . . Who said: Evil prospers because good men and women let it?''

He'd witnessed the vast expansion of intelligence organizations – some forced underground with each successive layer of public oversight – the fierce interdepartmental rivalries, fights for secret funds. He had admired the great practitioners of the art of intelligence, but he had seen so many officials cut themselves off from the real world behind the impregnable walls of secrecy and stunningly trivial enmities. ''I knew one man,'' he said, ''who really couldn't communicate with anyone unfamiliar with the special values, the unchallengeable rules.''

''This isn't helping me much,'' I interrupted.

''Wait. This man used to drink with his opposite number in the KGB because they had more in common with each other than they had with ordinary people. In the end, he defected –''

''The KGB man?''

''No. *Our* guy.''

The puzzling issue of Jerry Daniels, Scott Barnes, and the Bohica mission surfaced again. Shortly after I left *60 Minutes*, I saw David Taylor in the BBC's Washington office. ''Here's a new twist,'' he told me. Two Drug Enforcement agents had just confirmed to him that the Daniels Bohica mission took place with official encouragement. They asked to see Taylor in his office. Their names were Frank Panessa and Chuck Bonnyville. They wanted his help in reaching Scott Barnes. ''Said I could tell them more about Daniels and Bohica in connection with high-level CIA drug operations,'' said the BBC's man, between playing back audiotapes of the conversations.

''If looking for POWs was only a cover for some DEA drug operation, no wonder some intelligence group is trying to hush up the entire operation,'' I said. ''DEA would be even more concerned if they were investigating a drug operation disguised within Bohica, and found some other intelligence outfit was trying to run the drugs – " I suddenly remembered what Nick Rowe had told me, and quoted him. *"Official* action is taken against *criminal* drugs. *Unofficial* clearance is given to what's known as 'intelligence dope' for paying for covert action." Those who dealt in intelligence dope usually felt morally justified. The cause of defeating Communists seemed to them greater than the danger drugs posed to society.

Colonel Rowe (Star White One) had told me there were more than a dozen federal agencies responsible for halting the flow of drugs into the United States: "They fight over turf and don't always exchange information. If the Customs Service intercepts cocaine at a border point, for instance, they may run into problems following up on the case because some other department claims jurisdiction." He said it was easy for someone from Washington, flashing CIA or some other federal agency card, to muscle in. "That's how 'intelligence drugs' can be ushered through," I told Taylor.

"It's ludicrous," he said. "The country's awash in drugs. Vice President Bush is running a national campaign against drug abuse. Nancy Reagan makes speeches. The President just signed the Anti-Drug Abuse Act. Yet the situation's ten times worse than it's ever been."

Ross Perot had run a campaign against drug abuse in Texas and made himself expert on the traffic. So I called him to ask if there could be a clandestine world sanctioned by officials who felt everything, including the fight against drug addiction, was secondary to fighting communism. Did this explain the obvious failure of the supposed War on Drugs?

"Guys got in the habit of using drugs to raise money to finance anti-Communist operations," he said. "They can't break themselves of the habit."

Was Jerrold Daniels one of the "guys who got into the habit," in the sense Perot intended? Daniels had cried out in surprise and disbelief when the Bohica mission, one of whose official goals was to find prisoners, actually found them. That was Scott Barnes's story, adding that Daniels had been the CIA man who worked most closely with Vang Pao, the CIA's mercenary chief in Laos. Was he still in the habit of running anti-Communist operations in 1981? If so, a prisoner rescue would have raised awkward questions. His death was reported very soon after he returned from the mission.

I went to Bangkok to see if it really was Jerrold Daniels who died there from gas poisoning. I had worked out with Bill a system whereby one would always be with the baby. We would never travel together. If one had to meet a doubtful contact, our police contacts should be kept informed; or The Telephone Tree; or Red McDaniel. Before I left for Bangkok we had moved out of Washington to guarantee privacy.

The Daniels case was well worth further investigation. Daniels was known in Bangkok as "Hog." He had spent half his adult life working with Vang Pao's Hmong tribesmen, under the title of a U.S. government refugee officer. The Hmong (sometimes called Meo, from a Chinese word for barbarian) were a proud warrior people, living mostly in the mountains of Laos where the best opium was grown. They had been badly savaged by the many wars of Indochina. Other Hmong lived in northern Thailand and moved effortlessly across the Laotian border. Hog Daniels had directed the evacuation of the surviving guerrillas, and of General Vang Pao, when the CIA's secret war in Laos collapsed in the mid-seventies. This was when Ashworth had helped them settle in the United States. Daniels could tune into local thought processes, according to Vang Pao, who said, "He was like one lobe of a Hmong brain."

Shortly after the enigma of his Bohica mission, he was reported dead in Bangkok. The body had been found some forty-eight to seventy-two hours (nobody seemed sure) after death occurred, so that "it had time to balloon up and turn black like a 350-lb Negro," according to a Bangkok police report. "It was beyond recognition."

Alexander Haig, then Secretary of State, sent messages to

U.S. foreign posts that betrayed a seemingly excessive interest in someone who had been a seemingly lowly refugee officer. Daniels had died of carbon monoxide poisoning. "Approximate cause was faulty gas hot water heater." To deal with any more questions, Haig proposed, rather disarmingly, "the following comment be used: 'Out of respect for the family's wishes, the Department does not wish to comment.' "

Other State Department cables struck a less confident posture. The first alarm was in a message to Washington: "Bangkok Thai and English language morning papers dated May 2 report that remains found in apartment of USG employee are remains of Jerrold B. Daniels and death was accidental. . . . Embassy has been unsuccessful in locating Jerrold B. Daniels. . . . " Daniels had died, according to the Hmong funeral notice, on April 28. On May 3, the embassy informed Washington that, although Thai authorities were not certain the remains were those of Daniels, they had yet to provide the official cause of death. The fact that the body was not found for five days was left unexplained.

Declassified messages showed that the U.S. embassy in Bangkok spent U.S. $3,500 shipping the body, although it had first informed Washington that for a mere $350 it could be cremated and the ashes air-freighted home, all inclusive. The economy was rejected in a cable from the State Department.

On May 6, the embassy cabled the Secretary of State that "dirt from Laos and a letter from Eiland" were being routed through Hong Kong and Seattle, with a request to make sure the package made its connection to Missoula. "Separate telex follows with routing of Mr. Daniels' remains which is different than the above [sic]. Reasons explained to _____ via Telecon."

Michael Eiland was a covert-warfare specialist attached to the U.S. embassy in Bangkok. Sources claimed he had run special, highly classified missions into Laos and Cambodia, code-named "Daniel Boone." Men killed on these operations during the period from 1967 to 1973 were reported as having been lost on "border patrols." Any American taken prisoner was in trouble – he was not in uniform.

The Daniels body was shipped by a roundabout route, through the Port of New York, where it remained for twenty-four hours. Why it required a twenty-four-hour layover was never explained in any of the declassified documents. Nor was there mention of any official U.S. autopsy. Finally a body was buried at Daniels' home in Missoula, Montana, under his name. He would have been forty years old.

In newspaper files I found a modest funeral notice: "Hmong Rituals" would begin Saturday afternoon, May 8, 1982, in Missoula, and would continue right through the following Sunday. The pallbearers were listed as "The General," "Ring Man," "Terrible," "Worm," "Spider," "Glass Man" . . .

Thai Special Forces confirmed that "The General" was Vang Pao. They said there had been endless fights with Vang Pao's rivals, including General Khun Sa, over illegal drug routes and control of opium. Vang Pao's bodyguards were the other pallbearers at the Montana funeral. The Thais said the General treated Hog Daniels as a son. But what were Terrible, Spider, and the rest doing, besides carrying the coffin?

The coffin had been sealed in Bangkok and nobody had been allowed to see the body after that, not even Daniels' mother, Louise Daniels, who was treated as a Hmong clan ancestor. U.S. government officials, who were constantly present from the time the body arrived until it was safely buried, convinced the distraught mother that it would be best not to unseal the coffin.

A University of Montana biology professor, E.W. "Bert" Pfeiffer, who had made journeys into the borderlands of Thailand, told me that he had sniffed around the malodorous lead-lined coffin on its arrival in Missoula, until he was told to stop "in the name of national security"! But Pfeiffer, I thought, would always smell conspiracy. He seemed that kind of man. His background was that of someone who had more often poked his nose into wars in Indochina than into coffins.

I looked more closely into the circumstances of the death in Bangkok. One cable reminded me of my own experience with escaping gas. Some U.S. embassy staffers were said to have "played with the pilot light on the hot water heater in Daniels' apartment during a party," and perhaps caused the accident. Why had no U.S. agency investigated in depth a death that generated so much cable traffic?

Thai police insisted that a male had been found in an adjoining room, alive, and the official U.S. embassy version of events corroborated this. As Ross Perot had said in a confrontation with CIA staffers, "How could one guy, Daniels, die horribly, while the other, exposed to the same leak, walk away?" Experts expressed amazement that with gas leaking for five days the apartment had not blown up.

My Thai Special Forces friends said that the second man had been "too frightened to talk." They said Daniels had extensive files. Now the contents were missing. He had been angered by the refusal to properly investigate innumerable reports of American prisoners in the Communist-held areas. He was also angered by the way the Hmong had been used. "Many were destroyed in a kind of Holocaust caused by the secret war in Laos," I was told by one of the Thai participants in that war.

"What Jerry was really doing" was explained in one State Department cable that went to U.S. diplomatic posts from Geneva to Tokyo, from Paris to Mogadishu, Kinshasa, Jakarta, Guatemala, and stops in between. "He was staying," it said, "with his adopted people, the Hmong. After years of service with them during war, Jerry made a personal commitment to stay with them as they were forced to flee Laos."

However, a BBC documentary-film maker, Patricia Penn, had worked among the hill tribes of Laos and remembered Daniels as a senior CIA man. His Bangkok chief was "Refugee Coordinator" Mike Eiland. At another time, Eiland had been a colonel in the Bureau of Politico-Military Affairs at the State Department, and in 1978 he had turned up in Hanoi, taking photographs of the old American consulate on Hai Ba Trung Street. It was before that he served as a director of the secret "Daniel Boone" operations in Cambodia under Command and Control South (CCS) of MACV-SOG out of Saigon.*

And Eiland had coordinated Daniels' Bohica mission, according to Scott Barnes. His claim was ridiculed by the Pentagon, but at that time I saw no perceptible reason why Barnes should have known about Eiland's existence unless someone had been feeding Barnes information to serve some obscure purpose.

Travel vouchers showed Hog Daniels made frequent journeys home to Missoula, Montana, where Vang Pao had set up a ranch after viewing real estate with – of all people – Ed Wilson, the CIA officer subsequently jailed for his involvement with the supplying of illegal arms and plastic explosives to terrorists. It now turned out that Wilson, along with some of his business associates, had been involved with Vang Pao in Laos. Wilson was to voice astonishment to me later, when I saw him in jail, at General Vang Pao's decision to locate in Montana. "I'd taken him around Virginia looking at real estate," said Wilson. "And then the guy chooses fifty degrees below. Can you imagine? After the jungle heat?"

I returned from Bangkok late in the fall of 1986 with a sense of having learned a lot – and nothing.

Perot's own investigator into the Missoula burial recommended against exhumation. "The mother's gone through an awful lot," Perot was told. "After the burial, she was hounded by media inquiries along the lines of 'Don't you know your son was killed by his own people in the CIA?'

---

* CCS was redesignated Task Force 1 Advisory Element. *See* Glossary for a fuller account of the complicated ways by which secret warfare was concealed from the rest of the U.S. armed forces.

She's anxious to lay the whole thing to rest. It's rumored even Vang Pao is afraid the gossip might be true."

Perot's primary interest in Daniels was to learn if he had dealt with American prisoners. "I have to focus on the missing," he repeated yet again. At the same time, he wanted to know if missions like that of Daniels had included other duties.

A former reporter on the newspaper *The Massoulian*, Deirdre McNamer, told me how *she* became curious about Jerrold Daniels. "I thought, well, local boy dies in Bangkok, might be a story there.

"Soon after I started inquiries, I got a phone call. A man says, 'I understand you're looking into Daniels' death.' – Yes – The man says, 'There are certain people here who are very perturbed.' – Well, who are you? – The man gives the name 'Dan O'Dell of Virginia.' Then he warns me, 'It's not in your best interests to investigate.' I asked if that was a warning. 'Take it how you like,' says this O'Dell character. 'Do you need me to come out there and persuade you?'

" 'Yeah,' I said. 'Why don't you?'

" 'Jesus!' he shouts, like I don't know how to take a hint, and slams down the phone. Of course when I tried to trace him, there was no record of such a name in the whole of Virginia."

Deirdre McNamer was stung into asking more questions. That was when she got a better look at the University of Montana professor who became nosy about Daniels' sealed coffin, Bert Pfeiffer. She called the professor, who said he had some material on Daniels he would like her to see. "The professor agreed to show me his 'evidence' next day," said Deirdre McNamer. "Before we could meet, there was the university's first-ever bomb scare! The university was evacuated, and when Pfeiffer got back to his office, his files had been rifled."

Pfeiffer had obtained documents under Freedom of Information that showed he had been kept under surveillance by the FBI because of his anti-war activism. When I called

Pfeiffer, he struck me as a tough-minded academic, not what I had expected; not a soft-headed desk-bound skeptic. He had gone into Cambodia to investigate the use of Agent Orange at the time President Richard Nixon denied it was being used. He said, "I kept asking questions about Daniels. Finally the University Chancellor called me in and said, 'What on earth are you looking into? I've had calls from Washington about this, and you're to lay off.'

"I'm convinced Daniels was murdered. I don't know who did it, but no accidental death is surrounded by so much mystery and strange events."

I had no more to go on, but Daniels' death, soon after he was said to have seen POWs and determining to do something about it, fit the chronology of mishaps that seemed to befall anyone who went counter to official policy. There is no question that if Daniels, who had twice won the CIA's highest award for work in Laos, had publicly stated he saw live POWs, the official POW policy would have been blown right out of the water.

I was at the American Defense Foundation when Red McDaniel showed me President Reagan's response to the appeal smuggled into his hands by Betty Foley, wife of the lost airman Colonel Brendan Foley. I had first heard of her from John Brown – and about Reagan's noncommittal reply.

"Most of our efforts must be quiet and without publicity. We weren't helped recently by the news story about our mission in Laos . . . " the President wrote.

The letter was dated the late spring of 1981. The President himself was confirming that there had been a government-sanctioned mission to rescue POWs. Betty Foley, for her own good reasons, had kept quiet about it until now. The effect was to make me feel more confident about those sources who had told me about a government-sponsored Delta mission in early 1981. I asked Red if my same sources told the truth about an earlier Delta mission being abandoned by the government bureaucracy. "What *was* the President's role in all of this?"

"The President was probably sincere," he replied. "He can't *act*, any more than President Carter could. Reagan has to take the advice of the same bunch that doesn't want anyone independently poking around in the issue. That's why the Tighe Report is sealed up, tight as a drum."

Tighe and his commission of investigation seemed unlikely to be a nuisance. Perhaps also like Jerrold Daniels, the commissioners were sworn to lifelong secrecy. Despite earlier promises by DIA that the commission findings would be made public, its reports had been classified. Like Jerrold Daniels, the commissioners knew some ugly truths. Perhaps also like Jerrold Daniels, they had to wrestle with the agonizing question of how to deal with secrecy and with the way it is used.

By the end of September, 1986, when it became obvious to The Telephone Tree that the full Tighe Report would never see the light of day, vets and families pressed twenty-two congressmen to seek information on it. Capitol Hill in turn pressured Lenny Perroots of the DIA for a briefing. The night before Perroots' scheduled meeting with the congressmen, NBC TV broadcast a news item on the report, and included part of an interview with Tighe. He had given it weeks before, with the understanding that it was for use in a far-distant documentary. By running it now, NBC gave the impression that Tighe was discussing in public conclusions reached in the report. In fact, he had not referred to the commission's findings. This was not immediately apparent to DIA director Perroots, who heard about the NBC news item during a private dinner.

"He went ballistic!" said another dinner guest who was there. "He yelled, 'Tighe can't do this! He's stabbed me in the back!' "

Late that evening a military vehicle sped to Tighe's home. Tighe was startled by the high rank of the vehicle's passenger and by the demands he conveyed: "corrections" to his report, and answers to new questions that surprised him by their hostility. He was to have the answers and corrections ready by morning. Habits of a lifetime asserted themselves. Tighe worked through the night, since this seemed necessary to meet congressional needs and to protect national security.

The next day the *New York Times* gave DIA Director Perroots more reason for irritation with a follow-up to the NBC news item headlined "POWs Alive in Vietnam, Report Concludes." It was based on the NBC interview and quoted Tighe from the story: "A large volume of evidence leads to the conclusion that POWs are alive. . . . " It looked like a leak from Tighe. Tighe tried to straighten out the misunderstanding, but he was ignored. From Defense Secretary Caspar Weinberger came the accusation that Tighe was breaking secrecy and also lying. And Perroots struck, too.

Perroots gave the planned confidential briefing to the congressmen who had been pressed by the vets and families to find out just what was going on. According to some present, including Billy Hendon and Bob Smith (the Republican from New Hampshire), the DIA chief gave only the barest outline of Tighe's report, then launched into what Hendon called "a scurrilous attack against Perroots' own former colleague and mentor." Tighe was not there to defend himself, but he soon heard details from individual congressmen.

Meanwhile, the *New York Times* of the following day carried a report totally contradicting what Tighe had said in the interview and quoting Perroots: "No credible evidence, no strong compelling evidence that prisoners are alive." Some POWs *might* still be in Indochina, but, the *Times* story ended, "Perroots declined to speculate on whether they are prisoners or had decided to stay of their own free will." It seemed to me the government reserved the right, by such statements, to call any American who came out a deserter, as in the case of Garwood.

Few knew the price Tighe paid for his integrity. "General Tighe is so clean," Ross Perot said to me, "they just can't stab him in the back. His integrity is total."

So they destroyed a man with a boy's game.

General Tighe had fought hard for a new DIA headquarters. Finally, that fall, the imposing building was opened with ceremony. Tighe greeted Perroots in a friendly way. Perroots didn't say a word. No member of the senior staff spoke to either Tighe or his wife, Gwen, the entire day. The silent treatment was given to the retired intelligence chief for speaking the truth.

"I felt sick," said a DIA officer. "It was petty, it was cruel. It was punishment for not being one of the boys. Tighe had been cut out."

General Tighe's reaction to Perroots' behavior was "a violent, personal one," as Tighe himself described it. "Perroots insulting me, his deputy turning against me, old professional friends bad-mouthing me . . . Had I been *that* dumb? I remember thinking, 'Is this why old friends destroy you? Because their own careers are at stake? Don't honor and integrity mean anything any more?'

"I used to say my government would never behave dishonorably," Tighe ruminated. "Now I wonder."

Public opinion had aroused questions among federal lawmakers that made them think the Tighe Commission was necessary. But commissions and committees can also stall action. Bureaucratic complications struck again. Four months after Tighe submitted his final report in June 1986 – a report prompted by concern that if actions were delayed, American servicemen might die in prison camps – a congressional subcommittee convened.* Congressman Stephen Solarz, familiar to vets from his earlier chairing of the committee and to

---

* U.S. House of Representatives Committee on Foreign Affairs, Subcommittee on Asian and Pacific Affairs. Confusingly, the transcript of this subcommittee is called the Tighe Report.

me for the short shrift he had given to Billy Hendon and Bobby Garwood, was once again in the chair. Solarz asked Tighe to testify on October 15 in a closed session to consider his Tighe report – with strict orders to keep his remarks down to ten minutes.

As the hearings progressed, Perroots' deputy, Brig. Gen. Shufelt, made a singular statement that confirmed finally what had always been suspected: that an interagency team "managed" the public's perception of the missing issue.

"We are part of a team that President Reagan in effect put together," said the deputy DIA director. "That team is comprised of people in the White House." It was an unfortunate choice of phrase as the Iran-Contra scandal started to break into print. Blissfully unaware of this ticking bomb, Shufelt went on to tell the hearing that the White House team "is composed of the League of Families as represented by Ann Griffiths who is here today. It is also composed of people in OSD, State Department, and, of course, DIA."

Although no surprise, this was the first public confirmation of the government-approved status of the League of Families.

Before Tighe appeared, his erstwhile friend and colleague General Perroots attacked the Tighe Report as inconsequential and choppily written. He blamed Tighe personally. For many months after the hearing Tighe's remarks before the subcommittee were kept in Solarz's office. Little was heard of what he actually said. The mud stuck, and many on The Telephone Tree thought that Tighe's subsequent silence meant he could take no more. The fact was that he had been temporarily muzzled.

Eventually, Mike Van Atta spread word of Tighe's strong statement in the hearing: that *all his Task Force members agreed there were Americans being held in Indochina.*

Ross Perot had given his slot on the Tighe Commission to General Robinson Risner, the ace fighter pilot who spent seven years in Hanoi's jails. Perot anticipated that the Tighe Commission findings would be classified if they were critical

of U.S. government policy. Anyone involved would be prevented from speaking in public about such criticism. He and
the fighter ace agreed that it would be better to sacrifice
Risner's voice than Perot's. The League of Families, now
evidently a government mouthpiece, had not been involved
in determining the commission make-up, yet it issued an
official "Press Guidance", claiming that "Mr. Perot's schedule did not permit participation" in the Tighe Commission.

Perot's patience was dwindling. He had barged into the
Solarz hearing to force into the open what Tighe and his
commission members were unable to say because of the
classification gag. "Every member [of the Tighe Commission]
will swear under oath to what Tighe has said about live
Americans still in Indochina – and will say it in stronger and
more colorful language if allowed. . . . Let me put in perspec-
tive why the system is not working.

"A senior person in a sensitive position asked me, 'Ross,
don't you wonder how we live with ourselves?' I said as a
matter of fact I do. He said, 'It's simple, we set the screens so
tight that nothing can get through.' "

Perot came as close as he could to discussing secret-intelligence methods. He quoted an expert high in the military
who could not be identified: "When policy dictates that a
particular view should not be substantiated by intelligence reports, the requirements for accepting such reports are made
impossibly strict, and the reports disintegrate."

The words might well have been chiselled into a tomb-
stone marking the end of democracy, in Perot's private opinion. But he merely concluded by offering to answer
questions.

The chairman, Solarz, had only one: What were Perot's
sources? It sounded like an echo of the demand made by
Murkowski's committee. Sources could be silenced if they
feared their anonymity might be exposed by congressional
hearings.

"I must have their names," Solarz told Perot. "I'll subpoena them."

"Let me get their approval first," said Perot.

Solarz kept returning to the question. Finally Perot exploded: "Aren't we playing a game? I will do everything I can to help – "

Solarz: "The thing you can do right now is give us their names."

Perot kept his temper and said nothing.

Solarz tried again. Would it not be helpful if the testimony of Perot's sources were to be heard?

"This is like putting eighteen inches of concrete on a road already paved," snapped Perot.

The Texan wrenched the discussion around to something new. The Reagan administration's control team claimed to "revitalize the issue" by bringing home bones that frequently proved to be animal remains. "I don't know how *you* define cover-up, but you look at the standards required by intelligence officers to show there is one live American – then you compare those rigid requirements, almost impossible to meet, with what we send home in caskets. We've got a double standard. We close the books with the tiniest bit of information about a false set of bones. . . . "

"You indicated you knew some people who had information," interrupted Solarz. "Could you tell us who they are?"

"Here we go again," said Perot.

Solarz made a point of lecturing Perot on the law. There was such a thing as the Logan Act "which prohibits private citizens from engaging in negotiations on behalf of the government." It was as if Solarz already knew that Perot was contemplating ways and means of getting a response from Vietnam. "Don't – " warned Solarz, "don't you even think about trying it. . . . "

As the subcommittee ground on, behind the scenes another crisis was capturing defense department attention. An Iranian arms-dealer, Manuchehr Ghorbanifar, had been used by the CIA's director, Casey, as a channel to release hostages. Something had gone wrong. Millions of dollars were missing in a secret deal. Ghorbanifar was about to go public. The warning came from the senior CIA analyst on the Iran project, Charles Allen, in a memo on October 14, 1986. He added that some of the profit "in the secret arms deal was redistributed to other projects of the U.S."*

The Iran-Contra scandal was about to blow. And the Iranian contacts were reporting the probable existence of a four-hundred-page interrogation report, extracted from CIA's station chief in Beirut, William Buckley, who had been kidnapped March 16, 1984. Lt. Col. Oliver North, of the National Security Council staff in the White House, was selling arms to Iran, and after Charlie Allen's memo, North assured Casey that by such means hostages might yet be bought out . . . though it looked now as if even Buckley's body was lost for good.

When the whole Iran-Contra story began breaking in the Lebanese magazine *Al-Shiraa*, those familiar with the POW/ MIA issue were not surprised by the exposures. However, this was the first time the general public had had an opportunity to see how secret intelligence was being used to reinforce secret U.S. government policy, and how inconvenient intelligence reports – as Ross Perot had described it when he talked about POW intelligence – "disintegrated." The term referred to bureaucratic procedures for "retiring" documents until they disappeared.

"Nobody trusts anybody," Senator Paul Laxalt, the Republican from Nevada, told a group of veterans, including philanthropist Tony Duke and the retired Vietnam military-intelligence chief, Bill Legro. "There's a bunker instinct," said Laxalt. "CIA doesn't trust the National Security Council. The NSC doesn't trust the State Department. State doesn't trust anybody. NSC did its own thing because it sat immune in the White House."

---

* See *The Chronology: The Documented Day-by-Day Account of the Secret Military Assistance to Iran and the Contras,* by the National Security Archive, Washington, D.C., published by Warner Books, 1987 (p. 520).

"There's a bunch of people who are not being monitored," said Admiral Bobby Ray Inman, who had been director of the NSC from 1977 to 1981. He had had a long career in the CIA and naval intelligence, and he made no bones about making such statements in public during the subsequent weeks of debate. The leap to the concept of a secret government seemed farfetched, and yet more disturbing evidence began to surface, indicating something needed to be explained.

Back in 1983, Secretary of the Army John O. Marsh had written a top-secret memo to Defense Secretary Caspar Weinberger complaining about increasing CIA requests for Army support for covert operations. He wondered if the Army had legal authority to respond. Were the CIA's ventures designed to avoid congressional oversight and supervision? What Army activities in support of the CIA should be disclosed to congressional intelligence committees? Was the CIA using the Defense Department to avoid reporting operations to Congress? What about the War Powers Act, which required Congress to be notified of military engagements by U.S. armed forces? The Act did not apply to the CIA, which could "borrow" Army resources for military action which was then *not* reported to Congress.

Secretary Marsh insisted his memo was not designed to challenge covert action "as a tool of foreign policy." He was simply concerned that there seemed no proper legal review of the CIA requests.

The Defense Secretary took a month to reply. The decision on what to tell Congress, wrote Weinberger, "is the primary responsibility of the Director of Central Intelligence." That brought the Secretary of the Army full circle back to the cause of his anxieties: the absence of any real oversight of CIA-sponsored activities that involved the armed forces.

Colonel Earl Hopper saw even more serious implications in the lack of such oversight. He gave the example of Theodore Shackley, the former CIA chief in Laos during the covert war. Colonel Clayton had mentioned him to Ann Holland in connection with Site 85. "If you read his book, *The Third*

Option," said Hopper, "you can see he really recommends neither victory nor defeat – just a continuation of conflict where each side bleeds the other. A situation like that provides a perfect situation for covert commerce and 'a training battlefield.' "*

Shackley now ran a private company near the Pentagon backyard. It was called Research Associates International, in Rosslyn, Virginia. Red McDaniel went there to ask him some questions. Shackley had retired just when his CIA career seemed ready to be crowned by elevation to the top post of director. He had paid a price for becoming known as a zealot, after the Church Committee investigations into the abuse of secret powers during the mid-1970s. His trademark in Laos and in Vietnam had been a formal style of dress. He struck McDaniel as a man who never dirtied himself by direct action. Shackley studied the naval aviator, who had reputedly been one of the most tortured Americans in the history of war – and had never broken – and said, "Aren't you afraid to see me?"

Red, puzzled by the taunt, ignored it. What, he asked, was Shackley's view on men captured in Laos during his secret war? Shackley denied knowing anything about POWs and refused to talk about the war he'd run in Laos. Red reflected that if Shackley had been heading once for directorship of the CIA, it patently had nothing to do with his style in dealing with men who fight wars.

Red's curiosity had been aroused by Ann Holland, and her story of her husband, Mel. She told him that after her husband's commanding officer, Colonel Gerald Clayton, told her that Site 85 in Laos had been surrounded by poppy fields,

* In a *Vanity Fair* article of January 1990, Ron Rosenbaum described how Shackley set forth in his book, *The Third Option*, "what he learned from 'our experience over nearly two decades in such diverse areas as Cuba, the Dominican Republic, Vietnam, Laos, Cambodia, the Philippines, Zaire and Angola. [They] proved that we understood how to combat wars of national liberations.' Rosenbaum added: "Cuba, Cambodia, Laos, Vietnam – successes?"

she continued to push him for more information. He had recently surprised her during one of her attempts to get at the truth by saying: "That area was the biggest drug operation in Laos. . . . "

Clayton, as he had with me, directed her to Ted Shackley when she sought more information. With Iran-Contra breaking, it occurred to her for the first time that possibly the CIA had been involved in Site 85. Shackley did not answer her inquiries.

So I called Colonel Clayton again. This time, he burst into an angry tirade against Ann Holland, "this meddling woman who just doesn't know when to leave well enough alone."

CHAPTER 14

THE RADICAL, THE BILLIONAIRE, AND THE GREEN BERET

I thought I had built up some remarkably trustworthy sources, but my husband pointed out that I might be up against some clever disinformation artists. I felt it was time he met the man who could not be pushed around and could not be bought – Ross Perot.

Perot was giving the prestigious Forrestal Lecture at the Naval Academy in Annapolis in the fall of 1986. It was a soft Virginia evening in mid-November when Navy Lieutenant Mike McDaniel, Red's son, drove us to the lecture.

I also had plans to meet Danny Sheehan, someone who did not fit in this setting of deep conservative loyalties, but who did care deeply about integrity among U.S. government officials. Sheehan was chief legal counsel to the Christic Institute, the public-interest group known for its liberal leanings. It would be portrayed soon enough as an instrument of pro-Communist activists by a CIA veteran, Glenn Robinette, who was to tell an Iran-Contra inquiry he had been paid a large sum of money to develop derogatory material on the

Institute. Sheehan was to join up with Ross Perot in Annapolis, then fly back with him to Texas to compare notes. This put an interesting slant on the McCarthyite attacks against Sheehan, because Perot was seen as the all-American businessman hero and patriot.

Sheehan was investigating an incident in Nicaragua. That was about as far as you could get, geographically, from Americans lost in Southeast Asia. He felt, though, that he had stumbled upon a link. Perot had insisted on knowing about it, and asked Sheehan to meet him in this citadel of naval decorum.

"All I see is Navy brass." Bill looked around, pleased with the familiar scene of Navy spit'n'polish. He was already adjusting his tie. Months with me in a labyrinth of doubts made him appreciate being back among men he respected and understood. And Ross Perot fascinated him.

Perot's speech was about the courage and initiative of ordinary Americans. As he gave details of how his Electronic Data Systems employees improvised and executed the daring rescue of colleagues held hostage in Iran, it became clear to Bill that Perot was very familiar with a new era of intelligence operations and technology. However, he still placed the highest value on human intelligence, not gadgetry. Perot said that, in scratching together the rescue team, "I didn't know if anyone would go. Every single person, though, volunteered. And they did it for a very interesting reason. There was no money in it. Certainly no glory in it. Good way to get killed. They did it because . . . It – was – the – right – thing – to – do."

What Perot did not talk about publicly was that he had recently slipped through the guard around the President to deal with another hostage crisis – POW/MIAs. He had been given authority to function as a special investigator and to make a personal search through the secret-intelligence POW/MIA files. In an anteroom, Perot quietly told me that he had outmaneuvered the group controlling the issue by using personal connections. This made him a threat.

Perot said, "If I'm killed, my will is written so the bulk of the estate goes into the fight – the fight to get back our men, and the fight to expose what was done to keep them in Communist jails. So my death won't benefit anyone.

"You understand you can't follow me into classified areas," he added, "but we'll go on inquiring separately and comparing notes periodically."

A reception line of officers and their wives stretched into the corridor. Perot was affable with everyone. In an aside, though, he made one of those casual remarks that turn the world over. "When you look into the prisoner cover-up," he said quietly, "you find government officials in the drug trade who can't break themselves of the habit." Then he went back to small talk with a faculty wife. Perot had made his own connection between drugs and prisoners.

Bill wandered over to Danny Sheehan. Was that what he would be discussing with Perot? "Yes," said Danny. "I think I can prove how profits from drugs and arms financed covert wars in the name of American national security. Perot better be careful, if he says so, though. The men who play this game are deep in the bureaucracy, with unlimited resources. They're not likely to sit still while a maverick billionaire exposes their illegal activities."

At any other time, Bill might have taken Danny with a pinch of salt, but the Iran-Contra scandal was producing new disclosures every day. Long before it broke, Danny had obtained sworn affidavits that foreshadowed and went beyond the current investigations. Already, during the summer, a member of the U.S. Senate Foreign Relations Committee, Senator John Kerry, had called for a full-scale congressional investigation and spoke of "a private network" run from the White House by Oliver North and others in the National Security Council and linked to "an interlocking web of private bank accounts, airstrips, pilots, planes and anti-Communist guerrilla bases used in common by arms-smugglers, narcotics smugglers. . . . " The NSC had issued a statement that the House and Senate Intelligence committees "have reviewed the allegations which have arisen that Col. Oliver North is engaged in improper activities. These charges are patently untrue and both committees have found them groundless." Kerry spoke six months before the name of North became a byword, and three years before a Costa Rican parliamentary commission would charge that Oliver North and others contributed to the local drug problem by setting up the covert infrastructure in their country to supply the *contras* with arms.*

Another matter prevented Senator Kerry from pursuing his demand for a congressional investigation. A researcher, later suspected by Sheehan of being a former CIA agent, had won the confidence of Kerry's committee staff. Pretending his desire was to help Kerry, the newcomer searched freely through files and then spread the rumor that Kerry allowed his researchers to take money from "a public-interest group" closely allied with the Christic – the National Security Archive. The charge was not true. Kerry merely had information provided by the group in his file. The ethics committee was asked to look into the charge. Kerry was cleared but it stalled him until after the Iran-Contra hearings were long ended.

Sheehan had taken on a lawsuit that led to inquiries into a long history of alliances between U.S. intelligence figures and questionable businessmen, from Cuban drug traffickers to General Vang Pao, and to the CIA's secret wars in Asia. Until now, Sheehan had not seen a connection to the U.S. government group controlling the POW/MIA issue, nor did

---

* On July 20, 1989, the Costa Rican Legislative Assembly's Special Commission to Investigate Drug Trafficking issued its final report. The report stated that U.S. intelligence personnel had set up a covert infrastructure in Costa Rica to help supply the *contra* effort. That infrastructure, the report said, greatly contributed to the growth of drug-trafficking in that country. The report called for the banning of U.S. citizens who had helped to set up the covert infrastructure. Among the names cited was Oliver North.

missing prisoners seem to have much to do with the core of his own investigation. But he had collected information that Perot suspected could shed light on how it might be necessary for some people to stop all speculation on missing Americans being still alive. That's why Perot was whisking him off to pick his brains in Texas. Perot was a noncommittal collector of information. Because he tried to find out what Sheehan knew did not necessarily mean he supported him in all his efforts.

A white Navy car was waiting to whisk Perot and Sheehan to the Texan's private jet. In the darkness, the two scrambled into the car.

"What do you think of Sheehan?" I asked Bill as we watched the Navy driver ease away.

Bill laughed. "What a scene! Perot nipping through the Navy brass with Danny the Red!"

"Not *Red!*" I said. "Rebel, yes. Danny comes out of a respectable American tradition of using the law to bring about change." He had fought Karen Silkwood's case. Anything contentious – Attica, Wounded Knee, the Greensboro Ku Klux Klan affair, the Pentagon Papers. . . . Of course he would be labelled dangerous for taking sworn affidavits from government officials who suddenly woke up to what was going on. Sheehan was now speculating on why prisoners could be an embarrassment.

In Washington, after the Forrestal Lecture, we met a trusted colleague of Casino Man in an apartment hotel between the Potomac and M Street at Wisconsin. He had chosen to talk in a room without windows or telephone, just a refrigerator rattling away to frustrate eavesdroppers.

"Call me the Vicar of Bray. You know the verse," he said, thumping Bill's shoulder. "For Kings may come/And Kings may go/But I'll still be the Vicar of Bray, sir!"

"We'll put you in the index as 'The Preacher,' " said Bill. "I never met a *vicar* in America."

The Preacher was an American who had spent time with the British Special Air Service in Malaysia. He was risking his job at a very high level in the Pentagon, because he trusted Colonel Nick Rowe, who had told him to see us.

He was angered by "the secret policy on prisoners. It's run by a small gang," he said. "They run clandestine groups that have multiplied so nobody knows who's doing what to whom. They can activate investigation units you never dreamed of. They've had Perot followed. We've had twenty years of failures in my time with counter-terrorism. They've had twenty years' experience winning bureaucratic battles against us, and *not* against our enemies."

The Preacher was afraid that this group knew that the only way to damage their interests was to have an American prisoner rescued, causing a public outcry and a subsequent investigation. They would do anything to prevent this. His old foxhole buddy, Casino Man, had a plan to extract three specific prisoners. There was a great risk of failure if it should be betrayed.

Bill looked skeptical. The Preacher went on: "This secret group has such power to manipulate investigative agencies, the Mafia is kid's stuff. It doesn't have to use violence. People can be bought."

"How?"

"Through the billions generated by the drug industry and smuggled arms. Remote communities in this country play host to planes that carry in illegal drugs from abroad. The local sheriffs are bought off, the enforcement agencies are corrupted, and there's always someone hovering around to say, 'Hey, guys, this is a government covert program. . . .' So queasy consciences are eased."

"But if you know it, why can't *you* stop it?"

The Preacher took a walk around the windowless room. "Nothing less than a public outcry will stop it. What started out in Vietnam as a neat way to find money to fund covert operations has developed into a huge industry. The men and women who are involved, maybe they can't get off the merry-go-round. Maybe it keeps spinning faster and faster, they make more and more money, and even if they wanted to duck out, they can't." He stopped and moved to the door. "Here's a question I'll leave you with. How does it happen that since the start of the Reagan administration, and that War on Drugs under Vice President Bush, the amount of cocaine coming into this country has multiplied by about 1500 percent? From less than two thousand kilograms a year to about thirty thousand? Whatever his anti-drug program is, it hasn't been very effective."

I exchanged notes with Ross Perot. He was sitting in a Washington hotel. He phoned Bill Casey's office. "I want all your files on Nugan Hand, all on the Rewald-BBRDW case, everything on Jerry Daniels. . . . " He said to me later that "Million-dollar retainers are paid to big lawyers to cover tracks. Law enforcers too often have a price. Lawmakers need money for election campaigns. And the biggest money comes from drugs."

However, I wondered about Perot's fate as a special investigator if he continued to run counter to Bill Casey. Reagan's Central Intelligence director had already voiced doubts about this "outsider" and his qualifications for dabbling in secret-intelligence matters. Nobody could buy Perot, I was convinced, even if he went broke tomorrow. But he was not control-proof. Perot told me that two CIA men, both friends, had separately warned him that he might quietly disappear. They mentioned his kids. It was hard to tell if they were acting out of friendship. A friend high in the Justice Department told him the FBI was doing a complete check on him – "means *everything*, past and present." Perot called FBI Director Judge William Webster, who was soon to become Casey's replacement as CIA chief. "I'll tell you anything you want to know!" roared Perot in fury. "Just don't snoop behind my back."

Judge Webster laughed. "Don't be paranoid. We're not running any investigation. . . . "

Then Perot heard the ex-CIA agent Glenn Robinette testify

before an Iran-Contra inquiry on Capitol Hill that he had been paid $100,000 to develop derogatory information, "dig up the dirt," on Danny Sheehan on behalf of U.S. civilians with lifelong links with the CIA. There was no reason why the CIA's Judge Webster should have known about this. "But that, of course, is the trouble," said Perot. "Decent administrators are too nice to imagine abuses of power."

I asked him, "Is there a guerrilla war being waged against you?"

His eyes flashed. "I'm fighting a guerrilla war against *them*! I just go quiet for a while and tell people I'm totally minding my own business. . . . ."

I met with Earl Hopper, the disillusioned former executive-director of the League of Families, at Christmas 1986. He spread out a grease-stained chart like one of my father's old aviation maps, with dirty creases where it had been folded and stuck down the side of an old-fashioned flying boot. He took pride in the son who had been, like himself, a colonel steeped in honorable traditions: a son shot down in circumstances that were increasingly a puzzle because the intelligence bureaucracy now gave the father contradictory statements. Now he trusted outsiders like Casino Man more than the government.

"Our mutual friend," he said, referring to Casino Man, "*identified* three Americans at this point." He stabbed at the map. "Now we've got them moving. Their guides are indigenous personnel, operating in watertight units, passing the Americans from one unit to the next." He told me Casino Man's rigid rules for establishing proof that any prisoners were properly identified: blood types, physical markings, social security numbers, and photo comparisons. When I looked at the photographs, I could see that one of the three Americans seemed to be a man who had been established as missing from a shot-down reconnaissance aircraft. I did not know whether his family thought him dead, and I did not trust myself to ask them.

The other man in on Casino Man's operations was Colonel Nick Rowe. Rowe went into detail about the "secret" 1981 mission to Laos mentioned in President Reagan's personal note to Betty Foley, and about which I had now heard so much. "A special task force was set up by the Joint Chiefs of Staff to carry out two missions," said the Special Forces colonel. "Admiral Tuttle took what amounted to a blood oath never to speak to anyone, ever, about this – except to the immediate participants. The first mission was to fix, on the ground, the location and condition of prisoners, as recorded by SR-71 aircraft and RD-77 satellite photography. That's where the famous '52' signal came from. The second mission was to be a rescue by Delta commandos whose movements into the area were covered by huge joint-service exercises from the Philippines to Thailand. The government of Thailand cooperated on condition details of their role never be officially disclosed."

Meanwhile, said Rowe, the colorful Colonel Bo Gritz was preparing Velvet Hammer, his simultaneous reconnaissance mission, based on classified intelligence he had collected and, he said later, "unofficial-official government sources had verified." He was cooperating with the government, but was prepared to run his own mission should something go wrong. He was going after the "52" camp too, but apparently without the Joint Chiefs' knowledge. It was rumors of Gritz's involvement in this mission that had first stirred my interest in the POW/MIA issue.

Gritz's activities were reported to government officials outside the military. Rowe said, "They went on a rampage. Said these were 'rogue' operations, and demanded a stop to the Army's Intelligence Support Activity, which they accused of running Bo. By then, the Joint Chiefs' first mission, to reconnoiter the '52' area, was in Laos. Thereafter, the official word was that it found nothing – and the Delta forces were ordered home." The photos of reconnaissance, as Red McDaniel had remembered, were now dismissed as "Fort Apache" snapshots. At this stage I was confused. Apparently others were too.

Secretary of Defense Caspar Weinberger sent a top secret memo in early 1982 to Secretary of the Army John O. Marsh, ordering that ISA be dismantled within thirty days. In the end, Weinberger was persuaded to rescind his order to dismantle ISA because *it would be a victory for America's enemies.* The refrain was becoming a familiar in cases in which secret activities went unexamined.

But the Delta rescue was stopped dead in its tracks. Success would have given the Army's expanding ISA a boost. That's why ISA, according to Rowe, made secret plans for another mission – Jerry "Hog" Daniels' Bohica. Seemingly that mission, like the earlier Delta mission, was badly compromised.

I remembered Delta colonels who had told me that a rescue operation could have been carried out in both instances; that it had maximum chances of success. Rowe's version tallied with Judge Harold Fong's indiscreet remark at the censored trial of Ronald Rewald about the use of BBRDW funds raising "highly emotional POW/MIA matters" that ought not to be aired in public. Rowe said that Daniels' Bohica was never "a rogue operation," that it took intelligence funds from the Rewald financial empire and was therefore government supported. This tallied with BBC researcher Kelly's unearthing of the Rewald documents, which he had salvaged before government "sanitation experts", who were sent to weed out embarrassing material arising from the trial, could get to them.

Later, when Gritz was charged with illegal use of a passport, a Major Clarence E. Johnson would testify under oath that Gritz in 1981 was indeed on a mission, Bohica, and that the affiant, Major Johnson, was in the National Security Agency. Major Johnson swore he was present later when

Gritz was officially warned "he'd be in for a real shit-blizzard if he [Gritz] did not knock off all current activities."

"You'd go mad trying to unravel what's behind all this," Rowe said. "The defense system in this country's so big, complex, and uncontrolled that it invites conspirators – it's a major security disaster waiting to happen.

"So just concentrate on the one mystery that could explain all else. Keep asking: Why was Tighe's report altered? Why was the inquiry spun out for more than a year after your *60 Minutes* piece?"

I decided to go to the man who had the authority from the President and the interest to find out – Ross Perot, the only civilian who had been empowered to study classified intelligence. He was now facing one of the hardest decisions of his life. Could he talk with Hanoi and not fall foul of the Logan Act? As Congressman Stephen Solarz had reminded him, it forbade a private citizen to negotiate with a foreign power, but Perot was convinced that official negotiations had missed opportunities. When Henry Kissinger had suggested American prisoners from Laos could be brought out through Hanoi, the Vietnamese and the Laotian Communists had talked about the payment of reparations, and also a treaty. The government closed the books on the men. Could a private citizen open them again? Perot was increasingly sure, from the feelers put out to him from Hanoi, that he *could* accomplish something by methods that would keep the government from using the Logan Act to prevent others from taking action on prisoners. Perot explored the options.

Hanoi might conveniently "discover" its prisoners were held outside Vietnam – in Laos. That would avoid adverse American public reaction toward our former enemy. The Vietnamese were becoming desperate for capitalist wealth, now that all economic planning had failed, leaving the country in ruin.

Perot called David Taylor and asked him what he thought of buying Cam Ranh Bay.

Taylor knew the Texan respected his opinions, based upon the immense amount of work the BBC put into the POW/ MIA mystery, but he was taken aback by this question. He had a crazy impulse to say, "Yes, why not, Ross? Buy it!" Camn Ranh Bay, a natural harbor in South Vietnam, had been developed by U.S. forces into one of the largest seaports in the area. By early 1987, there were disturbing reports that it was now being used by the Soviet Red Fleet to such an extent that the Russians threatened U.S. naval interests in the Pacific and caused concern in Communist China.

"I should say it would be something of a coup," Taylor finally answered cautiously.

"It's just an idea," said Perot. The U.S. Navy would buy a lease on the seaport for an amount roughly equal to the money Nixon had promised in 1973 – the prospect of getting the base would outweigh the frequently expressed U.S. government stance against "paying ransom for hostages." Vice President George Bush eventually conveyed to Perot that the scheme had been rejected.

Reporters were now inquiring into the old controversy over CIA proprietaries. They had been stirred up by Scott Barnes's repeated assertion in the media that he had been hired by the CIA to kill Ron Rewald, the former head of BBRDW, in his prison cell. Once again it was the BBC that showed its independence. As a foreign news organization free from U.S. domestic political concerns, it publicly discussed the leading American and international figures involved in the Nugan Hand Group and Ron Rewald's financial empire.

Perot said, "Political considerations aside, the government is apprehensive about having to go rescue the folks in Indochina. They're held in multiple locations. How would you like to be in charge of twenty-five to thirty simultaneous rescues? Because if you don't get them all at once, the enemy is going to move or kill them." Hanoi had dispersed prisoners and beefed up their security after the leaks of the first 1981 rescue plan. He was sure that any large-scale military operation would fail. Instead, he would discuss things quietly with Hanoi. Let the Vietnamese wonder why they got conflicting signals from Washington, and why U.S. officials used every opportunity in negotiation and in public statements to say the U.S. government had no evidence of live prisoners.

Perot had not yet come to any conclusions when Colonel Earl Hopper, Sr., called me to report progress on the three Americans handled by Casino Man. "The three men are stopped," he said. "It will take several months to move them out of Communist or disputed territory."

"*Months!*"

"They're in bad shape. They have to come out only at night. They must almost never talk. They must accept being run by a handler. Each squad of handlers can be from a different tribe with a different set of motives. Each prisoner has to become a Jerry Daniels – think like his handler, become one lobe of the handler's brain. It's impossible, of course."

He sounded discouraged. "Our guys cling like babies to their mothers. They live in a world of senses we've forgotten how to use. The people of the hills and jungle can smell a Caucasian. Word travels fast, mouth to mouth. There's nothing to stop you being killed, any time, for no special reason. You're worth nothing. You don't exist. Nobody will avenge you."

I understood at last why Hopper was so close to Casino Man. The father of the downed Air Force pilot had given up all but the last remnants of hope of finding his boy. But he was determined to help the man who was doing something for the POWs about whose existence he had no doubt.

CHAPTER 15

THE VANISHING CABBIE

Robinson Risner met Bill at the Austin, Texas, airport. He had crayoned a large sign saying BILL STEVENSON to wave above the crowd.

Bill had last seen Risner on a *Time* magazine cover along with a report: "The Secret War in Laos." Risner was then a top-gun survivor of fierce dogfights with Soviet MiGs over Korea. At forty, already acclaimed the ace of U.S. fighter pilots in Indochina, he was shot down. The commanders of Hoa Lo Prison, the "Hanoi Hilton," knew his reputation and were waiting for him. He was hung from meat hooks and exhibited as a prize of war. His captors set out during the next seven years to reduce his physical and mental resistance until he could be displayed as evidence of American inferiority. Kept in isolation for five years, he had drawn strength from the biblical teachings of his parents when he was a boy in Pumpkin Center, Oklahoma.

None of this was evident now. Risner might have been a Rotary Club greeter. His scarred cowboy face passed almost unnoticed behind large spectacles sparkling with goodwill. Risner announced that he was taking Bill to the hotel. He talked while he drove, mostly about his return to a home similar to his boyhood home, where he was now raising horses after retirement from the Air Force. His wants were very few. A bit of land. Horses.

Bill forgot to say that he had changed hotels, that the Wyndham Park South was full and he'd been switched to the Residence Inn. They had lunch at the Wyndham anyway. "You said it was full," Risner said suspiciously. "Looks empty." He thought the switch had been a precaution on Bill's part.

Everyone was cautious these days. Ross Perot, too, had been forced to switch his plans when he realized he was under surveillance by government agents. Perot, authorized to search through intelligence files in Washington in his role of presidential investigator, spotted the watchers in a suite across from his hotel room. He took the emergency stairs and checked into another hotel. Thereafter, at the end of each day's research, the billionaire would return to the first hotel and wait for the watchers to settle in comfortably for the night. Then he would scuttle out to the backup hotel where he could work for the night in peace. Not even a billionaire is comfortable under surveillance, Bill thought. And perhaps Perot enjoyed outwitting the "spooks." It was, said General Risner, an outrageous situation for a free citizen to be placed in; but it was a fact of life.

The social chatter ended at the luncheon table when Risner removed his spectacles and revealed a face that now suddenly looked rock hard. "Just what is it you want?"

"You were one of General Tighe's commission investigators," said Bill. "You saw him trashed. The investigation was kept under wraps. Why would the government go to such lengths?"

A waitress hovered. Risner leaned forward, hand on knee, head bent in an attitude of prayer. He was saying grace. Bill had read the accounts of Risner's leadership from other prisoners in the Hanoi Hilton. Men in isolation cages contrived through codes improvised and perfected during years of captivity to conduct religious services in spite of the guards. Prison commandants had punished and even screamed threats of execution. The hymn-singing still continued. Each Sunday a volunteer yelled a sermon, another synchronized prayers by tapping on bars or plumbing. At each service, a different set of prisoners, elected by methods that baffled the guards, took charge. It kept the men sane. It drove the guards to fury. Risner documented it himself in *The Passing of the Night*, published by Random House in 1973, the year he came home.

Risner straightened up. "Your wife – ?"

"She's coming by a different route, arrives early evening." Another precaution. "Sometimes," said Bill, "I feel I've fallen into a spy thriller. That's one reason my wife asked me to see you. She felt you'd help me recover a sense of being in touch with reality."

"What's been so *unreal*?"

Bill told him, starting with the first warnings to me that I would "endanger national security" if I pursued a story on POW/MIAs that conflicted with the approved version. He ran through events since the moment Bob Garwood appeared in the guise of a certified deserter. "To this day, Garwood has never been debriefed in accordance with normal intelligence standards. If he ever is, we might find out more about why even you, General Risner, had to be silenced on the Tighe Task Force. . . . "

Everything was absorbed. The granite eyes, nestled in tiny pockets, never left Bill's face and gave nothing away.

After Risner worked so closely with Perot in the campaign to purge Texas of illegal drugs, and with Nancy Reagan in her war on drugs, and after the classification of the Tighe Report, he had been offered a post that in effect would have made him the country's anti-drug czar. He refused, wanting to keep himself as independent as possible. He wanted to settle the issue of POW/MIAs even more than he wanted to battle the problem of drug addiction. He had once believed that only fanatics became involved in the POW/MIA issue. Not now. Now, after being authorized to search through *all* secret intelligence on prisoners, he had become a convert.

"Can you see a Special Forces man in exactly an hour?" I asked Risner. I hadn't even put down my bag yet. He and his wife, Dot, had been waiting for me at the hotel with Bill.

"Certainly can," said Risner. "What's up?"

When I had arrived that evening, my bags had not come off the conveyer with all the others from my flight. While I was fretting about them, a taxi drew up and the driver said he'd check with the airline. The man was unusually helpful. We were ten minutes down Route 35 from the airport on our way to the hotel when he told me he'd been captured in Vietnam long *after* the war ended.

We were having a casual conversation about the mishaps that occur in life when he mentioned that he had been a prisoner in Vietnam; that he had served with Special Forces. That piqued my interest. I asked him if he knew Mark Smith or any of the other guys who got out in 1973, guys like Red McDaniel or Robby Risner. "No," he answered, "I escaped." My ears pricked up. "Really," I said. "How did you manage that? I understand it was extremely difficult." I told him I had heard that only Nick Rowe escaped from the Vietnamese during the war. Then he said that it hadn't been during the war. He had been captured in 1982, after a rescue mission. He escaped after a year, and he swore other Americans were still being held.

I'd then remarked on the strange coincidence that I was in Austin to see Risner, well known locally as a war hero and a member of a POW/MIA task force. The taxi-driver promised to come back at the end of his shift to meet us in the Residence

Inn. He seemed excited, even awed, by the prospect of talking to the famous Robbie Risner.

"Do you think he will?" Dot laid one hand on Risner's sleeve.

"If someone doesn't change his mind," said Risner. He fixed me with those startling gray fighter-pilot eyes. "You sure he couldn't have known you?"

"Don't see how. He started up the conversation by sympathizing because Continental lost my luggage. I wasted an hour reporting it. Then it showed up suddenly beside the carousel. By then the taxis had all gone.

"Except for this youngish guy. Cab 36. He'd been parked out of sight. Said there were worse things. His house had burned down at Christmas. After he told me he was an escaped POW, I must have sounded skeptical, because he showed me the burn marks inside his forearms where his sleeves were rolled up." I demonstrated. "Cab 36 said the scars were not from the fire."

He had dropped me at the hotel and gone, but I had his social security number, 451-91-8432, and his name, Jerry DuBose, of Roy's Taxicabs. I had obtained these details when he said he wanted to consult his buddies before seeing Risner. He was risking a lot personally, he said. He had been promised financial support to go through medical school by Special Forces. I said my experience had been, when people said that, they didn't come through.

"Ross can get him fire-proofed," said Risner.

"Then I'll call Perot now." I left to find a telephone, and caught Perot still in his Dallas office. I told him what had happened. "Gotcha," he said. It turned out he knew both the owner of the taxi company and the dean of the medical school DuBose said he had applied to.

Dot Risner watched the clock in the hotel lounge tick past the time for meeting DuBose. Dot had been the wife of another fighter pilot shot down over Vietnam: she had waited ten years before she received official word that he was dead.

"If Dot's first husband *does* come back," said General Risner, "I'll bow out gracefully. I love Dot. She's held me together. But if he gets out after all this time, he'll need her more than I do."

Dot's eyes travelled away from the clock. She had no great expectations: Cab 36 was never coming back. Dot Risner had lived a decade of life suspended while others decided if and when to declare her first husband dead. Now, with the suggestion of POWs still alive, the suspense had resumed, if it had ever really ended.

General Risner broke the silence. "If the administration won't act on the Tighe Report, the facts will be made known some other way – "

"When everything's been classified?" I asked. I saw him flinch. It wasn't easy for this man to question institutions he revered. He was being careful to disclose nothing specific from his own privileged investigation into intelligence as a member of the Tighe Commission. Yet he said, "I *know the men are there.*" It was what Tighe had said.

Bill called the dispatcher at Roy's Taxicabs and reported to us, "Cab 36 was turned in early and the driver left suddenly. Looks as if he's not coming."

Risner patted my arm. "Don't feel bad. Someone told him to break off contact. Tomorrow, after we finish working, why don't we all hang around the airport? Every taxi goes there some time. Whichever one of us spots your guy, hop in quick, hold him till the rest pile in."

So, the following day, before the evening rush hour, we went out to the airport. I felt like most people do after an inexplicable experience. Over and over I asked myself, did it really happen?

"That cabbie wasn't just trying to shoot me a line – he was almost uncomfortably respectful," I said defensively to Bill as we walked along the grass verge of the taxi ramp. "Yet did he tell a yarn I was meant to hear?"

Bill was sure I'd been set up. He pointed out I was in a vet's Washington office when the meeting with Risner was ar-

ranged. "Plenty of people know what you're investigating."
He broke off. "Hey! Did the airline ever tell you *exactly* what
happened to make your bag disappear for so long?"

"An agent was looking into it." I hurried ahead to see if the
man could possibly be there now. It had become dark. Cab
numbers were hard to read. Risner and his wife had chores to
do on the ranch. Every inquiry about a missing Cab 36 driver
had drawn a blank. The only explanation was that he was a
"gypsy" who picked up and dropped casual jobs. Bill called
out to me, "Can you hop a taxi back?" I signalled I would.

Later Bill would tell me what happened next. He had rented a
car to make some calls in town. As he drove to the hotel after
his calls, he brooded. Clearly, the Army's Intelligence Support Activity had gone against secret policy. Car 36's driver
must have served under ISA command. We had heard
rumors of a 1982 failed mission. Perhaps that's what he was
on when he was captured. The details of that rescue mission
confirmed what Bill knew already. Such details were never
made public. That must mean my encounter had been set up
by Special Forces guys to bring me together with an eyewitness. The cabbie, if he was a member of ISA, had sworn an
oath never to speak of ISA operations. Vows like this gave the
government a hold over the men. Since their benefits were
secret, like his medical-school fees, presumably they could be
secretly withdrawn if some of the men, disillusioned by
government actions, should feel they were entitled to break
their promises.

When Reagan's men first got into the White House, they
had shown every intention of carrying out the promise Reagan made on July 24, 1976, in a letter read at the annual
dinner of the League of Families. That promise was that, in
Reagan's first week as president, the new Secretary of State
"will start taking every reasonable and proper step to return
any live Americans still alive in Southeast Asia." That did not
seem to be the government's first priority, though. And when

Reagan's political-campaign manager, Bill Casey, moved into the CIA director's chair, suddenly Casey saw things the CIA's way too. Why?

Casey knew all about secret intelligence as a political resource. He had delivered the dirt that crippled Carter's presidency: the details of how the Teheran rescue was botched. So Casey would know better than most that raids into Indochina posed an extremely high political threat to the new president. A catastrophe in that region, where American emotions still ran very high, would destroy Reagan. And yet, in the first year of Reagan's presidency, 1981, Casey had shown sympathy with the cause. Then, insiders said, two or more rescue operations went wrong. Men like Colonel Bo Gritz were denounced as liars when they said they had been authorized by the government. ISA was ordered to stop large-scale rescue operation by Delta forces. . . .

Bill walked across the darkened parking lot, his mind still leaping ahead. Perhaps some clues were being carefully set down by contacts unwilling to break all the secrecy rules. Perhaps no single person *knew* the whole story . . . ?

A figure appeared out of the shadows. A woman. She said softly, "Pretend we're together."

He hesitated, and she whispered urgently, "It's okay, I'm not a hooker."

Someone in a uniform watched at a distance. The woman hugged his arm and, for the benefit of the onlooker, said in a loud voice, "The gang's in the bar, Bill." As she steered him to the hotel's front entrance, Bill wondered who she was and how she knew his name. The man in uniform moved closer. It was only the parking-lot attendant.

The woman said nothing until they were seated in the cocktail bar. "What is this?" he asked. "I haven't much time."

She nodded. She appeared to be under strain. She was carefully and neatly dressed in a straight black skirt and a black-and-white plaid jacket, an open-neck blouse, and patent-leather shoes with high heels. She might have been forty, perhaps more, hair long and blonde. She had a matching patent-leather shoulder bag that she dug into. She was agreeably pretty, but not in a conventional way; she had an attractive face with character. She put the bag away. There was a tightly packed envelope in her hand. "Let me buy you a drink," she said, sliding the envelope across the table.

Bill leaned forward, elbow and shoulder blocking the distant lighting, slipped the envelope out of sight, and said, "Can we meet later?" He was growing more worried by the second. He had left me where that damned cabbie could pick me up again. It *had* been a setup.

The woman said, "That's okay. I understand."

She looked so vulnerable that he added, "Let me check for messages. I'll rejoin you."

He was at the reception desk when he heard his name paged. It was me calling from the airport. "Just leaving," I said.

"Find anything?"

"Continental had no explanation for the way my bag was missing for a time. It was off-loaded properly. A nice man there suggested maybe another passenger accidentally walked off with my stuff and brought it back when he realized the mistake."

Bill returned to the bar. The woman had gone.

Up in the hotel room, he opened the envelope. It contained handwritten notes and the name and address of a woman. Later we nicknamed her "Franny." She was concerned about "huge amounts of money" carried by her former husband and his friends. They were noncommissioned officers in a secret military unit. Sometimes one or two of them were assigned to special duties abroad. She was afraid they'd been drawn into criminal activities.

There were several telephone messages in response to feelers I had put out. They came from the local fire chief, the deputy police chief of Precinct 5, the *Austin American Statesman* newspaper, a fire-insurance investigator, and a lady who said her dogs had knocked over a kerosene heater during Christmas and her house had burned down. All of them asked for me and left numbers where they could be reached.

"Who *are* they?" he asked me when I returned to the hotel. "All they talked about was fire – "

"The driver said his house burned down. There can't be that many homes go up in flames during Christmas in Austin. So I called locals who would have investigated, and no one with his name reported a fire."

"So all you've got is one elderly widow whose dogs caused a kerosene fire," said Bill.

"Anyway I did get somewhere," I said. "I got hold of Perot again. The owner of the cab company told him the driver simply took off. Left the keys in the cab in a side street and skipped town." I glanced at the notes given to Bill in the bar. "I know this woman!"

She had been an Air Force administrative specialist until the eighties. She first contacted me after my "Dead or Alive" piece. Franny had a need to talk. The calls started with her telling me that Major Smith and Sergeant McIntire were the best, that they were being shafted because "The Activity" was being shafted. They were good guys. But there were bad guys who were into criminal drugs, Franny had said.

There was a lot of girl talk. I got the picture of a woman who liked the rough and tumble of tough guys – especially the rough. She heard a lot in bed.

Bill looked at Franny's own notes again. She was now involved professionally in a form of public service that could indicate a woman of conscience. "Wonder what I should do with this?" he murmured. "She *must* be part of the Cab 36 feeler. But Franny's *notes* – they contain names, specifics. If we give these to Risner, we put him in a tough spot. He might feel he's got to hand them to the Army's Intelligence and Security Command. Then all these Army guys and Franny are in trouble. . . . "

I agreed. There were some things Risner ought not to be burdened with.

At the time of our visit, he was winding himself up to tell the country the whole story of how secrecy classifications had been misused. He was steeped in a tradition that did not wash dirty linen in public, and it was hard to go against that.

He had refused to betray his country to an enemy that made
him eat his own excrement, paraded him in chains through
Hanoi's streets under a hailstorm of blows and rocks, roped
him into a ball and rolled him off concrete ledges. . . . It was
hard, after all that, to come out in public with statements
critical of his own government, knowing too that he would be
accused of breaking secrecy. Yet he was to begin an arduous
campaign of telling public meetings that he had seen the
proof of Americans left alive, making speeches between
bouts of serious illness that steadily depleted his strength.

"You're like the man in my favorite poem," I had told him.
"You live in a strange time when 'common integrity could
look like courage.' "

"Who said that?"

"Yevtushenko."

"The Russian?" Risner winced. "Yup," he said after a
pause. "It's a good poem."

I wanted to talk to Franny again before deciding what to
tell Risner. If she would swear out an affidavit, then Risner
would not have to choose between lifelong loyalties and
private conscience. Franny and whoever was behind her
would make the choice for him.

But she called a few days later and asked me to burn the
notes she had given Bill. "Forget everything in them," she
said. "Forget anything I ever told you."

"Are you okay?" I asked, alarmed.

"I – I think so." She hesitated for a long time, and then
burst out, "One of those guys took me out on a date. But he
stopped on a side road and said *they* know everything. About
you. About what I've told you. He said they wouldn't think
twice about killing me if I ever talk again."

She was to phone again a week later. "If everyone acts like
a coward, nothing will ever be right again. . . . I will speak
out. But it has to be to someone with influence *and* integrity."

I remembered the Yevtushenko poem. Part of it goes:
"Courage has never been my quality. . . . /I did no more than
write, . . . /I left out nothing. . . . /And now they press to tell

me that I'm brave./How sharply our children will be ashamed/taking at last their vengeance for these horrors/remembering how in so strange a time/common integrity could look like courage."*

Ross Perot had that common integrity. And he wanted to hear Franny's story directly from her. She agreed. Later she provided documents for congressional investigators. Courage and integrity were what she needed in this strange time. By talking openly with prominent and honorable Americans, she was probably safe from physical danger, though not from slander. She submitted voluntarily to psychological and lie-detector tests. She said she wanted the experts to listen to the information she had collected so haphazardly and help her understand it. She still wanted to avoid disclosing matters her husband had confided that seemed, from her necessarily limited viewpoint, to be genuinely secret. As a result, the tests were not conclusive. Red McDaniel became doubtful about her overall accuracy. Bill, not usually generous in such judgments, argued on the contrary that she had been so mentally bludgeoned, she would be terrified of saying too much. Extreme nervousness often masqueraded as dissembling. The cabbie could have shed some light, but he had vanished.

---

* From *Yevtushenko: Selected Poems*, trans. and intro. Robin Milner-Gulland and Peter Levi, S.J. (Penguin Books, 1962), p. 81, copyright © Robin Milner-Gulland and Peter Levi, 1962. Reproduced by permission of Penguin Books Ltd.

CHAPTER 16

THE DRUG LORD

Perot called me one day in February 1987 to say that he couldn't find a trace of the Cab 36 driver. I, in turn, questioned him about his secret plans for flying to Hanoi. He said it was hard to focus, with the Iran-Contra story breaking new ground every day. "It's scandal time," said Perot.

During the months ahead, the Senate Subcommittee on Terrorism, Narcotics and International Operations would have less trouble focussing on a related subject: the importation of drugs by some who were involved in covert operations in other countries. Unfortunately, few in the media were paying attention when the committee revealed a series of "secret memos" General Paul F. Gorman had sent to the Defense Department in 1985 when he headed Southern Command, covering Latin America from Panama. He had written: "There is not a single group in unconventional warfare that does not use narcotics to fund itself."

His confidential memos had been ill-received by a government in which lip service was paid to the war on international drug traffickers, while the champions of covert warfare dominated foreign policy. Gorman wanted the Special Operations Division and the CIA to be used to track smugglers, not solely for adventures abroad. "There is an artificial membrane," he would testify to the subcomittee, "between intelligence relating to drugs and intelligence relating to military business" (II, p. 44).

After his 1985 protests, Gorman would say nothing more in public. He was dedicated to his security responsibilities and had no wish to encourage the communists. But, as he had written in his memos to the Defense Department, "We have to think beyond the Communist threat to the more acute problem of international drug rings and their effect upon ourselves."

Danny Sheehan was now involved in an investigation that suggested there might be a link between General Gorman's guarded memos and the government handling of the POW/MIA issue. The Christic Institute had launched a lawsuit under the Racketeer Influenced and Corrupt Organization (RICO) Act. I had once hired the couple in Sheehan's lawsuit for a documentary I produced in East Africa. Martha Honey was a sound-recordist and Tony Avirgan was a cameraman. The next time I saw them was in a press photograph. Avirgan was lying injured from a terrorist bomb, his wife trying to protect him from crowds. They were near the Nicaragua border. The picture had been taken during the May 1984 bombing attack on then-*contra* leader Eden Pastora. Eight people, including a U.S. reporter, were killed. Avirgan was among the wounded. With his wife he brought a civil suit through the Christic, alleging the bombing was the work of U.S. operatives. The suit had been filed six months before the Iran-Contra scandal broke, in May 1986, when Congress still accepted disclaimers from the National Security troika of Oliver North, Rear Admiral John Poindexter, and Robert McFarlane that the NSC had anything to do with the *contras*.

Sheehan expanded the case, using the RICO statute. Originally directed against organized crime, it allowed him to act as his own "private attorney general" to prosecute "a shadowy group whose activities until now have been a closely guarded secret." I recognized, in the broadening of the suit, some names I had encountered in my first "Dead or Alive" investigations. The suit claimed that the bombing was among the criminal exploits of twenty-nine individuals, including several government officials. It seemed to me that once Ross Perot began to question Sheehan, we found that we were all embarked separately on paths that converged upon one question – who is responsible for warping American values? Were we so busy fighting Communists, as General Gorman observed, that we were destroying ourselves?

There was a common thread of concern for American security running through the entire political spectrum. Those to the left of center worried about the abuses of secret power. Those like Red McDaniel, who was part of the Washington "inner circle" of Republicans, believed a strong defense depended on moral values which were now being corrupted. This was justified by those in the secret world that had been expanding since the Vietnamese Special Forces Command was set up way back in 1958. Then the CIA had supported and financed operations.

Many old CIA hands, and experienced Special Forces men and women, would have defended the use of clandestine weapons against a foe who constantly employed terror and deceit to undermine free nations. But somewhere between the fairly simple concepts of 1958 and today, some suspected we had started using such weapons against ourselves.

It seemed out of place, and was, in fact, unconstitutional, to put ordinary citizens under surveillance because they exercised their democratic right of seeking legal redress. Yet that's what increasingly seemed to be happening to people who tried to use the law to find out what intelligence the government had on POWs and on possible drug involvement by some of those who worked for the government. I would find that those who investigated the possibility of a connection between the two would be hit by a double whammy.

Somehow, the names of everyone who got involved with Danny Sheehan's lawsuit or Mark Waple's *Smith vs. The President* always became known. Then those people were singled out for the kind of intimidation described by Casino Man's friend, General Tighe, or Jerry Mooney, the National Security Agency specialist who tried to tell Congress about the more than five hundred POWs he had tracked up to the end of the war. If I hadn't seen these cases, I would have found it difficult to believe what was now happening to that highly decorated Vietnam vet sometimes known as "Jimbo," Colonel James "Bo" Gritz.

He had sworn out affidavits for both the Christic Institute and for the Mark Waple lawsuit. He had been warned by government contacts, he said, not to speak publicly any more about Bohica-style missions. He quoted Colonel Jerry King, then chief of the Intelligence Support Activity, as saying, "There are still too many bureaucrats in Washington who do not want to see POWs returned alive."

Six years after his first attempt at a rescue mission in 1981, he took a team of American volunteers into the Golden Triangle to bring back statements from General Khun Sa. The chief of the breakaway "Shan State" was naming federal government officials who allegedly knew how the Joint Casualty Resolution Center, the POW/MIA bureau in Bangkok, was a cover. He named Americans who, he said, had been trafficking in illegal drugs. Jerry "Hog" Daniels was one official named by Khun Sa who, at this time, was viewed by the U.S. government as a major drug baron, so that his statements were open to question.

Now Gritz was being investigated by federal agents, and was under subpoena to appear before a federal grand jury, in connection with allegations that he had misused his passport on his Southeast Asia excursions. In conversations with me at his home in Sandy Valley, Nevada, he gave an account of "harassment" of himself and of members of the team he had taken into the Golden Triangle. On the face of it, they seemed to have been ill-used. According to Gritz, one team member, Lance Trimmer, had been deprived of all his Burma notes, documents, and tapes while he was held by U.S. Customs, without charge, on the Canada-U.S. border.

Gritz was unquestionably flamboyant. He had appeared in Perot's Dallas office with running weights fastened around his ankles. He was soliciting help and explained that he had to keep fit for his arduous adventures. Yet Perot refused to join the chorus of jeers. "Gritz is an obstinate man. He's proven his bravery in war. He's stuck to his guns despite everything the government's done to him – and I'm satisfied he did work for the U.S. government on those 1981 missions."

In November 1986, Gritz and a CBS cameraman with whom I had worked, Wade Bingham, had been turned back by Thai authorities in Bangkok upon their arrival there from Los Angeles. By this time, narco-terrorism and illegal drugs had become a hot item at the top of the news every night. Gritz was trying to reach Khun Sa by way of northern Thailand, in the hope of recording his views on how to stop part of the drug trade. Both Americans had unblemished records. It seemed strange they should be refused entry by Thai Immigration, on advice from U.S. law-enforcement agencies. Bingham was at the top of his profession, and highly respected and well known throughout Asia. Nothing like this had happened to him before.

Bo Gritz had tried again and finally reached the warlord's base camp by a modern, well-paved highway – rather mocking the stories of others who had described arduous treks by mule-train. He gave me the names of government officials who had, he said, authorized him to question the drug warlord. Some of these officials later disowned him, once the investigation was launched. But not all. Defense-intelligence reports would later be made available to me in 1989 that demonstrated Gritz had been encouraged to look for missing American prisoners by government officials. He returned to the Golden Triangle in late spring 1987 to obtain a formal statement on film from Khun Sa, who now claimed to be commander-in-chief of the republic he had established by force of arms on the borders of Thailand, Burma, and Laos. It then became more evident why Gritz had been disowned.

Khun Sa claimed he wanted to end his own people's economic dependency on drugs. He added to his statement yet another appeal for U.S. support, and he sent copies to a lot of the media. "The world accuses us of being the main culprit for all the drug trade. We are eager to solve the drug problems [but] find high U.S. government officials and agents of U.S. drug enforcement wish us to continue. Our peoples want to grow food crops. They cannot switch, however, unless they receive help to tide them over the period necessary for substituting opium poppies."

Again, in June 1987, Khun Sa repeated to Gritz for the record, that he had evidence to show why the Golden Triangle was prevented from getting out of the drug trade. He requested again that the U.S. government help his people build a legitimate farming economy.

Videotapes of the Khun Sa interview were copied by Gritz's supporters in the United States. Most were former Vietnam vets with small businesses of their own. My husband, being familiar with Khun Sa's domain – some 765,000 square miles of hill country, perfect for growing opium poppies – viewed the tape with me. Bill had written about this territory in *The Yellow Wind, Travels in and Around China*, published by Houghton Mifflin, Boston, in 1961.

I asked if I could get in there.

After a pause, Bill said, "You'd probably need a *laissez-passer* like the old Chinese warlords used to issue for travellers passing through the fiefdoms in China." He pulled out old maps. He was actually enthusiastic about the idea. "Narcotics played a part in fighting the Japanese in that area. Bernard Fergusson, the former Governor General in New Zealand, led jungle commandos in the area during World War II. He took me through the documents on how promises were made to the Shan ethnic majority in Upper Burma. They'd get independence in return for fighting on our side. They were paid in part through opium. When the Chinese moved down, they expanded the opium business. Khun Sa is cleverly pushing 'Shan State' claims to independence that the Allies underwrote. . . . "

He restored an old red-ink line he'd drawn long ago across a wrinkled map of Thailand. "The so-called 'China White trail' – southwest China . . . the old Burma Road. Hills covered in red opium poppies under blue skies in the middle of December."

"China White heroin originates with the Communists?"

"Who knows? Most of the opium armies work both sides of the street. Back in the New York area, the police say ninety percent of heroin comes from Laos. You can see from the map that, to get out, the traffickers join up with the Golden Triangle route and so down to Bangkok. . . . "

The drug trade started before the CIA's secret war, and continued better than before, with groundwork laid by everyone who had ever come from abroad to fight there. Khun Sa had taken over from General Li Wen-huan, a Nationalist Chinese who persuaded the CIA in the 1950s that his forces wanted to 'return to the mainland.' It was a dream. 'Return to the mainland' was Nationalist China's theme song while exiled in Taiwan, and that's where General Li retired, very rich on opium. Khun Sa's army would never invade China, either. The Russians meddled with the shifting alliances in the area, but access was difficult so long as the Soviet Union was in conflict with mainland China.

"When you ask if China White originates with the Communists, it depends how far back you go. Opium was milked by the French colonial *Régie de l'opium* to fight the Communists of their day. Opium was the 'foreign mud' used by British merchants to open China's doors to trade, centuries ago."

I found there was a way to reach Khun Sa by going through Rangoon, the Burmese capital, where the government wanted to get rid of the drug warlord and occupy his "free state." My friend in the State Department's intelligence bureau told me, "You'd be very unwise to see Khun Sa. The U.S. government is going all out to convince the media that Khun Sa is one of the most vicious drug traffickers." My friend suggested I could draw my own conclusions from the four-volume report of the Australian Joint Task Force on Drug Trafficking. This had heralded the royal commission on Nugan Hand's reputed laundering of drug money. Some of that money passed through the Nugan Hand branch at Chiang Mai, the nearest respectable Thai location to General Khun Sa's territory. Khun Sa had lived there for a time. Why would a financial empire open an office in what was then a remote hill station?

An Australian diplomat met me in England to take me to a Khun Sa representative. I saw the Asian at the Ritz in Piccadilly in May 1987. He had a brigand's face, and the manners of an aristocrat. Yes, he said, Khun Sa would certainly receive me, because he genuinely wanted an exit from this trap his people had fallen into. "We see what's happened in Laos," he said. "It's the biggest of Communist producers of illegal drugs." He called Laos a rogue signatory to international agreements, absolutely refusing to give the United Nations any drug production figures. This was true.

I sent Khun Sa a set of questions. When I rejoined Bill, then in New York, a reply had come from Khun Sa, through our attorney-agent there, Paul Gitlin. It claimed that some American prisoners had been put into camps inside China, just north of the Vietnam border.

"The Russians said American prisoners *were* moved into China," I commented.

Bill looked surprised. I handed him an old newspaper clipping. It reported U.S. prisoners in Yunnan, the Chinese province adjoining Vietnam. The piece was by a well-known KGB agent, Vitaly Levin, who used the pseudonym Victor Louis.

Bill read from the article: "Hanoi has moved American prisoners to China, out of reach of any U.S. rescue attempts. . . . The camp exactly duplicates Vietnamese conditions so the prisoners remain unaware of their new location in China. . . . "

He scratched his chin. The dateline was February 1, just before the first 1973 release of American prisoners from Vietnam. " 'Victor Louis' was then Moscow correspondent for the London *Evening News*," said Bill.

"Why plant the story?" I asked.

"Russia was scrapping with China. Moscow propaganda wanted to stop China moving closer to the United States. . . . A report like this would make mischief."

"Victor Louis" had been built up by the KGB as a bona fide journalist filing to the West. The Central Committee of the Communist Party of the Soviet Union (CCCPSU) fed Louis hard news that wasn't important to Russian security. It built up his credibility. He had broken the news, for example, of the deaths of Soviet leaders. Few Western newsmen did not know Victor Louis was KGB.

I had also received the newsclip from Colonel Earl Hopper, Sr. He had failed to move U.S. authorities to investigate it while he was still running the League of Families. The official U.S. position at the time remained: there were no American prisoners in China or Russia. A highly placed source in the British government told us that he thought there were; and a Canadian government source claimed the Canadian government had conveyed messages from its Beijing embassy concerning such prisoners. They were described – in the intelligence parlance Jerry Mooney had told me about – as STs, Special Talents.

"But once Kissinger and Nixon began playing their 'China card,' the existence of Americans held against their will in China became a Washington no-no," I said.

"And I bet Victor Louis was instructed to embarrass the Chinese with the Americans through that report!" exclaimed Bill.

I remembered Red McDaniel's Russian visitors, the men who came just before the return of Kelly Patterson's identification card. They must have known something, as must my Russian film-makers.

I was at Red's home to discuss all this when he finally got confirmation that his navigator had been alive when officialdom said he was dead.

CHAPTER 17

BURIED LISTS

The shock was delivered by Mike Van Atta.

He staggered through McDaniel's side door from his car, carrying cardboard boxes stuffed with "secret" files, material on prisoners coaxed from wartime buddies who now had access to intelligence archives. By day, he still ran his own business. Then, almost nightly from three o'clock in the morning until dawn, he fed MIA intelligence into his home computers and tried through sheer persistence to crunch out some answers. A gruff, challenging personality, he took every opportunity to display contempt for government witnesses at congressional POW/MIA hearings. He would wear a lapel button inscribed "General Imbecile," and if any spectator shyly requested information, he would teach them to pronounce the name Im-Beh-Cheeleh, Italian-style, and suggest they call him at a Defense Intelligence Agency number. The number was that of a DIA officer whose handling of prison-camp intelligence provoked Van Atta's frustrated rage.

Sitting by Red's big old-fashioned fireplace, he fished out a dog-eared government document with symbols denoting Americans in various stages: missing, believed killed; believed to have died in captivity; known to be captive; thought to be dead; or maybe alive. The information was assembled from "indigenous" eyewitness accounts. It looked to me like the war condensed in a ledger whose smudged figures recorded no profit, only loss.

Mike Van Atta had gotten the document from the National Archives – simply by asking for it. It contained lists that had come to the archives from DIA and the Commander-in-Chief of the Pacific. The lists showed there were other families like Diane Van Renselaar's, whose men were known to be POWs by the U.S. government, at the same time as it declared it knew nothing about them up to and past 1973.

Red seized the file and retreated to a corner. Van Atta continued to dredge up official-looking papers. I was thinking this might be a good time to get him to talk about his part in the war.

Suddenly a stillness fell over the two men. Van Atta paused in the act of spreading some files on the floor. Red put down a list of names.

"Kelly would be *forty-five* years old today," Red whispered.

"Ah, you found him," said Van Atta.

There it was, the name of Red's navigator. Kelly Patterson – a prisoner; possibly died in captivity.

James Kelly Patterson. Special Talent. Qualified to sit in Red's A-6 and operate DIANE: Digital Integrated Attack Navigational Equipment. A man coveted by the Chinese and the Soviets. To them, DIANE had been a mystery back when he and Red were shot down in 1967.

"Patterson is *dead!*" McDaniel had been told when he was released from Hanoi's jails. "The kindest thing you can do for his parents is convince them this is so." And Red had carried this harsh message to his navigator's family and ended their six years' faith that Kelly was alive – somewhere.

Now Red said, "Kelly was never reported a prisoner. Yet here it is – 'a prisoner, *possibly* died in captivity'. . . . "

Red dropped the document on his coffee table, which was made of teak from the *Lexington*, the last carrier with a wooden flight deck. It had been Red's last command, I thought irrelevantly while I studied the names of others on the list. They were in tiny smudged print, each assigned a single line, no spacing. To describe how each was lost, the words had to be minuscule: "chute seen to open," phrases like that, followed by abbreviations for the location of shoot-downs and then stark letters like PDIC for "Presumed Died in Captivity." In this way, for an American who had travelled halfway round the world to fight, life ended in intelligence hieroglyphics.

Van Atta had made a glossary of logograms and acronyms to help vets and their families interpret such reports. He said, "Special Talents were taken to this island. . . . " He spread out a map of Lake Thui Bac, drawn on the basis of Vietnamese refugee reports. This was set beside an aerial photograph of the same area. The two were the same. The island was called Ho Thac-Bac; it was in the lake, by a river near Hanoi. It was said by Vietnamese defectors to be the holding area from which captured American technicians, Special Talents, were sent to China. I recognized it from Bobby Garwood's own description. He had given different spellings, but that counted in Garwood's favor because English translations were always erratic if they were not copied from standard military maps. When others had said Special Talents were sent to China and Russia, nobody paid attention.

General Tighe reported to the Solarz hearings that "we are getting reports the Vietnamese gave some of our men to the Chinese and Russians," and that part of his testimony had been deleted at government request. Instead, the League of Families issued another "Press Guidance" for its members: *Officially, no American prisoners were sent to Russia or China.* When I had asked Armitage in the Pentagon about repeated "sightings" of live Americans being surrendered to Chinese or Russian officers, he had denied it. And now – Van Atta's list! It confirmed that some in the government did know all along that STs were sent to Vietnam's more powerful allies.

Red's bonds with Kelly Patterson had been so powerful that he had always felt the back-seater survived the crash. Now he blamed himself for not trusting his intuition.

Red found the gap between desk-bound administrators and the fighting men was illustrated by the intelligence debriefers who told him to accept Kelly's death. This gap in understanding went back to the Vietnam War itself. Red found another clue after a lecture he gave at Colorado State University. A Captain Van Hough of United Airlines came up to his old Navy colleague. In a hurry to get on with their lives in different parts of the country, they had not seen each other since before Red was shot down. Van Hough had been one of the backup pilots who circled protectively over McDaniel and Patterson after they bailed out. He said to Red, "The whole rescue effort was badly botched by military command in Saigon. The admirals were livid."

I got the full story myself from Van Hough. He said Red McDaniel had only just come back from an Alpha Strike against Package 6, a bridge south of Hanoi. Then he'd been turned around for another Alpha Strike against a truck-repair depot. Alpha Strikes were flown to visual-flight rules, which meant sitting in the sights of the missiles and anti-aircraft guns growing in number along the bus route. The predictability of the route and their inability to adjust strikes to fit the changing enemy tactics angered the pilots, who were sitting ducks. Their targets were selected in Washington and the pilots were tired of risking their necks when they could *see* more valuable targets. One consequence was that now Red was down, and those giant brains in Saigon had ordered the Jolly Green Giant rescue helicopters based in Thailand to hold off while intelligence analysts studied the area.

"Those Jolly Green Gs would have gone," Van Hough explained. "For those guys, it was like finding your way to your own bathroom at night. They knew those hills and valleys. They knew which way to turn. They could do it blindfolded."

But U.S. Military Command in Saigon (MACV) finally sent orders to the rescue mission to stand down. McDaniel and Patterson had fallen into a high-risk area.

"The admirals went ballistic," said Van Hough. "They wanted McDaniel and Patterson back. Well, MACV didn't control the fleet, and the admirals decided to send in our own choppers. Navy helicopters were not built for long and tricky overland flights. . . . Still, we had to do something when the second day came round, knowing McDaniel and Patterson were hiding out in jungle, *waiting.* . . . " Red still had radio contact with U.S. aircraft, although he had no communication with Patterson, who had dropped on the other side of a mountain.

They'd been shot down on the birthday of Ho Chi Minh, the Communist leader in Hanoi. May 19, 1967, had been the worst day for pilots in McDaniel's Air Wing: seven shoot-downs. McDaniel was on his eighty-first mission. He was exhausted by the constant flying, but he was determined to complete his fair share of the Alpha Strikes. And now he was down.

On board the carrier, they rigged their own rescue plans. The ship's helicopters hadn't the range to fly all the way in and back again. So the pilots would fly extra machines loaded with fuel, the whole airborne fleet making a one-way trip to a mountaintop in Laos. There they would remove the gas from one helicopter, which would be scuttled, and top up the tanks of the rest. One chopper would go in for the downed airmen, and return to where another acted as tanker, holding fuel for the return flight to the carrier. "We would wind up having to scuttle two choppers," said Van Hough. "Everyone would cram into what was left." They were ready to launch when word came that McDaniel and Patterson had been captured.

"If we'd had authority from the start, we could have re-covered them," said Van Hough. "Our Navy communica-tions moved with fantastic speed in an emergency. Once, when I went down, I generated a whole *library* of naval messages between my Mayday and my being located and flown back to the carrier. You know, updates, authentica-tions, and double-checks. Saigon wasn't geared for that. They thought politically, not operationally." Van Hough was illustrating one kind of electronic tracking that was done of all prisoners by analysts like Jerry Mooney. He was also demonstrating, of course, the sort of emotion that fighting men invested in rescue missions – an emotion they did not feel was shared by those making bureaucratic decisions.

He said, "We once left one of our guys sitting in his raft because they decided back in Washington the rescue chop-pers would fly too close to China – and we mustn't provoke *those* Reds. So we had to sit listening to his beeper growing fainter and fainter, until it died. Of course, he died with it."

But Patterson had not died. Twenty years after shoot-down, Red confirmed from that chance encounter what had been already known to his squadron mates while he was heading into the jungle and a long darkness. His navigator was alive.

Red was driven by the sense of time lost. He had heard from survivors how the initials K.P. had been carefully mem-orized by witnesses who saw them carved into the underside of prison bunks. He had let his awareness of such evidence subside under the seeming certainty of the policy decision that Patterson was dead. His wife Dorothy wrote to me later, "Red started the toughest battle of his life right then, against an enemy with no face, an enemy behind closed doors and inside sealed filing cabinets, an enemy who attacked by innuendo and outright slander to destroy reputation and integrity."

As more and more stories like Kelly Patterson's surfaced, some in the media took a strong interest. So did the govern-ment, but it seemed the government's objective was to manipulate the media, if necessary, to maintain control of the truth.

One day not long after Van Atta's visit, Red told me that "the government's trying to suppress another television study of the issue." I received the news cautiously. It was easy for a producer to blame some vague censorship system for his own inadequacies. But, as Red elaborated, I found that I knew this producer: Ted Landreth, who had asked me to help with a full-length BBC documentary, *We Can Keep You Forever*. Because of my CBS commitments, I'd refused. Landreth told me now that the White House and the intelligence agencies had been only too ready to help. The BBC had invested a lot of money and a year's research into the project. The BBC's partner in Los Angeles, Lionheart, had overseen production. The program took its title from the statement of a Communist Vietnamese commandant to an American prisoner: "We can keep you forever."

Landreth said, "I wanted to do the decent thing. BBC researchers in Asia had uncovered evidence that the government might not have, and I wanted to be helpful in a good cause. A briefing was set for several government officials.

"They told me they were so glad to deal with someone who was going to do a responsible job, not like *60 Minutes* and ABC's *20/20* and the BBC News Division. I didn't realize I was falling into a trap. I thought, well, maybe their side of the story hasn't been told properly."

Landreth shared his sources with the officials. One such source was a Laotian refugee, who had been a prisoner in Vietnam. He "told a blood-curdling tale of two American POWs in his cell, one of whom died five years after the U.S. government said no Americans were left in captivity. The Laotian never asked for money or favors. Nobody had questioned him before, and when I asked if he'd repeat his story, he was more than willing. He had an old-fashioned loyalty to his former American comrades."

The reaction appeared to be one of gratitude. Time passed. Just before the program was ready to air, one of the government officials called Landreth and said, "I'm sorry to tell you this, but one of your witnesses has just recanted. The Laotian now admits he made up the whole story." Landreth checked with the Laotian, who denied absolutely that he had recanted anything. But he added that his family had received threats.

The Laotian had fought in the secret war for his country, and my husband sought him out. I looked up Bill's notes. "The Laotian, Sam," he wrote, "was under the protection of Bob, the principal of a rural school where Sam worked as a janitor. I could not believe Sam would keep repeating a story that got him into so much trouble *unless it was true*. He'd been so grossly harassed that he had to be prevented from committing suicide.

"Bob told me, 'I'm just a country school-teacher in middle America. I teach pride in our constitutional rights. I give the older children appropriate courses in how we govern ourselves, from local to federal levels. I really believed we were a free and open society. Yet here was the school janitor, being driven to despair by government officials who wanted him to stop telling what he believed to be true. If I wasn't guarding him, God knows where he'd be now.'

"If I'd had any doubts about the Laotian's honesty, I couldn't question Bob's integrity. He was a ruddy-cheeked, open-air type, not a big man and certainly not someone you'd expect to leap to the ramparts in defense of liberty. But he got hopping mad at what was being done to Sam."

We agreed to disguise names and places for the Laotian's own safety. It seemed absurd. He was clearly known to those who threatened that he would be sent back into Communist hands if he continued to talk publicly about his fellow American prisoners. Still, even now, I'm afraid to set down his name in cold print.

Sam was interviewed on film by an acquaintance of mine with NBC-TV News. Having heard that I had experienced efforts to convince me not to produce "Dead or Alive," she asked me, weeks later, if I thought she was becoming paranoid. She said, "I can't seem to get this item on air." I said no, I didn't think she was paranoid, and I told her some of the things I had experienced. "That makes me feel better," she responded. "I wasn't going to go into this . . . but my executive producer received a complaint from the government. They said I got the interview with the Laotian by passing myself off as a government agent."

That also was absurd. Anyone remotely familiar with the news business would know just how absurd it was. What rattled my friend, though, was that just for a tiny little moment her bosses had wondered . . . Could she have behaved unethically?

How much harder it must be for the Sams and the Bobs to fight such slanders.

Red McDaniel was also aware of the effort to discredit the documentary. His son, Mike McDaniel, still on active duty as an officer in the Navy, sent Red a copy of a memo his unit had received from the Department of the Navy and attached a note: "Dad . . . This is the kind of crap they are telling the public-affairs officers. . . . "

Issued by the Department of Defense, it was titled "Guidance – BBC Documentary, 'MIA: We Can Keep You Forever.' " It dismissed as false "several statements alluding to the possibility that U.S. personnel may have been moved to China or the Soviet Union." It denied that U.S. personnel with specialized knowledge, such as electronic warfare, were unaccounted for in any greater percentage than others.

The "Guidance" stated that "during the conduct of the government's investigations, the information presented by the sources had proven to be less than credible. There was little if anything in the way of new information presented. Virtually all information presented is known to the U.S.

Government, was previously investigated at length and found to contain no proof of Americans still held in Indochina."

Lionheart, the BBC's distributor in the United States, had a high batting average in judging its markets. It had confidently predicted that up to seventy-five percent of private television stations would buy the documentary. But local station managers reported being telephoned and urged not to run the film, "in the national interest."

A Lionheart executive told me, "Preposterous statements were made by a League of Families official. . . . Suddenly the same stations that were competing to buy the film lost interest." Lionheart's attorneys warned League officials that the BBC, Lionheart, and individual producers were prepared to defend their rights and reputations against League allegations that the producers admitted knowing the witnesses in the film were fabricators; that all witnesses in the film had been found by American intelligence to be fabricators. . . . These allegations had been tape-recorded.

Sam, the Laotian, did not have the BBC's resources and continued to live in fear that, despite his service as an American citizen, he could be shipped back to Laos, delivered up into the hands of those he'd fought against with the U.S. armed forces.

CHAPTER 18

THE BUSINESS OF COVERT OPS

Sam had fought for the United States in a war conducted secretly in his own country. He had suffered imprisonment for doing this. He had escaped and rejoined his American friends with news he thought they would want to hear. Why was he treated like an enemy? It seemed a simple question, but I could not find anyone to answer it.

"The explanation lies with whoever is formulating this policy," was the most Red McDaniel could suggest. But nobody seemed to know just who that was. I knew Ross Perot was unafraid of what Admiral Stansfield Turner had called "the CIA culture." Perot had reported adversely on security at the U.S. embassy in Moscow long before it became a national scandal; and although the Presidential Foreign Intelligence Advisory Board was often sneered at by "the sealed fraternity" described by ex-director William Colby,*

---

* Colby, in *Honorable Men: My Life in the CIA*, published by Simon and Schuster in 1978, wrote that the elitism within the agency nonetheless Perot had taken his membership very seriously.

He took it seriously enough that he would never be caught discussing what he knew with outsiders. So when I put the question about Sam to him, he suggested that I talk with the jailed CIA agent Ed Wilson, the man who had made the business of running CIA proprietaries a fine and profitable art.

Before I saw Ed Wilson in jail, late in the summer of 1987, I had another face-to-face meeting with Casino Man. There was a coldness in him until he described the first time he stumbled across American prisoners during an intelligence mission in the early 1980s. He could not help those prisoners without jeopardizing the mission, but he promised himself to work for their release. He showed me the complex system of observation and interrogation by which he had pinpointed a number of American prisoners, all of which he reported to his intelligence colleagues. But, he said, he was told to forget what he knew. The reaction of the government, he said, was a shocking betrayal of Americans who went to war in uniform, and of Casino Man himself. He no longer felt part of an institution that fought to destroy a well-defined enemy.

A few hours after this conversation, I was in the U.S. Penitentiary at Marion, Illinois, listening to CIA ex-agent Ed Wilson unwittingly reinforce some of Casino Man's claims.

Ed Wilson had been a business partner with other veterans of the secret wars in Asia who then moved along to running arms and peddling explosives in the Mideast. Wilson got caught and was jailed for selling C-4 explosives and terrorist weapons to Libya.

---

caused intelligence bureaucrats to clique together, "forming a sealed fraternity. They ate together at their own special favorite restaurants; they partied almost only among themselves. . . . They increasingly separated themselves from the ordinary world and developed . . . an inbred, distorted, elitist view of intelligence that held itself to be above the normal processes of society . . . beyond the restraints of the Constitution. . . ." (p. 87).

As Prisoner No. 08237054 he now sat in a concrete cubicle in a fortress-like prison. He was said to be frightened that his old buddies in something that he called "The Enterprise" might kill him. Yet he was bursting to talk about his time in Indochina and why, as he saw it, any genuine effort to recover missing American servicemen had to be blocked. He arrived in handcuffs, entered the small interview room, and turned to push his wrists through an opening in the heavy steel door to have the cuffs removed.

Then I was alone with him. He gestured courteously for me to sit down, and I glimpsed another person, the old CIA hand: a powerful physical presence. He was like a watchful all-knowing cat. He smiled wanly when I put the tape-recorder between us.

"All I want," I began, "is anything you know about missing Americans. Site 85, for instance."

"Ted Shackley was the CIA man in charge. He'd have tried to rescue his own CIA guys."

"But not Americans in uniform?"

"Shackley's a super-duper paper-pusher. When it comes to getting out and getting the job done, he doesn't know much about combat. He's a technocrat. He'd want the *technology* out of Site 85."

"And let the military guys go hang?"

Wilson shrugged.

"Is there any reason for covering up the way we abandoned them?" I persisted.

Wilson became cagey. "What we did selling arms, we did it sort of legal. I'll explain that," he said. "On drugs – I'm willing to tell the whole story but only providing you get a guarantee of immunity from _____." He named a foreign government. "They'd wipe me out otherwise."

"How could the smuggling of arms be made legal?"

His tone harshened as he described the ways in which arms were sold. The Iran-Contra hearings were in progress, and he interrupted himself frequently to clarify his ties with witnesses appearing on his TV set. For days now, he had watched that small box in his sunless cubicle, with nothing but his cot, his toilet, and the concrete floor. "If I'm guilty," he repeated, "they're guilty. . . . " He dropped several names, including that of a man he described as "once the most powerful guy in the Pentagon, Erich Fritz von Marbod."

For the next four hours, I taped Wilson's recollections. He had worked, he said, with those who believed in covert warfare in Vietnam. After the 1973 peace accords, the group had formulated an unofficial policy that said that sentiment must never again get in the way of fighting communism. The group had decided that past U.S. policy was the work of "pinkos" and Marxist sympathizers back in Washington. At the war's end, they moved enormous quantities of U.S. military hardware out of Communist reach. Where they finally sent this huge arsenal only a select few seemed to know precisely, though various stories were told to Congress.

"We'd learned that wealth and real power reside in a small basement room in the Pentagon that handles Defense Department supplies of weapons to foreign allies granted U.S. military aid," said Wilson. "This dinky unit down in the bowels of the Pentagon, the Defense Security Assistance Agency, DSAA, decides how the grant aid is spent. Take Korea – they get together over there and figure U.S. arms aid will be $600 million this year. The different services put in their bids. Finally the CIA and State and the rest get a consensus about types of weapons. Meanwhile the U.S. manufacturers are selling the hell out of their weapons to the guys in Korea, while back in Washington they're all kissing von Marbod's ass. . . . " Von Marbod was the first comptroller of DSAA.*

---

* The difficulties in bringing legal action against the misuse of such activities became apparent in two Pentagon investigations known as "Operation Ill Wind" and "The Fowler Case." Richard Lee Fowler was sentenced to two years in prison on January 12, 1990, for what the *Wall Street Journal* (January 18, 1990) described as "acting as the linchpin in an information-swapping scheme."

Wilson claimed that he found ready helpers in a game that bore a gloss of patriotism. "It started when the U.S. had to supply Israel, whether or not the American public agreed, in 1967," he said. "We learned how to funnel supplies this way and that. . . . For example, suppose I ship automatic pistols to Portugal with arms-control agreement here, but the stuff's really going somewhere that's under embargo. I have to get

---

The *Journal* reported that investigators tied in six big defense contractors with an inside-information ring dubbed "The Clique."

"You will see some additional activity in the coming months," said U.S. Attorney Henry Hudson of Alexandria, Virginia, who had learned to be cautious about bringing prosecutions against wrongdoers in this field. According to the *Wall Street Journal*: "The Justice Department had gotten cold feet, but a stubborn core of Pentagon investigators was still eager to go after The Clique. Congressional interest spurred them on, and the Justice Department's miscalculations bolstered their determination."

It had taken six years to bring Fowler into court, according to testimony at Fowler's trial which noted that, back in 1983, the Pentagon investigation was looking at Fowler, a midlevel budget analyst with Boeing Company, because of his weekly reports on what should have been confidential Pentagon decisions on forthcoming weapons' plans. The *Wall Street Journal* added that interviews with scores of government and defense-industry officials, in addition to the trial evidence, showed "a tight-knit circle of about a dozen defense executives violated U.S. military secrecy by ferreting out the Pentagon's multi-billion-dollar spending plans. . . . Involving executives of major companies, highly sensitive Pentagon data and billions of dollars in weapons contracts, the [Fowler] case is one of the most sweeping white-collar criminal inquiries in years. Prosecutors say The Clique may have compromised the military's long-range plans more seriously than the bribery and influence-peddling uncovered by a separate investigation known as 'Operation Ill Wind.' "

Details can be found in court reports and documents from the Fowler trial, contemporary newspaper reports of 1989-90, and the *Wall Street Journal*, January 18, 1990.

the stuff signed off over there in Portugal, by their police or Defense Department, and by someone in our embassy. Well, that costs ten percent in payoffs. Then I'm free to ship the arms anywhere. . . . When an ally needs DSAA planes, they go through our supply system with their computers, then we use them to trans-ship to the *contras* in Nicaragua or wherever. . . . The big money is creamed off in the resale. . . . "

He was talking now at such a clip, I was grateful for the tape recorder. He spelled out details of who did what, where, and when. "A lot of the information is in my court papers that are now under seal. _____ [a foreign power] wanted the papers sealed so they can keep the second tier in place."

Was he saying that a foreign country fostered the group? How could the super-patriots who had once worked with Wilson justify secretly working with a foreign government? Wasn't that treason?

We were observed by the prison's closed-circuit cameras. Wilson would not compromise himself by answering. Only a miracle or death would get him out of jail now. He knew too much.

His eyes betrayed a flash of fear. They were cold eyes, normally, even when he became a huge schoolboy, chuckling at how he'd hoodwinked the adults. Now, as he briefly confessed that perhaps there was an abstract system of justice slowly accumulating *all* the facts, those professionally remote eyes opened a fraction wider.

I took advantage of that glimpse of weakness. "Was it necessary to forget American prisoners? I mean, if their existence had been admitted, the American public would demand action. Then the offline sales of arms – and drugs – would be exposed."

"The drug trade is the lesser evil," said Wilson, eyes cold again, despite that affable smile.

"You knew General Vang Pao?"

"In Long Tieng. I used to see Vang Pao in his office. He would point upstairs and say, 'That's where the real war is!' He had seven wives up there, one from each Hmong clan. He was finally brought back to the United States. That's when Vang Pao stayed with me in Virginia."

Vang Pao and the Hmong were flown out. Why not American prisoners?" I asked.

"The CIA had no time to weep over prisoners. The Hmong were flown out because they could be infiltrated back into Laos later. This was an illustration of the secret power of the group," said Wilson.

"But all of a sudden Carter's elected. Big panic!" Wilson insisted that Stansfield Turner, President Carter's choice for the CIA, tried to rid the agency of what he considered excessive and unconstitutional secrecy and dirty tricks. "Some of them said, 'It's time we made some money.' "

The Nugan Hand Group was a big money-maker. "It was an old concept – done before, and will be done again," said Wilson. He had set up branches and companies himself, he said, then handed them over to the CIA. The first big money, after Nugan Hand opened base operation in Australia, was mutual funds from oil workers in Mideast countries. "They didn't want American Internal Revenue to skim the cream off their income. Then we got the military to invest, that kind of crap, so there were large funds swilling around to cover the CIA stuff. When the EATSCO [his company] thing blew up in my face, I was running a CIA proprietary. . . . "

There was nothing wrong, I thought, with military men sticking to their guns. But Ed Wilson was never a military man. I left the prison and flew on to meet with Bill, who was seeing some of the old Military Assistance Command Vietnam crowd introduced to him by Colonel Nick Rowe. They had outlined a loose organizational structure that operated within various government departments and on which the POW/MIA issue seemed to have foundered.

I thought there was nothing wrong, either, with like-minded covert-warfare specialists continuing to believe this was the conflict of the future. They followed The Third Option concept, outlined in the textbook of the same name by Theodore Shackley, published in New York by Reader's Digest Press. Perhaps the ideal secret war really was the kind in which you gave arms and advice to two sides, neither of whom you much liked, and let them bleed each other to death. The handsome profits this could yield for some had not been laid out in the original Third Option proposal. This envisaged the lean arm of muscular liberal-democracy fighting Communism in the Third World by winning hearts and minds, and stemmed from those highly classified operations launched throughout Southeast Asia in 1958 – and which were supposed to have ended in 1973. The CIA had started with an organization nominally created by the South Vietnamese government, the Special Exploitation Service (SES), whose task was to conduct highly secret operations in North and South Vietnam, Laos, Cambodia, South China, and the borderlands.

Bill had confirmed this from a Pentagon study on special-warfare units. He pencilled a sketch of the many sub-units that eventually grew out of the MACV–Special Operations Group (SOG). One, FANK (Forces Armée Nationale Khmer Training Command), had an authorized strength of only 423 and was deactivated on no given date, although official records listed deactivation dates for the other MACV-SOG commands around the time of the Paris Peace Accords in 1973. It was apparent, from the history of SOG, that titles were changed to mislead the public.

One of MACV-SOG's overall responsibilities was defined as "Keeping track of all missing Americans and conducting raids to assist and free them. . . . "

The accusation levelled by Casino Man was that decisions on prisoners were being made by some people who were only interested in CIA personnel. And Bill said this was borne out by a former special-forces commander who had given him the basis of the sketch he believed was accurate. "It purports to show what happened when special operations officially closed down," said Bill. "A sort of rogue branch of MACV-SOG – is the most secretive. Some in the rogue group supposedly made the decisions about dumping American prisoners unless they were CIA – and the decisions about when to stop bothering about any prisoners, or whether certain ones should be killed as dangerous to U.S. national security.

My friend said, when our part in the war seemed to be ending, it was decided to hold back prisoner information.

The reason for holding back prisoner information was to protect on-going activities. But the activities also generated a great deal of money. And although Ed Wilson was a convicted criminal, he had seemed to be speaking truthfully to me when he described the point being reached when patriotism and profit came together – at least for some.

Thousands of tons of U.S. weapons were moved out of Vietnam between the 1973 ceasefire and the 1975 evacuation of Saigon. Von Marbod had testified to this secret removal of arms and equipment before Congress. Some of the military hardware had been traced to Thailand, where it appeared to have been sold to overseas buyers. A new broom at the top of the CIA swept away some of these officials but never did disclose what was discovered about the fate of the missing arms. That, too, would have been "a victory for the enemy."

CHAPTER 19

THE SLEAZE FACTOR

Erich Fritz von Marbod, despite the German-sounding name, was born in Wenatchee, Washington State, in 1929. He had been a liaison officer with "40 Committee." This originated in 1955 with the National Security Council directives providing for oversight of secret operations by "designated representatives." After 1976 it had been replaced by the Operations Advisory Group, following the Presidential Executive Order that "no employee of the U.S. government shall engage in, or conspire to engage in, political assassination."

Von Marbod's 40 Committee job had been to work with the U.S. Phoenix program in Vietnam, which worked with MACV-SOG. Phoenix did not officially authorize assassinations by U.S. citizens. "Phoenix was about pacification, not assassination, Shackley insists," wrote Ron Rosenbaum in *Vanity Fair* of January 1990. Rosenbaum pointed out that former CIA chief and one-time Phoenix administrator William Colby "testified that about 20,000 alleged VC (Communist) cadres died as a result of these deadly visits to their villages." Critics of the program put the casualties as high as 40,000 and even 60,000 dead. *Vanity Fair* added: "But the CIA was not responsible for these deadly mistakes, Shackley says, because it just collated the lists. 'We did not have operational control over Phoenix,' he says. It was the other guys, 'the South Vietnamese military and police that did the shooting. We did collecting, collation, we were the evaluation mechanism,' he says. 'Assassination was not part of our charter.' "

On February 3, 1975, von Marbod, as Comptroller of the Defense Security Assistance Agency, did not mention his 40 Committee role to a Congressional Defense Appropriations Committee: "I manage military assistance programs for grant aid recipient countries and credit associated with foreign military sales," he said.

The FBI became interested in von Marbod after discovering his name in Ed Wilson's notebooks. Von Marbod announced he suffered from narcolepsy – a disease that causes one to fall asleep suddenly and remember nothing. He resigned abruptly in December 1982, after nearly thirty years in government service, and settled abroad.

Wilson had his own motives for blaming others. Unless he could get a retrial by arguing that he was only following what he thought was U.S. government policy, Wilson was in jail for life. According to Wilson, POWs and MIAs were a nuisance whose disappearance from the books would have to be explained away. Anyone snooping around the issue found evidence of other activities. He described those activities as being concealed by the careful exploitation of bureaucratic methods to promote members of what he'd called "a second tier" of government.

When von Marbod was examining U.S. arms in Vietnam after the war, one of Johnny Shaheen's friends had been with Task Force 157. Force 157, though camouflaged inside the office of Naval Research, was supposed to monitor Soviet shipping, but it also ran more than a hundred CIA proprietaries. Shaheen said his friend had regularly flown to Australia from Bangkok to deposit the funds raised by the sale of weapons and drugs to be used later for financing covert operations. The report of the Australian police inquiry into the Nugan Hand financial empire reported "many links connected with the group and individuals who are in turn connected in very significant ways with U.S. intelligence organizations, specifically CIA and Task Force 157. . . . At times those links appear to have been an intrinsic part of the then ongoing activity and have the appearance of direct involvement of the U.S. intelligence community itself." The Royal Commission appointed by the Australian federal government, however, stated there was no proof of CIA involvement. The Australian police kept their own counsel, since the matter had been raised to the level of diplomacy and national security.

An internal Pentagon inquiry found that a group of von Marbod's old colleagues had cashed in on his inside knowledge of Jimmy Carter's decision to give Egypt some $4 billion in military aid, reported Peter Maas in his book on Ed Wilson, *Manhunt.** That year, according to Wilson, he was made a partner of the insiders' Egyptian-American Transport and Services Corporation (EATSCO).

The group of people who formed the partnership could not have been naive about Ed Wilson's background. He had been fired from Task Force 157 by the then-director of U.S. Naval Intelligence, Admiral Bobby Ray Inman, after Wilson asked Inman in 1974 to steer a few contracts in his direction. The admiral's reactions were also chronicled by Peter Maas in *Manhunt*. Inman, who would become director of the National Security Agency and then deputy director of the CIA, dissolved 157 because it "reeked of bribery." He passed Wilson's name to the FBI as an obvious grafter. Shackley,

---

* Published in 1986 by Random House (New York), *Manhunt* explored the relationship between Theodore Shackley and Tom Clines, "two key high-level CIA contacts." Inman's comment on Task Force 157 is quoted on p. 57.

who was then deputy director of CIA operations, according to Ed Wilson, appealed on Wilson's behalf for "a reprieve." Later, Shackley would deny that he had any kind of involvement with Wilson, claiming that his friendship with the convicted former CIA man came about because their wives were social friends.

There was a custodial account in Bermuda for Wilson's own Liberian-registered company, International Research and Trade. I heard some familiar names among the registered directors cited by Wilson. When I had asked Wilson if his own name was there, he laughed. "I learned long ago to keep my name off everything possible. I moved money through IR&T to my security firm, Systems Services International, and that's how EATSCO was formed."

The *New York Times* obtained grand-jury transcripts showing von Marbod approved exclusive U.S. government contracts for EATSCO in 1979, authorizing an advance payment of $13.5 million for shipping costs. Investigators alleged all the money was put into a Swiss banking account, at taxpayers' expense. A series of advances followed, totalling $71 million.

The story of Wilson and EATSCO broke in the *Times* after President Reagan took office in 1981. Reagan's new CIA director, Bill Casey, as good as accused the *Times* of serving communism by publishing the facts. Outside investigators became accustomed to hearing that "any questionable billings probably went into covert operations that we cannot talk about." Auditors nonetheless found EATSCO fraudulently billing the Pentagon for some $8 million, in addition to making inflated profits.

General Richard Secord, who had been involved in arms sales as Deputy Secretary of Defense for the Near East and Southeast Asia, was suspended from his arms-sale duties. After a grand-jury investigation, he was reinstated in 1982, despite the Pentagon's General Counsel. When Frank Carlucci became National Security Advisor, the March 1987 issue of *Conservative Digest* raised some questions. The magazine's Contributing Editor, Kathryn McDonald, wrote:

> The selection of Carlucci . . . while his predecessor [Robert C. McFarlane] is under investigation with respect to the Iran arms transfers, and alleged diversion of funds, is absolutely amazing – considering Carlucci has ties . . . via his protege Erich von Marbod. . . .
>
> Keep in mind that these people are associates of Edwin Wilson who amassed tens of millions of dollars by illegally selling weapons, explosives and expertise to Libya's Qaddafi and other Third World pariahs.

The *Conservative Digest* had investigated a "sleaze factor" in depth after publishing an article in December 1985 by former New Hampshire Governor Meldrim Thomson, charging that "elements of our government have deliberately debunked live-sighting reports and keep the facts from the American public." Many Republicans who were aware of the POW issue were troubled. It was common knowledge to them that some of the people mentioned in McDonald's article had begun their business deals in Southeast Asia under the same cloak of secrecy that encompassed the missing. The August 1986 *Conservative Digest*, in a cover story, insisted there were hundreds of Americans still alive in Southeast Asia, held against their will.

"There's a secret world that protects itself," Jerry Mooney had once told me. Mooney was the intelligence analyst who claimed he had tracked some six hundred American prisoners up until the last day of war. He said, "I have the electronically filed intelligence on the prisoners, but secrecy rules prevent me from publishing them." There were few in the secret world Mooney was talking about who signed anything.

There was an echo of this, on another issue involving secrecy and covert action, during the Iran-Contra hearings when General Secord appeared on ABC-TV's *Nightline* and was asked by Ted Koppel, "You spent a lifetime in covert operations?"

"That is correct," said Secord.

"People would say, 'Ah, Secord, sly dog, never signed anything.' "

"That is correct," said Secord.

Admiral Inman's first complaint about Ed Wilson to the FBI was apparently not to be found in that agency's files, despite its reputation for never losing paper of any kind. "If the FBI had investigated," said Bill, "Wilson would have been stopped dead in his tracks years earlier."

He was sitting with me in the legal library of his New York agent, Paul Gitlin, comparing notes. We were coming to the reluctant conclusion that within security-blanketed bureaucracies, the truth could be whatever you decided it should be. In Wilson's case, billions of dollars in foreign trading would have been lost if the CIA man's wings had been clipped earlier. Within a culture set up to eradicate evidence of covert missions, though, if someone got caught doing what he shouldn't, the problem was erased as easily as pressing a button. We'd been wise to dig into the case of Ed Wilson because it illustrated on a small scale what might happen to something embarrassing like misuse or non-use of POW/MIA intelligence services. The institutions buried their mistakes in mystery because they were so highly classified. MACV-Special Operations Group, for example, remains a top secret to this day in the minds of many who served it. But there were some who were determined now to break through the secrecy as the only way to get some action on MIAs.

If the MACV-SOG failed in its assigned task of keeping track of imprisoned and missing Americans, was it the result of incompetence? If MACV-SOG intelligence was never properly followed up in later years, could one still believe this was also bureaucratic incompetence?

These questions were being asked of government officials by a group of vets who could not be easily fobbed off: John

Brown's own investigation team, including Tony Drexel Duke, the philanthropist, and Bill LeGro, the former military intelligence chief in Saigon. They were on the same trail as McDaniel, Perot, and Hendon, but there was a subtle difference now in the increased response they got from officials. Iran-Contra had shown them that the intelligence agencies were capable of cover-up – to suit their needs. The team had spent five hours questioning a CIA official and more time still with DIA. They had heard from senior State Department officials how impossible it was to get around a made-in-1973 policy on prisoners. They had confronted numerous intelligence, political, and military notables.

At a meeting with a Deputy Secretary of State, LeGro had said, "It's beyond dispute, from all the evidence I've seen, that American prisoners are still alive in Laos and Vietnam. It's bizarre that government-to-government negotiations are carried out by low-level Pentagon and National Security officials." He then named some of those who had tried to stop production of "Dead or Alive." LeGro and his companions kept a record of the information they gave to those they met. Then, when the truth emerged, the officials could not deny knowledge of it.

Sometimes officialdom pushed the vets to extremes. On one occasion Brown and John LeBoutillier, the former congressman and founder of Skyhook, were waiting in the lobby of the Sheraton Carlton Hotel in Washington, D.C., when the then-Secretary of State, George Shultz, passed them on his way to the barbershop downstairs. On impulse, Brown and his companion followed and caught Shultz in a tilted chair, trapped in a white sheet, with a manicurist's grip upon his hand. Brown stood in front of him and said, "Mr. Secretary, with the greatest respect, I want you to hear this."

He then proceeded, with LeBoutillier's help, to recite facts about prisoners. "We just want it on record," said Brown, "that you have been informed, so you can't say you didn't know when the people find out." Then the Secret Service moved in, leaving a red-faced Shultz silent in his barber chair. As the security men hustled the intruders out, one told

Brown: "I'm a vet too. . . . I'm glad you did that, though you've probably gotten us into a lot of trouble. . . . "

This sort of comradeship vaulted barriers of rank and social position. Men like Brig. Gen. Harry C. "Heinie" Aderholt seemed to me to be at war with themselves. He'd been given a free hand with his "Air Commandos" and his secret aerial warfare operations. He defended his old buddies associated with the Ed Wilson scandal. But overriding this was loyalty to wartime comrades. He ridiculed the Joint Casualty Resolution Center (JCRC) in Thailand. "It's a farce," he told me. Scott Barnes had told me Aderholt had been in business with Armitage in Thailand and that he had often seen the two together. But recently an anonymous letter had denied that the head of covert ops for the Pentagon ever had more than one lunch with Aderholt. I was skeptical of Barnes's information, but now Aderholt confirmed his long-standing relationship with Armitage.

Richard Armitage had just that day called him, he said, from the Pentagon. "First time we've talked since we split up. The only time he had a job outside the military, he was in business with me."

Armitage had gone to great pains to disclaim having been in business with Aderholt after my *60 Minutes* piece. "He says he scarcely knew you," I told Aderholt. "Remembers vaguely having lunch with you once."

Aderholt was pained. "We had offices in Bangkok and Washington. I know Dick Armitage very well. Our company was called Sea-THAI.

"I'd fallen out with him over the prisoner issue after I called him with specific information. Dick jeered, said, 'Oh no, not again! You got more buffalo bones?' He knows as well as I do we left our boys behind."

"Then why does he continue to say there has never been any evidence of live prisoners to act on?" I asked.

"Dick never did anything to dishonor himself, but I disagree on this matter of the prisoners. I lost thirty of my own men, either prisoners or missing. I personally knew men who were being held in caves. The CIA waged its own war and couldn't get the men back. . . . " Aderholt corrected himself. "The priority for getting them back just wasn't there. How could we desert them? We were getting first-rate intelligence up to the very last day of the war. We claim to know everything about the Soviet Union. Yet we can't penetrate a two-bit country like Laos?"

"What about our counter-terrorist activities," I said.

"That's why I'd like fresh blood in that office," replied Aderholt. "The search for prisoner intelligence is used for other things. . . . The Special Ops people are worried. There's been a long series of unexplained failures. And who are these people in the bureaucracy who strangle every prisoner rescue bid at birth?"

I said I had only discovered their existence because my "Dead or Alive" segment broke the silence.

Aderholt nodded. "They tried to discredit me when I was beating the drum for prisoners. I was accused of cross-border violations in Asia. Same charges that were made against Colonel Howard. And Smith and McIntire – "

One name kept popping up. The man had enormous financial resources. I wanted to use his name. "If you do," I was warned, "he's capable of intimidation by threatening legal action. He could lose the case, but he'll gamble that the legal costs will be so great, nobody will want to risk publishing his name."

I had run into such cases in TV news, when a threat of legal action could chill enthusiasm for a story. I asked Ross Perot. He agreed there was overwhelming evidence of the man's involvement in questionable deals that were made possible by his eminence in public affairs. "But you *can* buy justice," said Perot, "if you're rich enough." It was the sad conclusion of a disillusioned but still patriotic American. So I called this man Sleeper because, although no longer in a powerful government position, he still commanded large resources.

"He seemed to be at the center of the group formed at Three Corners," said Colonel Nick Rowe. "Its philosophy stemmed from the defeat in Vietnam, and a conviction that the CIA could have won by other methods."

I wondered out loud about the usefuless of intelligence agencies if they failed the men and women who did the fighting. Rowe gave me a funny look.

"Secrecy becomes an end in itself," he said. "You can't make use of what you know because it's secret. We can't make use of what we know about those lost in Laos because the whole war there was secret. You know we even lost American girls there?" I replied that women's names had been recovered during research by Earl Hopper and his Task Force Omega. "You ought to take a thorough look at Laos," said Nick Rowe.

I put this to Ross Perot, who said he'd asked DIA for "everything it knew about Laos." This was while Perot still had presidential license to delve into the intelligence archives. He had summoned government experts. "They ran out of things to say after three minutes," he said. "You could put what they knew about Laos on the head of a pin. Laos was this Big Black Hole."

Perot was sitting in his Dallas office, rocking gently in his chair. He said he'd again brought up Jerrold "Hog" Daniels, the CIA man, and rescue missions with Daniels' Laotian guerrillas. "Those guys got real emotional," he said.

"Emotional?"

"If someone says your husband's going to be killed, you get emotional. You follow me? They were upset."

Perot's investigation, even though it was authorized by President Reagan, was running into road blocks. The administration seemed not to have expected that Perot would do the gritty research himself and discover that government officials were actively slandering people who told the truth. The billionaire gathered facts, but he could not disclose official sources without breaking a code of secrecy he believed was possibly self-serving and frequently self-defeating. He could not publicly show the evidence that Colonel Howard and Smith and McIntire spoke the truth, for instance. He would be giving away secrets. He played the game. He presented the facts to those entitled to see confidential information, trusting they would do the right thing. This, he hoped, would defeat those trying to manage the old POW/MIA policy.

But President Reagan was insulated from Perot's facts. Perot felt that Vice President Bush reduced contacts with his old friend. Perot was challenging the infallibility of institutions. Their guardians must have seen him as trying to expose gross failures. I could imagine the arguments that would multiply against him. The public must never doubt the competence of the intelligence machinery it could not see. Anything that threatened this trust also threatened national security.

I was soon to hear of a case that would definitely have led most people to doubt the competence of the intelligence machinery, either to police itself or to protect ordinary citizens from the influx of possibly harmful materials into the country. It would also illustrate, however, the intelligence bureaucracy's superb "cover-up" skills and CIA's seemingly total immunity when it came to shipping things in and out of the country – even when it was suspected of moving drugs.

A former U.S. Army sergeant, now with the FBI, was warned not to worry about certain kinds of military shipments from abroad. He sent me a copy of the original FBI report of an investigation into the alleged transport of illegal narcotics that ended with a formerly senior government official being bundled onto a CIA plane from Houston, Texas, to Washington, D.C., on March 17, 1985. No such incident was publicly acknowledged by any U.S. government agency.

According to the report, acting on the basis of information from a nearby airfield used by the U.S. military, a three-man team had been hastily organized by the FBI office in Austin, Texas. At 0845 on the morning of that March day, it intercepted a convoy of eight vans, two pickups, a backup car, a "chase car," and one "escort unit." The FBI had authority to stop only a certain truck in the convoy and search it for drugs.

During the search, the chase car drove up. The driver jumped out and said he was the convoy supervisor. It was the man I dubbed "Sleeper."

"I examined his I.D. and then he became aggressive and said I had no authority to search," the team leader wrote in the report that nobody would later officially acknowledge. The FBI man instructed his teammates to rip out panels of the suspect truck, and Sleeper tripped one of the searchers and then swung at the team leader. "He cussed that we were 'fucking up his job.' Using my neck choke hold, I held _____ to the ground."

Sleeper identified himself as a government security officer and called the searchers "stupid idiots" interfering in a national security operation. A passing Texas highway patrol officer stopped. Sleeper, who was already pinned to the ground, said he would have the officer arrest the FBI team. Instead, the patrolman saw the FBI's credentials and prudently withdrew. "The entire convoy had circled back and drivers were standing around," said the FBI report. It was rush hour, and "cars passing us were slowing down and this was becoming a security risk. I ordered the convoy drivers back to their units to proceed to their destination – Houston. I handcuffed _____ ." The rest of the convoy could not be searched, and no drugs were found in the suspect truck.

Sleeper put up a violent struggle until he was cuffed and thrown into the back of a Ford Bronco. The FBI team leader reported to the CIA station chief in Houston about an hour later, and two CIA men were detailed to escort Sleeper to a

CIA "Evergreen" aircraft, which landed him in Washington before lunch. So far as the FBI in Texas was concerned, the case had been kicked upstairs.

The incident was "a Keystone Kops mix-up," I was told by the source. "Covert warfare cargoes flown in and out of that Texas airfield are left alone by the policing agencies. There's a thing called the 'trust act' where contract workers say they won't take advantage of the secrecy and do anything illegal like smuggle drugs. . . ."

It was pure coincidence that a copy of the report reached me. Every official, except the source, professed ignorance. I had to consider if it had been fabricated. If so, why? It was just the kind of incident Ross Perot would have investigated in the past. But he was getting indications that his mandate to investigate prisoners meant just that. He was not supposed to look into anything else. He didn't have the easy access to material that he'd had at the beginning of his investigation.

CHAPTER 20

GETTING "BO"

The Iran-Contra hearings during the spring and summer of 1987 offered some insight into why there might be other reasons for secrecy about prisoner intelligence. Many of the people involved in the scandal had held positions in Southeast Asia during the United States' long military involvement. Robert C. "Bud" McFarlane, who had recently resigned his position as National Security Advisor, had been closely involved in the Paris peace negotiations on prisoners in early 1973.

I was walking from the Caucus Room one day when a man came up to me. I knew him as someone who had sworn out an affidavit for one of the lawyers trying to build a case that might force the government to release certain confidential documents.

"I was thinking up there how JFK and his brother Bobby ran their own little show," he said. "When Kennedy was president, Bobby was in this interesting position. As Attorney General he could put anybody anywhere he wanted. I'd been in Treasury as an agent. Then I was put into Customs and Excise. Always investigating. Then I was put into Narcotics and sent to Laos – "

"*Laos*? When was this?"

"After we messed up in Cuba and we were left with all these anti-Castro experts in drug trafficking – Bobby wanted me to analyze the power structure of the opium traffickers in Laos and the Golden Triangle. It was long before the U.S. got involved in Indochina, and we decided Vang Pao was the best man. . . . "

"How'd you know he was telling the truth?" Bill asked that night when we met in the Nam Viet restaurant on North Hudson Street in Arlington, Virginia. The proprietor, Thoi Nguyen, has a large circle of customers with a professional interest in Vietnam. Arlington is sometimes described as the CIA's annex. I said I'd no idea if the informant was honest, but I assumed he must be willing to stick to his story as a court witness. Bill commented drily that the last person who swore out an affidavit on the subject had just been killed.

His name was Stephen Carr. He had been giving information to Senator John Kerry, who was conducting his own inquiries into allegations of drug-funding of CIA operations in Central America. Carr had direct knowledge of covert cocaine and arms deliveries. He had been warned by the CIA, he said, that he must stop giving information to the investigators. His body had been found in Van Nuys, California, on December 13, 1986, and at first it was said that he had died from swallowing three bags of cocaine. Because he had received a frightened call from Carr, and because there were so many strange elements in the case, Senator Kerry had an investigator intervene after the first perfunctory autopsy. Two more autopsies followed, and all three proved Carr had not swallowed three bags of cocaine. But a small mark on his elbow, reported by police to be a scratch, proved to be from a needle injection. Carr was not known to use needles, and in any case it made little sense for him to inject himself behind his elbow. On the other hand, someone else could easily jab him there. Despite these confusing discoveries, the case was closed.

"Another of Senator Kerry's informants called his office," Bill went on. "Worked with Carr loading covert planes. He said he *knows* Carr was killed. It was the same kind of call Carr made to Kerry just before he died. Carr had sounded terrified. Of course there's no proof of anything and maybe both guys lied. But one's dead and the other's hiding."

At 3 a.m. on March 5, 1987, David Taylor got a phone call from Scott Barnes.

"David! David! You've got to help! They finally got me!"

Taylor groped for a light. He was in Washington. How could he possibly help Barnes, who lived in a remote part of the Sierra Mountain foothills in Kernville, California?

"My God, they're out there, David! They've stabbed me – " The phone went dead.

The BBC producer called the Kernville sheriff's office and was told the police were on their way.

Three minutes later, Barnes called again. He was screaming now. "David. I'm bleeding ... There's been a lot of shooting. The police here can't sort this one out. There has to be someone in Washington can help." Barnes had lately claimed to be advising some people in the government on drugs, but he had been secretive about names and Taylor had no idea who to contact. A telephone operator cut into the line to say that an ambulance was on the way. "This is bigger than you realize!" gasped Barnes.

He received emergency treatment for a ten-inch stab wound in his stomach. "The knife was meant to nick the bottom of my heart," testified Barnes later. "I'd have bled internally because all you'd see would be a small external cut. It's a technique. . . . "

Sheriff Larry Kieier told the BBC the incident was "minor." Taylor commented, "The police of Kern County had no ambition to tangle with federal agencies."

When Barnes got home from the hospital, a former Air America crewman from Laos awaited him. The visitor, said Barnes, helpfully pointed out that bullets buried in the door-frame had been fired by a marksman from the cover of bushes with exquisite precision, aimed just close enough to Barnes's head to convey an unmistakable message. And – say! – wasn't that stabbing surgical!

The fortuitous visitor knew all about Jerrold Daniels. Barnes called Taylor again while the man was there. "He says Daniels was killed for knowing what I know," said Barnes.

Taylor told him to put the visitor on the line. "Who are you?" he asked.

"Just a concerned friend."

"Barnes nearly gets killed in the middle of nowhere, and suddenly a *concerned friend* appears and points out how expertly Barnes actually did *not* get killed?" Taylor exclaimed.

Scott Barnes had been living hand-to-mouth. His name had been blackened in media stories about his alleged duplicity. Nobody would employ him. His Kernville house was his only possession, protected by California state law against bankruptcy proceedings. He had been living there alone in spartan conditions. After the visit from the Air America man Barnes claimed he received a call from a former CIA agent. "Awful funny the way Carr died," said the former agent. To Barnes's ear, there was something "awful funny" in the way he said that, and he recorded the conversation.

Barnes was now being pressured to testify before grand juries that were looking into alleged activities by Bo Gritz and his associates. He told me that investigators for the Iran-Contra hearings were asking him for information.

"I've been told I'd get blanket immunity from the first of January '72 to this day. . . . I can go into the witness protection program, but I'll belong to them for the rest of my life," he said.

"What are you talking about?" I asked.

"I can't talk on the phone."

Barnes seemed so steeped in the habits of conversation used by the group of clandestine warriors with whom he had spent most of his adult life that every telephone conversation between us was loaded with code words and slang. However he did seem to me to be telling the truth, since he did not hesitate to repeat things that were damaging to himself. And I had not forgotten that Chris Gugas, the retired CIA polygraph expert so highly regarded by General Tighe, said he had reviewed Barnes's documentation and polygraphed him – and as far as he was concerned, Barnes was not lying. I wanted to find out why someone with Barnes's history was involved in the Bohica mission.

"Can you meet me in Washington?" I asked him.

"I'm so broke I can't even make it fifty miles to the Bakersfield Airport."

So Dorothy McDaniel and I bought Barnes a ticket, and Dorothy promised to put him up for a while, because Red McDaniel wanted to see him too. In the days that followed, sitting in the McDaniels' Virginia home, he talked about new, compact sabotage explosives, methods of selling embargoed weapons by clever paperwork, his expulsion from a foreign country for attempted espionage, his work among drug gangs for the Bureau of Alcohol, Tobacco and Firearms and for a District Attorney. Names and details spilled out in convincing detail, together with what looked like genuine documents. His only display of emotion came when he spoke of Jerrold Daniels, the Bohica mission, and an order to kill American prisoners that he claims he saw.

Barnes's experience with prisoner intelligence, he said, began in 1974. He was officially a private E3 Military Policeman, but he had twice been commended for his undercover work for assisting organizations not part of the military – such as the Bureau of Alcohol and the Seattle Police Department. "In Washington State, at Yakima," he said, "I did certain classified work and saw top-secret messages from Indochina to Washington *rewritten*. They related to intelligence on American prisoners, as tracked by the armed services on the ground in Indochina." Barnes said he did not question the ethics of this until much later, after Bohica, but it helped him to understand how information from Bohica could have been changed or allowed to disappear in the government's labyrinthine bureaucracy.

After a while at Yakima, Barnes said, "I was told to leave the service, go home to Redondo Beach." He was moved into BET, the Bikers' Enforcement Team, "which involved the Secret Service and all federal and state law-enforcement agencies," to work with the Hell's Angels. Some Angels distributed illegal narcotics. "That," he said, "was how I got to know Vang Pao."

I said that the Laotian general was not someone you just got to know. Barnes laughed. "Everyone knows that Vang Pao was the CIA's man in Laos during the war. What they don't know," Barnes claimed, "is that he continued the war for a small group of people."

Barnes explained that the Laotian general had kept his network of agents operating in Laos long after 1973. These agents, according to Barnes, kept the resistance groups supplied with arms, spied on the Communists, and assisted U.S. intelligence with various off-line missions in Southeast Asia – particularly in Laos and Cambodia. "Vang Pao always had pots of money to contribute to off-line activities," said Barnes.*

"Did the money come from the production and export of drugs after the war?" I asked.

Barnes quickly changed the subject. "Vang Pao always knew prisoners had been left behind. That's why he was willing to set up the Laos end of the Bohica mission. But only

---

* Vang Pao's resistance forces were reported in 1990, in newspapers around the world, to be claiming successes in guerrilla operations inside Communist Laos.

because he didn't know the CIA would be involved."

Barnes explained that Vang Pao and the group of intelligence people he had been associated with in Laos during the war had had a falling out with the CIA during Carter's presidency. In reorganizing the CIA, Carter's CIA director, Stansfield Turner, had demoted or removed, amongst others, the people he thought had been involved in off-line activities that contravened the law and were kept hidden from congressional oversight committees. In many cases, Turner found the director of the agency himself had not been informed of certain activities.

Barnes said it was his job to get Vang Pao's assistance for Bohica and to be the liaison man between the general and the mission when it got to Laos. The general agreed because he knew Bo Gritz was genuinely interested in prisoners. Gritz had been vocal about his skepticism of the CIA. Barnes claimed this made Vang Pao trust there would be no agency involvement in the Bohica mission.

Throughout his stay at the McDaniels', Barnes was nervous about calls from former associates who were "concerned about his safety." He was worried that something might happen to him if he was forced to testify about his previous association with these callers in Laos. He was also being called by men who worked for investigative bodies that were looking into Iran-Contra.

I said, "What in the world do they want to know about Laos for?"

Barnes responded by pulling a sound tape out of a travel satchel. He explained that he had been tape-recording his conversations with former colleagues.* As he put the tape on the radio tape-recorder in Red's office, he said meaningfully that men like the clandestine expert I was about to hear had moved their activities to other parts of the world.

---

* Scott Barnes gives reasons for taping conversations like this in his book *Bohica* (with Melva Libb), published by Bohica Corporation, Canton, Ohio, 1987.

"When Reagan came into office the covert activities that had been made illegal under Carter became legal all over again," he said. "Jobs like political assassinations in other countries were farmed out to freelance operatives under a new directive. All the old crowd lined up for jobs – it was real nice, until Iran-Contra."

The tape began. I recognized the man who was speaking and called him "The Ear." The exchange had taken place shortly before Barnes's stabbing, and began with The Ear discussing published reports that a governmental official, who was involved in the POW/MIA issue, was being investigated. "If [he] gets in trouble, then Vang Pao gets in trouble," said Barnes, referring to the former drug warlord, leader of the CIA's Laotian forces – and friend of Jerry Daniels. "Then the whole network gets in trouble."

"Yup," said The Ear. "That's right." He talked of the inability of the U.S. government to act in Central America because of fiscal restraints. Vang Pao's money couldn't be used in Laos any more, he added. "I'm in touch with a dozen different – ah, elements. One has everything from end-user certificates to some capability of parts and equipment and so forth, can be put into a local infrastructure, can be built upon with a military base. I've got all of these elements that I'm juggling, but – someone's got to take the risk. Guatemala's the only place I know where you've got the tradespeople, communications, transport, and some sort of national organization and security."

Barnes asked if dollars could be flown to an airstrip, exchanged for local currency, and then forwarded. "Is that a big problem?"

"Currency's got to be located somewhere where it's available," said The Ear. He speculated about bringing in arms that had been left in Thailand. "Shit," he said. "It's like Laos fifteen years ago. We put in enough weapons to arm every man, woman, and child, three times over. . . . " The Ear thought there were enough arms left to supply the kind of operation he had in mind in Guatemala.

Vang Pao had all this money, but he couldn't use it in Laos, The Ear said. "If VP [Vang Pao] has access to a capital base, let me know. We'll be able to put it to good use in a national-security-related project which is truly commercial. . . . "

I stopped the tape and listened to the last sentence again. I wondered what a "national-security-related project which is truly commercial" was. Was that what Bohica had been about? I wondered. And had the discovery of POWs been a threat to commercial profits? I returned to the tape to hear a description of the kind of people who go into the national-security-related businesses.

"It requires people who know what the hell they're doing in the security business, counterinsurgency and the paramilitary area."

Barnes asked if things would ease off, now that Frank Carlucci was the National Security Advisor.* Carlucci had now taken over from Robert C. McFarlane, who had been implicated in the Iran-Contra scandal.

The Ear replied, "Carlucci's a top-notch bureaucrat who is called in there [the White House] to do damage control. He's going to call in people he knows and can trust, and he's going to put together a different operation. . . . [But] these guys [the kind of people who go into the national-security related business] are not what they were ten, fifteen years ago. And neither am I. But at least I've got my health, and I can regroup and redraw my scenario."

"All this VP [Vang Pao] money . . . ?" Barnes said.

"Now that's the kind of a thing I would welcome, along with some of the key people. I have no objections to it. But – you know, to put – to put any kind – to put any kind of a going, er, operation still connected with the source of the money – is of this date, and with Iran-Contra questions leading anywhere, the kiss of death. . . . " The Ear grumbled. "They're going to monitor everything at this stage. . . . "

---

*   In other circles, Carlucci's appointment was controversial, since he had at one time been associated with Erich von Marbod.

The Ear's voice had lifted as he described his partners in Guatemala "with the only infrastructure in Central America that could be built on, with security interests which will require both aircraft and patrol craft on the water, plus I've got fixed-wing requirements to haul crops to market and equipment that's going to be needed to build these – ah, different activities."

Barnes said that sounded like a good cover.

"That's right," said The Ear. "So give us the feedback." He sounded hungry for Vang Pao's money.

The Ear's exchange with Barnes made one thing clear: he believed Barnes had a long-standing relationship with Vang Pao and the group of semi-private covert operatives that The Ear represented. It also indicated that Vang Pao's money had financed a lot of activity in Southeast Asia. I wondered just how many "national-security-related projects" that were "truly commercial" there had been during the long run of the secret war in Laos and Cambodia. One thing was certain, the rescue or other repatriation of POWs could never meet The Ear's requirements for a truly viable project.

Meanwhile, it was becoming even more clear that, from 1981 on, different parts of the military and their intelligence branches had considered intelligence on POWs so credible that they made plans for highly secret and elaborate reconnaissance and rescue missions. One after another of these attempts failed, until the Reagan administration lost its enthusiasm for the POW cause. President Reagan had won a huge victory in part because he ridiculed Carter's failed attempt to rescue the Iran hostages. The Reagan administration's attempts to rescue prisoners were failures on an even larger scale. Some in the Pentagon still believed there had been deliberate sabotage involved.

My source for this information was a man who had been directly involved in one of the missions. I met him through Colonel Nick Rowe. He was a military counter-terrorist expert I named "True Man" in my notes. True Man was very high in clandestine warfare, and he made it obvious that he would not have been speaking to me if he had not felt the country was threatened by misuse of intelligence on the POW/MIA issue and by a larger conspiracy than a POW cover-up. He said, "The effect is to sabotage U.S. covert actions. Those actions are secret, so the public cannot judge. But you ask who benefits if it isn't America's enemies. . . . "

He started with the first Delta mission in the spring of 1981, whose failure President Reagan had confirmed to Betty Foley. The Joint Chiefs of Staff planned an elaborate two-stage operation: reconnaissance and rescue. The rescue would be done by Delta commandos in cooperation with the Army's Intelligence Support Activity (ISA) and the Army's Special Operations Division.

Bo Gritz, said True Man, had come up with some of the original intelligence. I told True Man that I had encountered a lot of skepticism about Gritz's actual involvement with the government on this mission. True Man insisted that Gritz's team brought out the initial evidence of twenty-five or so POWs in a camp in central Laos. The rescue plan was aborted through no fault of the Green Beret.

Intelligence on the American prisoners came from DIA. It was incredibly strong. True Man mentioned the SR-71 high-altitude reconnaissance planes and RD-77 satellite photos of the prison camp which had persuaded Red McDaniel there were prisoners. Those satellite photos, he claimed, confirmed the ground intelligence Gritz had first brought to DIA. DIA took it very seriously. "To this day," he said, "that kind of intelligence on prisoners is still coming in. Two of my former subordinates are directly dealing with POW/MIA matters at this moment, and they're extremely disturbed by what's going on. They have ground intelligence covering every inch of Vietnam. They have absolutely no doubt there are POWs alive to this minute."

Bo Gritz distrusted the government's intentions and organized his own rescue mission (Velvet Hammer) on a stand-by basis, said True Man. Contrary to official Pentagon reports, Gritz did not embark on his own mission until the official one in the spring of 1981 had been aborted. When he did embark on his own, he said, he was preceded in Laos by Voice of America reports announcing his arrival. The prisoners had been moved when the team got to the camp. When Gritz got back to Thailand, newspapers around the world had been informed that he had single-handedly planned and botched the mission. There had been no U.S. government involvement at all, said the press.

According to True Man, neither Bo Gritz nor the then-ISA chief Jerry King gave up the idea of rescuing the prisoners that they both strongly believed were there. A new plan emerged. This would be Grand Eagle, better known as Bohica. Apparently without informing the Joint Chiefs of Staff, ISA agreed to provide Gritz with the support and equipment needed to help document evidence of prisoners in Laos.* When the Pentagon discovered ISA's cooperation with Gritz, it ordered the mission put down. That's why Gritz had not gone to Laos with Scott Barnes in October of 1981 as planned.

I asked, "Did the Bohica mission become rogue or was it taken over by someone else?"

True Man did not know what happened to the mission, although he had heard reports that it was taken over by the CIA and became a cover for something else. He did know, he said, that the "episode killed a whole lot of careers. ISA came close to being terminated. It almost killed Jerry King."

In 1981, the year of Bohica, Jerry King, as head of ISA, had been highly regarded by top Army commanders who wished to build up a global counter-terrorist capacity. After Bohica,

---

* In his book *Secret Warriors: Inside the Covert Military Operations of the Reagan Era* (G.P. Putnam's Sons, New York, 1988, p. 80), Steven Emerson says, "ISA officials have argued that they did notify the Joint Chiefs and received tentative approval for Gritz to collect intelligence. They have adamantly insisted that their support of Gritz was not a 'rogue operation.' "

King had to take the heat. "Bungling in Laos" was blamed on ISA. An adverse report on ISA activities, from the Inspector General in the Department of Defense, was based on the activities of Colonel Bo Gritz. It was only through the persuasive powers of a few high-ranking Army officers that the order to terminate ISA was rescinded.

According to True Man, it had been a new man at the Pentagon, brought in with the Reagan administration, who had found out about the planned Bohica mission and had presented it as a rogue operation to Secretary of the Army John Marsh and Secretary of Defense Caspar Weinberger. Weinberger had almost immediately decided to terminate ISA. True Man said the new Pentagon official, who had won his spurs by campaigning strongly for Reagan and Bush, was reputed to be a double-ranker, a CIA official who simultaneously held the Pentagon position. The alleged double-ranker had advanced rapidly to a position of some decision-making power on covert activities having to do with prisoners. True Man echoed what Colonel Al Shinkle, the Air Force intelligence officer, had told a congressional committee in the late seventies about his difficulties in Laos: "The single greatest obstacle to collecting information [about U.S. prisoners] is not the enemy: it is the CIA's steadfast refusal to let U.S. military intelligence mount a viable and effective intelligence collection system. . . . "

True Man said, "Without our own effective [military] intelligence collection system we are not only dependent on the CIA for intelligence, but for the decisions that are made in response to the intelligence."

Six years after the Bohica fiasco True Man still felt that, left alone, ISA and Bo Gritz had had a good chance of rescuing the prisoners Scott Barnes claimed he saw in Laos.

I remembered something Scott Barnes had said at the McDaniels', referring to the time period when he was involved in helping to set up the Laos end of the mission. "Bo Gritz was so gung-ho on getting back prisoners. We were afraid he'd compromise the mission's real aims." This did not square with Barnes's own expression of POW concern, but it would be borne out by transcripts made available after a trial in 1989 found no foundation for U.S. government charges that had been brought against Bo Gritz after he had returned from yet another POW reconnaissance mission.

True Man's parting shot had been to advise me once more to re-examine my information on Bo Gritz. No one, he said, would have gone to so much trouble to discredit the man if he had not the evidence of prisoners in 1981 and the skill to find them. I decided to speak to Gritz again.

Was Gritz easily fooled? My husband had once been told, by the chief of Britain's Special Operations Executive, General Sir Colin Gubbins, that soldiers were poorly trained for clandestine missions because "our traditions and experience are built on mutual trust. Treachery you expect only from the enemy."

Gritz was a career soldier. He had just passed the benchmark of forty in 1981 at the time of Bohica. The legendary years in Vietnam were fading. General William C. Westmoreland had portrayed him as a national hero in his 1976 book, *A Soldier's Story.**

Gritz was not after fame and glory when he concluded there were still Americans in captivity. He had had a distinguished post-Vietnam career. He risked losing future promotion when he undertook that secret mission that would never win him the publicity that his enemies at home later said he craved. He was invited to resign from Special Forces to work undercover in 1978 on the strength of proposals "so sensitive they could result in a real inquisition if word leaked out." This was in the days of the Carter administration, when not even lip service was given to the possibility of prisoners being alive. Gritz had showed me a copy of a letter on

---

* Published by Doubleday, New York.

Defense Intelligence Agency stationery containing those words and an appeal to Gritz "to prove beyond a doubt our men are still captive. Then the system will do the rest."

Before the Iran-Contra scandals broke, I gave credence to suggestions that the letter was forged, but the hearings had shown quite clearly that all kinds of schemes were possible. The system had done the rest until those schemes were exposed by someone totally outside the system – the Ayatollah. If Gritz had to operate without official or provable ties to any U.S. government agency, it would be normal practice for the government to repudiate "paper trails." Later, trial transcripts recorded that Gritz had indeed met with the DIA author of the letter to discuss further action. I asked him to give me his version of the events of 1981 that True Man had already outlined.

President Reagan had been excited about the rescue of prisoners at the start of his first term, said Gritz. Their presence in Laos had been indicated by foot patrol and by air surveillance in 1981, before Reagan's inauguration. Admiral Jerry Tuttle briefed the President on SR71 Blackbird aircraft and Big Bird satellite pictures.

Gritz put together a "private option" team, Velvet Hammer. From another source I had a copy of his confidential submission to the President of an extraction plan: "The operation must free POWs while allowing the Communists to save face [since they] have so far refused to acknowledge holding any Americans. To bludgeon them over the head with a humiliating defeat would make for more antagonism. . . . Use of federal troops to cross borders could legally constitute an act of war. . . . If a military rescue failed, the United States would be open to worldwide ridicule. . . . The U.S. government can honestly deny direct involvement. . . . "

Then, on March 4, 1981, according to Gritz, Admiral Tuttle had informed him that "The President is going to make the rescue using official forces." Gritz took from this that the government reconnaissance mission had confirmed intelligence he had initially brought to the government. "It will not be necessary," he quoted Tuttle as saying, "to use the private option. . . . You step down."

Then President Reagan lost interest.

"Advisors closed ranks around Reagan," said Gritz. "They didn't want any action taken at all. They persuaded him that politically it could destroy him if a mission failed. And, conversely, if the public learned Americans were still alive and we couldn't get them out, that would destroy him too. But those advisors really had other objectives." His Velvet Hammer mission was compromised. Bohica was taken out of his hands and became a CIA operation when Jerrold Daniels took charge, under the name of Michael J. Baldwin, and Scott Barnes joined the rescue-mission team.

A lot of POW families and veterans had not been affected by the smear job done on Gritz. They knew he was a stubborn man and kept abreast of his activities in the hope that some day he would succeed in rescuing POWs. By 1987 he had launched two more rescue missions and was in the middle of another kind of investigation that could offer possible answers to why every POW rescue effort seemed to be compromised.

Elvus Sasseen of Yukon, Oklahoma, called me. "Bo Gritz has been warned by that bunch in the White House. They don't want to hurt him, but they will unless he destroys all his tapes of Khun Sa in the Golden Triangle. They're going to bring charges against him and keep him so tied down with legalities he won't have time for anything else – unless he plays ball and keeps his mouth shut."

Elvus often phoned me like this. He was a small-town middle American, who had always taken things pretty well on trust, believing in the essential goodness of his fellow Americans – until he lost his cousin, Technical Sergeant Patrick Shannon, at Site 85 in Laos. He once wrote me, "My cousin grew up with me, back in Cordell, western Oklahoma. My dad was thirty-five years the prosecutor there. A lot of my folks were local prosecutors, and a lot of others were preachers to keep them in line. My dad gave me a strong sense of ethics, and the pure feeling that America's strength is in fidelity to ethical standards. What's good in America comes from plain, honest folks like Patrick Shannon. I didn't much like the way those other folks in Washington refused to level with us about what really happened. He was just written off. So I started to look into what happened out there in Laos. . . . "

Elvus devoured everything he could get on Asia. He began pestering officials. He became friendly with men who'd fought in Special Operations. He talked to returned prisoners. Pretty soon The Telephone Tree was calling *him* for information. His phone bills rocketed, until he was spending some twelve thousand dollars a year trying to satisfy his increasing curiosity.

"What are the charges against Gritz?" I asked him.

"Started out with things he'd done while training Afghan rebels. . . . " Again Gritz had exposed himself to legal action by undertaking "private" covert ventures that could be officially denied. "The subpoenas are out to bring him before a grand jury. There's a charge of 'misuse of passport.' "

Scott Barnes had said that in carrying out covert assignments he'd had to break the law. Now that Barnes wanted to cut out of such activities, he was being pressured by the threat of prosecution for breaking the law. Was the same thing happening to Gritz? Yet Bo had commanded Special Forces in Panama from 1968 to 1979. His records said he had been "responsible for unconventional warfare in Latin America and strategic protection of the Canal."

As Elvus said, "He's an outstanding soldier. He brought back the black box from a U-2 that crashed in enemy territory during the Vietnam War. . . . " Elvus ran through a long list of decorations for valor.

"Does he get any prizes for ordinary common sense?" I asked.

"He doesn't have the sense to give up when the folks in Washington tell him he's beaten," replied Elvus.

CHAPTER 21

SCOTT BARNES TELLS
HIS STORY

I could not believe "the folks back in Washington"
would want to beat up on Gritz – unless they thought he'd
"gone rogue," as they say about intelligence operatives when
they give politicians heartburn. Scott Barnes did not have
Gritz's outstanding military record, but as I went over my
notes of the conversations with him held at Red McDaniel's
house, and his version of Bohica, even Barnes seemed to me
to have tried to carry out orders.

"I'm just not sure *who* you thought you were serving," I
had said after I had looked at the personal files Barnes
brought to the McDaniels' home. If Barnes had an obvious
fault, it was his readiness to voice hatred for military uniforms. He despised uniforms, he had said one day, unaware
that behind him in a cupboard were Red's naval uniforms,
including that of a carrier captain, and the striped pajamas of
Communist imprisonment. With Jerry "Hog" Daniels now

316

dead, and everyone ridiculing Barnes, I had taken an awful lot of what he told me at Red's house on good faith, but I had continued to record our conversations.

We had gone over Barnes's career repeatedly. There were no serious discrepancies with what he had said during voluntary submission to truth-drug tests for Mark Waple and the BBC and, later, the Christic Institute. He had first become conscious of illegal drugs when he worked undercover among the Hell's Angels. When I pushed him to reveal who had taken over Bohica after ISA had been cut out, he claimed, "DIA kept telling me the Bohica mission was to meet several objectives, although I thought POW reconnaissance was the most important. We had a 'Presidential Charter.' " If true, this meant they were reporting back to the National Security Council in the White House. If Barnes remembered correctly, it meant that DIA was getting reports on Bohica and analyzing the intelligence. I remembered Gritz's claim that the CIA had taken over. But that would not have prevented intelligence from going to the DIA.

First Barnes had to deliver a package to Bangkok on June 15, 1981. "At that time, Oliver North in the National Security Council was working on a project with a former CIA guy in Thailand, who later registered with the State Department as a foreign agent for Thailand. I was given his name as one of the contacts if I needed independent verification of any order." Barnes found Gritz's team at the Nana Hotel in the Thai capital.

"I later met a helicopter pilot for 'Grand Eagle,' which was still the formal code name for this mission," Barnes said. "The pilot told me he 'flew things' into the Golden Triangle for covert operations under Drug Enforcement Agency cover. He took me into what he called the CIA's office at the U.S. embassy." Barnes said he was given a small box encased in a rubbery substance and told that he should deliver the package in Cambodia to the Khmer Rouge. "We were working with the Khmers, Task Force 80,* and JUSTMAG,† which was a military group of U.S. and Thai officials," Barnes said. Barnes claimed that it was there that he met Col. Paul Mather of the Joint Casualty Resolution Center. "This Colonel Mather let me know that, unknown to the American people, the war had not really ended. It was just over so far as the folks back home were concerned." Mather would later deny all of this.

Barnes claimed to have crossed near the Three Corners into Cambodia. "I had an escort of U.S.-supported guerrillas. They showed me U.S. arms and equipment in a tunnel, drawn from supplies flown into Thailand originally from Saigon. Said the region was overrun with agents and partisans of every kind." Barnes delivered the package, he said, and on his return to Bangkok was told he had passed muster. He could report to Bo Gritz in the United States that everything was proceeding smoothly. "I got paid big bucks," he said.

At Hermosa Beach, crowded with people, near the statue of a California surfer, Barnes met the burly, self-confident Bo Gritz. Over beers, Barnes repeated what he had seen and heard, then left Gritz to go to General Vang Pao's office in Garden Grove, California. The walls of the building were covered with bulletins about Vang Pao's own secret war in Laos. The general ran through the equipment Barnes would be taking, including atropine. "You stick it in your leg when you're exposed to gas," said Vang Pao. Barnes had a queasy feeling that he would soon find himself in the region. He was right.

---

* Task Force was a Thai military unit created in 1980 to supervise displaced Cambodians. (See *Cambodia*, a report of the Lawyers' Committee for Human Rights, published in New York, 1987.)
† When I checked through my file of joint service high command unconventional war task-force operations (MACV-SOG) later, I found that the highly classified sabotage and psychological and special operations group set up in March of 1971 had never been deactivated. It had also never been acknowledged.

In September 1981, according to Barnes's account, Gritz showed him $426,000 in large bills and said, "This money's for bribes, medicine, weapons. . . . " Barnes met other American members of the team. "I told myself I'd only go as far as Bangkok with them," Barnes said. "There seemed an awful lot of equipment to be delivered to Vang Pao's Hmongs. . . . Then Bo Gritz was ordered to remain in the U.S., and suddenly I was swept up by events. The rest of us were issued ordinary blue passports, but we also got red diplomatic passports in case of emergency."

In Bangkok for the second time, Barnes claimed "the CIA man for the mission, Colonel Mike Eiland" was pointed out to him in the hotel lobby. Eiland, he said, was the man in charge of "Daniel Boone" secret operations into Cambodia during the Vietnam War.

Barnes said he was directed to Bangkok's Don Muang Airport, where a Thai officer stamped his passport *Departed 24 October 1981* and said, "As far as anybody knows, you left the country." The officer took him to another part of the airport with a team member, J.D. Bath, a former Green Beret. From there, the two men flew directly to Udorn, the Thai air base used by the U.S. 432nd Tactical Reconnaissance Wing during the CIA's secret war in Laos. A radio base was set up at Nakhon Phanom (NKP),* and Barnes and J.D. (Bath was known by his initials) were then escorted by a U.S.-trained Thai intelligence agent named "Southern Chicago" to the Thai village of Ban Pheng. Here Barnes was identified by Vang Pao's men.

"Our mission was classified as Grand Eagle, but we used Bohica in communicating through NKP to a classified CIA

---

* Nakhon Phanom is a sleepy little town separated from Laos by the Mekong River. There is considerable traffic across the river, and only cursory controls. When we visited there in early 1990, it was possible to cross into Laos with nothing more than identification papers.

telex number 24893," said Barnes. Each time Barnes mentioned CIA, he gave it special emphasis. "We were also given access to a Department of Defense DIA number." He gave me the numbers to jot down. Their communications equipment appeared to be sophisticated, with automatic coders, but Barnes was not to see it put to use. He was taken on another journey, instead, where he became separated from J.D. and Southern Chicago on the Thai banks of the Mekong, opposite the Laotian capital of Vientiane. There, waiting near a Buddhist monastery filled with guerrillas, he was approached by an American who called himself Michael J. Baldwin. This was Jerrold "Hog" Daniels. "We're going into Laos immediately," he announced. "Without the rest of the team."

The trek across the river and into the jungle was made with some thirty of Vang Pao's guerrillas. "We wear boogie bags," Hog Daniels told Barnes. "Inside are bare essentials – dehydrated high-protein food, water-purification pills, compass . . . If all hell breaks loose, you drop everything else and you *boogie!*"

Patrols always moved ahead. After three days, a patrol leader announced they had arrived. The guerrillas moved into new positions while Daniels unpacked high-tech Litton/ Hughes equipment and moved it to the top of a knoll. "He assembled cameras – one had the longest lens I'd ever seen; then radio equipment with what looked like a satellite dish. . . . In a valley below, I saw what seemed like a triangular camp, surrounded by a fence with a watchtower at three points. One building was larger than the others and was surrounded by large drums. Outside the walled compound were fields, one to the left and the other facing us, where men worked under armed guard. At the furthest point there was a kind of tunnel into the thick jungle.

"Suddenly Daniels shouted, 'My God! Look!' I took the binoculars and saw two Caucasians under armed escort, walking to the compound. He shouted, 'We really *did* leave them behind!' He actually cried," said Barnes with emotion.

"But he was very professional. After a while he began recording with parabolic 'ears' and ordered me to fire the long-lens camera, which just ate up film. We recorded and photographed until our view of the prisoners was obstructed by the buildings."

Vang Pao's men showed their contempt when ordered to withdraw. "We keep telling your people about prisoners, but they do nothing," the translator told Barnes.

The journey back was long and arduous. Daniels divided up the exposed film and told Barnes he was to get one lot of pictures to the CIA contact, using an address near Washington in Vienna, Virginia.

On his return to Thailand, Barnes said he was shown a decoded order that the "merchandise" was to be "liquidated." The prisoners had been referred to before by the code word "merchandise." Barnes said he had no idea where in Washington the order came from or how one would liquidate the prisoners, but he announced he wanted nothing more to do with the mission. "I was taken over by armed men," he said. "They took me to the U.S. embassy in Bangkok."

Barnes had always maintained that if he ever entered the embassy compound, he would never leave it alive. At the last moment, with help from one of his mission colleagues, he had run up an alley on Wireless Road where the embassy is located. With Thai money in his pocket, he grabbed a taxi to Bangkok's Don Muang Airport. There he was told his open Pan Am ticket had just been cancelled by the issuing agent. He rushed to Japan Air Lines and pulled out all the U.S. dollars he had left. It was enough. "I was in such a panic, I never argued about how a ticket in my name could be arbitrarily cancelled," said Barnes.

Back on home ground, Barnes called his CIA contact. "He told me to mail the photographs, but when I started to say I didn't know we were going to be ordered to kill, and that I couldn't understand the purpose of a mission with guerrillas so heavily armed with assault weapons, he turned to ice. He said, 'You don't know me. You don't know anything. Just take your money. . . . ' "

Barnes's story was denied by U.S. officials. But J.D. Bath confirmed to David Taylor later that he had been with Barnes when the order was received "to liquidate the merchandise." He added, though, that Barnes was "a flake and misunderstood – the order had nothing to do with prisoners." J.D. Bath refused to discuss it any further. Later, he refused to answer any further questions from me.

What was worrisome was Barnes's ability to pick up so much detail. He reminded us of a certain kind of con artist. Perhaps his personality had seemed ideal for secret operations. He used a phenomenal memory to recreate reality. And he really believed in what he said.

Casino Man counterbalanced our skepticism by saying he had known Barnes in Vietnam. According to Casino Man, Barnes had worked with Command and Control North, the super-secret unconventional warfare group in Laos and North Vietnam. And Barnes himself talked knowingly about CCN. The highly classified group had been directed from the U.S. embassy in Saigon in operations that included "neutralization" of alleged Communist officials. At the time I discussed it with him, CCN was still only mentioned in the vaguest terms by my security-conscious contacts in the Pentagon.

One of Barnes's Pentagon contacts during the Bohica mission had been Colonel, later General, Bobby Charles Robinson, at that time Commander of the Pine Bluff Arsenal for Nuclear, Chemical and Biological Warfare. Barnes said that when he came back from the Bohica mission he told Robinson about the order they had received to "liquidate the merchandise." Robinson, he said, denied there was ever any authority to kill Americans. According to Barnes he then said, "From now onwards, you and I no longer know each other."

The story was given some credence by Dr. Mathew Meselson, the Harvard authority on chemical and biological warfare. He had known General Robinson very well. He felt that if "Robbie" was involved in the Bohica mission, it could well have had as one of its objectives the planting of fake evidence – to make it look as if the Soviets were using chemical weapons in Southeast Asia. Meselson said, "He was capable of planting evidence – he was so worried that we were falling behind the Soviets in chemical warfare."

This raised a new issue. I asked Barnes if planting evidence had been part of the mission.

"Jerry Daniels was upset," Barnes replied evasively. "His friends, Vang Pao's men, were getting gassed by the other side. I know part of the mission was to plant 'Yellow Rain' for tests in chemical and biological warfare. Vang Pao's men had a word for it – *kemi,* for chemical weapons.

"A whole lot of people wanted to wipe out what's left of Vang Pao's men in Laos," said Barnes.

I then learned that General Robinson had died suddenly from a gunshot wound to the head in January 1985. The USACIDC public affairs officer, Lt. Col. Robert Flocke, said the report was still secret. It had to do with nerve gas and suicide. The police of Fairfax County, Virginia, where Robinson died so violently, said their investigations began as "possible homicide." Others had made them report it as suicide. Asked for the identity of the "others," a police sergeant said, "We can't say. But I know he was working on something very sensitive in Indochina."

Soon after I had reviewed my notes, Barnes phoned from his California home. He reported back almost immediately that the situation regarding his safety had not gotten any better. He told me and David Taylor, who was still in Washington, that the vague group of former "friends" from his covert ops days in Laos seemed to be closing in on him.

The sheriff of Kern County, California, John Smith, called David Taylor in Washington to ask his impressions of Barnes. From that conversation, the BBC man concluded that police had a skewed picture of events on the night Barnes was stabbed. The sheriff said he had seen reports that quoted Taylor as having denied knowing much about Barnes. "That's totally untrue," said Taylor, and he told the sheriff that he felt Barnes was being framed.

Taylor was alarmed. He had just learned from Barnes that two Drug Enforcement agents had "wined and dined" him near the China Lake naval weapons center, and at first Taylor thought they were the same two men who had come to the BBC's Washington office to ask help in locating Barnes.

"But *these* two drug-enforcement agents spoke to Barnes about getting special work in Central America," Taylor told me. "They would put to good use his expertise in moving currency, guns, and drugs. That was the exact opposite of what the two agents professed when they came to my office." Taylor had a tape running when the agents entered his office, and he now reviewed it. The two who had come to see him were listed as Senior Inspectors from the Drug Enforcement Agency's Internal Security Office named Frank Panessa and Chuck Bonnyville. "They shocked me by claiming that, whatever else the mission had been asked to do, Bohica involved a very high-level drug operation coming out of the CIA," said Taylor.

Panessa and Bonnyville were investigating a long way back into illegal drug trafficking, which they said involved top Drug Enforcement Agency officials. Taylor now worried that these other "officials" could take countermeasures against Barnes, and that he might have unwillingly set up Barnes by advising him to trust "two DEA agents coming up to see you." Barnes was trusting the wrong "drug-enforcers." He would wind up confused and frightened by these other two unnamed agents.

Bonnyville and Panessa were clearly doing an honest job of investigation. Chuck Bonnyville had questioned Ross Perot and Arlington detective Jim Badey about some of the information they had collected. Bonnyville also questioned some of my other police contacts. This had been going on for at least five months. Those questioned all felt there was a large-scale, bona-fide inquiry in progress.

Barnes was being softened up, though, in a clever psychological war of threats alternating with enticements, to return to the world of covert activities. He called me frequently during this period with accounts of job offers from "secret sources." He was flattered when a high government official asked him to back away from the subject of Bohica's other missions, because, Barnes claimed, "I was going against national security."

Barnes had started counselling young drug addicts for an organization called KICK. But when I questioned him about this, he sounded more and more baffled: "I've been put in an office with no exterior signs. I've never yet seen a drug addict. My bosses tell me to read books all day. They've also put four security telephones in my house. . . . I'm not scared at night any more now," he added. "Someone always stays with me."

It was impossible to get information on KICK. No telephones were listed under that name.

Early one morning, Barnes called again. "It's all over," he said. "I never saw American prisoners. I never went into Laos or Cambodia. I never did anything. It's all over for me. Believe me, whatever I've done, I'm paying for it now. For me, it's all over."

He called David Taylor. "I've just heard a tape recording," he said. "I'd swear it was myself. But I never made such a tape. On it, I deny everything. They've got me saying I lied. How can I win against that?"

Taylor said, "If you can't talk on the phone, I'll come to California right now."

"No," replied Barnes. "It's better we not meet again. I've got to live with the stigma that my children have this kind of father. . . . Dangerous people are running this country."

The only exit left for Barnes would seem to lead back into the covert world. But he later made public appearances to repeat what he had told me. His unusual combination of talents had been developed during the Vietnam War. Now the climate was rapidly changing and the conduct of covert operations was changing also.

CHAPTER 22

THE PARTY LINE (OR ELSE)

$\mathbf{B}$ill wondered why we were fighting other people's wars. We had both put aside and postponed other work projects, which made no economic sense at all. And yet his contradictory impulse was to say that we couldn't just forget what we now knew. He remembered the wars fought for preservation of freedom, and wondered what those who'd died would think today of those who were cowed into silence. What also upset him was the abuse of a tradition inherited from England – the system of grand juries.

They began as people's forums, to stop the King's Prosecutor from abusing his power. The system survived in the United States as a protection against an English monarch's tyranny. It was the means by which citizens heard accusations against persons said to have committed a crime, so that indictments might be issued if there was sufficient evidence. Technically, grand juries existed as a subdivision of the judicial system. But now it seemed as if the grand jury system was being used to *suppress* investigations. Men like Scott Barnes and Bo Gritz were being subpoenaed. They had usually done Special Forces type of work in trouble spots from Afghanistan to Latin America. It seemed possible to silence people who opposed government policy by just going through the motions of preparing a grand jury hearing.

There seemed to be a range of legal weapons to stifle dissent. The threat of a lawsuit, expensive in time and money, discouraged many who wanted to make public what they knew. Military law could be adjusted to curb anyone inclined to ask too many questions. Men could be punished on the basis of false accusation only. Their careers could be destroyed. That was the case in the humiliation of Father Charles Shelton, son of Colonel Charles Shelton, whose wife Marian had cofounded the original League of Families with Dorothy McDaniel and had been so outspoken for *60 Minutes*.

Charles Shelton, Jr., was the eldest of five children. He'd been offered a prestigious position as a Catholic chaplain at a new U.S. missile base in Belgium early in 1987. He was thirty-three, the same age at which his father, Colonel Shelton, was shot down. The day before Father Shelton was due to leave for Belgium, he was told by an Air Force orderly that "the Judge Advocate's put you on administrative hold."

Father Shelton figured that the delay might have to do with an outstanding speeding ticket. Four days after he had paid the traffic fine, a lieutenant colonel flew down from Washington to inform him that an airman had accused him of homosexual solicitation.

Shelton said the Commander of U.S. Tactical Air Command in Belgium heard of his predicament and called to express support. "We're holding the slot open for you," he said. "You're the best chaplain for the job. We'll wait for you." The congregation of 1,500 was one of the largest in the armed forces; a plum for a young officer. "You're highly respected," said the commander.

Father Shelton spoke out at every opportunity about abandoned Americans to servicemen who were concerned about their own status if ordered into trouble spots where there had been no formal declaration of war. They knew the chaplain's father as an Air Force hero. Shelton, Sr., was the only American serviceman who remained officially classified as a prisoner-of-war, thus representing some 2,500 Americans officially still unaccounted for in Indochina. As I had learned when I started my research, Title 37 of the U.S. Code does not permit someone presumed dead to be classified a POW. Section 555 of the law, regulating procedures about missing servicemen, provides only two options. If the man can be reasonably presumed to be alive, he keeps his missing status. Otherwise, a finding must be made that he is dead.

Father Shelton had drawn attention to this anomaly during a speech to airmen shortly before the accusation of homosexuality was made against him by the airman, who turned out to be under investigation as a barracks-room thief – one of the worst offenses in the eyes of military men. The accuser's service record carried his own admission of male prostitution and attempted suicide. Father Shelton told Captain Felix Losco, the area defense counsel on the base at Keesler in Mississippi, that he would fight back if charges were brought.

Then the next blow fell. The Franciscan order to which Shelton belonged advised him to resign, before his career as a priest, too, was affected by false innuendo, and to return to his old parish at St. Thomas Catholic Church in Riverside, California. The accusations had been taken to the headquarters of clerical matters for the military in Washington, where, it seemed, nobody wanted to hear his side of the story. It was more important to avoid a scandal. Otherwise, his lawyer was told, ecclesiastical sanction would be withdrawn. Without that, a clergyman's service career is ended.

Captain Losco told me he did not believe the case would go anywhere. Father Shelton was not a homosexual. His moral probity had never before been questioned. The only evidence came from a discredited source. There was no case.

But pressures were being applied. Captain Losco spoke freely to me one day. The next day he said his superiors in

Washington had just forbidden him to talk to me. "If I'd realized everyone wanted me to clam up, I would never have talked to you in the first place," he explained.

When I queried Captain Losco's superior, Lt. Col. Gary Grunick at Maxwell Air Force Base in Alabama, he had not yet been told that there was a ban on discussing the case. He was so sure Shelton would win, he told me he had wanted the court martial to go forward quickly to vindicate him. "No formal charges were ever brought," he said. "The accuser had such a bad record, I'm sorry we never had the opportunity to put him under a microscope. As for Father Shelton, his strongest defense is his character."

Sworn statements were sent to me from USAF officers who believed Father Shelton was being framed. His immediate neighbors testified to his hard work on behalf of airmen who got into trouble. Airmen testified that they had previously complained many times about the man who made the accusation: they felt he would say anything, just to have the theft charge dropped. All these documents were given to Air Force authorities, along with impressive letters of commendation from other service chaplains of non-Catholic denominations.

It didn't make sense. I set out to see what Father Shelton could have done to bring this persecution on.

He told me that, some months earlier, while stationed at Keesler, he had been asked to counsel a sergeant based in the Philippines. "The sergeant said he'd been involved in a medical evacuation team, which in early 1986 had flown to the North Vietnam port of Haiphong in a C-130 to pick up prisoners," Father Shelton told me. "Two other flights had gone to Hanoi. All the planes carried Red Cross, not USAF, markings. A total of eighty-six men were flown to the Philippines, where they were put into special wards at a military hospital. He said the men were Caucasians. Not one weighed more than a hundred pounds. Some were so sick, they died soon after evacuation. They all had difficulty speaking English.

"The man seemed to realize suddenly that he might be breaking security. He said, 'I could lose my job.' I told him, 'You could lose your life, too.'

"I made some inquiries of my own. I heard about a young woman electrical engineer who had been assigned special work at an Air Force hospital in the Philippines, in a 'classified' floor. Some of the inmates spoke with her. They said they were prisoners-of-war from Vietnam . . . but now they were still prisoners. She conceded it might have been a 'psycho ward,' but she did think it was odd that all of them imagined they were POWs. . . . An Air Force colleague confirmed there was a classified floor at that hospital."

Father Shelton knew it was possible this was disinformation planted by someone who wanted to discredit him by having him spread wild stories. So he gave them no circulation. What he did talk about was the persistence of reports on several hundreds of missing prisoners, including his father. Another thing the chaplain talked about was the fact that Hanoi desperately needed commercial links with the United States. The Communist regime had wrecked its own economy.

He said some of this in a speech at Myrtle Beach, South Carolina, on September 19, 1986, then flew back to Keesler Air Base to address a parade of some 5,000 airmen. "As I approached the podium, something happened to me that was unprecedented. A general ordered me, 'Stick to the speech.' Soon after, friends warned that I had the reputation of a rabble-rouser. I found myself no longer invited to speak to service gatherings."

Because Father Shelton did not wish to get his informants into trouble, I made my own inquiries and tracked down an Air Force technical sergeant in the Philippines. He told me the classified section of his base hospital had been entered by a female Air Force electrical engineer he had known since schooldays and trusted completely. "She said the first inmate looked like a concentration-camp victim, and another man on the floor said they were POWs, and 'he'd never see civilization again.' " The sergeant said that another friend had been in charge of tracking the C-130 flights to Hanoi and Haiphong, and confirmed they had picked up what looked like Caucasian prisoners.

"Can *you* give me an answer?" the sergeant pleaded. "It doesn't make any sense to me at all."

I traced the woman engineer to Hawaii. The girl would not confirm what the sergeant had said. She had been warned not to break secrecy rules.

I called the chief chaplain at Shelton's old base, Colonel James Millsap. "I found no evidence of misconduct," he told me. "Father Shelton is an outstanding gentleman. But he needed to learn there are some things we say in the pulpit and some we don't."

"Like – ?"

"Like talking about his father. . . . When you're in the armed forces, it is important to speak the party line."

By 1987, Ann Holland felt trapped. She had promised her husband that no matter what happened, she would be true to the secrecy agreement he had signed when he was taken off the Air Force books and placed on civilian contract. Most of her knowledge regarding Site 85 came from classified material, and she wanted to have the truth publicly debated. She was sure the U.S. government was "guilty of a massive fraud" but hid it behind secrecy rules.

Since the *60 Minutes* segment had aired, she had sent me her own painfully acquired documents. They revealed an extraordinary effort by friends in the armed forces to help her dig out facts. A senior U.S. Army officer who had served with distinction in three major wars, in combat and military intelligence, said, "Remember, lots of areas in Laos, like Site 85, are remote. Communists come seldom, and then to collect taxes and rice. Even in that one cave where American captives have been reported, the Communists don't have much communication equipment. There's a Russian plane comes once a week. The prison guards are in the boonies. . . . One CIA rescue effort was abruptly cancelled.* There were to be six prisoners rescued. One died of a bleeding ulcer. They were Site 85 personnel. They were separated from another three prisoners in another cave. ALEX [code name for a ground observer] has a friend there captured in 1978, three years after Saigon fell, and *was set up to be captured,* but that's real low profile. The six Air Force guys captured are on the mountain at Phou Pha Thi. . . . ''

James Shirah, the self-styled ''anthropologist,'' who had spent half his life in covert action, now told me the name of the DIA officer who had debriefed the Vietnamese Communist who had spent half his life in covert action. Shirah had known him for five years. ''He later worked with a secret intelligence group run out of a New York State university,'' said Shirah. ''The big kids operated it, mostly using Thailand as a base for Indochina. . . . The Vietnamese defector swears he saw one American taken prisoner, his battalion commander thought he saw at least two.''

Commander Hugh Taylor, a retired U.S. Navy pilot who later became a newspaper editor and spent many years seeking answers to the Site 85 mystery, claimed, ''The U.S. government lied, threatened, and purposely withheld information from the wives and families of the men left behind at Site 85. Families were prevented from finding out each other's identities to foil any attempt to correlate what little they knew, and were warned to stop trying to find out what happened. There are reports the Americans at the site were

---

* A Special Forces (Delta) colonel confirmed to Ann that there had been another aborted rescue attempt of a prison site in 1982 involving the Delta team. I suspected it was the same rescue attempt Jerry DuBose, the Austin taxi driver, had described to me. The intelligence gathered before the mission listed a number of prisoners who had been Site 85 personnel. The Delta colonel professed not to remember the names of the prisoners.

denied defensive support because their presence posed a threat to local CIA-supported drug operations. . . . "

Hugh Taylor had a personal interest. During the Vietnam War, he had been approached to fly unspecified missions. Those who advised him against the seductive offer of intrigue and adventure – he was very young then and admired the secret services – later told him he was lucky. Had he volunteered to be sheep-dipped, he would likely be counted among the missing, his fate concealed from friends and family.

Just like Melvin Holland.

Both Commander Taylor and Ann Holland had run into puzzling roadblocks to do with the issue. Taylor wrote a book about Site 85. The outline, he said, got back to the government. Taylor was told the publisher no longer wished to print the book.

Ann was approached by someone who called himself a Paramount movie producer. "We're making a film on Site 85," he told her, whereupon she talked to him at considerable length. Then she called me. It was the first time I had heard Ann break down. All these years she had been given the runaround. An Air Force representative had always pumped her for information she got from other sources, but he never gave her anything back. . . . This time she had quietly pumped the producer. "He told me that the same man disclosed to the film-makers things about my husband that he'd never told me." Ann was understandably upset.

She had learned this much from the film producer: "Melvin and another American fought a rearguard action to allow badly injured men to reach a CIA helicopter while Site 85 was under attack. The chopper began to lift off without them. One of the fatally wounded on board, Echberger, kept yelling, 'Don't leave! Don't leave! There are still two men down there!' The chopper wheeled away. 'Mel Holland's still down there!' were the man's dying words. The chopper never went back."

Sergeant Peter Cressman, 1971.

A page from one of Peter Cressman's drafts of his letter to a public official, outlining his dilemma. The drafts, never finalized, were returned to his family with his belongings.

A 1956 shot of Phou Pha Thi (later location of Site 85) taken by Canadian Major Charles Coutts (retired) while he was stationed in Laos with the International Truce Supervisory Commission. He noted that already the site was "completely surrounded by the Pathet Lao" and was supplied by air drops.

Phou Pha Thi dominates the surrounding Laotian countryside.

This shot of a helicopter landing at Site 85 on Phou Pha Thi was taken by Air America Captain Ted Moore in January 1968, just months before the site was overrun.

Staff-Sergeant Mel Holland
with sons Rick and John,
November 1965.

The Holland family,
Christmas 1966. Mel Holland
left in 1967 for Thailand and
then Site 85.

John and Rick at The Wall,
standing next to their father's
name.

Ann Holland and family
gather for the presentation of
the Bronze Star (V for Valor),
March 1984.

Lieutenant-Colonel Charles Ervin Shelton, the only officially listed U.S. prisoner of war. He was shot down while on a mission over Laos. (U.S. Air Force)

This photo of Charles Shelton, taken shortly before his shoot-down, was on a film in his camera, which was returned to his wife with his belongings. It shows him wearing a "sanitized" uniform.

The Van Renselaar family, December 1967.

Diane Van Renselaar and son, Erik, today,
holding a picture of Navy lieutenant Larry
Van Renselaar, whose plane was shot down
on September 30, 1968.

Two MIA Case Studies

Below: Captain James Grace was shot down over Laos on June 14, 1968, and declared MIA. When he did not return in 1973, his family accepted that he had been killed. In 1988, his wife saw this picture from a Soviet propaganda film on prisoners, made during the war. She and his closest friends claim that the appearance, stance, and movement are those of James Grace. The inset shows Grace in 1969. (Large photo: No. 77 in the DIA Unidentified Prisoner of War Book)

Opposite top: Master Sergeant Jacob Mercer, 1967. His AC-130 gunship was reportedly blown up in midair in 1972, but his dogtags, when returned, showed no burn marks or other such damage. (National Forget-Me-Not Association)

Opposite bottom: In May 1985, Mercer's wife was shown this photo for identification purposes. She insists that the stance, the cheekbones, and the eyes of the bearded man in the picture are those of her husband. The photo was brought out of Laos by the man sitting on the left, who claimed to be the nephew of the prison commander, and claimed, as well, that the bearded man was Mercer. Mercer's wife says she has received more information since 1985, but no government action has resulted. (National Forget-Me-Not Association)

Colonel Nick Rowe.

Bobby Garwood and Monika Jensen-Stevenson, November 1988.

The producer claimed that he'd seen the intelligence to back up this story. She said, "The worst thing of all, the studio saw separate intelligence reports that all agree Mel was taken alive. . . . And the Air Force has always known it. The Air Force representative always cautioned me to say nothing, ask no questions. . . . Now he's doing all the talking to Hollywood. And the film's producer, who turns out to be a former Air Force intelligence officer, won't share certain details with me."

Once again, however, an unseen hand jinxed both movie and book.

Ann hoped there was someone strong enough to rise above politics, who also had the necessary intelligence background to force some action. She sent Ross Perot the most complete of all the accounts on the fall of Site 85. She summarized her appeals to President and Mrs. Reagan for news of her missing husband. When Iran-Contra broke, knowing that many of the people called on to testify had specific knowledge of what happened at Site 85, she had written the first of two letters to the President. She thought that perhaps the President, if no one else, could influence the Senate interrogators to question those with the knowledge she desired about their earlier involvement in similar activities in Laos. She wanted to find out specifically if Site 85 had turned into the same kind of scandalous fiasco as Iran-Contra, and if that was why her husband had written, "They lied to us . . . real bad." With no intention of implicating anyone specific in an Iran-Contra-like scandal, she wrote to President Reagan for information:

> I have been trying for almost 19 years to find out the truth about what really happened to my husband. . . . I never wrote to President Johnson in 1968 because I had been told by my military advisor to keep quiet, they were working on it. I believed him until 1970 when President Nixon told the world we had never lost any men in ground combat in Laos. I realized then that those men

had been written off as expendable. They may have been expendable to our country, but my husband was not expendable to me. I was 28 years old with five small children to raise. I was an orphan when I married him and he was all I had. He was not only my husband and the father of my five children, he was my best friend. Surely you can understand why I can not let him be written off.

This brings me to the reason for writing this letter at this time. It has taken me this long to locate some of the men who have knowledge of what happened to the men at Site 85, Phou Pha Thi, Laos, on March 11, 1968. Those men will be available to you in the next few weeks. I believe those men know that not all eleven men left behind at Site 85, died. . . .

The men I am referring to who were aware of the covert operations in Laos in 1968? John Singlaub, Harry Aderholt, Rich Secord, Ted Shackley and Tom Clines. Please sir, I realize the Iranian arms problem has first priority, but will you please take the time to ask those men about Site 85?

Ann Holland knew nothing about the activities of the men as they related to Iran-Contra to other charges, she simply believed that these men should have had some knowledge of Site 85. She got no reply.

CHAPTER 23

PEROT MAKES A MOVE

Perot was receiving a lot of information like Ann's from the families of the missing. He had always been careful to protect such information – even when pressed to reveal it by people like Congressman Solarz. Events would now prove that his prudence had been wise.

Relations between Bush and Perot had gone downhill ever since the Vice President had asked Ross Perot how his POW/MIA investigations were going.

"Well, George, I go in looking for prisoners," said Perot, "but I spend all my time discovering the government has been moving drugs around the world and is involved in illegal arms deals. . . . I can't get at the prisoners because of the corruption among our own covert people."

This ended Perot's official access to the highly classified files as a one-man presidential investigator. "I have been instructed to cease and desist," he had informed the families of missing men early in 1987.

"I've forced myself to drive a stake in the ground and say I must always come back to the prisoners," he told me. "I had proved there was overwhelming evidence we left men behind; high probability some were still alive; and zero possibility of getting them back by force.

"I was left with one option. Negotiate. I didn't want to hurt this cause because people with power thought I was tying it in with other matters."

There had been numerous government attempts to negotiate during the Reagan administration. In the last year there had been a flurry of such activity because the Vietnamese had told a group of congressmen at the time of the Veterans' Affairs Committee hearings, that there might be prisoners in areas not under the control of the central government. But each negotiation focussed on the return of remains. Perot, like many of the POW families, was frustrated because the chief negotiators never seemed to ask the Vietnamese about live prisoners.

Now Perot, without negotiating himself, was about to lay the ground for negotiations on live men. In Texas they would have said he was going to "make a deal."

Shortly before Vice President Bush told him to "cease and desist" in his role as special presidential investigator, Hanoi's ambassador and acting permanent representative at the United Nations, Bin Xuan Nhat, had asked to see him. Several meetings had taken place. Hanoi hoped Perot would fly over. He went to the White House with the news. This was on February 2, 1987, and he offered to go at his own expense. He did not want to be named a negotiator.

But then White House correspondent Sam Donaldson reported on ABC-TV News that Perot had asked for presidential backing for a trip to Hanoi to discuss missing Americans. "White House officials say they have tried to cooperate with Perot for some time on the MIA issue. But they say there is strong disagreement among Perot, the MIA families, and responsible officials of the National Security Council staff. They say what Perot seems to be asking for is the prime role in the overall effort and although the President wishes him well, officials here say *that* [the prime role] he won't be given."

Donaldson later apologized to Perot, saying he'd been misled by an official in the National Security Council who described Perot as having delusions of grandeur with ambitions to run foreign policy himself. After this, the League of Families took to calling him Texas Billionaire Secretary of State Perot.

Later that spring he had flown secretly to Hanoi and returned with modest proposals from the Vietnamese leadership that would result in the release of prisoners. He reported to President Reagan and waited in vain for a response. In June he spoke to me in his Dallas office.

His rocking chair creaked angrily. As far as he was concerned, he had come agonizingly close to getting back prisoners. Hanoi was in no shape to reject any reasonable face-saving solution. The country was so *poor*. He looked through the vast windows of his library-office at the wide blue horizon of Texas and brooded on the wealth of talent here, capable of transforming that distant, destroyed economy. With the former enemy begging for help, it should have been possible to solve the issue at once. Instead, the opposition had learned all the details of his journey and was now taking steps that would neutralize its effect.

I felt vindicated in my sense that any information shared with others inevitably reached the government group that stopped actions likely to challenge the official line. So when I asked Perot if he could tell me more, I already agreed with his reply.

"I'd like to – " He stopped rocking. He was visibly upset. "I have to be careful. . . . "

Knowing his fondness for horse-traders, I had an urge to make a deal myself. I had just talked to Casino Man, whose three escaping Americans were now at Camp 5 along a chain of hideouts. There they were stuck, exhausted and uncertain if the next team of indigenous escorts could reach them through the thick jungle. I knew some names now. They were names I recognized, with families I knew. The news would be worth something to Perot, but if I told him, I would be breaking my own promises.

I had come again to Dallas because Perot had told me guardedly by phone of a news leak. A proposed mission to Hanoi by retired General John W. Vessey, former chairman of the Joint Chiefs of Staff, had been announced as soon as it seemed there might be a public outcry over Perot's independent action.

"I arranged the Vessey mission," he said. "But now the White House has postponed it. My whole effort could be sabotaged."

Perot described the secret talks in Hanoi that spring, which led to the proposal of Vessey as a presidential envoy on POW/MIA matters. Perot had been taken aback by the Vietnamese leaders' familiarity with his own background. They spoke of his long fight to free Americans – "just like your namesake, Governor Ross of Texas." It was as if the Hanoi leaders had been in Perot's office, where, on one of the walls, hung a framed plaque honoring Texas Governor Sul Ross – "a foremost humanitarian [who] spent time and means to liberate prisoners held captive by Comanche Indians in the early days of the Texas Republic. One of those released was Cynthia Ann Parker, who had been imprisoned for 25 years."

Hanoi's foreign minister, Nguyen Co Thach, had seemed to regard this visit as the equivalent of an excursion into Indian territory. "Why are you here?" he asked Perot when they first met on March 25.

"Because you invited me," said Perot. He sat squarely facing the minister. "I want to get prisoners released." He broke off. "Why are you laughing?"

"We were told you're a direct man," said Nguyen. "We didn't know you were *that* direct."

"This matter could be resolved immediately," said Perot. If the Vietnamese wished to avoid the embarrassment of producing prisoners they had said previously did not exist, they could "discover" them in Laos or Cambodia. He accepted without comment the diplomatic response that of course Hanoi exercised no jurisdiction over those two neighbors.

It became clear that the Vietnamese craved Western "respect." That was evident from the warm reception they gave him. They wanted only modest gestures from the United States. Perot asked if Thach's government would feel comfortable negotiating with General Vessey. They knew Vessey, a mud soldier whose battlefield commission was won at Anzio. Vessey was a battalion commander in the Vietnam War, later director of military support for the CIA's secret war in Laos.

Nguyen said Hanoi's leaders would wish to send someone to the United States in return. Could their most famous young Vietnamese pianist give some concerts?

Perot felt sure a piano player would not be any threat to American security.

Then they asked if one of their bright young men could come to America to study capitalism.

Again Perot couldn't see this as posing a danger to the United States. The young man could be buried in some neutral embassy, to avoid U.S. government restrictions on visitors from the Socialist Republic of Vietnam, which it still did not recognize.

Was there anything else?

Yes. Could General Vo Nguyen Giap address the U.S. War College?

Perot gulped. Giap was the man behind the Tet Offensive. On January 30, 1968, Giap launched simultaneous attacks on major U.S.-held cities, towns, and bases. Some U.S. military men said the U.S. lost the war from that day. Others argued that Giap's offensive was a tactical disaster; what cost America the war was the effect the Tet offensive had on opinion back home, where the will to win was already faltering. Giap had calculated this. He remembered how his victory at Dien Bien Phu turned public opinion in France against continuation of *its* war. American military men would jump at a chance to debate all this with the Commander-in-Chief of the North Vietnamese Army, the most famous of their old enemies. He was seventy-five and not expected to live long. U.S. students of guerrilla warfare might well curse an opportunity lost to hear Giap's side of the story from his own lips.

Perot sat back in his chair, rocking silently.

"Was that *all* the Vietnamese wanted?" I asked.

"Yup."

Vietnam had one of the world's largest standing armies. Her leaders were said to be unbending, barbaric. Their requests appeared to be simply a way to earn American respect. If they couldn't get diplomatic recognition, perhaps the United States would at least recognize that their society could produce a great classical pianist and a military strategist, and that they were Vietnamese, not Russian, and needed economic alternatives to dependence on the Soviet bloc.

"Did they admit they had our men?" I tried again.

Perot stopped rocking. "They said something to me that went so much to the heart of the matter." He pitched forward. "It confirmed . . . *The men are there.* . . . " He refused to elaborate, because he wanted to keep the doors open.

His eyes had tears in them. He shook his head. Some group in the government, he believed, had tried to sabotage all this.

When Perot had first received feelers from Hanoi in November 1986, he had recommended to Vice President Bush and others in the administration that the proper way to break the deadlock on U.S. prisoners was to send high-level negotiators. This, he argued, would show the U.S. government was serious about the POW/MIA issue, and that Vietnam did have our respect. Such a move would have taken the issue away from those officials who were finding no solution. The invitation had come from Hanoi, and Perot had informed the White House. It was then that Donaldson did his ABC report. "I waited and waited. I wasn't getting green, yellow, or red lights. I felt like this was an opportunity falling off a building," Perot recalled gloomily.

So he had filed a deceptive flight plan for his private jet. The date of departure given was a day after his actual planned departure. He now knew everything he did was monitored by the government. "They have enormous surveillance resources, as you know."

Two days before he was to leave by commercial flights booked under another name, he heard from Howard Baker, then White House Chief of Staff. "We had to meet in a D.C. hotel in the dark because Baker was trespassing on the turf of National Security Advisor Frank Carlucci by even speaking to me. Baker said, 'You can go, but go on your own.' I said, 'You know all about the Logan Act. . . . '* Baker was extremely friendly. 'Try to get them to deal with us,' he said. 'But remember, *you have to go on your own.'* "

Perot was infuriated and said, "At the end of the war we just abandoned those men. Our government froze like deer then, and it's freezing now. Howard, you're all deer. You figure if you stand still, nobody sees you. Okay, I'm not going to Hanoi. . . . "

Then he went.

Another pause settled over Perot's office.

"Did President Reagan ever know the facts?"

"Reagan talked to me much earlier," said Perot. "Said he'd heard I wanted to get to the bottom of this. Nancy chimed in to ask if anyone was still over there, and I was as forceful as I could be. I said there was no doubt they'd been left behind, and recent good human intelligence indicated they were still there. I said, 'But we won't find out unless we move. . . . We've got to make the effort while Ronald Reagan's still in office.' "

When Perot got back from Hanoi, he went straight to the White House to report. He found the agenda for his meeting

---

* Perot, of course, had been publicly warned by Congressman Stephen Solarz at the Tighe Commission hearings that the Logan Act prevented private citizens from negotiating on their own with Hanoi.

with the President was phrased to give Reagan the impression he was there to discuss financing Reagan's memorial library! Frank Carlucci, soon to become Secretary of Defense, was present with his nominated successor as National Security Advisor, General Colin Powell. They were not the sort of staffers you would expect to be interested in memorials.

Perot swept aside any talk about books. "Mr. President, I want you to get this straight from me. *You've gone back on your word.*" That got Reagan's attention.

Carlucci interrupted to say that Mr. Perot had just been to Hanoi. It was as if the President had never known about Perot's prolonged efforts to get presidential support for his journey. Perot went along with the pretense anyway, and quickly ran over the few simple requests made by Hanoi. He said again that American prisoners had been held long after the war ended. Reagan had broken his promise to get to the bottom of things. Prisoners could be brought back quickly and easily if advantage was taken of the Communists' willingness to react *informally.*

Carlucci had anticipated all of this. "In the President's pockets," Perot told me, "were these little three-by-five cue cards, just in case Reagan didn't understand that the cause of the prisoners was already in good hands. The President began pulling these cards out of his pockets. They had the correct responses written out to anything I brought up.

"Look – " Perot dug into his desk drawers and flourished White House photographs taken at the meeting. They showed Perot staring incredulously at Reagan, the man he had once championed, while Carlucci hovered over the President, who was staring down at something in his hand. The expression on Reagan's face was also one of utter astonishment.

Perot laughed, then shrugged. "Well, President Reagan consulted these cards and he said, 'We'll have to get the Communists to see General Vessey.'

"I said, 'I'll do that, Mr. President. Tomorrow. I've got a man standing by in Bangkok.' The answer was another mumble, and another look at his cue card."

Perot tried another tack. "I said to the President, privately, while Carlucci's attention was taken up with a query from his office, 'Just give me the wink if you can't do this thing formally.' I got no wink, though this was the man who'd made informal gestures famous."

Finally, Perot had said, "Mr. President, is this how you want to go down in the history books? Even if it's a hundred years from now, do you want people to read that you did *nothing* to bring them home?"

He got no response except a further mumble. "It was all futile," Perot said.

Perot's disenchantment was now complete. He had tried hard not to believe the reports that the President had been forced to backtrack on his promise to properly investigate this issue. But Perot was no longer able to dismiss the evidence that the government was giving counter-terrorism and covert action priority over our men held in captivity. The government had to prepare against the public's learning about Hanoi's willingness to meet General Vessey. "A story was leaked that Hanoi was delaying the Vessey mission," said Perot. "You can imagine the impact on the Vietnamese. These negotiations were so delicate – well, it was as if, after handling very fine bone china, someone dashed it onto a concrete floor."

In May, Richard Childress, the colonel in charge of POW/MIA affairs for the National Security Council, flew to Hanoi amid official announcements that he was arranging a forthcoming visit by Vessey, following months of negotiation. One man in charge of official POW/MIA policy thus recovered the initiative.

"The truth was," said Perot, "the first Hanoi heard of the possibility was when I suggested it on March 25." He expected the Childress group to return to the stiff, bureaucratic style of past meetings when Childress, Griffiths, and Armitage had insisted upon long semantic discussions about precise official language to describe trivialities. These discussions would lead to meaningless communiqués, and the Vietnam leaders would return to their customarily guarded attitude and ideological rigidity.

In July, a month before General Vessey was finally to go to Hanoi, he spoke to me from his Minnesota home. He was blunt. "Those statements that Hanoi wanted to postpone my mission were false. They're anxious to go forward, and I'm ready. I'll sit there, weeks or months, to get this resolved. . . . "

As it turned out, Vessey's mission lasted only from August 1 to August 3. It included some of the Tighe Commission members. Among the other delegates were Richard Childress and the League of Families director, Ann Mills Griffiths, both of the POW/MIA interagency group. What had started as an informal attempt to bridge a gap between two nations became a return to what the Vietnamese regarded as a joke.

Vessey told them that many Americans believed Vietnam still held prisoners. The Vietnamese maintained they held none. They emphasized they had their own distraught families, their own missing men: 1.4 million war-disabled, half a million war orphans, and many destroyed hospitals and schools.

Some of the other U.S. delegates said later that the talks were interrupted constantly by Childress and Griffiths – as Perot had expected. The two would challenge a word and then huddle in a corner to argue its meaning. The same complaint was made by the Vietnamese, but more politely. Deputy Foreign Minister Nguyen Dy Dien was quoted later by the *New York Times* as saying, "In negotiations sometimes there is only one word in the text, and it can take hours to remove it and replace it with another word. . . . I told the American side the important thing is action."

I spoke again to James Shirah, the intelligence analyst who had been with the super-secret Blackwatch project in Laos. He was in despair. "There's a kind of bribery going on," he said. "Serving officers who have all along kicked up a stink within the bureaucracy about the prisoners have been told it's an unwinnable fight, and to give up, and accept the offer of whatever they want in government appointments.

"I don't think the truth can ever get out. There are just too many scandals that bureaucrats can't risk having exposed. For example, the CIA files in Laos that were acid burned and that I copied and deposited in the archives in Hawaii – they held all the intelligence on nearly 600 American prisoners that the U.S. government officially said did not exist. The code name for prisoners was Brightlights. Maybe in the year 2088, file number 5310-03-E will resurface to shame us."*

On Wednesday, September 30, 1987, Congressman Solarz chaired another hearing of the Subcommittee on Asian and Pacific Affairs. General Vessey, Presidential Envoy, reported on his mission. Background was provided by Ann Mills Griffiths. Vessey gave an account of what Vietnam could use in the way of American artificial limbs and other aids for the disabled.† Griffiths took the opportunity, which seemed strangely out of place, to accuse Red McDaniel of disseminating "false or misleading information" about prisoners. Chairman Solarz attacked Red's POW/MIA fund-raising appeals

---

* Shirah would later turn over that file number and related information to investigators working for Senator Jesse Helms (Rep., N. Carolina) and Charles Grassley (Rep., Iowa). Their 1989-1990 inquiries would delve into the POW/MIA cover-up.

† Some months later Casino Man sent me copies of the incorporation document for a Connecticut-based foundation set up to deal with the Vietnamese on the matter of artificial limbs and other aids for the disabled. Ann Mills Griffiths was listed as the woman in charge.

for the effort to publicize the POW issue. "We want to have someone from the Justice Department investigate whether there is a potential case of mail fraud here," he blustered. Nothing came of this attempt to intimidate Red. One thing Chairman Solarz did not discuss was that the Vietnamese had made an offer to allow the United States to set up a branch of JCRC in Hanoi and that the State Department had not allowed it because the Vietnamese had not yet pulled out of Cambodia.

Congressman John G. Rowland, a Republican from Connecticut, protested this attack on Red McDaniel's good name. Congressman Frank McCloskey, a Democrat from Indiana, joined him. Then Rowland made some attempt to voice the frustrations of others. "I am quite frankly sick of this," he said. "We were snookered by the Vietnamese in 1973. . . . Now, fourteen years later, where have we come? We debate whether the Vietnamese are telling the truth [about] live Americans. . . . Bobby Garwood came out in 1979 when we were told they had no live Americans. The Vietnamese continue to say 'no live Americans in captivity.' "

Vessey had told me in July that Ross Perot "single-handedly" arranged the Vessey mission with the Vietnamese. At the September hearing, however, he said, "I was selected by the President in February to be his special envoy." That was a month before Perot had arrived in Hanoi. "In May," Vessey told the hearing, "Dick Childress from the National Security Council staff went to Hanoi to get agreement on the conditions for my visit." By shifting dates, the "Texan Billionaire Secretary of State" had been pushed into obscurity.

When I tried to reach Vessey later, I was told that he was "somewhere in Europe on something to do with war memorials to those who died in World War II." It was a job that would keep the retired general busy, and I didn't speak to him again.

His position was disappointing after his 1983 speech in which he said if the country asked enlisted men to do dangerous jobs and risk their lives in combat, the country had to make it very clear it would "get back our prisoners and account for the missing. . . . *Accounting for the missing in the past is a part of that promise to those who serve now.*"

There was also an eagerness to label Americans left in Vietnam as deserters – as Bobby Garwood knew too well. This took care of any promise to get back prisoners. At the Vessey hearing, Chairman Solarz asked Ann Mills Griffiths about French prisoners held by the Vietnamese after *that* war had ended. "Was it a Garwood-type situation where people ambled up to some foreign-looking person and slipped them a note . . . ?" he asked. The sly phrasing infuriated former prisoners like Red McDaniel.

I remembered that Bill had seen exactly how French prisoners – often said by the U.S. Defense Department not to exist – were treated. "Hanoi," he had told me, "called them *ralliers* – converts. To me, the men were browbeaten and trying to stay alive, and if it meant pretending to believe Communist ideology, that's what they did.

"In Hanoi's mythology, such men would convert when given the chance to study 'the truth.' So Hanoi encouraged the Western classification: 'deserter.' We play Hanoi's game if we say a brainwashed prisoner is a deserter. . . . "

CHAPTER 24

GARWOOD DEBRIEFED

It seemed as if Solarz and the others in the government POW hierarchy were also still playing the kind of "game" that President Carter's National Security Council staffer Michel Oksenberg had talked about in his 1980 memo to then-National Security Advisor Zbigniew Brzezinski – a game that had more to do with "good politics" than facts about live Americans still in Southeast Asia. Garwood's return had forced the government to give lip service to the possibility that prisoners might yet be alive. But he had been turned into the not-so-subtle symbol for any POW who might still come out.

Solarz showed his contempt for men who had gone to war in Vietnam and their families by intimating that any POWs still behind the bamboo curtain would have had the option of "ambling up to a foreign-looking person . . . and slip them a note" about wanting to go home. It seemed outrageous that, along with the struggle to obtain information from the government, the families of the missing now had to struggle to guard the reputation and character of their men. However, what Solarz intimated about Garwood was in the process of being disproved. After almost ten years of procrastination, the Defense Intelligence Agency would soon be prodded into debriefing the one real live prisoner who had come out of Vietnam – but only after a debriefing had already been done by General Tighe, someone with the reputation for being the best in the business. And DIA would admit to Garwood what they had known all along – that he was not the only prisoner, and they had known it when he came back.

General Tighe was, of course, retired now as director of DIA. With Dr. Chris Gugas, the retired CIA polygraph expert, he had finally conducted a debriefing of Bobby Garwood in California late in the summer of 1987. Ross Perot's electronic experts had checked the tapes and transcripts for fidelity. I had picked up a copy of the debriefing at Dallas during a stopover on my way to Bangkok, where Bill was waiting for me. He had called me to suggest I tie up some ends of research with Thai and Laotian Resistance workers who had been involved with prisoner reconnaissance. Casino Man had also contacted him and suggested we meet on what was now his home ground. I had not found time to study the Garwood debriefing and little realized the implication of what I had been carrying.

Bill took the transcript, and after scanning the first page, he looked up. "This interrogation should have been done here, in Thailand, when Garwood arrived from Hanoi in '79. . . . How did *this* come about?"

It had come about because Tighe, the former DIA chief, prayed very hard for guidance during Easter Mass. He'd been harangued by vets to do more about abandoned Americans. The Easter sermon sounded like God's answer. The Monsignor had preached about a Communist prison camp, where Americans were so badly tortured and malnourished they were on the point of giving up. Among them was a chaplain who made them rise at dawn – Jews, Catholics, Protestants, everyone – for a surreptitious service. It gave them new strength, said the Monsignor. . . . "No matter how tough the going, if you believe you are right, you must push on."

General Tighe had asked the priest later if he had some personal reason for choosing such an unlikely subject for that day. "He said no, he'd just felt compelled to speak – he didn't even have any connection with the military. . . . " Tighe had his answer.

Debriefing Garwood became his response. It had been nineteen months since I had brought him together with the disgraced Marine at the 60 Minutes interview. At that time, Tighe had been fighting unwinnable battles within the intelligence bureaucracy. Now he was exhausted to the point of doing serious damage to his health. His family had begged him to let it go. But he had been a common soldier who was promoted to noncommissioned rank in the field, and this meant more to him perhaps than the glamorous promotions that followed. NCOs were the backbone of the fighting forces, and from them he had learned the vital importance of moral fiber. The Easter sermon forced him to fight on. He called Dr. Chris Gugas, who had been on his task force (and who, as mentioned earlier, set up lie detectors for the CIA), to say it was possible that Garwood was the first demonstrable victim of biased or incompetent intelligence methods. Patiently he took Garwood back through his fourteen years in captivity while Gugas double-checked for signs of deception. There were none.

Bill read the transcript with growing astonishment.

The Marine had remembered things with simple clarity. Often he did not think he would remember until his interrogators took him back to a specific time and place that triggered his emotions. As he often had, when talking to me, he began with memories of "Ike," and the time they had spent together.

"It was raining, raining very hard. Cold and wet rain," he began. "Our eyes met and we recognized we were fellow Americans. First time in my life I ever cried over an individual. He weighed less than a hundred pounds, because I was able to lift him up. He was beaten all over and he couldn't see very well. He had to put his face up close to see. I found out later he was as shocked by my appearance as I was by his. I was scared to death he'd die and I'd be alone again. It was raining and cold and the Communist guards laughed because we cried and hugged. . . . I stopped feeling sorry for myself when I heard how long Ike had been in captivity. . . . "

As I read, I could hear Garwood's language when he first spoke to me. I remembered his voice and speech patterns as he sat in the Georgetown house and in the restaurant later. Although he covered some of the same ground, he had disclosed to Tighe details of deeper significance than I could have recognized back then. His interrogators were experts who knew the questions to ask.

"It was a thirst, a hunger, with me to know who these people were that captured me. The cruelty, I just couldn't understand that. . . . Ike said for me to survive the ordeal ahead – he was telling me not as a superior but as a fellow American – he had an obligation to pass on to me all he knew about survival. Ten words of Vietnamese a day to begin. After I learned a hundred words, I had to construct sentences.

"He taught me to recognize jungle vegetables and make soup and green jungle tea. I would divide a meal up, and when he couldn't see, I'd give three-quarters to Ike. He was so sick, and I was terrified he'd die and leave me alone again."

Ike said a prisoner should do everything to let the U.S. government know he was alive. Then it could act. Garwood gave his dog tags to South Vietnamese who were being released. *"I know they reached U.S. intelligence – they turned up at my court martial."*

This alone put a different complexion on things. The dog tags were a message. This was the first I had heard of them.

"Ike and I were always on display. Lots of North Vietminh regulars in full dress green came through the camp," Garwood told the Tighe team.

"I'd do work runs or tidy up the guard kitchen, anything to steal food. . . . Cutting wood, bamboo, or carrying leaves, I could forage to keep up strength. We never saw the sun because of the jungle canopy."

Two Puerto Ricans were brought in. "They were told they were victims of American imperialism just like the Vietnamese. They got special privileges." This was a familiar technique, to divide the men and make it easier to win their cooperation. It was later used on Garwood. "Later, one testified against me at the court martial, and what was really strange, he testified to what he supposedly heard me say to the Communist guards, and yet he didn't speak English and I didn't speak Spanish. . . . " The Puerto Rican had been described to me by Edna Hunter, the head of the POW center for psychiatric examination of returned prisoners, when I talked to her at the beginning of my research. He had been afraid that he would be accused of collaborating with the enemy unless he testified against Garwood. She said all who testified at Garwood's trial admitted to her they had behaved much as Garwood did.

Ike was caught after one escape attempt and beaten unconscious in front of Garwood. "He was put in stocks outside the hooch. . . . As he was dying, he said, 'Bob, they're never going to release anybody. Play along with them and maybe they'll take you to a village and try to use you as propaganda. Go along with it. The closer you get to Hanoi, the better opportunity you have to escape.'

"He encouraged me to do everything and anything to stay alive . . . so long as it didn't hurt another American . . . just so I could get out and tell the American people what happened to us there. I promised."

After Ike's death, Garwood did not make another close friend. After two years of disuse, his English "was beginning to break up." He was isolated from other Americans. Newly captive U.S. prisoners looked on him with suspicion – "One thought I was Russian." Prison commanders were upset when Garwood tried to instruct the newcomers about prison

life, and segregated him when "Americans almost outnum-
bered guards and they realized I could have organized a
revolt. . . . Those claims about Americans working for the
Communists were propaganda to try and create American
turncoats." It was cruelly simple to divide prisoners against
one another.

Garwood was uniquely informed on the prison system
because he had passed through a number of camps and work
farms. At one camp, "the American prisoners had all been
captured in Laos and were taken each day to work at a farm
set up by the Cubans. There were French prisoners there who
must have been in the system a lifetime."

He found he could provoke guards into betraying
information.

"They were always saying Hanoi wouldn't be so stupid as
to return all prisoners. . . . They'd nothing to lose. They'd
show the U.S. to be liars by producing us when it suited
them." Tet, the biggest Vietnamese holiday of the year, was
always a good time to exploit lax security. The festival was
like Christmas and New Year's Eve rolled up in one. "The
guards would get shit-faced on black-market booze. I was
like part of the furniture and heard what they said."

Once, suspecting there were American prisoners on the
other side of a hill, Garwood said to the guards, " 'Hey, I
don't give you guys a hard time, not like the Americans over
there.' And they'd fall for it." By Tet 1974, he knew there
were twenty hooches with one American in each on the other
side of that particular hill.

He got to know Communist personalities: "Scarface –
Pham Van Cuong, a real torture hunter . . . Mr. Ho, who had
his own bodyguards and doctor. . . . " He heard Ho describe
the American prisoners "in the outhouses" as pilots who
were "obstinate, uneducatable." The word "educate" was
used in the sense of "political re-education through hard
labor."

When Garwood began fixing vehicles, he not only got out
of camp to make repairs on the road; he talked with Viet-

namese drivers while crouched near or under a damaged truck. "Drivers, because they've got wheels, they're something special. They get around. They gossip." He learned military and prison-camp geography. He found out about the big prison at Son Tay, target of an American rescue mission during the war. It had become a police academy. He fixed the locations where he had seen Americans herded into large Chinese trucks.

He gave a verbal picture of one enormous prison camp to which he was sent. "Camp 5 it was called, spread right through these mountains. The mountains had been stripped of trees and planted with tea bushes by French prisoners. You go to a man-made lake by going back across the river, cross where the ferry is at Yen Bai, go down six and a half kilometers, cross the railroad tracks (that's the same railroad from Hanoi that goes up to China), then finally you're at this man-made lake, built by the Chinese. . . . Thac Ba is about half an hour by an old motorboat."

Garwood came by his knowledge through deciding no one was ever going to come to his rescue. "Once I knew official U.S. government policy was that no American prisoners remained behind, I came to the conclusion 'Bob Garwood, get the hell out of Vietnam any way you can. . . .' And, taking that attitude, I agreed to help set up a Czech generator at Camp 5. I didn't know diddley squat about putting one together. . . . But actually the parts were marked and all you had to do was fit them together like a Tinkertoy. . . . "

Garwood was suddenly in demand.

"I brought light to the whole camp. When I saw my first light bulb, I just about freaked out. A piece of civilization! I thought they were going to hug me for it. They didn't have technicians, and they'd wanted that place lit up for all the prisoners they were expecting. About 60,000 [South Vietnamese] shuffled through there, and about 20,000 remained in Yen Bai. The whole former Saigon administration except Mr. Minh was held right there in Yen Bai.

"Funny thing about it, I'd always thought I was lucky if I could change an electric-light bulb. But I snowballed my way through it. . . . In Communist minds I could now take a generator apart blindfolded and put it together again. And there I was, praying every day the thing wouldn't blow up."

The camp commander told him, "If anything happens to that generator, it will be considered sabotage, and for that – 'extreme, the most extreme punishment.' " Garwood commented: "With that kind of punishment, you're lucky if you get a firing squad." More South Vietnamese prisoners were brought in. "The Communists wanted me to teach them everything I knew about generators. I was to break down a second generator so it could be transported in small sections. This was a really big generator and I thought, 'The jig's up.' But God was looking out for me. These new prisoners were still loyal SVA [South Vietnamese Army] officers, hadn't been brainwashed yet, and there were some technicians among them. I told the guards I had to be alone, mustn't be distracted. Then I told the new prisoners I didn't know a damn thing about this generator. They laughed and laughed. Thought it was funny. Two electricians and three mechanics among them knew more or less what to do. That's what saved my butt. So I spent a week with them playing cards and talking about what happened to their senior officers, Big Minh, and the downfall of Saigon and so on." This was the camp that General Van Phat, the former South Vietnamese general, had written to President Reagan about. He was in the camp with Garwood. He had written that Garwood was a prisoner.

Thus, in 1987, Garwood told of the fate of America's allies abandoned in 1975. Perhaps the delay was unimportant to Washington, or perhaps the information was already known to the U.S. government. It might have been valuable, though, to thousands of Vietnamese refugees who settled in America. They felt as strongly about their imprisoned relatives as did the POW/MIA families. It would not be until 1990 that some of the South Vietnamese prisoners from "reform" camps began to trickle out to Bangkok under a new agreement by which the United States gave them sanctuary.

In another prison camp a compound had to be built just to enclose the newly assembled generator. "This camp took its name of 776 from the date of opening: July 1976. Captured American vehicles were bringing American and Vietnamese prisoners by the hundreds into 776. The camp commander said they were forming a motor pool from U.S. vehicles. All I'd ever done was drive a jeep, but I stood at attention and said yessir when he told me each and every vehicle would be my responsibility, especially if any broke down on the road. I tried to get out of that by saying I couldn't be responsible for bad drivers who might strip gears, burn out a starter, blow a battery. There are a million things. . . . The camp commander finally agreed and said, 'Just don't let any vehicle blow up.' "

Camp 776 was scattered over one hundred square miles, and contained twenty-two different camps. Each camp housed 2,000 to 6,000 prisoners. Any escape attempt here led to immediate execution. POWs were coming in by truck and train. One night Garwood was rousted out "to go fix a truck broken down on Route 1. On the way, a train was stopped on the tracks. . . . I counted twenty boxcars. Some opened, prisoners just fell out, packed inside like sardines.

"I fit in the crowd, watching." He wore Ho Chi Minh sandals and black prison garb, and he was stooped and gaunt and he could joke in their dialect. Having seen the film of Garwood in captivity, with his language skill and his uncanny ability to mimic the gestures and mannerisms of his captors, I could believe he'd fit in the crowd.

He was standing beside his Chinese-made jeep. One of the boxcars flew open and "out fell Caucasians. Thin, bearded, blue jackets and pants, with flip-flops. I heard things like 'Where the fuck are we – China?' This was street language, not British English. Everyone around me just gawked. This had been kept a secret from the people by the Communist administration. So everyone's taken by surprise. These weren't POWs from Saigon. They were long-time POWs."

The debriefing had filled out Garwood's story, but it begged one question: Why was Garwood kept in suspense in Hanoi for four weeks, unsure if he was to be executed, when Hanoi had already agreed that an American military transport could pick him up on February 22, 1979?

During that month's delay, it was agreed that Garwood should fly out by commercial airliner to Bangkok, instead of by the U.S. military plane. This made him seem a free agent. The Hanoi government by then saw that it had as big a stake in discrediting Garwood as anybody else: for the Communists now knew, from their conversations with him in this period, that he possessed extensive knowledge of other U.S. prisoners. During the delay, the U.S. government had time to prepare the court martial. From the time Garwood touched down in Bangkok, he was under close Marine guard. After he was tried and sentenced, nobody was ever going to take action on tales told by a traitor.

Garwood had been so effectively trashed that it had been hard to persuade anyone to reconsider the judgment on him ... even compassionate men who had become critics themselves of the policy on prisoners, like General Risner and Red McDaniel. Even Ross Perot had insisted that if he got any Americans out, they must be real prisoners and not defectors or drug addicts.

All these men now knew that the trashing procedure followed in Garwood's case could be applied to any remaining prisoners who might be brought out, and that anyone who took up the cause took the risk of having his or her character assassinated, no matter how impeccable that person's personal life. Despite this, General Tighe acted with his usual integrity. He knew certain people had been trading on Garwood's eagerness to prove his patriotism, and were advising Garwood to go to Hanoi with a congressional group to discuss other prisoners. Tighe saw a possibility that Garwood could be detained in Vietnam, and, as a convicted collaborator, would have little protection. Tighe's message was: "Garwood must not go. He will never return. Tell him that!"

Casino Man was exposed to danger, too, if he went into Communist territories. It was impossible for him to have direct contact with the three "particular guys" he was bringing out. I heard nothing until a message was sent to southern Thailand where we had been visiting old Thai friends. The nearby border jungle was well known to Bill from his years in neighboring Malaysia. Casino Man was waiting there.

The former CIA man still had the gray ghost look that I had noted during our first talks in Las Vegas. He wore the light tan clothing of an Old China hand now: silk shirt, striped tie with old-fashioned Windsor knot, tailored suit, and neat brown shoes with a high military polish. None of the baggy safari suits and elephant's-ear desert boots of the newcomers to Asia. He sat granite-faced under a sun umbrella made of thatched palm leaves, well away from the Moslem marketplace. A station wagon stood in the shade by the mosque. The driver and another man squatted against palm trees at a discreet distance.

"I never thought you'd get my message," he said.

"You mean you never thought I'd come."

"I still wonder why you're so committed," he said.

"If you're still worrying about my motives, let's stop right now!" I retorted, getting up.

Casino Man apologized. "One of the prisoners was a former buddy. When I told the Company what I'd seen, I was told to shut up. When I refused, I got into big trouble. Otherwise I'd still be part of the team, blind to where it's being led."

"Where is it being led?" I sat down again.

"To where American security is in real danger."

"How do you prove that?"

"With the perfect test case. Nothing else in American life is wrapped as *legitimately* in secrecy as our intelligence systems. So how do we know if they're properly or honestly run?

"The prisoners provided my perfect test case," continued Casino Man. "They're a lawful concern for every American.

"Inside the Company, I was blocked. So I developed my own resources – vets in intelligence, vets in law enforcement, my own contacts out here . . . and concluded the Company's routine business is in the hands of bureaucrats who know they're safe if they go along with the crowd."

Casino Man outlined the day-to-day intelligence since the first Americans were captured. *"We just don't use it,"* he said, lighting a Burmese cheroot. "I wouldn't have seen the signs if I hadn't been shocked when my report on those prisoners was deliberately torn up." He sucked long and hard on the burning cheroot.

This tangled jungle on an ill-defined border was once the retreat of Chin Peng's Communist Chinese forces in Malaya. No white man could pass through undetected. Casino Man operated from a distance. He hovered on secured frontiers and worked through local agents whom he knew and fully trusted. He could not confide his plans. One false step might send tremors along the tenuous lines he had cast into hostile territories beyond his sight. What he feared above all else was that his agents might be betrayed by his own side. A couple of years ago, I might still have refused to take him seriously. Now I knew too well the world against which he rebelled.

He had brought a discouraging report from the field. The three American prisoners he was trying to bring out were in a "free zone," unable for the moment to move to the next station on the escape route. "They're not in Communist hands," he said. "They're in limbo. And that's where they might have to stay if we don't get a clear signal from Washington that the men are wanted. The handlers don't want money – just respect and American support for their own cause."

Hanoi was also waiting for a clear signal, said Casino Man. Business deals had been made between a small group of

Vietnamese Communists and American entrepreneurs in the period after the Paris peace agreements were signed in 1973 and before the fall of Saigon in 1975. Those deals were likely to be activated any day, once Vietnamese troops were withdrawn from Cambodia. "If the deals go through, *no* American prisoners will come out alive," Casino Man added bitterly. "Not with so much at stake."

He was franker than he had ever been before. He was more at ease in this other world; he didn't need the noise of Las Vegas slot machines to drown his voice. The clatter of mahjongg ivories as Chinese gambled on the veranda of a beach restaurant was enough.

A lot of pieces came together while he talked. He said some Americans were known as "Chosen-by-God-to-stay." The phrase was *"Buon Nhans,"* in a dialect used in the region held by General Khun Sa. Some taught school. Some worked in the fields. There were other Americans who were in Vietnam as "Blessed-by-God-and-Ho-Chi-Minh," or *"Thuoc Hoa Va Ho Chi Minh."*

He was interrupted by the Chinese driver of the station wagon, who sauntered over and spoke softly to him. Casino Man nodded. The driver left. Casino Man continued. "The trouble started with that special-operations group based in Thailand up to 1973. It had its own infrastructure, camps, communications. There was violent resentment in this group at the way public opinion was mobilized against continuing the Vietnam War by what they saw as Communist propaganda back home. The guys built a shield of patriotism for themselves. I worked for them, but never put the whole thing together until 1982, when I realized how people wrapped personal aggrandizement inside a belief that it was fighting godless communism."

He said he understood how Nugan Hand business fronts operated, because he had his own practical experience. He said, "Rewald's company of Bishop, Baldwin, Rewald, Dillingham and Wong – BBRDW – was 'tailor-made for the

CIA,' according to Bill Casey. And you realize, when Nugan Hand collapsed in Australia, it continued to operate a branch in Honolulu right up until the collapse of BBRDW? When the Australian government investigated the charges of laundering drug money, the Nugan Hand crowd simply dissolved and then reconstituted themselves. One purpose was to make big money for themselves. But there was always this gloss, this pretense of generating money to support anti-Communist 'freedom fighters' wherever the U.S. Congress won't vote them an adequate budget."

By this time, I had read everything published on Nugan Hand. Admiral Bobby Inman, former director of the National Security Agency and deputy director of the CIA, had said in Washington on September 30, 1980, and again in January 1981, that further investigation of Nugan Hand would lead to disclosure of "a range of dirty tricks against foreign governments." Out of my own inquiries, I could form a picture that corresponded with what Casino Man now said.

"Decisions are still by a small group. The group is within the overall bureaucracy – the CIA, the State Department, DEA, DIA, the Pentagon, the White House. Critical documents attract the input of the members, so that when a document goes forward to the top, it only *looks* as if everyone had input."

"Can you give an example?"

"The discussions on MIAs with the government in Laos and Vietnam. . . . You'll see that no matter how successful outsiders like Ross Perot are in Hanoi, the only channel for U.S. government action remains under the control of the group. It wants to dictate the timing of diplomatic recognition, and the opening up of business in its own favor. Once that happens, forget the missing men."

Casino Man stirred. He had a long drive to make down the Malaysian east coast. "I'll go first," he said. "One of my men will follow you to the border post. You'll be quite safe."

I watched him step carefully up the sloping beach, the sand

impeding his progress, his shoulders hunched. A dogged man. But the chances of getting his "guys" out were rapidly diminishing.

I thought of "Kayak," an American pilot in Laos during the secret war. The Americans were finally pulling out, and the CIA airstrip was overrun by terrified Hmong who knew what the advancing Communists would do to them. In the confusion, Kayak was left with no aircraft of his own. Still, he had promised a Hmong soldier that he would get the man's wife and child out – somehow. Kayak shepherded them onto a crowded transport aircraft. He was told by the supervising CIA officer, "Case officers and Americans only." Kayak tried to argue, but orders were orders. He said, "If they get off, I get off." The CIA man said, "Suit yourself," so Kayak took the Hmong woman and child back off the plane. The tall figure trudged into the swirling dust, the child in his arms, the woman holding on. Those who watched knew the American pilot was doomed. "He had no need to do that," said the CIA man.

But it wasn't true. Kayak had a need to do that, just as Casino Man had such a need too. Both were part of an America with decent instincts. In their minds at least, theirs was a country that would never walk out on its friends.

When Bill had first arrived in Bangkok, he had called at Hanoi's embassy. To his surprise, he was invited back to meet a political officer. The last time he'd had dealings with Hanoi, he was asked to leave the country.

"The Vessey mission had no authority," said this official when they met. "It was not able to negotiate on matters that concern us. It did not exhibit a proper respect for the government of the Vietnam People's Republic and we did not see a reason to discuss American prisoners any further."

In this almost casual way, our misgivings were confirmed. What had started out as an informal channel had been wrecked, as Ross Perot feared. The White House team, not

General Vessey, had insisted on linking the question of American prisoners to the withdrawal of 140,000 Vietnamese Communist troops in Cambodia. This offended Hanoi. The U.S. negotiators were low-level. They made General Vessey seem an appendage without real power as a presidential envoy. So the Vietnamese shot down the Vessey mission. Well, that was their story.

A little less than a year later, Bill found his little visit to the embassy had made an impact. He got the visa he had applied for two years earlier.

CHAPTER 25

VIETNAM REVISITED

"I'm going to Vietnam," Bill said in the autumn of 1988.

"Hanoi won't let you in."

"Mr. Foo of Quebec's already fixed it!" He laughed at my expression. Hanoi had always ignored his visa applications until the Vietnamese embassy in London suddenly instructed him to contact Francis Foo in Canada. Who? Foo arranged travel to Vietnam for residents of the United States, because there was a ban on travel-agency business with the Communist regime. Foo prescribed a route through Detroit to Bangkok where "a man called Sam will meet you. . . . Give him three thousand *American* dollars to cover basics. Don't carry any other currency into Vietnam, and only small bills."

I was uneasy. "Why would Hanoi let you in after the way you wrote about their treatment of Western prisoners?"

"Times have changed," said Ross Perot when we told him. "You want to meet the top man? Call me from Bangkok while I fix it."

I still didn't like it. "Bobby Garwood was warned by General Tighe not to go back because he'd be killed," I reminded Bill.

"Garwood's not a literary figure." Bill handed me a booklet printed by the Hanoi Foreign Languages Publishing House. I read my husband's name and the title: *Breakfast With Uncle Ho*. I flipped through the pages. "They've taken out your criticisms – "

"So – ? It opens the door."

The booklet contained an extract from his book *The Yellow Wind*, which was originally a profile on Ho Chi Minh in the *London Sunday Times*. Suitably and drastically edited, it was now a text used by English-language students. I could not imagine the regime had really thrown Bill's past criticisms down a memory-hole.

Yet Hanoi was letting him go to China Beach, where Garwood's story began – at Marble Mountain . . .

In Bangkok, as promised, the man named Sam brought papers authorizing entry to Vietnam. "We don't stamp passports," he said. "Visitors don't usually want their governments to know they've been to see us."

Sam had worked for the CIA during the "secret war" in Laos. "I was only a clerk with Air America," he added with a giggle. Now he worked for Vietnam. Until lately, travellers to Hanoi had had to fly through China. If they wanted to escape Western attention – if, for example, they were destined for Vietnamese training centers for subversion and terrorism – it was the convenient way to go.

Bill read the passenger list for the 10:10 a.m. Thai Airlines flight while Sam looked the other way. The passengers seemed a mixed bag: African nationalists, Mideast "businessmen," East Europeans, and Scandinavian technicians. Sam drifted back to his Bangkok office. Two hours later, at Hanoi airport, Bill was pounced on by security men.

He was left to stare through the bars of the holding shed at a pot-holed tarmac and the runways. They seemed never to have been fixed since he had landed here first in an old Junkers-52 trimotor with the French Air Force. There was still the French colonial smell of blocked urinals, the same primitive system of painted light bulbs to signal passengers through wooden guard posts. The country was desperately and visibly poor. The passengers had swept past him, eyes fixed forward like children anxious to please teacher, but with tiny smiles of glee over an "imperialist" being caught out. Bill began to regret the message he had sent, requesting an interview with the toughest of the old Party hard-liners – to talk about American prisoners.

A cultured voice interrupted his thoughts. "Apologies." He turned and faced the man from The Office in Charge of Foreigners. *"Security* thought your papers were out of order."

The Officer in Charge was dressed like an artist from the Paris Left Bank. His eyes twinkled. *"Security* has yet to catch up with our new policies."

The word *Security* was used in a way that implied some powerful authority, momentarily out of step. Bill had just read diplomatic reports from Hanoi, analyzing tension between old Party zealots – those who had wanted to keep POWs – and young rebels who saw Vietnam as the poorest country on earth, while next door, Thailand, with fewer natural resources, was blooming into the fastest-growing economy in Asia. *Security* still served the zealots: an omnipresent network of police spies and informers. But times were changing. When Bill finally went through the barriers, a young woman in security uniform took his copy of the *Bangkok Post*. But not in order to confiscate heretical messages from the wicked world outside. With her co-workers, she settled down to study color pictures of the King of Thailand and his family.

Making the transition from the Thai kingdom to this land of commissars was like falling into a coal-black cellar. Bill had never been able to fully swallow Garwood's account of how corruption crept through Hanoi's dark alleys, and how even a prisoner could work through the black-market network. Now nothing seemed impossible. That night in the Cuban-built Victory Hotel, where Garwood in 1979 smuggled out his plea for help, Communist officials came to Bill's room, offering to change his dollars. Everyone survived by using the underground economy. The chambermaid was an army officer and taught three French classes a week for extra money. The girl in the bar taught mathematics. They were all moonlighting.

The Office in Charge of Foreigners listened politely to Bill's requests, couched in a tortuous language he thought he had forgotten: a language of indirection and supposition . . . "Suppose I were to meet Truong Chinh, the man closest to Ho Chi Minh? Suppose I were to bring up the matter of prisoners?"

In the middle of the second night, Bill was shaken awake. "Get dressed," said a man in an unmarked uniform.

It was all eerily familiar. The sudden nocturnal summons, the feeling of conspiracy. It had been like this when he was taken to see Ho Chi Minh. Now Ho was in his mausoleum, gray marble and sandstone brooding over Ba Dinh Square. The official car sped Bill on, past the former French governor's palace where Bill had breakfasted with Ho, and finally stopped at the stilted, open-sided house where Ho worked until the end of his life, each morning feeding the fat carp in the ornamental pond below. Now, in Ho's old study, sunk in a wooden armchair, was the shrivelled form of Ho's old deputy, and – some said – Ho's true boss, Truong Chinh.

Truong hated the Americans. Always had. Always would. Bill remembered the slogans Truong gave to road workers: "Think of every rock as an American head to crush."

Why was this virulent anti-American now on display?

The conditions of the meeting were that it should be kept absolutely confidential. But the promise was between Bill and Truong, and later it would be broken by an event neither foresaw.

Bill travelled south after his meeting with Truong. The rigidities of northern rule loosened. He was puzzled by Truong Chinh. Obviously the old man – he was in his eighty-first year – had intended to convey a message. Yet it conflicted with the current Party line, which was to be nice to the Americans. When Bill had tried to photograph the prison where Red McDaniel spent so many years, a security man stepped out of the shadows to stop him. Bill hopped back into the foreign ministry's Toyota. However, his escorting official said, "It's okay, point your camera through the back window as we drive away."

No casual conversation could be dismissed. It was like communicating by code with an old enemy who wants to be friendly but has to transmit through a fog of ancient hatred. Truong Chinh represented the past, but he still had the power to frighten a new generation of bureaucrats.

Bill's companions were the Hollywood actor Jeff Kober and Dana Delaney, who was to win U.S. television's best-actress award in 1988 for the series in which both appeared: *China Beach*. At the real China Beach, they climbed into Marble Mountain, at the heart of the former U.S. base near Da Nang. Dana shivered: "It's full of ghosts." One ghost was that of Bobby Garwood who'd been first held in the Communist military hospital here, under American noses. Again Bill was impressed by the accuracy of Garwood's memory.

Later, alone with a Da Nang official, Bill was asked by the former army captain: "Would Americans be friends if this thing about prisoners could be finished? . . . Some of us thought the prisoners were reformed. But they were like the converts of Christian missionaries in the old days. Rice Christians, they were called, because they did it for the rice. They were hungry. Like our Rice Communists."

Rice Christians? Rice Communists?

Ho Chi Minh City in the south intensified the sense of a nation at war with itself. Its old colonial name of Saigon was obstinately employed by the young. Its streets were alive with youngsters trading items smuggled from countries paying lip service to the U.S.-led embargo on trade. "Notre Dame the Second," the Basilica of Our Lady of Peace, was once again crowded with Catholic worshippers. A radio placed in Bill's room could be tuned to the Voice of America, the BBC, and Australian newscasts.

"We want the Americans back," said a former Saigon lawyer, "because Russian imperialists have no money. American imperialists have all the money." He was one of many visitors to the open-sided shop of a black marketeer The Duck, famous in French colonial days. He looked and sounded like Peter Lorre. "You are not Vietnamese," he said, "until you have been in prison." He had been in and out, and the secret-police chief who'd put him in was now living in The Duck's cellar.

Luke, the prison expert, was brought up for a meeting with Bill. It all seemed alarmingly open. Luke had been toppled for "corrupt practices" and, after time in one of his own jails, emerged a non-person who was denied the right to work officially. He was now part of The Duck's extensive black-market operations. If he was still reporting to the secret police, The Duck took the risk calmly: "If I go back to jail, what difference does it make? I get fed, and I don't have to work."

The few dollars Bill paid him were a fortune to the disgraced security boss. Luke was a small, thin man with lean features that seemed without character until he was caught unawares, and then his face hardened and the eyes turned mean. He talked as if he had been waiting to get all these things off his chest, and at such times he maintained the air of a friendly, sick old man. But when Bill suddenly said, looking at a map Luke had drawn of prisons throughout South Vietnam, "Those were French prisons!", then Luke drew back and showed black stumps of teeth in a snarl. "Of course," said the prison expert. "We learned from the French imperialists."

The map Luke drew resembled Billy Hendon's "Measles Map." Bill photographed it. The symbols representing Communist jails coincided with about three hundred separate detention camps of the French era. Vietnam had been, above all, a land of prisons.

"We had thousands of Americans after the release of 1973," said Luke. Even though the South Vietnamese government lasted another two years, the Viet Cong were everywhere and seized Americans when they had the chance. "Many were taken here in Saigon, pulled out of whorehouses and beer parlors, dragged down into the tunnels of Cu Chi. Many were moved through tunnels to the north while the war went on, and they often died because conditions for us were even worse and we could do nothing for them."

He claimed that "important prisoners with special skills" were taken north. Other Americans were put to work in reform-through-labor camps. In 1981, after the Reagan speech declaring that prisoners were a priority, the security authorities feared U.S. rescue missions. So the men had been scattered throughout the interior. "We thought it was impossible for information about them to leak out. Until 1985, I knew about groups of Americans in several locations."

Luke seemed not to expect more money. He reminded Bill of other officials who, when the dam burst, had been eager to talk, as if temporarily unhinged by the presence of someone who would listen. He did not ask the purpose of Bill's inquiries. He indulged in one moment of philosophy. He said, "It would help nobody today, not us nor the Americans, to let go of captured soldiers now. They're better dead."

"Why did you keep them?"

"The French paid to get their men back, over many years. The price we asked from the Americans was too high."

"How much?"

"Those four or five billion dollars Nixon promised."

After Luke returned to his cellar, The Duck said, "Tomorrow he could be arresting me again, but the black market is more powerful than anything. It runs the country. American intelligence uses it all the time."

The Duck waddled between shelves, cabinets, glass-fronted cupboards crowded with his strange and forbidden prizes: opium pipes, tins of Russian beluga caviar, French champagne, animal skins, and rows of books between whose bindings were concealed gold and silver coins and thick wads of Vietnamese *dongs* and U.S. dollars. He was so casual about it all, so unguarded, that Bill decided he must have police protection. And if so, where did that put Luke?

"He's foolish," said The Duck. "He came here from the north and put many people in jail, and they don't forget. He was denounced by Party comrades in the south." The Duck sat down with Bill and said: "You should believe what Luke says about American prisoners. He still speaks with authority. Unfortunately, he dare not tell you the worst."

"Which is?"

"Nobody wants them." He dropped his voice even lower. "The police still run this country. They compete with Western intelligence. They buy information on the black market. They think American intelligence does not want the prisoners back. There is just that madman Truong Chinh. He wants to punish Americans. He hangs onto the prisoners for that purpose. His enemies in the Party hate him. They need American help. Every time this country moves closer to America, *he* smashes everything. In the south, Truong is hated. Truong called us decadent for doing business on the sly. . . . "

Truong Chinh had sent waves of terror through the south at intervals. His power was still feared. But in Hanoi there were young leaders who did not want Vietnam to be divided again.

When the time came to leave, The Office in Charge of Foreigners suddenly lost its efficiency. Bill and his Hollywood companions waited at the Ho Chi Minh City hotel, watching the clock tick past the hour when their Air France flight should be taking off. He wondered if an earlier incident had started a security crisis.

The trio had intervened with plainclothes police trying to drag off a small girl. She screamed, "I don't want jail!" Passersby looked the other way. She was being arrested for selling "illegal maps" and faced a year in prison, according to The Duck. While Jeff Kober and Bill drove the police off, Dana Delaney took photographs.

Now Bill reflected that security police do not like foreigners to interfere. Security was loyal to Truong Chinh. Security especially did not like its picture to be taken by American TV stars.

But the foreign ministry, with its argument that capitalists had to be stomached, would oppose the security-police demands. "We need money," the foreign ministry would say. And security would reply, "Security must have the highest priority." And the argument would rage until they all missed their plane.

Then The Officer in Charge appeared with transport. They hurtled out to Tan Son Nhut. The airliner had been mysteriously detained. Bill and his two friends were rushed through formalities. His escort said in farewell, "The police have trouble controlling crime. Security fears a Chicago crime wave. . . . We must be vigilant."

And he added, squinting at Bill, "There is always the possibility of raids to rescue prisoners. And we do not want another invasion."

In those last words, Bill thought there might be some explanation for the inscrutable delay.

Then he read the announcement from the official Vietnamese News Agency. Truong Chinh had suffered "an accidental fall, resulting in death an hour later." The champion of the old guard was gone.

What strange reasons moved Truong Chinh like a puppet in an Asian shadow play? Bill ran back over the meeting in Hanoi while the Mekong Delta wheeled under Air France wings. Down there was the face of Vietnam known to bomber crews, combat infantrymen, and now tourists. The jungle roof hid layer upon layer of vegetation down to the jungle floor. And the earth masked another subterranean world, too. Those war tunnels symbolized thousands of years the West hardly knew. "We only see what the Vietnamese want us to see," he thought. When the United States first became involved with Vietnam, the name was not on U.S. maps: it was labelled "French Indochina." At the Yalta Conference in 1945, which divided the world into spheres of influence, President Franklin D. Roosevelt had asked the Chinese leader, General Chiang Kai-shek, "D'you want Indochina?" And Chiang replied, "They do not assimilate," for he knew what Roosevelt did not: that there was no Indochina – only a Laos, a Cambodia, and their dominant neighbors, the Vietnamese, whose dynasties had defeated every invader and absorbed Mongols, Hindus, and the Chinese.

Until thirty years ago, there was not a single English-language book on Vietnam's history published in the United States. The soldiers who later poured into the Indochina region knew as little as their leaders. Many Americans who were captured felt they were in the hands of killing machines.

Searching this land for prisoners was an almost impossible task without help from the Vietnamese people. Some of their leaders were playing a guessing game right now: guessing, perhaps, that President George Bush's administration would prefer not be embarrassed by the truth, either through returned prisoners or through a documented accounting that showed just where and in what numbers the men were left behind after the 1973 release. The Truong Chinh diehards would have made the United States pay, if not by redeeming Nixon's promise of aid, then in political embarrassment. The new guard just seemed to want to rid themselves of a nuisance in whatever way would be most economically profitable.

"Truong Chinh pulls the strings that make Ho perform," Bill had once written. And that last night in Hanoi, it had seemed he still tried to pull strings, though his hands were frail. He'd been hedged in by anonymous figures. His voice quavered. Yet he still struck fear in many hearts.

Untold numbers had been imprisoned, re-educated, or done to death for uttering the heresy Truong Chinh had spoken to Bill: "Il faut avoir . . . we need new policies. . . . We must learn capitalism to carry out Marxist teachings." His French was awkward but he hadn't wanted an interpreter's intervention.

He must have known about inquisitions. Truong had been "first commander and builder of the nation," which meant he had purged at will. He had devastated the farming economy with imported theories of agrarian "reform." He had tried to win the war against Americans by sole reliance on the doctrines of peasant uprising. But it was Soviet-supplied tanks, SAM missiles, heavy artillery that swept into Saigon. When Ho Chi Minh died in 1969, Truong was pushed aside. By 1986 he had talked his way back as General Secretary. He was Party "advisor" at the end. In the meeting with Bill, he parroted the new Party line, but the real Truong burst through the mask when Bill asked: "Why don't you let Americans go?"

There was no word for "prisoner" in Truong's lexicon. An enemy soldier who persistently refused to cooperate with his Communist captors was a criminal. He said, "Nobody in an appropriate position in the government of the United States has ever come here to request the return of missing personnel."

"Can I speak with Americans?" Bill asked. He held his breath, remembering a similar request to see French prisoners. He had been banned later for reporting that the Frenchmen had to pretend to be re-educated to survive; the reward was that they were then no longer called "prisoners," although all of Vietnam remained their prison.

Truong Chinh was making no effort to answer. Only his fingers flickered like bleached bones in the dim light of a solitary lantern.

"Let them all go." It was the only thing left for Bill to say, and the opportunity was dying fast. "Then you and the Americans can put all this behind you." It was the argument Ross Perot had used.

The man in the armchair breathed noisily. He had already given a glimpse of his diehard hostility. Now he made a statement whose ambiguity slipped past the would-be translator, past the hovering comrades who had staged this show to demonstrate the change of heart in modern Vietnam. General Secretary Nguyen Van Linh had said he could guarantee "there is not a single American prisoner held in this country."

But Truong had said, "It is possible we shall embarrass the American government some day by sending some back."

CHAPTER 26

WHAT THE GOVERNMENT ALWAYS KNEW

It was the last day of November 1988. We were staying in an old house high on a windy hill in Bermuda. I shook Bill awake. "Get on the extension and see if this is Bobby Garwood."

He stumbled into another room and found a phone.

"Your wife says I don't sound like me," said a man's voice.

The voice was too confident, too Californian, and too buoyant. There was no trace of Garwood's seemingly ineradicable Vietnamese accent. "Ask me about things only I could know," said the caller.

I replied, on the other phone, "Give me details of all our interviews."

Bill listened to the exchange, and finally tottered off to bed again. He had long ago become accustomed to strange calls in the middle of the night.

"I'm sorry," I said a few minutes later. "But *that wasn't Bobby!*"

"So why'd he call here?"

"Wants to see me. Here."

"Lunatic!" snorted Bill, and went back to sleep.

What made me suspicious of the caller was his account of events in Washington when he had met General Tighe with me. He spoke of a second encounter with a CBS-TV crew later that same day, at the same hotel. I knew this was not possible, since no other CBS crew would have tried to interview someone I had lined up exclusively for *60 Minutes* without asking my permission.

In the morning, when I told this to Bill, it was too late. The man who said he was Garwood had arrived.

Bill had never seen Garwood except on film, never talked with him except by phone. We watched the caller negotiate the slippery flagstone path between the orchards and the house. Then I recognized him.

"*Bobby!*"

He had filled out. He looked *good*. He moved with confidence.

Garwood started talking as we entered the library. He continued to talk on the beaches, and later walking our daughter home from nursery school. It seemed that finally, after all these years, he had recovered his identity and was no longer uncertain about what had happened and why. I said, "It was idiotic, but I just didn't see how it could possibly be you when you first called. You tripped yourself up about that second CBS crew."

Garwood shook his head. "No. They caught me in the corridor after I left you with Tighe and Ed Bradley. They wanted to do a news interview. I said the only interview I was doing was for *60 Minutes*, but I was polite and answered their questions."

"That wasn't a CBS crew," I said. Later I confirmed with CBS News that nobody had been sent to interview Garwood that day.

That evening our Vietnamese neighbors came to dinner. Until the very last days in Saigon, the husband had stuck honorably to his post in the anti-Communist South Vietnamese cabinet. He had scarcely escaped with his wife and small children; all had spent months in refugee camps. Garwood plunged into a prolonged discussion in fluent Vietnamese and I watched him revert to the man I had first met. Even his facial muscles somehow altered when his tongue delivered the glottal diction. The Vietnamese husband turned and said, "He comes from _____ ," naming a small district in the central highlands.

"He's *American!*" I reminded him.

The Vietnamese nodded. "Of course, but when he became a Vietnamese, it's like he was born in that place. He has the exact dialect." He had named the place where the imprisoned Garwood had first started to speak Vietnamese with his captors.

It struck us, too, that the security police in Vietnam had reason for their suspicion that Garwood was a CIA agent. He was a big man, and the last few years of hard physical labor had developed powerful muscles that gave him a heavy build. Yet, when he drew his knees up, hunched over, began fluttering his hands and conversing in Vietnamese, his appearance underwent an extraordinary change. In black pajamas, conical hat, and Ho Chi Minh sandals, he could still pass for a peasant of Tonkin.

When the guests had gone, Bill asked, "Why *are* you here?"

Garwood sat back. "I want to tell you – after General Tighe and Dr. Gugas debriefed me, I was put through an intensive debriefing by DIA *at last.*"

The debriefing involved two marathon sessions, clocking a total of one hundred hours. They had begun in the office of the director of DIA, General Perroots, a year earlier, and they continued into February 1988. It had taken Bobby this long to reach the conclusion that he had a right to let me, the reporter who had originally wanted to tell his story, know the truth about how he had been used and set up by the government.

"What I've come to tell you," said Garwood, "is that I was never a traitor, never a collaborator, in the judgment of those who condemned me."

Several government experts had helped in the belated debriefing. One took the trouble to come to see him privately. "I'm a former jar-head, Bob," Garwood quoted him as saying. "An old Marine. I understand . . . I watched my buddies get killed. We never had reservations about you. We knew for a fact you were a prisoner-of-war. . . . We know they broke you and we know how they used you – often you didn't know how. There was never a doubt about you. I checked all the rumors about you, the bad ones. Absolutely no validity to them."

It was what Tighe had always maintained, but less bluntly, when he said that the intelligence the government possessed matched Garwood's. The only thing he had not done was break security to tell what that intelligence was. I remembered that, during the *60 Minutes* interview, Tighe had refused to condemn so-called defectors, saying, "If the man broke, we should be first to say, 'There but for the grace of God go I,' and give him a chance."

Garwood had asked, "If you knew this, why didn't you come forward at my court martial?"

"You were a necessary sacrifice," the man had answered. "You were lucky. You got out. Others didn't. It was important at the time to discredit you, send a signal to the Communists that we weren't going to listen to your reports about other Americans. . . . "

When Garwood reached this point in the narrative, he became more visibly the man I remembered in Washington, suddenly nervous and unsure. He stood up, brushed his eyes, and said, "But why did they have to make me a sacrifice? Someone knows. Do you?"

I didn't really, but I presumed it had been so the Vietnamese and their allies would continue to be kept in the dark about the U.S.'s vast capacity for collecting intelligence. I did not want to even contemplate what other reasons there might have been. But Casino Man's words about "commercial deals" rang in my head.

Garwood excused himself and found his way to the up-stairs veranda that looked down on a calm, moon-washed sea. He was smoking a cigarette when I joined him.

"They always had precise intelligence," he said, "on every camp and prisoner. They showed me photographs of myself in some of the camps. They told me things even I didn't know, about men like my black-market boss. They said if I told this publicly, they'd deny it."

In our bedroom, I said to Bill, "He doesn't know you've just been in Vietnam. . . . "

"It's funny he suddenly shows up just when I'm back. Who paid his trip?"

"He makes fifty bucks an hour as a mechanic in L.A. He's frugal. Incidentally, Perot offered him two thousand a week to work on the POW issue, but Garwood turned down the money. Said he'd help, but didn't want to make anything out of it."

"You got that from him or from Ross?"

"From Perot."

Bill was impressed. General Tighe's debriefing notes fitted in with Garwood's personal disclosures tonight. He was impressed, too, because Garwood had started to climb out of his lonely nightmare with dignity. Bill had watched how people reacted to Garwood: black Bermudian workers fell easily into conversation with him. Garwood had developed a remarkable vocabulary, and his use of big words flattered rather than condescended to the ordinary people he'd encountered. It seemed as if instinctively they knew he was far older than he looked.

He had broken out of his reserve at one point with our Vietnamese neighbors when he said with sudden passion: "I beat the Communists at their own game. I'm the only American who ever made them into fools. I broke *their* system — *they* didn't break *me*."

It had been a brief display of cockiness, but the claim was not challenged by our Vietnamese friends, who knew better than anybody what Garwood had been through.

By dawn, Bill had worked out the full significance of what Garwood had revealed. It made strange events less inexplicable. U.S. intelligence had penetrated Vietnam with such efficiency that it could follow the movements of its own captured soldiers. There was a *technical* argument for keeping silent about the prisoners in order to prevent the Communists from learning of this coup. To protect a great secret, sacrifices must be made. But *who*, then, was saved? *What* was saved?

To keep the great secret, the Jerry Mooneys had to be silenced. To keep the secret, Mark Waple's lawsuit on behalf of Major Smith and Sergeant McIntire had to be crushed. To keep the great secret, Red McDaniel was accused of misusing the American Defense Institute. Bo Gritz faced charges of illegal activities arising from his training of Afghan rebels. When it suited the government to disown a man in covert operations, he stood naked before the law. But surely the great secrets of a nation were meant to protect the rule of law and individual conscience?

Casino Man's mystifying escape route for the three American prisoners was designed to evade both the enemy and Casino Man's own colleagues. None knew better than he the absurd lengths to which secrecy can be taken. Even Casino Man might have continued to subscribe to the theory of the great secret if he had not seen those prisoners first hand in the early eighties, and if those unaccounted for had not included a close and courageous buddy. Then Casino Man forgot loyalty to the institution and became an angry individual. "How can you serve your country, right or wrong?" he had once asked me. "Men who were lost in a war they'd been required to fight can't be discarded because of some higher national interest. . . . There is no higher national interest." Casino Man stopped serving his country when a part of it followed a policy that was for him morally wrong.

Why had the government suddenly debriefed Garwood so thoroughly, nine years too late to act on what he knew?

Garwood now believed that most of the interrogators were sympathetic to him.

He said, "When Ed Bradley interviewed me for TV, he started right out by saying, 'Many people would consider you to be a traitor.' In those days I did feel that I had collaborated. For six years in prison there wasn't even a conflict going on between my country and Vietnam, and I'd had to find ways to survive. But I *was* a prisoner. That much I've got confirmed at last. I feel free."

He was talking at breakfast. The unspoken theme, in Bill's mind, was betrayal. This man had been betrayed. He had entered into a compact with the armed services of his government. He would fight its wars in exchange for a guarantee that he would be brought home with all reasonable speed, or his family would be given a body to bury or a true accounting.

The government expert had told Garwood that hardly a day passed when "I don't feel bad about all this," and Garwood thought the man meant that he was distressed to see the honorable rules of war pushed aside by a skewed view of codes of conduct.

Had he meant something quite different and much more sinister?

Bill sat silent while Garwood explained that for a long time, according to the debriefers, U.S. intelligence suspected Garwood was being turned into a Communist propaganda tool. They tracked him through camps known to specialize in psychological pressuring; they forecast that he would emerge in the Soviet Union to be displayed in Moscow. They were puzzled when no propaganda films or documents came back, mystified when Garwood just kept being moved to new camps.

"We didn't know what the Communists were saving for you," they told Garwood now. "That's why we zeroed in on you, kept closer tabs."

There was no voicing of concern for Garwood or other prisoners. He said, "They regarded us as guinea pigs. They didn't come to get us out or try to pressure our captors."

An idea struck Bill. "Why did they target you to be killed?"

"Perhaps when they thought I was going to be put on show."

"Was this ever discussed?"

"No. They really wanted to get information. And they'd show me satellite pictures, ground photographs, and sometimes try to trick me. They had all kinds of names of Vietnamese I'd come into contact with – all working for them."

Bill looked at me. We were both beginning to think the same thing. If Garwood had been under constant surveillance, and nobody had tried to rescue him, what was the purpose of all that good intelligence? Did it exist simply as the perfect system, beautiful in itself, so valuable that it could never be used?

And if Garwood had been a guinea pig then, was he still a guinea pig when he finally came home?

The debriefers had said that the Vietnamese intelligence chiefs had become convinced that Garwood was a spy: that he *must* have learned their language in America at a special school. Hanoi still did not believe it was a lucky break and some courageous initiative on the part of Garwood that allowed his message to get out: that the Finn had not been part of a secret U.S. intelligence operation.

If the Vietnamese thought this about their enemy, might American intelligence, in turn, not also think Garwood could be a Vietnamese spy? A young, impressionable American, selected to be taken prisoner, and slowly converted to serve his captors? All the arguments used to explain why Hanoi still thought Garwood an American spy could be reversed: How *could* he learn such fluent Vietnamese in prison? Had all those years after the 1973 peace agreement been spent training Garwood to return to the United States as a spy for Hanoi?

Garwood interrupted these thoughts. "I'd really like it if you could give me that film. The one they made of me in Hanoi, before they would let me go."

"It's in a safe place. General Tighe said it would save you. It proves you were a prisoner."

"They said I was the last prisoner."

"And they waited this long to tell you, because they were watching you the whole time, Bobby. They deprived you of pay but kept you in the Marines. You couldn't officially work; you had no medicare. You were being forced into a corner. And if you had been sent back to the United States to spy for Vietnam, the economic pressures would have forced you, sooner or later, to turn to your real masters – if they exist."

"If you knew how much I hate communism – " said Bobby, pushed into anger. "They told me, 'This year, Bobby,' they said, 'you're in the clear.'" He paused and remembered something else he said they had told him. "You're on the plus side now, Bobby. But be careful, because contact with the wrong people can put you in the minus. . . . "

He could have meant by "they" either his own side or the Communists. He was, in fact, still talking about the interrogator. Bill studied the face of a young man pitched into middle age without going through the normal intermediary stages. There were so many vulnerabilities. The truth about Garwood was simple and clear. There was nothing faintly evil in his background. But his own side had created myths that fed their own suspicions. He had come back from the dead, a challenge to the policy that – for whatever reasons of political expediency, bureaucratic mindset, well-meaning efforts to preserve the morale of the armed forces, commercial gain, or inverted intelligence logic – required that none survive.

CHAPTER 27

A MATTER OF ETHICS

All through the late spring and early summer of 1989 there were strong rumors in Washington that the new Bush administration was finally moving toward an opening of diplomatic relations with Hanoi. The rumors were strengthened by the fact that some with inside information about the coming re-establishment of diplomatic relations had for the past two years been scouting out business possibilities in Vietnam. One such scout had obtained rare permission from the State Department to travel to Vietnam for his company, Henry Kissinger's Kissinger and Associates. There was still a ban on official American travel to Vietnam, as Ross Perot had found out when he had asked the government to allow him to go to Vietnam legally. Perot had been told to go on his own, but Kissinger's man had, in 1987 and 1988, been carefully briefed by the State Department for his trips. He was Lawrence Eagleburger, whom Bush had appointed Deputy Secretary of State after his inauguration.* Word on the POW grapevine was that if Kissinger opened for business despite U.S. trade embargoes, there must be hope. The old enemy was losing his demonic mask. The mask had been useful to frighten Southeast Asian allies of the United States into joining the embargoes, though few did much to stop the growing trade in smuggled goods. Even Colonel Richard Childress would leave the National Security Council to become "a consultant on Asia affairs and investment," according to the announcement in the Time-Warner publication, *Asiaweek* of January 5, 1990. It described Childress now as "formerly with the top-level U.S. National Security Council." It quoted Childress: "We have a new war, and that is in Cambodia."

POW families were not against the opening of diplomatic relations, but they were disturbed by the U.S. government's single-minded focus on Hanoi's withdrawal from Cambodia and a pronounced leaning on the part of the negotiators toward some sort of alliance with the Khmer Rouge, the Communists of "Killing Fields" fame, who were also determined to get revenge on the Vietnamese. What the families and vets wanted was that the United States insist on a total accounting of MIAs and a return of prisoners before diplomatic relations were formalized. Most were willing, however, to have arrangements for the return of prisoners couched in a face-saving way for the former enemy.

During the government's negotiations with the Vietnamese, Red McDaniel was approached by a Vietnamese man who was living in Paris, through an attorney. The Vietnamese, he said, were interested in diplomatic relations, yes, but they were more interested in economic rejuvenation for their country. Red, they knew, had offered a reward for the return of American POWs, and they thought he might be able to find someone who was interested in making a deal.

---

*   After his confirmation as Deputy Secretary of State, Eagleburger excused himself from making decisions on countries he had done business with for Kissinger and Associates.

The Vietnamese feeler brought an American to Paris to consider this new proposal. In Paris the commander of a Communist garrison in southern Vietnam offered, in confidential meetings, to deliver some 150 American MIAs he said were confined in his region. The general set a price tag of US$2 million per head. US$4 million was deposited in a Swiss bank to show good faith, and one of the Vietnamese was walked through the Geneva bank to see for himself.

The first overtures to Red McDaniel were made near the end of 1988, and the negotiations were excruciatingly slow. Red McDaniel ran the operation. Precautions were taken to prevent leaks. New state-of-the-art scramblers were installed on phones at the American Defense Institute. Special recording equipment was smuggled into Ho Chi Minh City in the hope of getting evidence that the alleged prisoners really did exist.

Dominating the later negotiations was new tension in Southeast Asia. With the Vietnamese withdrawal from Cambodia, would the Khmer Rouge, burst out of "refugee" camps along the Thai border to knock over the weakened Cambodian government? The arms reaching these camps were conveniently blamed on China. The policy to back the Khmer Rouge against Vietnamese forces was pursued, however, by U.S. covert-warfare advocates stuck in the mind-set of the 1970s and Third Option ideology.

"The Khmer Rouge are beyond the Nazis," said the president of the Federation of American Scientists, Jeremy Stone. He claimed Pol Pot still ran the Khmer Rouge, which, he said, had killed two million out of the three million inhabitants of Cambodia. He called on the United States to support the Vietnamese-backed government of the Marxist, Hun Sen.

This was precisely what U.S. policy had opposed. President Bush nominated Richard Armitage to take over the Southeast Asian desk at State. Armitage was still involved in the POW/MIA issue from his post in the Pentagon as chief of covert action. The nomination was withdrawn amid rumblings inside the State Department that covert action had led to the current mess in Indochina, including Cambodia. Bush then nominated him for other posts: Secretary of the Army, and then Secretary of the Navy. In each case, there were objections within the government. Finally Armitage resigned from his post in the Pentagon, in which he had for so long been involved in POW/MIA policy and covert operations.

Hanoi had trouble reading the signals. It wanted desperately to break out of the economic and diplomatic straitjacket strapped around it by the United States, so strangely allied with Communist China. It had assumed the POW/ MIA policy in Washington influenced all else.

In Paris, the Vietnamese presented the deal on prisoners as if the government was not involved. If it was decided the release of prisoners could help improve relations with the United States, arrangements could be made to fly out the men. If Hanoi sensed a backlash of American public opinion, the Communist government could deny the existence of any official negotiations. Hanoi was well aware of American opposition to anything that smacked of buying back hostages. Plausible deniability was not exclusively a Western device.

I was set to fly to Vietnam with Red if he reached that next stage. I had been approached independently by a former high-ranking Vietnamese government official who said Hanoi wanted long-term economic benefits more than it wanted U.S. recognition. His last post in Vietnam had been in the South Vietnamese government as a cabinet minister, and now he held a position of great trust in an American international corporation.

It was all perplexing, but no more so than other events in the five years since the report on Lance Sijan's ring set me on this long trail. I was no nearer to solving the mystery of the ring, but I knew much more about the families of the missing men. I no longer dismissed their seeming obsessions. I had only to think of Ann Holland, who had obeyed an instinct so overwhelming that she never stopped believing her husband, Mel, had survived the fall of Site 85.

Ann had written a final letter to the President in the White House:

> Since I have never received an answer [to my last letter] I can only assume (1) you were never made aware of my appeal, (2) whoever handles your correspondence did not feel I need an answer or (3) my letter cannot be answered truthfully. . . .
>
> Sir, if you, as Commander-in-Chief of our country, cannot get answers to my questions, then who can? And if you cannot answer my questions, then how do you propose to bring back our forgotten American heroes who were left behind in 1973?

I also read letters that were said to have been written currently by American MIAs and brought out through the Ho Chi Minh City trader, who was bringing out "proof" that 150 American prisoners really existed. They were written in bad English on scraps of paper. A government analyst would say they were fake, because of the jumbled sentences and bad spelling. To me, those awkward phrases sounded like Garwood long after he got out of Vietnam. His sentences had come out backwards, too. And prior to his capture, his spelling was awful.

By October 1988, the Vietnamese said they had withdrawn all their troops from Cambodia. Instead of getting the anticipated relaxation of U.S.-led embargoes, however, they heard a barrage of accusations from the United States: that they had left behind combat-ready forces in Cambodian uniform; that they were getting massive doses of Soviet arms to prop up their Cambodian puppet, Hun Sen. . . .

Suddenly Red's contact with the Vietnamese in Paris ended. Deeply concerned, he published a letter in the *Asian Wall Street Journal* that he hoped would jolt Hanoi into seeing the integrity of making a deal to release prisoners. He called on Americans to wake up to the divergence between U.S.

foreign policy as it was presented to the public and as it was practised:

> The repeated declaration since 1980 has been that the recovery of POWs is the top national priority. Higher priority has been in reality placed on the conflicting policy to support military action against the Vietnamese-backed government in Cambodia. None of the evidence on POWs has been made public because the public would reverse those priorities. The Vietnamese desperately want favorable aid and trade. If we unite with them to oppose the Khmer Rouge, we may find both problems resolved simultaneously.

This was a remarkable plea from a man who had suffered as much as any American at the hands of the Communists in Vietnam. It came from a man who could still speak of the Vietnamese as "the enemy," while believing in his heart that the enemy of his missing comrades was now to be found among zealots backing the Khmer Rouge. Those zealots wanted nothing so much as to wipe out the humiliating defeats they had suffered at the hands of the Vietnamese Communists, even if it meant backing the murderous Khmer Rouge. U.S. defeats had been blamed on "bleeding hearts" in Washington. The zealots had no intention of being defeated again because hearts bled for missing soldiers.

In Bangkok, Bill questioned again the lieutenant-general in the Royal Laotian Army who had turned in the Lance Sijan ring – Bill called him "Chuck" to hide his identity, because he continued to work with resistance groups in Communist territory. Since he and Bill had met at Lucy's Tiger Den, which now had been closed, Chuck had stopped dealing with the U.S. Joint Casualty Resolution Center (JCRC). He said the Center wanted nothing to do with American prisoners from the war. He quoted from a letter sent by "Christian Laotians" who were offering to bring out MIAs whose location they knew. This duplicated one of the letters carried from Ho Chi Minh City by the intermediary in the Red

McDaniel negotiations in Paris. Bill commented on the coincidence.

"They sent out copies by different means," said Chuck. "They write each letter at great length, very careful, trying to make no mistakes. They are sincere. The copy I saw was addressed to JCRC, but I never delivered it. The CIA is not interested in sincerity."

Bill remembered that Chuck knew of another ring. It had been given to Curtis Daniel Miller by his wife. Miller's AC-130, call sign SPECTER-13, was flying an electronic-intelligence mission out of Thailand. The crew were therefore "sanitized" and did not wear uniforms. They had crashed near the Ho Chi Minh Trail on March 29, 1972. Sue Miller had long ago asked me to bring up with Armitage in the Pentagon a report that Miller's ring had been found. Armitage had assured me the ring was a fake.

But then Sue Miller called to say she had just got the ring, engraved with the words "Love Forever Sue."

She had been told first that her husband was captured. His name, however, was missing from the list of repatriated Americans in 1973. "I felt so strongly he was alive," she told me, "I wasn't surprised when a decent sort of man from the Pentagon came to tell me confidentially that Curt fell into the hands of the Pathet Lao."

Two Air Force officers had appeared without warning on her doorstep in October 1983, and had said they needed to speak urgently to her about Curt. "I almost fainted. I couldn't go through it all again – more questions raised, more answers never given. They hit me with intimate questions about my marriage . . . I was in a state of shock. . . . Then I realized they were looking for answers – I couldn't possibly guess to what questions. . . . " Although she was afraid to get her hopes up, she wondered if they were trying to verify details in a message from her husband.

Her callers finally said Curt's ring had been recovered. Could she describe it? She blurted out the inscription: "Love Forever Sue." They showed no reaction and said they couldn't let her have it. A matter of ethics, they said. It wouldn't be proper to pay for its recovery from a refugee in Bangkok.

Nevertheless, Sue did track down the "refugee" with the ring. She did not tell me how. She did tell me she never paid a cent for it. It was precisely as she'd had a jeweler refinish it, just before Curt went back – with a delicate florentine treatment, featherlike, unmistakable.

"That ring was real," said Chuck when Bill recalled all this. "But American intelligence did not want it to be real."

Bill asked how it was inscribed.

"Love Forever Sue," said Chuck.

"Why didn't you bring this up earlier?" asked Bill.

"One has to be careful." Chuck took a deep breath. "Americans come to me saying they are agents, working on prisoners. But they don't really want to hear. . . . You have an expression, to kiss someone off. That happens to your boys. Their families kiss them goodbye, but your government kisses them off."

However, some U.S. government servants had not kissed the boys goodbye. Colonel Nick Rowe, for instance. In early 1989, he was military advisor to the Philippines armed forces. He used that position to keep track of unofficial activities by other Special Forces men like Major "Zippo" Smith, who was now into his third year of operations inside Communist-run territories. Rowe had become embittered since that first time I spoke with him at the Special Warfare Training Base at Fort Bragg. "We have all the intelligence on our MIAs," he'd said then. "With Reagan as president, we'll get them out."

Colonel Rowe had always played by the rules. You were loyal, you didn't run to the media with complaints, and your trust was reciprocated. That had been the way the rules used to work. Now he saw charges brought against Colonel Bo "Jimbo" Gritz by the U.S. government. That April, Gritz faced a grand jury.

Gritz's mistake, as Rowe saw it, was that he had gone into the Golden Triangle to question the drug warlord Khun Sa about MIAs, and had come out repeating Khun Sa's charges that some U.S. officials were using secrecy to traffic in illegal drugs. The U.S. government had threatened Gritz, said his lawyer, Lanny Wade.

Charges were brought against Gritz in Nevada, a state "notoriously lax about resisting certain political pressures," observed Wade. Yet the worst the state could do, after a long ordeal of grand jury questioning, was to prosecute Gritz for a minor felony: using another person's passport. Use of a false passport was standard operating procedure for clandestine operations; and Wade let it be known he would fight the case on the basis that Gritz was ordered by the White House to falsify his passport to carry out a national-security mission to see Khun Sa. This permitted the defense to obtain DIA records on the Khun Sa mission's origins. Wade was also then able to question White House personnel, who invoked national security in order to avoid public testimony. The government officials active in the POW issue were permitted to testify *in camera*.

Wade, the defense lawyer, told me, "In open court, I would have torn him to shreds. *The DIA material showed the mission was given the highest priority.* Childress answered directly to the President on MIA matters. I now had the evidence of a meeting in the President's office, a meeting that came to the conclusion that Gritz could probably do what nobody else could . . . get back a prisoner from Khun Sa."

The classified reports made it clear that Gritz incurred government wrath when he tried to link "a POW/MIA cover-up" with Khun Sa's allegations that U.S. government officials dealt in illegal drugs. Gritz was warned, according to Wade, that "if they find out about this in Thailand, heads will roll."

A former National Security Agency man, Major Clarence "Chuck" Johnson, swore an affidavit: "I was aware Bo Gritz left active duty at the request of Lt. Gen. Aaron as a commander of Special Forces and as U.S. Army intelligence chief. I was informed by Bo in November 1978 that General Aaron had asked him to temporarily leave uniformed service to determine the status of POWs. . . . Bo did submit his request. . . . From that time until now, I have been in close personal contact with Bo, and am aware of his activities. Throughout this nine-year period, I have served as a cut-out and back-up to Bo's operations, a role which is standard operating procedure for intelligence assets outside official channels."

He swore to being present at meetings between General Aaron and Bo Gritz. At my meeting with General Perroots in late 1985, the officers surrounding him had tried to persuade me that the DIA letter, signed by Aaron and arranging for Bo to be sheep-dipped, was a forgery!

Major Johnson testified that with the discovery by Gritz's reconnaissance teams of "30 U.S. POWs at _____ on line, Laos, in April 1980," efforts were made to stop Gritz by the intelligence services. Gritz then moved into the Army's Intelligence Support Activity (ISA, or "The Activity") with a case officer, Dan Myer, code-named Shipman. "ISA was unreported to Congress," swore Johnson. "And [was] therefore unlisted as an official intelligence activity."

In April 1987, Major Johnson said he was asked by Gritz to go to Thailand to acquire "various records of interviews with Khun Sa, naming U.S. officials involved in the illegal trafficking of arms and drugs." Johnson kept careful notes and on May 19, 1987, according to his affadavit, listened in and chronicled a telephone call to Gritz from a security officer in Washington, Joe Felter, who apparently said to Gritz, "They say you're in for a real shit-blizzard unless you knock off all current activities. . . . You've got no options. . . . You're going to be 'taken care of.' No one wants to hurt you. But you've got to erase and forget everything. . . . You are going to hurt the government and get hurt unless you do exactly as I say."*

---

* Johnson states in his affidavit: "Affiant recognized Felter's voice from previous telephone conversation. Although it is not

Two other members of the Gritz team confirmed listening to these words. Both agreed Gritz was also told, "Look, Jimbo, we're all just trying to help you. Nobody wants to put a war hero in jail. . . . They're ready to crunch you big-time. You're gonna serve fifteen years as a felon – four files of aggravated charges and hostile witnesses. . . . Just get your ass on the first thing smokin' this way. . . . Don't talk to anybody. . . . "

Gritz was acquitted on April 18, 1989. He had already been harassed by grand jury investigations into his training of Afghan rebels – another assignment that could be made to look illegal if repudiated by his own government. It seemed to Colonel Nick Rowe a remarkable way to reward a man greatly honored for dangerous behind-the-lines operations in Vietnam, who had once commanded all Special Forces in Central and South America, and who had willingly given up a fast-track career to go under cover and search for POWs.

Rowe made his views known. He was already angered by the sudden stand-down of a Delta force ready to strike into Indochina to rescue men. Twelve days after Gritz's acquittal, the press reported that Colonel James "Nick" Rowe, aged fifty-one, U.S. advisor on how to counter Communist terrorists, was gunned down and killed early in the morning after he left his house in Manila by Communist terrorists.

Major "Zippo" Smith, working on his own, continued to send back reports from the field. These went to Ross Perot now. The lawsuit *Smith vs. The President* had been defeated in the Supreme Court. It had seemed more and more like *lèse-majesté*. Government lawyers, as if working for the Crown, had all the time and resources to wear down Smith's stubborn but increasingly hard-pressed lawyer, Mark Waple.

To Smith, it seemed that only one thing would jar America: a living, breathing prisoner. He was equally certain that his

---

usual practice for the affiant to make written notes of conversations, a concern existed in affiant's mind for the potential of government interference due to the sensitive nature of Khun Sa's statements." The complete text of this affidavit is in Appendix 4.

opponents would stop at nothing to prevent him or anyone else from thus causing a great public outcry. *"You are going to hurt the government,"* Gritz had been told. And Bobby Garwood, having got out of Vietnam against all odds, heard the first words from a fellow American when he landed in Bangkok: *"Don't talk about other American prisoners."*

So now Smith trusted nobody. He worked only with local Laotians, Cambodians, and Vietnamese that he had recruited himself. He lived rough, suffered bouts of malaria; and he reported to Perot the survival of Americans he had seen in open-cut mines or teaching school in remote valleys. They were always guarded. Garwood had watched Americans boarding railroad cattle-trucks. They now worked, Smith believed, in iron foundries at Da Nang. They were known, said Smith, to U.S. intelligence. They had to be. They also had to be sacrificed to the cause of winning the wars America lost in the 1970s. Secret intelligence, Smith said bitterly, was not serving those who needed it. That was the final futility.

He sent back a photograph of himself. He looked like a phantom. Since he was a retired officer, he could have sought medical aid from Special Forces camps still operating secretly in northern Thailand. He knew now, though, that U.S. Special Forces had been drawn into a joint-intelligence activity, Force 838, that functioned without the Thai government's official knowledge.

A complex intelligence apparatus was spending unreported funds on resistance to the Vietnam-backed government in Cambodia. Clandestine warfare continued to threaten America's good name in order to serve the purposes of a small group that was pursuing its own private policy in Indochina, directed from Washington through a top-secret unit in Bangkok.

It was becoming clear to Smith why so many good Americans like himself had been made targets of lies and disinformation worthy of the Soviet Union at the height of its own disinformation operations against "the enemy." By some bizarre inversion of values, Smith and all who dared challenge U.S. government policy in concealing intelligence on missing Americans had become "the enemy." Americans lost in Indochina must die soon. They were less important than continuing covert wars that eroded Vietnam's strength in the buffer zones of Laos and Cambodia.

But any reliance upon the natural elimination of living evidence was badly shaken in November 1989 when two World War II Japanese soldiers, now in their seventies, emerged from guerrilla country on the borders. In 1989, the outlawed Communist Party of Malaysia (CPM), operating on the Thai border in thick jungle, came to terms with the Thai Fourth Army.

After forty-five years in the jungle, these two old soldiers suddenly reappeared, giving new heart to Smith, who still clung to the quaint belief that nothing could be more wicked than a government hoping time will erode any evidence of its dereliction. Asian Communists had twisted their prisoners' minds into submission by saying, "We can keep you forever." That threat was again disproved.

CHAPTER 28

THE SECRET WAR

"If they find out about this in Thailand, heads will roll."

Those words from a government official suddenly illuminated the POW/MIA mystery. Thailand was a good and close ally. It was not likely that it would ignore charges that U.S. officials had made any kind of arrangement with Khun Sa, who was regarded there as a notorious drug warlord and brigand, who often assaulted Thailand's borders and made claims on Thai territory.

Thailand had been the base for secret warfare in Southeast Asia since the mid-1950s. The tiny kingdom was awakening to what this really meant; and so were we. Bill was travelling with combat troops in the winter of 1989. They were inspecting a jungle factory making artificial limbs for Thai soldiers.

Bill asked a general how there could be so many disabled soldiers. "We lost *whole battalions* of troops in Laos. They were called 'mercenaries' because the war was secret. They didn't wear uniforms, which meant they could be executed if captured. We *had* to get our wounded back."

An advisor picked up the theme that evening. "If we hadn't stopped certain American activities, we would be in the same condition now as Cambodia and Laos. We'd be destroyed. Do you know the slaughter in Laos was worse than the Khmer Rouge killings? No, you wouldn't, because it took a movie to make the world aware of the genocide in Cambodia."

The Thai kingdom, by resisting French colonialism in the previous century, had lost Laos and Cambodia as buffer states. Both countries had religious, racial, and historic links with Thailand. "They've become battlegrounds," said a former United Nations High Commissioner for Refugees, now retired. "The Hmong people don't really exist any more, because of the secret wars the CIA promoted."*

---

* The cultural genocide of the Hmong in Laos was only officially acknowledged in early 1990 through a scholarly work in the journal of The Siam Society, whose President was the King of Thailand. An Israeli anthropologist from the Hebrew University of Jerusalem, Erik Cohen, had spent years studying the changing needlework of Hmong survivors of the secret wars, and in examining "anguish and distress" expressed by the few surviving Hmong women in their folk art, he mentioned in passing how "war disturbed and eventually destroyed" the Hmong communities in Laos. He wrote of harsh communist reprisals against the Hmong after the CIA "organized and equipped a Hmong army under General Vang Pao." He wrote of Hmong homes "napalmed" in anti-communist operations, but all this was discussed within the context of his learned paper on what happened to folk art among ethnic groups "experiencing major cataclysmic events." He estimated that fifty thousand Hmong survived to be resettled in America "centuries away from their mountain homeland." Observing that Americans commonly fail to distinguish between refugee groups, he added that "the most dramatic manifestation of distress among the resettled Hmong was 'sudden death syndrome,' " a still-mysterious phenomenon in which young people simply died in their sleep, disconnected from their past. There was something

The Thais had joined in those secret wars, persuaded that Communist guerrillas were ready to advance on all the borders: difficult borders of mountains and jungle, exposed to revolutionary forces from China, Burma, Malaya, and the Indochina states. Thailand had been the base for training Hmong hill people, the special concern of Jerrold "Hog" Daniels. The work began in 1956 when "White Star Action Teams" prepared men, women, and children for counterinsurgency operations in Laos. U.S. instructors, if asked, were to say they were doing "relief work." A Program Evaluation Office (PEO) covered operations from 1958 to the end of the Vietnam War. "The only way to combat Communism in places like Laos is through covert-action groups," Thai Special Forces were told. Even earlier, the CIA had provided heavy weapons and naval vessels to General Phao Sriyanonda, who became the most powerful figure in Thailand, trafficking in illegal drugs for CIA clients.*

"The CIA, through its affiliated Sea Supply Company, was responsible for supplying the police with tanks, armored cars, planes, boats, helicopters and firearms, and it trained a Thai paratroop division," reported another Thai advisor, in a 600-page internal document, reviewing a period when the kingdom was overwhelmed with a secret U.S. presence.

Narcotics . . . The cultural genocide of ancient peoples . . . And this sudden vision of thousands of artificial limbs. It amounted to a substantial reason to discourage investigation into the fate of missing Americans.

Pierre Jambro, the United Nations Commissioner for Refugees in Thailand, said the "refugee" camps on the Thai

---

frighteningly appropriate in the way this all slipped out in a study of "Laotian needlework," and the professor's conclusion that "a close relationship appears to exist between political events and folk crafts."

* Surachart Bamrungsuk, "United States Foreign Policy and Thai Military Rule, 1947-1977 (Thesis, Cornell University, 1985). Published in Bangkok.

borders harbored groups armed and trained to fight for control of Laos and Cambodia – the Khmer Rouge dominated such groups. Familiar names came up, of Americans who had taken part in secret missions into the other two Indochina states during the Vietnam War. The U.N. High Commission was taken aback, in the wake of Vietnam's withdrawal from Cambodia, by the offer of transport by U.S. companies implicated as CIA proprietaries in the Iran-Contra scandal. "Nongovernment agencies" offered their help. Some were identified by UN officials as U.S. intelligence fronts.

"Americans who came to the refugee camps to interview possible eyewitnesses in connection with MIAs were not interested in prisoner-intelligence," said a former Thai commissioner on refugees. "They were Americans recruiting for the secret armies."

This kind of information was coming out now because of remarkable changes in Thailand. It had always boasted of its success in defying colonialist expansion. There was a natural reluctance to see itself as having serviced the United States in the exercise of its power in Asia. At the end of World War II, the Office of Strategic Services (OSS), forerunner to the CIA, was heavily influenced by the belief that Britain sought to panic the Thais into coming under direct imperial British control. The United States decided to become Thailand's guardian.

Americans seemed to start with the advantage that King Rama IX was born near Boston, Massachusetts, in 1927. But as a schoolboy during World War II he had lived in Europe, and followed in detail the British use of commandos when the British Empire stood alone against the Nazis. The King later studied British secret operations based on a belief that a monstrous tyranny could be sabotaged by brave men using their brains. He came to Bangkok with his elder brother after the war. The brother, who was heir to the throne, was found shot dead on the eve of his coronation. The younger brother became Rama IX at the age of eighteen. Still a schoolboy, he had to feel his way into a job that gave him no direct or political power. He was an idealist who believed there had to be moral strength at the core of any defense system.

By the time President John F. Kennedy declared Laos to be the keystone in this defensive arch in Asia, seasoned Thai military rulers had been won over by vast quantities of anti-Communist aid. C.L. Sulzberger of the *New York Times* called the CIA's chief client, Police-General Phao, "a superlative crook." A later Thai prime minister, Kukrit Pramoj, said Phao was "the worst man in all Thai history, and that's saying a lot!" As the CIA's man, Phao marketed the opium crops of anti-Communist Chinese bands in the Golden Triangle. His CIA-trained Border Patrol Police escorted the opium caravans for the big Chinese dealers in Bangkok, who rewarded Phao with directorships on a score of corporations. He rigged the gold exchange and ran the slaughterhouses, where the squeals of dying pigs are identical to the cries of murdered humans.

In all these years, King Rama IX had to move cautiously. United States involvement in Vietnam ruled out any head-on clash with his generals. In the retreat from Saigon in 1975, though, he saw that the United States "had a short attention span." In the neighboring kingdom of Laos, the failure of covert warfare ended with King Savang Vatthana starving to death in a prison camp. His royal Laotian armed forces had become indistinguishable from CIA-run forces.

King Rama IX had celebrated his sixtieth birthday in 1988, to a massive outpouring of national affection amid the most auspicious signs. He had completed the fifth twelve-year astrological cycle. The King's way of fighting vice and other evils was the Buddhist Middle Way. He won over insurgents on the borders with ambitious land-reform programs. His friend the Buddhist abbot of Wat Tham Krabork, a crusader against opium, was sought out by the Golden Triangle's best-known drug warlord, General Khun Sa, who repeated what he had told Bo Gritz: that he would end his own followers' dependency on drugs with outside help. Opium-growers in

Thailand had been shown by Rama IX how to cultivate new crops of exotic fruits and temperate-zone vegetables for foreign markets at far greater profit than the pittance they were paid by the drug traffickers.

But still operating from Thai soil were the advocates of covert war against Communism. Their activities had literally paved the road for Khun Sa from the Golden Triangle to Bangkok's middlemen in the drug trade, when it was built as a "strategic highway." The Thai Office of Narcotic Control was in 1990 still fighting a flood of heroin from Laos. Police-General Sawat Amornwiwat estimated the flow at 2,000 tons, double the previous year's total production. In the clean new wind blowing through Thailand, the police directorate no longer tolerated corruption. Nor did they tolerate those who pretended to fight Communism to cater to vice.

The struggle for a middle way continued. Laos was the major source of heroin destined for the United States. Anti-Communist guerrillas drew on recruits trained in the "refugee" camps, and smuggled the drugs to finance operations. The Communists of the Lao People's Revolutionary Party were just as guilty. One of the region's most notorious heroin "master-chemists" ran a soft-drink company to cover the manufacture of the most popular heroin brand sold in New York.

Rama IX's projects for weaning border hill-tribes from growing opium crops had attracted delegations from his Communist neighbors, who wanted to see what commercial alternatives could help them escape from economic dependence on opium. Others in Bangkok still followed the old CIA view that covert warfare was the only way to combat communism. The Thai press no longer tiptoed around this subject, as it had when powerful military politicians subscribed to, and benefited from, the covert-warfare theory. "Everyone knows the old CIA believers are back," said a Bangkok columnist. "They are not on the diplomatic list, and they still don't go through our immigration formalities, so if there's a congressional inquiry, they can deny being here." The chief criticism against them was that after nearly forty years they had proved ineffective.

THE CIA IS NOT THE USA read the headline in "Thailand's independent newspaper," *The Nation,* when it reminded readers in October 1989 that

> The Bush administration steadfastly maintains that aid to non-communist resistance [in Cambodia] is non-lethal. Yet General Dien Del, commander of the rightwing Khmer People's National Liberation Front (KPNLF) said last week that U.S. weapons including anti-tank missiles enabled his troops to penetrate deep into Cambodia and knock out five Soviet-made tanks. . . . U.S. lethal aid has been and is being supplied to the KPNLF covertly by the CIA [but] whatever the CIA does is covered by layers of plausible explanations that give Washington plausible grounds for denial.

Among the new fronts was the allegedly anti-Communist Cambodian Working Group that the *Bangkok Post* called "the covert key to military aid."

Thais who had been reluctant before to talk about U.S. prisoners now said it was always obvious to them that missing Americans were not wanted back. "They'd only open this whole can of worms," said a Thai national-security advisor, echoing General Alexander Haig.

The withdrawal of Vietnamese troops from Cambodia had stirred up clandestine groups drawing from a pool of some 400,000 Indochina refugees in Thailand. The secretary-general of the Thai national security council, Suwit Suthanukul, said in Thailand there were 290,000 Cambodians under UN border-relief organizations and 106,000 Cambodians sheltered by the UN High Commission. There were another 76,000 from Laos. Non-government agencies were one channel for arms. At the start of the dry season in November, heavily armed "refugees" had already taken up positions in

Communist-controlled territories for "the final onslaught."

"The final onslaught" was the concept of a clandestine-warfare enthusiast who came to see Bill. He was a disciple of Theodore Shackley, the former CIA chief in Laos, and of "The Blowtorch," Ambassador Robert Komer, who had been appointed by U.S. President L. B. Johnson to kick off the Phoenix program in Vietnam. He said, "When we first became active in Thailand, the Thai Independent Movement was operating out of Communist China for the same purpose that other Communist fronts were proclaimed in free Asia. We stopped China's expansion, but we lost Vietnam.

"You've got to weigh these dangers against crusading on behalf of Americans who may or may not exist, who may or may not be collaborating with the enemy."

Bill objected that, officially, the U.S. war had ended fourteen years ago. Prisoners could hardly be accused of collaborating with the enemy now. They were simply surviving. As for the existence of American prisoners, this had been substantiated in daily U.S. intelligence reports during the postwar years.

"But we're talking about letting Vietnam get away with the same old Communist tricks," said the other man. "We have to stop any Hanoi-backed government from continuing to control Cambodia. We have to keep arms, supplies, and advisors going in there. The way to democracy is only through the battlefield."

Bill's caller was concerned that "muckraking" in the MIA issue would encourage newsmen "like Mort Rosenblum," an American who had just published *Back Home: A Foreign Correspondent Rediscovers America*. Rosenblum was concerned that, outside of Washington, the American intellect was being hit by government distortions. "Our credibility," wrote Rosenblum, "has been . . . battered by lies, distortions, 'damage control,' erased tapes, secret hypocrisy and broken promises. . . . "*

---

* *Back Home* (New York: William Morrow, 1989).

There was no arguing against the covert-warfare advocate. A public scandal – over the destruction of the CIA's "assets" like the Hmong, the origins of the Khmer Rouge slaughter in Cambodia, the illicit drug trade – any of these moral issues must take second place to defeating Vietnam.

Just at this point, I received the best evidence that Casino Man's "merchandise" had been in good condition as recently as the past summer. His obsessive commitment to getting them out, his allegiance to what could only be walking skeletons, kept him on the right side of the narrow line separating those he regarded as carrying out the proper function of the CIA from those who had misused the institution. Years ago, he had recruited "controlled assets" in the service of the United States. Such assets had been betrayed when the intelligence files were left intact by Americans in their haste to leave Saigon. He had not forgotten, any more than the Thais could forget – as one intelligence advisor told Bill – "the way Americans were shown on the television news kicking Asians off the evacuation helicopters." Nobody wanted to become a controlled asset again.

Casino Man's "particular guys" were bunched up in Laos. The Communist rulers in the capital of Vientiane had poor control over remote valleys and mountains. They had not been eager to admit this, any more than their sponsors in Hanoi wanted to confess that administration in the provinces was shaky at best. The "new thinking" laid down by the Soviet Union had turned Vientiane into a strange amalgam of beer, bars, and boogie-woogie, but all skin-deep and lashed together to lure businessmen from non-Communist Asia. Beyond the seedy nightclubs along the Mekong, Caucasian "illegals" and escaping prisoners could hide in Communist-free pockets.

There were similar pockets all over the former Indochina states. Almost every day, the Thai government located Thai prisoners and paid roughly U.S. $1,000 to get each one out. Most were now fishermen who had been arrested by Communist gunboats. The Thai government did not regard its captured citizens as assets who had flown out of control. To

those Americans who were zealously won over by the arguments for covert warfare, uniformed Americans who became
prisoners were not assets at all. Assets, in their parlance, were
CAs – Controlled Assets, recruited among Asians, whose fate
could be seen in the skulls piled up on the site of the old
Khmer Rouge torture chambers near the Cambodian capital
of Phnom Penh. Controlled Assets could be denied if taken
prisoner – "The U.S. government knows nothing about
them." Their services could be abruptly forgotten to suit the
expediencies of each new twist in secret strategy.

The truth rose above the surface of lies in late 1989, after a
new Thai prime minister, Chatichai Choonhavan, challenged his foreign ministry's entrenched policies on Indochina. There was a perception that Thailand had been led into
policies laid down in Washington, D.C., by a group whose
objectives in Southeast Asia never came under public review.

The situation was first hinted at by the former CIA director,
William Colby, who had conducted operations during the
Vietnam War, in his joint appeal with the president of the
Federation of American Scientists, Jeremy J. Stone. Colby
pointed out the danger of U.S. support for the guerrilla forces
based on Thailand's borders, and dominated by the Khmer
Rouge. He asked if the U.S. really wanted to revive war with
Vietnam. The United Nations General Assembly again per-
versely voted on November 16, 1989, for an interim administration in Cambodia that would include the omnipotent
Khmer Rouge. The Federation of American Scientists
charged, in the *New York Times* of the same day, that the
White House continued to use U.S. financial and intelligence
resources to fight Communist Vietnam. The focus of the
secret wars had become Cambodia, the moment Vietnam
withdrew its troops in the hope of escaping U.S.-enforced
isolation.

"The Cambodian Working Group, a highly secret unit in
Bangkok . . . coordinates every move. . . . Working with the
Group are CIA operatives from the U.S. Embassy in Bangkok
and officials from the highest levels of the Thai, Malaysian

and Singaporean governments," wrote Stone, the Federation president.

"The Working Group is the conduit for all lethal material and financial aid . . . except for that coming from China. It reviews battle plans, approves specific weapons, disburses direct cash payments and reimburses resistance leaders. . . . Weapons [are provided] through a quasi-private weapons company in Singapore. And the United States pays for virtually everything."

He wrote that the general offensive launched into Cambodia after the Vietnamese withdrawal had been carefully planned and organized by the Working Group. Those running secret U.S. policy had pressured Thailand "not to pull the rug from under the war itself."

This statement, combined with ex-CIA director William Colby's earlier protest, for the first time alerted the public in Thailand to the danger of secret policies run by a second-tier U.S. government, backing a coalition overshadowed by the genocidal Khmer Rouge.

"The U.S. Government is intervening in Thai politics by backing its hardline Foreign Minister, Siddhi Savetsila, against its prime minister, Chatichai Choonhavan, to keep the war going," wrote the Federation president the next day in his second *New York Times* article. "Secret details on the Thai involvement shed new light on the importance of supporting the peaceful initiatives of the [new] Thai Prime Minister."

Khmer Rouge leaders, loyal to the lunatic "Marxist," Pol Pot, were allowed to travel from their jungle bases to offices and warehouses in Bangkok where their arsenals were overseen by a U.S. intelligence entity, disguised under the number "838."

The charges were followed at once by a statement from Thai foreign minister Siddhi Savetsila that the Cambodian conflict "will no longer be a top priority for my ministry."

So ended the mystery of why I had triggered such a campaign by government officials; a campaign that touched me far less than it affected the lives of so many who had blundered unknowingly into forbidden territory. America's wars in Southeast Asia had not ended with the fall of Saigon. By drawing attention to those who said U.S. intelligence had up-to-date information on missing Americans, I had unwittingly disarranged someone's idea of "national security." Such Alice-in-Wonderland logic led to Garwood's persecution because he kept trying to force into the open the knowledge gathered by what DIA's General Tighe had called the best human-intelligence network imaginable. The former DIA director just happened to believe that if it existed, it ought to be used to benefit Americans who needed it most.

I now understood Scott Barnes's claims about his first secret mission into Cambodia, before his Laotian mission, and why he got into difficulties when he talked out of turn about seeing American POWs. He had described how the CIA's Jerry "Hog" Daniels became upset by the discovery of prisoners – the real purpose of the mission, he had always claimed, had been to pursue clandestine military objectives. Daniels had been known as a "refugee" officer helping in the POW/MIA issue. Barnes's contention all along, now supported by our Bangkok sources, had been that sections of the agency for POW/MIA affairs had been used to cover secret wars.

"Sections of JCRC were corrupted into a bureau to bury evidence of prisoners in order to protect the secret of further clandestine operations," claimed the source who had supplied details to the Federation of American Scientists. "That's why Daniels died – either by his own hand, or by others determined to silence him. He couldn't live with the knowledge that American agencies supposedly performing humanitarian services were in reality dedicated to more killing."

Daniels' praises had been sung by General Alexander Haig, while he was Secretary of State, who described him as an American dedicated to Indochina's refugees. Now it turned out that the refugees, herded into border camps, had been undergoing tough and continuous training ever since war drove Cambodians, Laotians, and Vietnamese over

Thailand's borders. Under secret agreements, the British Special Air Services (SAS) based in Malaysia had helped to train guerrillas whose resistance in Cambodia inevitably strengthened the Khmer Rouge.

When the truth came out at the end of 1989, the British foreign secretary, Douglas Hurd, announced that his government was satisfied all Vietnamese troops had indeed withdrawn from Cambodia, despite the Cambodian Working Group's propaganda campaign to convince the world that this was not so. British policy on the region underwent an emergency review. Questions were asked about SAS units involved in collaboration with the Working Group in Bangkok.

Resistance broadcasts sought to portray the Vietnamese-backed government in Cambodia as being led by a Khmer Rouge "killer," Hun Sen. But Elizabeth Becker, the historian who chronicled the years of massacre by the Khmer Rouge under Pol Pot, gave the lie to this propaganda in an article for the *Washington Post*, reprinted in the *International Herald Tribune* on October 25, 1989. As an adviser to the Cambodian Documentation Commission, she had sifted through files left behind by Pol Pot after he fled from the Vietnamese invasion of 1978; and she said with the authority of those documents that Hun Sen was out of commission after losing an eye during the Pol Pot purges. He had never participated, she said, in the genocide.

I supposed Henry Kissinger prepared the way for the distortion of truth when he declared that he had been told there were no U.S. prisoners in Cambodia on April 9, 1976. As William Shawcross wrote in his book *Quality of Mercy*, "It was the policy of American administrations to say as little as possible about their role in Cambodia. . . . From the White House's point of view, this was sensible enough – those years of warfare saw the destruction of Cambodian society and the rise of the Khmer Rouge."* Three years later, Lt. Gen. Vernon

---

* William Shawcross, *Quality of Mercy* (New York: Simon and Schuster, 1984, pp. 48-9).

Walters, a deputy CIA director, admitted that "in Cambodia, several U.S. personnel were known to have been captured and never accounted for"; but the groundwork by then was firmly laid for ignoring the fact that many U.S. personnel were lost in secret warfare in Cambodia. General Walters's statement referred only to the men who were recorded as missing prior to the end of the official conflict in Vietnam.

Up against such heavyweight authorities, what chance did ordinary Americans have if they challenged the doctored records? None. Not until the weighty authority of the United Nations came down on their side in mid January 1990. The Security Council met in Paris to discuss Cambodia, unable to ignore leaks about secret warriors stoking up the fires in Southeast Asia again. The U.N., it was agreed, must play a greater role in Cambodia.

Suddenly, it was Thailand that was blamed for America's drug problem. "Corruption poses a significant problem in Thai enforcement efforts," Melvyn Levitsky, assistant secretary of state for international narcotics matters, testified before a joint hearing of the U.S. Senate Foreign Relations Subcommittee on East Asia and Pacific Affairs on Terrorism and Narcotics in March 1990.

"You'd think the Americans had just discovered illicit drugs," a Thai narcotics-control chief, General Chavalit Yodmanee, told Bill. "Every time I turn around, there's a new 'drug war czar' in Washington. I have to brief him, when it should be Washington briefing me." The Thais were now taking all the blame because the Golden Triangle was finally acknowledged to be the chief source of heroin smuggled into the United States. The Senate subcommittee heard evidence that the United States embassy in Bangkok had been "less than frank," but this was blamed upon a desire to avoid offending Thailand's national sensitivities. General Chavalit, a policeman since 1956, educated in England and trained by Scotland Yard, said the basic problem was the American drug market and America criminal skills "creating a flood which, if American law enforcers cannot control with all their enormous resources, this small country cannot be expected to stop all on its own."

The process of shifting blame on everyone else, as the Thais saw it, was dangerous. On March 15, 1990, the U.S. government announced the indictment of "General Khun Sa, the opium warlord." Many Thais feared that this opened the way for another military operation, similar to that in Panama. The Thais' military forces were accused at the same time of corruptly supply the Khmer Rouge in their renewed attacks in Cambodia. Nothing more was heard of the Cambodian Working Group, and instead it was reported that the Beijing regime, with help from middlemen in Singapore, supplied the anti-communist guerrilla forces.

Five months earlier, as Vietnamese troops began a well-publicized withdrawal from Cambodia, a twenty-one-nation conference in Paris had suspended negotiations to head off civil war. Then, few members knew how Cambodia had been turned into Tom Tiddler's ground by lethal busybodies. The leakage of those "secrets" led to the 1990 reversal of course. Such leaks were regarded as "criminal" in the Bush administration, observed the editor of the *Washington Monthly*, Charles Peters.

The leaks undermined the secret policy to defeat Vietnam's interests: and to blame Cambodia's "warring factions" for failing to agree on how to live together. In fact, they were desirable leaks. They served Americans well. They strengthened the hands of those in the CIA as much as in the State Department who wanted to get back onto something like a moral track. They were the same kind of leaks that made patriotic Americans sense, long ago, they had a moral right to demand answers about missing men. If they had been treated with common civility, our country might have been saved much grief. Instead, they were told to stop making squalid nuisances of themselves, and warned that they were making a big mistake.

My own "mistake" had been to refuse to heed the government warnings against proceeding with a *60 Minutes* item. Its title now took on a grim significance: "Dead or Alive?" I had fought for my original title: "Unwanted – Dead or Alive." I could understand now that the word "Unwanted" would inflame those controlling the POW/MIA issue.

The simple actions of so many other Americans did not seem sufficient cause for retribution from our own country's secret services. Their questions had unwittingly provoked a hidden monster. In the end, I suppose a kind of moral victory was won – by all those wives, mothers, and children who were made to feel like traitors for seeking clear answers; by stubborn men who had served loyally in U.S. armed forces and who had made the hardest of choices between service loyalties and personal conscience; by lawyers like Mark Waple, who believed not even the President of the United States was above the law; and by Dorothy and Red McDaniel, who suddenly and in deep dismay discovered that the security of the nation was endangered by a loss of integrity at the very heart of its defenses.

Some day, Americans like Casino Man and Major Smith will prove *they* were the true loyalists, upholding ideals on which our defense institutions are based. I would hate to think national security is in the hands of those who say America can only be safe if top-secret labels are plastered over all intelligence reports, regardless of the welfare of the American people. My own comparatively mild ordeal taught me that the real America still consists of brave individuals who will fight for their beliefs against zealots who fund murky foreign wars with deniable assets and disposable soldiers.

PLAUSIBLE DENIABILITY

"T he following information is being handwritten because we are no longer using our computers for this investigation, for security reasons," began the note. It had been sent to me from a U.S. Congressional committee in Washington, D.C., that, during 1989, had begun aggressively to question the possible abuse of official secrecy to conceal POW/MIA intelligence reports. The two federal legislators who spearheaded this effort, Senators Charles Grassley (Iowa) and Jesse Helms (North Carolina), held key positions on judiciary and foreign-relations committees. They were both Republicans who believed that personal conscience and the national interest took priority over political expediency or self-serving government use of secrecy labels. Sadly, their precautions were intended to protect them from influences within their own government. All through 1989, staff investigators on their congressional committee had run into obstacles similar to those I have described.

They were disturbed by the official campaign to discredit Major Mark Smith after he placed intelligence on American prisoners before his superiors. By September, Grassley had a six-inch-thick "classified" file on Smith, including the allegations that were made against him and were investigated by the CIDC, the army's Criminal Investigation Command. I had already heard all about this from Smith's lawyer, Mark Waple. The file also contained Smith's allegations about the suppression of prisoner intelligence.

Senator Grassley finally concluded that they must talk with the Army's CIDC case agent, Tracy Usry, who, after prolonged investigations in Korea and Southeast Asia, had cleared Major Smith of all charges. Senator Helms's office called the Army Congressional Affairs department on Friday, September 15, requesting a briefing. The army liaison officer saw no problem with arranging for Tracy Usry to review the case for the senators the following Monday or Tuesday.

There was a hitch, however, as the handwritten note from the committee went on to tell me: "The Army suddenly realized we had their only copy of the documents. . . . the contents were most embarrassing to the Army, but the Army didn't know for sure since it didn't have a copy. . . . All day Monday, Senator Helms's staff dealt with the Army, and it became apparent the Army was beginning to squirm."

Senator Grassley felt the Army was fighting a delaying action to cover itself. On Tuesday, September 19, his staffer, Kris Kolesnik, called the general counsel in the Army's Congressional Affairs office requiring the presence of Tracy Usry in the senator's office, "by 1300 hours that same day."

"We have to get a copy of the Smith file from the Records Center in Baltimore," responded the counsel. "That will take the rest of this week. Then we have to sit down with Usry and go over his report line-by-line. It's hard to say when Usry will be available to the senators, but it will be quite some time."

Kolesnik made a counter-proposal. "Bring anyone you like to Capitol Hill, and we can go over the material together, because we've got a copy." When this offer was rejected, Kolesnik suggested to the counsel that the only logical reason for delaying matters must be that the Army wanted to coach Usry in what to say and what not to say. The Army's general counsel denied this. "Then don't be surprised if Senator Grassley shows up at Bailey's Crossroads," countered Kolesnik before hanging up. Bailey's Crossroads was Tracy Usry's base. His acting commander, Colonel David Humbert, was informed several times of the senator's intentions to come personally to the base, but "They thought we were bluffing," Kolesnik told me.

Finally, Senator Grassley crammed Kolesnik and a staffer from Senator Helms's office into the back of his orange 1977 Chevette and hurtled over to 5611 Columbia Pike, where the commanding general had vacated his office. Colonel Humbert, standing in his place, was confronted shortly after the 1300-hour deadline. Surely, Grassley suggested, the colonel did not want to get involved in "what's tantamount to interfering with a Congressional witness." The colonel agreed, and let Tracy Usry return in the senator's overcrowded car to Capitol Hill.

So it came about that senators finally saw the material that I had urged my *60 Minutes* executive producer to review four years earlier. It would have made it impossible for him to dismiss Smith as an Army looney. Usry made it absolutely clear that Army-inspired allegations against Smith were untrue.

Finally, in late 1989, CIDC case officer Tracy Usry was officially detailed to the Senate Foreign Relations Committee. He had waited five years to break the official barrier. His professional wish all along had been to pursue Smith's own allegations – namely that intelligence that might be embarrassing to the U.S. government was discredited, because the sources were made "plausibly deniable."

But even the minor triumph of obtaining Usry and his material was almost wrecked when Senator Helms was told "by the highest quarters in the defense department" that he should stop his inquiries for reasons of national security. There is was again: the last refuge of scoundrels, an appeal to patriotism. Unimpressed, Helms insisted that he wanted Usry's knowledge and investigative skills put exclusively at the lawmakers' disposal. The cat was now out of the bag about the senator's interest – and investigation.

By November, there were bursts of official activity. The Joint Casualty Resolution Center (JCRC) sent a team to Hanoi amid self-righteous statements that the Bush administration was determined to settle the MIA issue. General Vessey returned to Hanoi for a brief but well-publicized visit, seeking American remains. By December, the U.S. government was being distanced from any support given to any guerrillas who had continued to fight Vietnamese forces in Indochina.

Meanwhile, investigators for senators Helms and Grassley told me details of a report from Hanoi specifying the survival of twenty American prisoners as recently as November 1989. Their existence had been reported by an American who was interviewed by the investigators after her return from humanitarian work in Vietnam. The investigators confirmed that she had delivered details – names, addresses, and U.S. service identification – to the highest authorities in Washington, D.C. They requested that I keep the information confidential while they waited to see if any action would be taken.

Tracy Usry now told me that he had continued his own inquiries ever since he became convinced five years earlier that Major Mark Smith had been falsely charged in order to discredit his story of abandoned men. As part of the senators' overall investigation, he gave name, chapter, and verse for the case built up against those who had misused U.S. national security. His partner, an active Secret Service officer, told me how efforts were made to discredit Usry once he made known his belief in Smith's story. Usry has in his possession the letter from his commander acknowledging that the accusations made against him could not be substantiated. In many ways, it had been the courageous position Usry adopted that originally influenced Bill to take my early arguments seriously. He had waded through Usry's voluminous files on Smith and McIntire; files that later were said by the U.S. Army to be confidential.

One action brought sadness. Diane Van Renselaar had kept her hopes alive since the 1987 bureaucratic slip-up that revealed that the government always knew her husband, Lars, was not killed, but had been taken prisoner. Now, suddenly, his body arrived from Vietnam – on what would have been his birthday. She took friendly witnesses to receive it. The naval officer in charge was cryptic. "This," he said, "is a clear case of murder."

Lars's fingers and toes were missing. His body had been embalmed, and perhaps stored in the infamous Hanoi warehouse that had been described by The Mortician to Congress. Diane's privately hired, independent experts told her Lars had been held captive for some time: his teeth were in far worse condition than when Diane had last seen him. The amputation of fingers and toes "is evidence of the torture and punishment we tracked," said Jerry Mooney, the National Security Agency analyst. "American prisoners who fought deep interrogation or repeatedly defied work orders had parts cut off, piece by piece."

That was another of the many things Mooney had wanted to say during all the years when he was warned of how he could be shamed and ridiculed if he told what he knew.

APPENDIX 1

Open Letter from Robert Garwood to the House Subcommittee on East Asian and Pacific Affairs

June 5, 1985

MESSAGE TO: The Congress of the United States of America

ATTENTION: Congressman Stephen Solarz, Chairman
House Subcommittee on East Asian & Pacific Affairs

FROM: Pfc. Robert R. Garwood, USMC

I want to briefly outline what I know about American prisoners who are alive and being held against their will in Vietnam. Allow me to call to your attention the attached 'Washington Times' article dated May 21, 1985, as an accurate summary of what I saw and heard of other Americans while I was in Vietnam. I am concerned that you as congressmen have not taken steps to bring my brothers, fellow American prisoners, home. It's time for you to outline what actions you have taken, besides holding hearings and writing letters, to rescue these live POWs. I fought communists in a war in Southeast Asia in which Congress walked away in 1973 and left me, as well as many other Americans, behind.

I have been told repeatedly by officials of the U.S. government to be quiet and only privately discuss my knowledge of Americans that were held back by the Vietnamese. After almost six years of silence, I decided to publicly disclose my first-hand knowledge of other Americans still in prison camps in Vietnam, in a December 4, 1984 article in the 'Wall Street Journal'. Much to my surprise, I received little attention from Congress as a result of this alarming disclosure that I had seen 60 to 70 other Americans between 1973 and 1978. On March 22, 1985, I held a news conference in Washington, D.C. and gave names, dates, and locations of the other Americans I knew who were still in Vietnam to Congressman Bill Hendon for transmittal to President Reagan. To date, I am given to understand that the President's advisors have refused to permit a meeting between the President and Congressman Hendon to discuss the live POWs I saw. I cannot understand why a President who declared the POW/MIA problem to be this nation's highest national priority, would allow his advisors to stop information from reaching him that I saw several other Americans still held prisoners by Vietnam.

421

I met in a closed session with members of a House subcommittee on May 15, 1985, after what I understand was an intense lobbying effort by some of my friends to set up this meeting. I cannot understand what you are hiding! I was interrupted and instructed by Congressman Gilman, in an elevator full of congressmen, not to discuss openly my sightings of live American POWs held in Vietnam. I cannot understand why you want to keep it quiet that you left live Americans as POWs in Vietnam and have not taken steps to rescue them! I freely volunteered to come forward in open session and swear under oath that these American POWs I saw with my own eyes want to come home to America. They want to be rescued. You simply cannot write these live Americans off as war casualties. I understand that Congressmen Soloman and Solarz want to see me again in closed executive session on June 12, 1985.

Listen closely! The only reason I came forward six months ago with a public disclosure of my eye-witness accounts of U.S. POWs, was to help bring these Americans home. Not to be ignored, not to be hidden away in a back room, and not to be told by congressmen to be quiet. It's my understanding, from other POWs as well, that we received better treatment when it was publicly known that we were important to the American public. It would be a betrayal of American values and the Constitution of the United States if you as congressmen were not doing everything in your power to bring these Americans that want to come home, home. It has been six months now since I came forward and pray, tell me, (1) what have you done to bring these Americans home?; (2) why you walked away and left us there?; and (3) why do you want to hide from the American public, the proof that we left live American prisoners of war still in Vietnam? Please tell me.

I am prepared to testify in open session where the American people can judge the truthfulness of my information. I am unable, at this time, to meet with you behind closed doors. I would like to receive a written, formal response to the three questions I have asked in this letter.

Thank you for your interest. Please bring home the live POWs!

Sincerely,

Robert R. Garwood
P.O. Box 182
Vienna, VA 22180

APPENDIX 2

Letter from Ronald Reagan to Mrs Anthony Drexel Duke

In this letter the National League of Families is identified as a member of the government Interagency Group.

THE WHITE HOUSE

WASHINGTON

July 7, 1987

Dear Mrs. Duke:

Your letter to Nancy concerning the POW/MIA issue just came to my attention. Thank you for sharing your concerns.

Let me reassure you of my personal commitment to achieve the fullest possible accounting of our servicemen still missing in Southeast Asia. The priority effort we brought to this issue early in my first term has resulted in more progress since the end of the war, but we are not satisfied. Hanoi possesses far more information than it has been willing to share, information the families deserve to receive in order to end their uncertainty. I recently

appointed General Jack Vessey (Ret.) as my
personal emissary to Hanoi on this issue and we
are attempting to establish an agenda with the
Vietnamese at this time to ensure a successful
trip.

Internally, intelligence priorities are at the
top and we have increased full-time staff on
this issue throughout the government by several
fold.   The effort is government-wide and does
not rest in any one agency due to the complexity
of the issue.   The Department of State chairs
the Interagency Group, which includes all
agencies and the National League of Families,
while the Department of Defense acts as
Executive Agent.   The NSC staff participates in
all meetings and provides active oversight for
me.   This process has served us well.

Nancy and I appreciate your interest and
support as we share your deep concern.   We will
continue to do all we can, recognizing that
ultimately the full answers still lie with the
Communist governments in Southeast Asia.

Sincerely,

Ronald Reagan

Mrs. Anthony Drexel Duke
3 Pound Hollow Road
Glen Head
Long Island, New York   11545

APPENDIX 3

Extracts from an Affidavit by Jerry Mooney

RE: SGT JOSEPH A. MATEJOV, ET AL.
     THE MISSING IN ACTION AND
     PRISONERS" OF WAR RESULTING
     FROM THE VIETNAM CONFLICT.

STATE OF MONTANA   )
                          : ss.
COUNTY OF ROOSEVELT   )

MY NAME IS JERRY J. MOONEY. I CURRENTLY RESIDE AT 324 EDGAR STREET, WOLF POINT, MONTANA, 59201. I AM 49 YEARS OLD, MARRIED WITH TWO DAUGHTERS AND FOUR GRANDCHILDREN. BETWEEN 28TH OF APRIL, 1957 AND 1ST OF JUNE, 1977, I WAS ON ACTIVE DUTY WITH THE UNITED STATES AIR FORCE. I RETIRED AT THE RANK OF E8, SMSGT. DURING MY 20 YEAR MILITARY CAREER, I SERVED AS AN INTELLIGENCE ANALYST AT VARIOUS OVERSEAS LOCATIONS IN EUROPE, AFRICA, THE NEAR EAST, THE FAR EAST AND SOUTHEAST ASIA. FURTHER, I PERFORMED THREE STATESIDE DUTY ASSIGNMENTS WITH THE NATIONAL SECURITY AGENCY.

I MAKE THE FOLLOWING STATEMENT CONCERNING SGT JOSEPH A. MATEJOV, ET AL., THE MIA'S AND POW'S RESULTING FROM THE VIETNAM CONFLICT, OF MY OWN FREE WILL AND WITH FULL UNDERSTANDING IT IS EQUIVALENT TO SWORN TESTIMONY AND SUBJECT TO THE PENALITIES OF PERJURY:

DURING THE VIETNAM WAR, THERE WAS A POPULAR PROTEST SONG THAT CONTAINED THE LYRICS: "WHERE DID ALL THE YOUNG MEN GO, A LONG TIME PASSING?". FOR 16 LONG YEARS, SGT MATEJOV'S MOTHER, MARY MATEJOV, THE OTHER FAMILY MEMBERS, AND TOO FEW CONCERNED CITIZENS HAVE ASKED THAT SAME QUESTION OF OUR GOVERNMENT CONCERNING THE MIA'S AND POW'S FROM THE VIETNAM WAR. OUR GOVERNMENT, IN CONGRESSIONAL COMMITTEES/COMMISSIONS, A PRESIDENTIAL COMMISSION, JUDICIAL COURT ACTIONS, AND OFFICIAL STATEMENTS OF RESPONSIBLE GOVERNMENT OFFICIALS, HAVE BORROWED FROM THAT PROTEST SONG THE OFFICIAL U.S. POSITION: "TO GRAVEYARDS EVERYWHERE"...

THE SURVIVING CREW MEMBERS OF THE EC47Q DID NOT GO TO A GRAVEYARD ANYWHERE. THEY WERE CAPTURED ALIVE AND IDENTIFIED IN A CATEGORY KNOWN AS "MANNA FROM LENIN, MB-MOSCOW BOUND"! THEY WERE IDENTIFIED AS POW's. BUT POLICY AND POLITICS AT THAT TIME, ABANDONED THEM, FOR "VIETNAM,'AS I NOW REALIZE, BECAME THE "WALK AWAY WAR"...

SOME OF THE INTELLIGENCE INFORMATION RELATING TO THE EC47Q INCIDENT WAS PROCESSED, EVALUATED AND REPORTED BY MY SECTION. FOUR OF THE CREW, THE "BEEPS" (BACKEND ELECTRONIC PEOPLE), SURVIVED THE INCIDENT AND WERE CAPTURED ALIVE. IN CONVERSATIONS WITH DIA ANALYTIC COUNTERPARTS, THEY CONCURRED, STATING THAT BACKUP OPERATIONAL DATA SUPPORTED THE INTELLIGENCE. FOUR HAD SURVIVED AND WERE CAPTURED BY ENEMY FORCES. THIS WAS A SIMPLE, UNCOMPLICATED TRUTH ARRIVED AT BY THE EXPERIENCED EXPERTS OF THE TIME, BASED ON THEIR PROFESSIONAL REVIEW OF ALL AVAILABLE DATA, WITHOUT THE INTERFERENCE OF POLICY OR POLITICS.

SOMETIME LATER, INFORMATION APPEARED IN THE PUBLIC MEDIA INDICATING THE FOUR SURVIVORS OF THE EC47Q HAD BEEN CAPTURED BY THE PATHET LAO. THIS WAS POLITICALLY CONVENIENT TO OUR GOVERNMENT, FOR THE FOUR EC47Q SURVIVORS COULD THEN JUST DISAPPEAR INTO THAT RECOGNIZED MIA/POW "BLACK HOLE" IN LAOS, AS DID SO MANY OTHERS. HOWEVER, DATA I PROCESSED AND EVALUATED WAS NOT PATHET LAO, BUT NORTH VIETNAMESE! BECAUSE OF ENEMY FORCE DISPOSITIONS AND TACTICAL COOPERATION IN SOUTH LAOS, THE PATHET LAO HAD INVOLVEMENT IN THIS INCIDENT. BUT IT WAS THE NORTH VIETNAMESE WHO EXERCISED THE COMMAND AND CONTROL OF THE FOUR SURVIVORS OF THE EC47Q; MATEJOV, CRESSMAN, BRANDENBURG AND MELTON. THIS WAS CRITICAL AS IT ENABLED AN IMMEDIATE, DETAILED EVALUATION OF AVAILABLE DATA. IT CORRELATED KNOWLEDGE OF ENEMY INTENTS AND CAPABILITIES RESULTING IN AN ACCURATE AND PROFESSIONAL ASSESSMENT. TO THE BEST OF MY RECOLLECTION IT WAS AS FOLLOWS:

EC47Q SHOOTDOWN, 5 FEB 73

"THE EC47Q INTELLIGENCE COLLECTION MISSION WAS, IN ALL PROBABILITY, FLAK TRAPPED, A DELIBERATE PRE-PLANNED ACTION, RATHER THAN A TARGET OF OPPORTUNITY. THIS IS SUPPORTED BY (------) ACTIVITY SHOWING AN ENEMY INTEREST AND PROBABLE INTENT AGAINST THE MISSION PRIOR TO THE INCIDENT. THE PROBABLE UNIT INVOLVED IN THE STRIKE WAS THE (...ND) REGIMENT WHO HAD CONDUCTED A SIMILAR FLAK TRAP IN LAOS IN LATE MARCH 1972 AGAINST A C130 AIRCRAFT. INFORMATION INDICATES THE "BEEPS"; MATEJOV, CRESSMAN, BRANDENBURG AND MELTON, SURVIVED THE STRIKE AND WERE CAPTURED ALIVE. DATA FURTHER REVEALED THE CAPTIVES WERE IN THE CONTROL OF THE

NORTH VIETNAMESE AND THEIR MOVEMENT WOULD BE EITHER TO HANOI
OR THE SPECIAL POW CAMP NORTHWEST OF VINH AT (CN --- ---).
IN THEIR MOVEMENT, PRELIMINARY INTERROGATIONS WOULD PROBABLY
BE ACCOMPLISHED BY THE (...TH AND ...RD) DIVISIONS IN THE
(--- ----) AREA AND THE (---TH) DIVISION IN THE (-- ----)
AREA. IT WAS FURTHER ANTICIPATED, THAT DUE TO THEIR CURRENT
SPECIAL KNOWLEDGE, AND PAST EXPERIENCE, THEY WOULD BE
HANDLED AS "**MANNA FROM LENIN**", WERE **MB (MOSCOW BOUND)**, AND
WOULD EVENTUALLY BE PROCESSED THROUGH (--- ----) LAOS".

UPON COMPLETION OF THIS ASSESSMENT, IT WAS DISCUSSED
WITH A COUNTERPART ANALYST AT DIA. DURING THAT CONVERSATION
I MENTIONED, "WELL, THEY (THE SURVIVING EC47Q CREW MEMBERS)
ARE GONE FOREVER. WE WILL NEVER GET THEM BACK". THE
ANALYST I WAS TALKING TO REPLIED, "YOU BETCHA!"

THOSE TWO STATEMENTS (...THEY ARE GONE FOREVER...AND
YOU BETCHA") REPRESENTED AN UNDERSTANDING BY EXPERTS I
ASSOCIATED WITH, THAT CERTAIN PRISONERS HELD BY THE ENEMY,
"**MANNA FROM LENIN**", WERE GONE FOREVER. THIS WAS BECAUSE OF
THE TACTICAL, STRATEGIC, AND/OR SCIENTIFIC/ECONOMIC VALUE
THEY REPRESENTED TO THE ENEMY AND THEIR ALLIES. THIS SHOULD
SURPRISE NO ONE, LEAST OF ALL, OUR GOVERNMENT. IN THE ARMS
RACE OF MILITARY POSTURES, CAPABILITIES, AND DISPOSITIONS,
IT IS NOT OUR QUANTITY THAT ENABLES US TO MAINTAIN A BALANCE
OF POWER WITH HOSTILE NATIONS, BUT OUR EXPERT
QUALITY-HITECH. IT IS ALSO TRUE, THAT OUR ENEMIES, AS WELL
AS FRIENDS AND ALLIES, HAVE RISKED ESPIONAGE, BLACKMAIL,
SUBVERSION, ETC., TO OBTAIN SECRETS AND CAPABILITIES. IN
THE VIETNAM WAR, MANY OF OUR MEN, TRAINED AND WITH HANDS-ON
EXPERIENCE IN THAT HI-TECH AREA OR WITH SPECIAL KNOWLEDGE
CAME FLOATING DOWN IN PARACHUTES LIKE "**MANNA FROM LENIN**"
INTO THE COMMAND AND CONTROL OF THE ENEMY AND IT'S ALLIES.
SIMPLY PUT, THEY WERE FREEBIES, AND TO DENY THAT THE ENEMY
AND IT'S ALLIES WOULD TAKE ADVANTAGE OF THIS "FREEBIE"
SITUATION IS AN ANALYTIC CRIME OF GROSS INCOMPETENCE.

THE SURVIVING FOUR CREW MEMBERS OF THE EC47Q SHOOTDOWN
WERE CARRIED IN THREE UNOFFICIAL ANALYTICAL WORKING AID
LISTS? THEY WERE

(A) THOSE MIA'S KNOWN TO BE CAPTURED ALIVE. A LIST OF
OVER 400 NAMES OF MIA'S OF WHICH APPROXIMATELY 305 WERE
LISTED AS POW'S. ONLY ABOUT 5% WERE RETURNED AT HOMECOMING
I.

(B) THE "WHO TO ASK LIST" ON MIA/POW'S. THIS LIST WAS
DEVELOPED IN 1972/73 TO PROVIDE SUPPORT TO OUR HIGH LEVEL
NEGOTIATIONS, IF REQUESTED. SIMPLY PUT, IT LISTED OVER
1,000 MIA/POW'S BY NAME AND WHO, WITHIN THE ENEMY'S MILITARY
FORCE DISPOSITIONS, WOULD HAVE KNOWLEDGE OF THEIR FATE.
SPECIFICALLY, IT WOULD HAVE ENABLED OUR NEGOTIATORS TO ASK,
WITH COMPETENCE AND AUTHORITY, NORTH VIETNAMESE NEGOTIATORS;
"WE KNOW THAT YOUR (...) DIVISION, (...) REGIMENT, (...)
COMPANY ? WAS INVOLVED AND HAS SPECIFIC DETAILS ON THIS
MIA/POW (MATEJOV, CRESSMAN, ETC.), HOW ABOUT IT?" NO
REQUEST FOR THIS TYPE OF INFORMATION WAS EVER MADE?

(C) THE WARM BODY COUNT SCENARIO FOR 72/73-A COLD
SURGICAL LIST WHEREIN ANALYSIS WITHOUT, HEART OR HOPE, MADE
KIA DECLARATIONS FOR CERTAIN MIA'S NOT RETURNED AT

HOMECOMING I AND CONTINUED POW STATUS FOR OTHERS WITH CAUSE. IT WAS PROMPTED BY A PERCEIVED CHANGE IN POW POLICY BY THE NORTH VIETNAMESE IN 1972, AND IN ANTICIPATION OF SUCCESS AT THE PARIS PEACE TALKS AND WAS REQUIRED TO ENSURE OUR MILITARY WITHDRAWAL FROM SEA.

MY IMMEDIATE SUPERVISORS KNEW I MAINTAINED THESE LISTS. BUT IT WAS NOT UNTIL THE SUMMER OF 1974, FOLLOWING A POSSIBLE POW SITUATION IN LAOS, THAT THEY WERE REQUESTED. MY SUPERIORS WERE INFORMED WHERE I HAD FILED THESE LISTS AND THEIR FUTURE HANDLING AND DISPOSITION IS UNKNOWN.

IF SOMEONE WOULD HAVE TOLD ME 16 YEARS AGO THAT IN 1989, THERE WOULD BE AN MIA/POW CONTROVERSY, I WOULD HAVE REPLIED "YOU'RE CRAZY". PRESIDENT NIXON'S STATEMENT FOLLOWING HOMECOMING I, "THAT ALL OUR BRAVE MEN WERE BACK HOME AGAIN", WAS ACCEPTED BY US ONLY AS A POLITICAL STATEMENT WITH LITTLE IMPACT ON POLICY. FOR AT THE SAME TIME, AND CONTINUING UNTIL AT LEAST 1976/77, THE HIGHEST NATIONAL PRIORITY WAS TO "ISOLATE, LOCATE, IDENTIFY AND RECOVER AMERICAN POW'S PARTICULARLY IN LAOS". THIS REQUIREMENT WAS NOT ONE OF THOSE "EYES ONLY", BEHIND CLOSED DOORS POSITIONS, BUT WAS TASKED THROUGHOUT THE RANKS AND AT ALL OPERATIONAL LEVELS WITH COMMITTED AND DEDICATED RESOURCES. BUT OPERATIONS, BY THEMSELVES CANNOT ACCOMPLISH THIS OBJECTIVE, THAT IS, THE RETURN OF OUR POW'S. IT MUST BE SUPPORTED AND ACTED UPON BY POLICY AND POLITICS. AND THERE LAYS THE CAUSE AS TO WHY OUR POW'S HAVE NOT COME HOME, AND WHY IN 1989 WE CONTINUE TO HAVE AN MIA/POW ISSUE, ONE OF POLICY AND POLITICS WITH A TRIAD OF OFFICIAL POSITIONS.

1. FIRST THERE WAS THE BAMBOO CURTAIN. THEY ARE ALL DEAD. A SIMPLE WAY TO CLOSE THE DOOR ON AN EMBARRASSING AND POTENTIALLY COSTLY SITUATION IN REPARATIONS AND ACCOUNTABILITY TO THOSE WHO SERVED AND FOR THE WAR. NO NEED TO MAKE THE MIA/POW ISSUE THE LAST BATTLE, INTERNATIONALLY. IT WOULD BE TOO COSTLY.

2. SECOND, THE BRICK WALL. SIGHTING REPORTS, ALTHOUGH THE LEAST RELIABLE OF SPECIAL INFORMATION AND THE MOST DEBATABLE , HAD TO BE EXPLAINED AWAY. EASY ENOUGH WITH AN ACKNOWLEDGEMENT THAT SOME MAY STILL BE ALIVE BUT REMAIN BY CHOICE. SIMPLY PUT, TRAITORS. OF COURSE, NO MENTION IS MADE TO THE FACT THAT THE GOVERNMENT'S ACTIONS OVER THE YEARS, THAT IS, DENYING THEIR EXISTENCE, COULD BE CONSIDERED COLLABORATION AND CONTRIBUTED TO SUCH DECISIONS BY SOME POW'S.

3. THIRD, THE STEEL SHIELD OF NATIONAL SECURITY, A POLICY TO PROTECT US ALL. SIMPLY ITS PREMISE IS, GOOD WILL BEGETS GOOD WILL - WE WILL NOT DEAL OR NEGOTIATE FOR HOSTAGES. THIS NATION WILL NOT BE BLACKMAILED. IF THOSE WHO HOLD OUR POW'S WISH TO "GIVE THEM BACK" WITH NO STRINGS ATTACHED, WE WILL ACCEPT THEM. HOWEVER, WE WILL NOT CONSIDER ANY PAYMENT FOR SUCH AN ACTION EVEN THOUGH SUCH A PAYMENT MAY BE A LEGAL OR MORAL OBLIGATION AS A RESULT OF ACTIONS DURING THE WAR.

CONFRONTED WITH THIS UNDERSTANDING, PERHAPS MY STATEMENT IN 1973 FOLLOWING THE EC47Q INCIDENT THAT THE SURVIVORS "WERE GONE FOREVER" NOW APPLIES TO ALL POW'S. THE

HISTORY OF THE ISSUE TO DATE SEEMS TO SUPPORT THAT 1973 CONCLUSION.

BETWEEN MY RETIREMENT IN 1977 UNTIL MID 1985, I GAVE LITTLE THOUGHT OR CONCERN TO THE MIA/POW ISSUE. THE HIGH LEVEL REQUIREMENTS TO LOCATE AND BRING OUR MEN HOME WOULD BE ACCOMPLISHED? FURTHER, LIVING IN AN ISOLATED AREA OF MONTANA, NO NATIONAL NEWS RELATING TO THIS ISSUE WAS AVAILABLE. THUS FOR 8 YEARS, I LIVED WITH CONFIDENCE AND FAITH THAT OUR GOVERNMENT WAS DEEPLY COMMITTED TOO, AND WOULD BRING THE MEN HOME. IN 1985, CABLE T.V. CAME TO WOLF POINT, MONTANA, AND WITH IT, EXTENSIVE CONVERAGE OF NATIONAL AND INTERNATIONAL NEWS. IT WAS AT THAT'TIME, I VIEWED A NEWS REPORT CONCERNING THE THOMAS HART INCIDENT AND HOW THE GOVERNMENT CLAIMED THAT ALL THE REMAINS HAD BEEN RECOVERED FROM THE CRASH SITE EXCAVATION IN SOUTHERN LAOS. I KNEW THIS TO BE IN ERROR, FOR I RECALLED MY RECORDS LISTING SURVIVORS FROM THAT INCIDENT.

MY INTEREST RENEWED IN THE MIA/POW ISSUE, I DID SOME CHECKING AND FOUND, TO MY TOTAL SHOCK, THAT ALL HAD BEEN DECLARED DEAD AND THERE WAS STRONG GOVERNMENT INSISTENCE THAT NO POW'S REMAINED. INITIALLY I PLANNED TO CONTACT THE DIA, AN ORGANIZATION I HAD A GREAT DEAL OF RESPECT FOR BECAUSE OF THE EXPERTISE IT HAD DEMONSTRATED TO ME IN OUR CONTINUOUS CONTACTS DURING THE WAR, AND CHALLENGE THIS CURRENT POLICY POSITION WITH A REVIEW OF MY HANDS-ON KNOWLEDGE AND EXPERTISE CONCERNING THE ISSUE. HOWEVER, I LATER DECIDED TO JOIN IN THE SMITH, ET AL., PLAINTIFFS, LAWSUIT AS A LEGAL MEANS TO CONFRONT THE GOVERNMENT TO AVOID A CLOSED DOOR, CONTROLLED ATMOSPHERE AND GIVE THE ISSUE SOME PUBLIC EXPOSURE "JUST IN CASE" A COVERUP OR INCOMPETENT EMPLOYMENT OF POLICY AND POLITICS WAS INVOLVED...

IN LATE JANUARY, 1986, I TRAVELED TO WASHINGTON D.C. TO TESTIFY BEFORE THE SENATE VETERANS AFFAIR'S COMMITTEE CONCERNING THE MIA/POW ISSUE. PRIOR TO MY DEPARTURE FOR WASHINGTON, I RECEIVED THREATS NOT TO GO. THE NIGHT PRIOR TO MY TESTIFYING, I RECEIVED THREATS TO "GET OUT OF WASHINGTON". THIS PROMPTED CAPITAL HILL POLICE PROTECTION DURING THE REMAINDER OF MY VISIT TO WASHINGTON.

THE MORNING OF THE DAY I WAS TO TESTIFY, I WAS CONFRONTED BY OFFICIALS OF THE JUSTICE DEPARTMENT AND SECURITY OFFICERS OF THE GOVERNMENT. ESSENTIALLY I WAS TOLD I WAS BEING "BAD" AND FROM NOW ON NOT TO DISCUSS MY KNOWLEDGE OF THIS ISSUE WITH ANYONE UNLESS I HAD THEIR PERMISSION FIRST. NOT ONCE DURING THE COURSE OF OUR BRIEF CONVERSATIONS DID THESE OFFICIALS MENTION OR SHOW WILLINGNESS TO DISCUSS THE REAL ISSUE, THE MIA/POWs.

DURING THIS SAME TIME FRAME, AT GOVERNMENT INSISTENCE, MY ORIGINAL AFFIDAVIT WAS WITHDRAWN FROM THE COURT, REWRITTEN AND RE-SUBMITTED FOR "SECURITY REASONS". MUCH OF THE DATA THAT WAS DELETED FROM THE ORIGINAL AFFIDAVIT WAS EXTRACTED FROM "UNCLASSIFIED" PERFORMANCE APPRAISALS GIVEN TO ME BY AIR FORCE PERSONNEL CLERKS AT ANNUAL RECORDS' CHECKS. UNCLASSIFIED THEN, BUT NOW CLASSIFIED BECAUSE IT WAS BEING USED IN THE MIA/POW ISSUE'??

In January, 1987, the BBC broadcast "We Can Keep You Forever" was aired. Following that broadcast, the DOD released a public statement referring to those of us who had appeared in that broadcast as "less than credible"...

The events of the last 3½ years have been both frightening and disgusting regarding the MIA/POW issue. I have been to the Executive Branch of Government only to be ignored, intimidated, threatened and discredited. I have been to the Legislative Branch of government hearing much concern, but seeing no official action in leadership, responsibility, and accountability. And I have been to the Judicial Branch of Government, only to be told that they have no legal jurisdiction, for the issue is an exclusive matter of policy for the Executive Branch. The latter is the most disturbing to me. The Courts, the soul of our democracy and human rights, are ignoring their responsibility in favor of policy.

I do not know if any laws have been·violated in the actions taken concerning the MIA's and POW's. That is for

lawyers to argue, juries to decide, judges to rule and historians to debate. But, at the minimum, as a 20 year professional, and concerned, committed American citizen, I firmly believe our government is guilty of violating "The Covenant".

"The Covenant" was explained and instructed to me by a supervisor at my first overseas' duty assignment. Simply, the primary responsibility of the government to the people is to keep the peace. When government fails, for whatever reason, we the people give government the right to exercise the terrible responsibility to risk our lives in warfare. In turn, we the people demand from government their awesome accountability not to waste us. During the "No Win" policy and politics of the Vietnam War and in the resolution of the MIA and POW issue, the government has failed to fulfill its accountability to the Covenant. Those who served in that war know it, as does **JOSEPH A. MATEJOV**'s mother, MARY MATEJOV.

Further Affiant saith not.

DATED his 26th day of March, 1989.

Jerry J. Mooney

JERRY J. MOONEY

SUBSCRIBED AND SWORN TO BEFORE ME THIS 26TH DAY OF MARCH, 1989.

NOTARY PUBLIC FOR THE STATE OF MONT.
RESIDING AT WOLF POINT, MONTANA
MY COMMISSION EXPIRES: 11/10/90

APPENDIX 4

Affidavit of Clarence Edward Johnson

AFFIDAVIT OF CLARENCE EDWARD JOHNSON

STATE OF OKLAHOMA }
------------------:SS
COUNTY OF OKLAHOMA}

CLARENCE EDWARD JOHNSON, BEING FIRST DULY SWORN UNDER OATH, DEPOSES AND STATES AS FOLLOWS:

1. AFFIANT IS A FORMER U.S. ARMY OFFICER, RETIRED IN THE GRADE OF MAJOR, CURRENTLY A RESIDENT OF OKLAHOMA CITY, OKLAHOMA. AFFIANT'S LAST MILITARY DUTY ASSIGNMENT WAS WITHIN THE U.S. NATIONAL SECURITY AGENCY (U.S. ARMY INTELLIGENCE AND SECURITY COMMAND) AT FORT MEADE, MARYLAND AS AN INTELLIGENCE OFFICER.

2. AFFIANT PERSONALLY KNOWS LTC "BO" GRITZ (HEREINAFTER REFERRED TO AS "BO"), AND MAINTAINED CLOSE CONTACT WITH HIM WHILE BO SERVED AS A CHIEF OF CONGRESSIONAL RELATIONS IN THE PENTAGON. AFFIANT IS AWARE THAT BO LEFT ACTIVE DUTY AT THE REQUEST OF LTG HAROLD AARON, DEPUTY DIRECTOR, DEFENSE INTELLIGENCE AGENCY (DIA). AFFIANT PERSONALLY KNEW LTG HAROLD AARON, AS A COMMANDER OF SPECIAL FORCES AND AS ARMY INTELLIGENCE CHIEF AND DEPUTY DIRECTOR, DIA. AFFIANT WAS INFORMED BY BO IN NOVEMBER, 1978 THAT GENERAL AARON HAD ASKED HIM TO TEMPORARILY LEAVE UNIFORMED SERVICE SO HE COULD ACT IN THE PRIVATE SECTOR TO DETERMINE THE STATUS OF US POW'S.

3. AFFIANT IS AWARE THAT BO DID SUBMIT HIS REQUEST FOR
RELEASE FROM ACTIVE DUTY. FROM THAT TIME UNTIL NOW, AFFIANT
HAS BEEN IN CLOSE PERSONAL CONTACT WITH BO, AND IS AWARE OF
HIS ACTIVITIES. THROUGHOUT THIS NINE YEAR PERIOD, AFFIANT
SERVED AS A CUT-OUT AND BACKUP TO BO'S OPERATION, A ROLE
WHICH IS STANDARD PROCEDURE FOR INTELLIGENCE ASSETS
OPERATING OUTSIDE OFFICIAL CHANNELS.

4. DURING THE PERIOD JANUARY THROUGH JULY, 1979 AFFIANT DID
RECEIVE FROM BO MESSAGES WHICH WERE PASSED ON TO GENERAL
AARON. THE MESSAGES WERE READ BY AFFIANT AND CONSISTED OF
POW PROGRESS REPORTS. AFFIANT WAS ALSO A WITNESS TO A
MEETING BETWEEN GENERAL AARON AND BO IN JULY, 1979 IN
WASHINGTON, D.C.. BO DISCUSSED DIFFICULTIES IN BRINGING A
FOREIGN NATIONAL NAMED GIANG INTO THE U.S. FOR ELECTRONIC
VERIFICATION OF POW INFORMATION. GENERAL AARON SAID HE
WOULD SEEK ASSISTANCE FROM GENERAL EUGENE TIGHE, DIRECTOR,
DIA. I RECEIVED COPIES OF GENERAL TIGHE'S LETTER TO DEFENSE
SECRETARY HAROLD BROWN, AND SECRETARY OF STATE VANCE'S
NEGATIVE REPLY IN SEPTEMBER OF 1979. BO REPORTED THAT HIS
ASIAN RECON UNITS HAD LOCATED 30 U.S. POWS AT
LAOS IN APRIL, 1980. CIA WAS TO CONFIRM BY OVERFLIGHTS.
TARGET CONFIRMATION WAS RECEIVED IN NOVEMBER, MAKING THE
REPORT "A-1" INTELLIGENCE. AFFIANT MAINTAINED
LIAISON WHILE BO WAS IN FLORIDA PREPARING FOR A PRIVATE
SECTOR RESCUE EFFORT. ADMIRAL JERRY TUTTLE, DIA, CAUSED BO
TO STAND DOWN AFTER WHITE HOUSE DECISION TO USE "DELTA"
FORCE, FORT BRAGG, NORTH CAROLINA. IT WAS AFFIANT'S
UNDERSTANDING THAT ADMIRAL TUTTLE RECOMMENDED THAT BO RETURN
TO ACTIVE DUTY AS A MEMBER OF THE JOINT CHIEFS' PLANNING
STAFF.

5. BO REPORTED TO AFFIANT THAT HE HAD BEEN RECRUITED AS AN
INTELLIGENCE ASSET BY THE INTELLIGENCE SUPPORT ACTIVITY
(ISA) IN MAY 1981. DAN MYER (CODE-NAMED "SHIPMAN") WAS HIS
CASE OFFICER. ISA WAS UNREPORTED TO CONGRESS AND THEREFORE
UNLISTED AS AN OFFICIAL INTELLIGENCE ACTIVITY UNTIL MARCH,
1983. BO INDICATED THAT HE HAD PREPARED ISA RECON TEAMS IN
OCTOBER, 1981 FOR INFILTRATION INTO LAOS. BO HAD USED J.D.
BATH AND THREE OTHER AMERICANS TO CONDUCT TRAINING IN
THAILAND. AFFIANT PERSONALLY KNOWS BATH. BO INFORMED
AFFIANT THAT HE WAS SCHEDULED TO LEAD A PHOTO-INTELLIGENCE
TEAM INTO SOUTH-CENTRAL LAOS IN DECEMBER, 1981.

6. AFFAINT MET WITH BO ON OR ABOUT DECEMBER 9, 1981 AT A
WASHINGTON D.C. MOTEL. BO STATED THERE WERE "PROBLEMS" WITH
DIA. HE WAS TO SEE ADMIRAL BOBBY INMAN, AFFIANT'S OLD BOSS
AT NSA, THEN DEPUTY DIRECTOR, CENTRAL INTELLIGENCE AGENCY
THE NEXT DAY AT THE WHITE HOUSE.

7. BO STATED TO AFFIANT IN JANUARY, 1982 THAT ISA WAS TOLD
TO OFFICIALLY STOP THE POW RESCUE EFFORT, BUT THAT ISA CHIEF
(CODE-NAMED "CRANSTON") HAD OKAYED BO'S PERSONAL EFFORTS
WITH ISA SUPPORT. IT WAS AFFIANT'S UNDERSTANDING THAT
CRANSTON OFFERED TO BRING BO BACK ON ACTIVE DUTY AS AN ISA
DEPUTY.

8. BO NOTIFIED AFFIANT IN AUGUST OF 1982 THAT CIA HAD
APPROVED SUPPORT OF A RESCUE MISSION IN LAOS. BO CAME BACK
FROM LAOS IN MARCH, 1983 AND RETURNED SPECIAL CIA EQUIPMENT.
AFFIANT WAS TOLD BY BO THAT A CODE MACHINE WAS RETAINED BY

THE EXECUTIVE OFFICER, GORDON WILSON, AND A PORTABLE POLYGRAPH MACHINE, SOME F-3 NIKON CAMERAS, AND ONE SET OF PVS-5 NIGHT VISION GOGGLES WERE RETAINED BY BO. AFFIANT PERSONALLY SPOKE WITH GORDON WILSON IN OKLAHOMA CITY, OKLAHOMA DURING LATE 1988 ABOUT BO'S PENDING TRIAL. GORDON CONFIRMED TO AFFIANT THAT THERE WAS FULL USG KNOWLEDGE AND SUPPORT OF THE GRITZ OPERATION, AND THAT HE (GORDON) HAD PERSONALLY BRIEFED PRESIDENT REAGAN ON THE OPERATION. AFFIANT BELIEVES THAT WILSON WAS CONCERNED ABOUT REPERCUSSIONS FROM HIS PRESENT GOVERNMENT ASSOCIATES, SHOULD HE SURFACE AND TESTIFY AT THE UPCOMING TRIAL. BO NOTIFIED AFFIANT IN APRIL, 1983 THAT HE HAD COORDINATED FURTHER POW SUPPORT THROUGH GENERAL JOE LUTZ, US ARMY SPECIAL WARFARE CENTER, FORT BRAGG, N.C..

9. BO CALLED AFFIANT AND ASSOCIATE, JOHN HEYER, TO NEVADA IN MARCH, 1984 TO CHECK THE IDENTITY OF A POW WITH A FAMILY MEMBER. BO TURNED OVER THREE DOCUMENT SETS FOR AFFIANT'S SAFEKEEPING AT THAT TIME. THESE SETS CONSISTED OF THREE U.S. PASSPORTS AND MILITARY IDENTIFICATION IN THE NAME OF "COOK", (PROBABLY SUPPLIED, IN AFFIANT'S OPINION, BY THE ADMINISTRATIVE SURVEY DETACHMENT (ASD) AT FORT MEADE, MARYLAND). AFFIANT WAS LATER ASKED BY BO TO DESTROY THESE DOCUMENTS, AND DID SO BY PULPING AND BURNING THEM IN 1984. BO INFORMED AFFIANT THAT HE PLANNED TO SECURE "CLEAN" IDENTIFICATION IN THE NAME OF "CLARK" THROUGH A LOS ANGELES, CALIFORNIA COVER ARRANGEMENT FOR THE PURPOSE OF A POW RESCUE ATTEMPT. BO SENT A DOCUMENT SET IN THE NAME OF "CLARK" IN 1987 FOR SAFEKEEPING. THAT SET WAS RETURNED TO BO AT HIS REQUEST IN 1988.

10. BO VISITED AFFIANT IN OKLAHOMA CITY IN 1985 TO OUTLINE A PLAN OF RESCUE OF THREE US POWS, CODE-NAMED "BROKEN WING". AFFIANT TRAVELLED TO THAILAND IN LATE 1985 TO SUPPORT THAT PARTICULAR RESCUE ATTEMPT.

11. BO REPORTED TO AFFIANT IN AUGUST, 1986 THAT WILLIAM (BILL) BODE, SPECIAL ASSISTANT TO THE UNDERSECRETARY OF STATE FOR SECURITY ASSISTANCE, HAD CONTRACTED HIM TO TRAIN AFGHAN GENERAL STAFF OFFICERS.

12. BO INFORMED AFFIANT IN OCTOBER, 1986 THAT A WHITE HOUSE NSC STAFF OFFICER, CODE-NAMED "TANGO", HAD CONTRACTED BO TO TRAVEL TO BURMA AND CONFIRM REPORTS OF US POWS UNDER CONTROL OF ONE GENERAL KUHN SA. BO RETURNED IN JANUARY, 1987 AND STATED TO AFFIANT THAT HE HAD GIVEN "TANGO" THREE VIDEO TAPES WHICH SHOWED THERE WERE NO POWS WITH KUHN SA. BO TOLD AFFIANT IN JANUARY, 1987 THAT HE WAS RETURNING TO BURMA TO FOLLOW UP ON A BUY-OUT OF FOUR POWS THROUGH THE PREMIER OF LAOS, AND TO MAKE A FURTHER VISIT TO KUHN SA. BO INDICATED TO AFFIANT SOME CONCERN THAT "TANGO" (BY THEN KNOWN TO AFFIANT TO BE TOM HARVEY) HAD STATED THAT THE US GOVERNMENT HAD "NO INTEREST" IN PURSUING THE POSSIBILITY OF STOPPING SOME 700-900 TONS OF OPIUM FROM ENTERING THE FREE WORLD EACH YEAR, AND DISCLOSURE OF INVOLVED US OFFICIALS.

13. BO CALLED AFFIANT IN LATE APRIL, 1987 AND ASKED AFFIANT TO TRAVEL TO THAILAND FOR THE PURPOSE OF BRINGING BACK TO THE UNITED STATES VARIOUS RECORDS OF INTERVIEWS WITH KUHN SA WHICH NAME US OFFICIALS INVOLVED IN THE ILLEGAL TRAFFICKING OF ARMS AND DRUGS. AFFIANT TRAVELLED TO THAILAND, ARRIVING IN BANGKOK ON OR ABOUT 14 MAY, 1987.

AFFIANT STAYED WITH BO UNTIL DEPARTURE FROM THAILAND ON OR
ABOUT 21 MAY, 1987. ACCORDING TO AFFIANT'S RECORD, DURING
THE MORNING OF 19 MAY, BO RECEIVED A TELEPHONE CALL FROM ONE
JOE FELTER AT THE PLACE WHERE WE WERE STAYING. AFFIANT
RECOGNIZED JOE FELTER'S VOICE FROM PREVIOUS TELEPHONE
CONVERSATIONS. (ALTHOUGH IT IS NOT USUAL PRACTICE FOR THE
AFFIANT TO MAKE WRITTEN NOTES OF CONVERSATIONS, A CONCERN
EXISTED IN AFFIANT'S MIND FOR THE POTENTIAL OF GOVERNMENT
INTERFERENCE, DUE TO THE SENSITIVE NATURE OF KUHN SA'S
STATEMENTS). AFFIANT AT THAT TIME HAND-COPIED THE FOLLOWING
CONTENTS OF THE ENSUING CONVERSATION BETWEEN BO AND JOE
FELTER:

FELTER: "...HARVEY HAS BEEN IN TOUCH...ALSO SOME GUY FROM
STATE NAMED DAVIS... THEY SAY YOU'RE IN FOR A REAL
SHIT-BLIZZARD UNLESS YOU AGREE TO KNOCK OFF ALL CURRENT
ACTIVITIES......YOU'VE GOT NO OPTIONS IN THIS THING....I
KNOW BOTH SIDES...YOU'RE GOING TO BE "TAKEN CARE" OF....NO
ONE HERE WANTS TO HURT YOU....WE ALL WANT TO HELP YOU...BUT,
YOU'VE GOT TO AGREE TO ERASE AND FORGET ALL YOU'VE DONE
THERE.... COME EAST,   NOW, AND   BRING EVERYTHING   YOU
HAVE....DON'T DELAY OR TALK TO ANYONE. YOU ARE GOING TO
HURT THE GOVERNMENT AND GET HURT UNLESS YOU DO EXACTLY AS I
SAY..."

BO: "...JOE, HAVE YOU GOT ANY IDEA OF WHAT I'VE GOT
HERE?.."

FELTER: "...I DON'T KNOW, AND I DON'T CARE....I KNOW JUST
ONE THING...UNLESS YOU AGREE TO ERASE AND FORGET EVERY THING
YOU'RE DOING, YOU'RE GONNA HURT THE GOVERNMENT..."

BO: "...WHOSE GOVERNMENT?...NOT THE GOVERNMENT MY DAD DIED
FOR....."

FELTER: "...LOOK, JIMBO, WE'RE ALL JUST TRYING TO HELP YOU.
NOBODY WANTS TO PUT A WAR HERO IN JAIL....BUT YOU'VE GOTTA
GET ON THE FIRST THING AVAILABLE AND COME EAST....WE'LL MEET
AT THE APARTMENT AND SORT THIS THING OUT...MAINTAIN A LOW
PROFILE, AND DON'T TELL ANYONE WHAT YOU'RE DOING..."

BO: "...WHO ALL IS GOING TO BE AT THE APARTMENT?...

FELTER: "...YOU KNOW ME BETTER THEN THAT. IT WILL JUST BE
ME AND TOM HARVEY...STOP ALL YOU'RE DOING, BRING ALL YOU'VE
GOT, AND COME NOW..."

BO: "...OKAY, DEAR CITIZEN, I'LL COME. I'LL SHOW YOU WHAT
I'VE GOT. THEN TELL ME TO "ERASE AND FORGET"..."

FELTER: "...LOOK, JIM, I'M ONLY TRYING TO HELP YOU...
HARVEY AND THE OTHER GUY SAY IF YOU DON'T STOP WHAT YOU'RE
DOING, AND BRING EVERYTHING EAST, YOU'RE GONNA SERVE FIFTEEN
YEARS AS A FELON...THY'RE READY TO "CRUNCH" YOU BIG-TIME....
I DON'T WANT TO SEE THAT...THEY SAY IT'LL BE FOUR FILES OF
AGGRAVATED CHARGES AND HOSTILE WITNESSES....JUST GET YOUR
ASS ON THE FIRST THING SMOKIN' THIS WAY....MAKE SURE YOU
BRING EVERYTHING YOU'VE GOT, AND DON'T TALK TO
ANYBODY...HARVEY SAYS EVERYTHING WILL "GO AWAY" IF YOU'LL
JUST FORGET ABOUT EVERYTHING YOU'VE BEEN DOING...DON'T BLOW
THIS ONE, JIMBO..."

BO: "...OKAY, JOE, I'LL GET IN TOUCH WITH YOU ONCE I'M STATESIDE..."

FELTER: "...OKAY, JIMBO, I'M SERIOUS...HARVEY SAYS THEY'LL BRING FULL-BLOWN AGGRAVATED CHARGES UNLESS YOU COOPERATE AND DO EXACTLY AS THEY WANT...I'LL SEE YOU HERE..."

BO MADE ENTRIES OF THE CONVERSATION IN HIS LOG, AND INSTRUCTED AFFIANT TO PRESERVE THOSE WHICH AFFIANT HAD MADE. BARRY FLYNN WAS ALSO A WITNESS TO THE CONVERSATION. LANCE TRIMMER WAS PRESENT, BUT WAS NOT A PARTY TO THE CONVERSATION. WE ALL DISCUSSED WHAT HAD BEEN SAID IMMEDIATELY FOLLOWING THE CONVERSATION, AND IT WAS DECIDED THAT SEVERAL COPIES OF ALL DOCUMENTATION WOULD BE MADE, AND COPIES OF THE DOCUMENTS WOULD BE BROUGHT BACK TO THE UNITED STATES BY SEVERAL SEPARATE PERSONS.

14. AFFIANT DID VIEW AND TRANSPORT DOCUMENTS IN THE FORM OF PHOTOGRAPH NEGATIVES, MOTION PICTURES, VIDEO CASSETTES, AND AUDIO CASSETTES FROM THAILAND TO THE UNITED STATES. LATER, IN THE COMPANY OF JOHN HEYER, AFFIANT DID DELIVER COPIES OF THE DOCUMENTS TO THE CHAIRMAN OF THE SELECT COMMITTEE ON INTELLIGENCE, SPECIFICALLY TO THE OFFICE OF THE HONORABLE DAVID BOREN, AND TO SEVERAL OTHER CONGRESSIONAL COMMITTEE CHAIRMEN.,

15. SINCE JUNE OF 1987 AFFIANT HAS BEEN AWARE OF CONTINUING GOVERNMENT EFFORTS TO MUFFLE BO THROUGH THREATS, AND, AS JOE FELTER SAID, "CHARGES AND HOSTILE WITNESSES".

FURTHER, AFFIANT SAYETH NOT.

Clarence E Johnson
CLARENCE E JOHNSON

SUBSCRIBED AND SWORN TO BEFORE ME THIS _25th_ DAY OF

JANUARY, 1989.

NOTARY PUBLIC IN AND FOR SAID COUNTY AND STATE.
My Commission Expires _March 13, 1990_ .

GLOSSARY

"The Activity": Term used to describe a group of U.S. specialists who continued activities in Southeast Asia after the U.S. withdrawal from Vietnam. Also the name by which the U.S. Army's Intelligence Support Activity was known, although there is no known connection.

Air America: Central Intelligence Agency proprietary airline, flying aid to covert-warfare mercenaries.

American Defense Institute (ADI): Based in Washington D.C., this non-profit organization and affiliated American Defense Foundation (ADF) work for strong national defense policies. Clearing-house for defense information to Congress and the public. Educational arm conducts non-partisan worldwide military registration drive to encourage serving men and women to exercise right to vote.

Bishop, Baldwin, Rewald, Dillingham & Wong (BBRDW): Investment firm in Honolulu. When income-tax investigators refused to accept claims that BBRDW carried out secret U.S. government tasks abroad, the firm's top man stood trial. Presiding judge withheld certain evidence because it might stir up emotions on POW/MIA issue. Rescue missions were said to be financed through BBRDW.

Brightlights: Code-name used in White House and National Security Council for servicemen whose fate is officially unknown following the wars in Southeast Asia. It was reported in 1989 in DIA message traffic to the White House when it referred to live POW/MIA intelligence. The use of "Black" as a prefix in military/CIA operations indicated "highly classified." "Blackjack" followed by a number series designated cross-border operations under the overall name "Shining Brass" for Laos.

Bureau of Intelligence and Research (INR): U.S. State Department's intelligence section. Comparable to the British Foreign Office's now-defunct Intelligence and Research Department (IRD).

Central Intelligence Agency (CIA): During the Vietnam War, absorbed talent from U.S. armed forces and ran Controlled Assets (CAs), recruited from local inhabitants in Southeast Asia. Top officials included veterans from its predecessor, the World War II Office of Strategic Services (OSS); but also a new breed who theorized that Communist covert warfare had to be countered by new clandestine methods, somewhere between conventional and nuclear conflict, with CIA-trained and armed resistance groups.

Christic Institute: Public-interest group, based in Washington, D.C., that uses law to bring about change.

Command and Control North/Central/South (CCN,CCC, and CCS): These three field commands during the Vietnam War carried out highly classified clandestine operations throughout Southeast Asia (*See below*: Special Exploitation Service, Special Operations Group, Studies and Observations Group). In 1971 CCN changed to Task Force I Advisory Element and CCS to Task Force 3. United States Army Criminal Investigation Command (USACIDC).

Criminal Investigation Command (USACIDC): U.S. Army Command with authority to look into cases that may go on trial. If an individual is cleared by a CIDC investigator, details of the case should be made available to concerned citizens, such as U.S. Congressmen.

Defense Intelligence Agency (DIA): Sometimes known as a "traffic director," DIA collects intelligence by open and secret means and should communicate information to relevant clients. In the case of

U.S. armed forces personnel, it cannot initiate action to rescue prisoners. DIA analyzed POW/MIA intelligence.

Defense Security Assistance Agency (DSAA): Described by jailed CIA agent Ed Wilson as "This dinky unit down in the bowels of the Pentagon . . . decides how grant aid is spent" on U.S. arms for foreign governments. Wilson may be prejudiced, but his definition is not in dispute.

Drug Enforcement Agency (DEA): Highest profile among more than a dozen U.S. federal agencies responsible for stopping the flow of illegal drugs into the United States. In fights for turf, DEA often feels need to maximize publicity, especially in foreign operations where it has been embarrassed by reports of U.S. intelligence agents using DEA "cover." Former Congressman John LeBoutillier swore an affidavit that he was offered DEA cover by the White House. There were fifty-eight federal agencies and seventy-four congressional committees "currently engaged, each with its own agenda and armies, on various fronts of the drug war" reported editor Lewis Lapham in *Harper's* magazine, December 1989.

Egyptian American Transport and Services Company (EATSCO): Set up by jailed CIA agent Ed Wilson to handle contracts foreshadowed by Pentagon insider-information. High-level Pentagon and CIA officials were named as partners when Wilson was investigated for illegally selling explosives and terrorist weapons to Libya.

Electronic Data Systems (EDS): Texan billionaire Ross Perot rescued his own EDS employees from a Teheran prison. He later sold EDS to General Motors, having founded the computer-service company with a thousand dollars.

Federal Bureau of Alcohol, Tobacco and Firearms (ATF): Its officers sometimes overlap the Drug Enforcement Agency's actions against illegal drugs. It acts against smugglers of arms and drugs where appropriate. The battles for turf arise over interpretations of what is appropriate.

Forces Armée National Khmer Training Command (FANK): U.S. group in Cambodia that began as part of Studies and Observations Group (SOG). (*See below.*) By 1989, it was replaced by the Cambodian Working Group (CWG) in Thailand, described in the *Bangkok Post* as "the key" to clandestine operations against Vietnamese-backed forces.

Grand Jury: A panel of U.S. citizens who review evidence and decide if a case should go to trial.

40 Committee: A committee of responsible U.S. citizens designated to oversee secret U.S. operations. U.S. congressional inquiries following the Vietnam War led to demands for a more democratic way to render U.S. government officials accountable for clandestine activities.

Intelligence Support Activity (ISA): Sometimes known as The Activity, is not to be confused with what Casino Man called "The Activity," meaning an unofficial and unauthorized group using U.S. secrecy regulations to conceal self-serving aims. ISA had grown to some extent out of a reaction against "The Activity" freebooters, and represented the U.S. Army's concern about the CIA's record in Vietnam. ISA caused heartburn, however, because it challenged CIA clandestine activities abroad; and it also seemed to offer a means of circumventing U.S. Congressional oversight of the known and conventional intelligence agencies.

Interagency Group (IAG): Formed to give the White House a consensus, in theory, on any given problem. Prisoners, being a problem of growing importance in domestic politics, had to be studied from the viewpoints of different government agencies and the armed services. The POW/MIA problem left over from the Vietnam War required an Interagency Group conveying White House political concerns to the agencies and armed forces. Requests for action on getting back possible prisoners would rotate through the IAG, which could respond with the current administration's reflections upon what the political cost might be to the party in power if the public became agitated over its handling of the POW issue. "Hostage crisis" was a phrase burned into presidential minds. (*See* National Security Council.)

Joint Casualty Resolution Center (JCRC): After Paris peace accords in 1973, continued to resolve missing Americans in Southeast Asia. After growing criticism from families of POWs and MIAs, JCRC sent a team to Hanoi late in 1989. An account of what JCRC has accomplished, beyond bringing back bones, is eagerly anticipated.

Prejudiced descriptions of its never-to-be-revealed accomplishments are said to be "utter rubbish."

National League of Families: Started during the Vietnam War to make the U.S. administration act on behalf of prisoners, not then the hottest political topic. Later, it was described by a deputy DIA director as carrying out U.S. government policy.

National Reconnaissance Office (NRO): Said officially not to exist, by a DIA official who removed a reference to it from statements made on Capitol Hill by Representative Douglas Applegate (Dem., Ohio). Applegate had said that NRO spy-in-the-sky intelligence had shown the presence of live American prisoners in the Vietnam area.

National Security Council (NSC): This has grown enormously since it was conceived as a convenient way to brief the U.S. President on security matters. There were fears that the Iran-Contra scandal resulted from the NSC's size, impenetrable vaults, and assumption of power in areas in which secret actions could be veiled by pleas of "national security."

Phoenix Program: This thinly disguised CIA operation was run through the U.S. Military Assistance Command in Vietnam – Special Operations Group (*see below*). The precise number of Vietnamese civilians, suspected of being "Communist sympathizers," who were killed or jailed through information it collected is in dispute. It was conceived "to win hearts and minds," but seems mostly to have counted bodies, the exact number being a state secret.

Search Location and Annihilation Mission (SLAM): Fell under the U.S. Special Operations Group (*see below*). Its tasks included kidnapping and killing those who helped the enemy in Vietnam, as stated in a Pentagon manual.

Skyhook II: One of many private organizations seeking U.S. prisoners in Southeast Asia, this was headed by former New York Congressman John LeBoutillier, who swore an affidavit claiming he was offered "DEA cover" in Asia if he cooperated with U.S. government officials to discredit a POW/MIA advocate.

Special Forces Detachment, Korea (SFD-K): Conducted operations in Southeast Asia, among other U.S. Army duties. Some officers detached to Thailand said that secret intelligence on U.S. prisoners in Vietnam and Laos was suppressed. Their superiors denied this and the men were investigated by the CID (*see above*). Two had outstanding Vietnam War battle records. All were finally cleared of charges of criminal misconduct.

Special Operations Group: Had five primary responsibilities in Vietnam, including "to keep track of all imprisoned and missing Americans and conducting raids to assist and free them. . . . " According to congressional investigators, the operational name was Special Operations Group, but the title Studies and Observations Group was used to mislead the curious, according to a 1990 study. SOG was listed as a "MACV-J5" activity, but actually came directly under the Joint Chiefs of Staff. In 1967, operations in Laos were under field supervision of CCN. Vang Pao's Hmong army was "considered a CIA-Lao operation in conjunction with CCN" reported the 1990 study.

Task Force 157: Officially part of the U.S. Naval Research in Vietnam, it ran CIA front companies and was dissolved by a director of U.S. Naval Intelligence, Admiral Bobby Ray Inman, who became deputy-director of the CIA. Inman said 157 "reeked of bribery." It was officially said to be monitoring Soviet ship movements.

Veterans of Foreign Wars (VFW): A venerable U.S. organization that represents veterans who served overseas in wartime.

NOTE TO READERS

U.S. government intelligence on its military personnel captured in Indochina was still officially classified as of early 1990. American families were still unable to get information freely on missing relatives, although many of these families struggled for years, sometimes resorting to protracted legal battles, to obtain the information they sought. When it was obtained, its nature often persuaded them that official silence served no recognizable purpose of national security. This silence extended to men known by the U.S. government to have been executed in captivity. Their families were not informed.

The authors have dealt with only a handful of cases from the many files made available to us from those families who doggedly extracted facts about those they had lost. Our files contain the stories of hundreds more, thanks to the work of POW/MIA activist organizations and to their friends inside government agencies who helped them trace individual cases and to pierce official obfuscation. We dealt with men and women who spent the major part of their waking hours cross-indexing the available information, organizing film and photo archives, and building up computer data bases that constituted a formidable intelligence resource. Their ingenuity and stubborn devotion should be characteristic of intelligence work in general.

We are under a burden of indebtedness to such great Americans; they shared so generously their time and their findings. They helped us check details against lists of prisoners and the missing, some obtained through the National Archives, Machine Readable Branch, and some retrieved from "retired" official files.

It seems unfair to single out any individual. The reader will have met some of our sources already. Jerry Mooney, the NSA analyst, has since sworn affidavits repeating information he provided for this book, hoping the government will challenge his memory in open court.

We also had available to us government publications on the subject. All the hearings mentioned in the book were printed in the *Congressional Record*. Some were special reports also printed in the U.S. Government Printing Office or by the White House. Examples of special reports are: *Americans Missing in Southeast Asia: Final Report Together with Separate Views of the Select Committee on Missing Persons in Southeast Asia* (December 13, 1976); *Report of the Special Committee on Southeast Asia* (September 7, 1978); *Prisoners of War/Missing in Action in Southeast Asia: Recent Developments and Future Prospects* (Hearing before the Subcommittee on Asian and Pacific Affairs of the Committee on Foreign Affairs, House of Representatives, August 8, 1984); *Tighe Report on American POWs and MIAs* (Hearing and Markup before the Subcommittee on Asian and Pacific Affairs, October 15, 1986); and *Drugs, Law Enforcement, and Foreign Policy*: Panama (Hearings Before the Subcommittee on Terrorism, Narcotics, and International Operations of the Committee on Foreign Relations, United States Senate, February 8-11, 1988). We relied extensively on the Congressional Research Service and the Library of Congress: Prisoners of War/Missing in Action – Congressional Research Division.

While I was at *Sixty Minutes*, the Department of Defense (U.S. Marines) allowed me to borrow the entire Garwood court-martial transcripts for a period of over two months. The Department of Defense also made available their *POW/MIA Fact Book*. From the White House we obtained the *Report on Actions of the U.S. Government in Pursuit of the Nation's Goal of Obtaining as Full as Possible an Accounting of American Servicemen Still Missing as a Result of the War in Indochina* and the *Report Concerning Misinformation on the Issue of American POW/MIAs in Southeast Asia.* The Jimmy Carter Memorial Library has the record of National Security Council correspondence regarding Bobby Garwood's return from Vietnam and the POW/MIA issue. Lists of prisoners and MIAs were obtained from the National Archives – Machine Readable Branch, where some of them might still be available.

Certain information was provided to us by men and women who, for reasons we respect, wished to remain anonymous. Blind attributions, of course, raise questions about the reliability of the information. Where these occur, the reader is assured that sworn statements and other documents exist to back up each story. With their permission, official Pentagon sources like True Man and The Preacher were indentified by us to bonafide investigators on the staff of Senator Charles Grassley (Rep., Iowa) and the Senate Judiciary Subcommittee as well as investigators working for the Senate Foreign Relations Committee. Key documents disclosed to us by Casino Man were verified for us, with his permission, by those investigators. The identities of Casino Man and others code-named in our book have been verified by others who appear in the narrative, including Colonel Earl Hopper, Colonel Bill LeGro, and Captain Red McDaniel.

We have tried to make clear where conversations were notated or taped at the time. Sometimes we edited for brevity. We recorded at least eighty interviews and drew on tapes accumulated over the years by the American Defense Institute's Red McDaniel, constituting some hundreds of hours of video- and audio-taping time. Other notes were made available by John Brown, with verification from Colonel LeGro, Tony Drexel Duke, and several military and other intelligence officers.

Space limitations obliged us to deal briefly with the prosecution of Colonel Bo Gritz, after reading through hundreds of pages of official papers made available by his lawyer, Lanny Wade. This alone could fill a fascinating book. The complete file on DIA correspondence cast a different light upon stories told *in camera* by White House and National Security officials. That DIA correspondence was never intended to be seen by the public.

The deeper we probed, the more frequently we were approached by self-described "government investigators." They offered to help us, or else they asked questions. We were able to check their credentials in most cases, usually through third parties who frequently warned us that they were not who they claimed to be, but were on fishing expeditions to find out how much we knew. What might have seemed on our part like undue suspicion was echoed by the Senate Judiciary Subcommittee and the Senate Foreign Relations Committee in 1989.

We had been approached by Senators Charles Grassley (Rep., Iowa) and Jesse Helms (Rep., North Carolina) to help them examine the issue as outlined by Red McDaniel. The committees' own staffers asked if we would share with them certain information. We could prove it had already been given to the Federal Bureau of Investigation while its agents looked into some specific matters in 1989. The Capitol Hill staffers said they needed to have collateral proof of such information given to the FBI, because they suspected similar material had been held back, possibly on dubious grounds of "national security."

Because Senators Grassley and Helms took such a strong and stoutly independent interest in the issue, we agreed to help. In return, their own investigators used the authority of Congress to see documents, access to which had been blocked for others. They cross-checked, and officially confirmed, material we had obtained through excellent but unofficial sources, especially relating to specific activities in Southeast Asia that had been held secret. They gave us further confirmation of prisoner-rescue efforts, and of the prolonged efforts by government officials to misrepresent the whole picture of POW/MIA secrecy.

The Capitol Hill investigators told us that it was plain as a pikestaff that matters of legitimate public interest, reported to the Justice Department by properly authorized government agents, had been retarded at some higher level. In one specific case, all that one investigator could get was "a self-serving document that cleared DIA of any wrongdoing." He asked the relevant Department of Justice official for the full file. The official said he would have to take this up with another government department, and later withheld the complete file because of "a third agency's" objections.

In time, files die as well as men. As General Tighe, the former DIA director, had said to us: "The great danger is that all the data will be retired, and finally lost to history." That provided the best reason for discharging our debt to all those who helped us. We hope this book will help them rescue some truth from the ashes.

NOTES

Overview: The Story

Page 1   — Richard Nixon's promise is a matter of public record: the letter to Prime Minister Pham Van Dong of Vietnam, dated February 1, 1973, was finally released May 19, 1977, by the Department of State.

Page 2   — The fact that the capture and imprisonment of live MIAs was monitored by U.S. intelligence is treated in the text through Jerry Mooney, a former National Security Agency official who was involved in tracking prisoners. See later Mooney material. Mooney has spoken extensively to the authors and to investigators of the Senate Foreign Relations Committee. He has also issued a series of sworn affidavits backing up his statement. The authors have his affidavits in their files.

                    — Associated Press announced on April 7, 1973, that the Senate voted to bar aid to Vietnam unless approved by Congress. Congress did not approve.

Page 3 — Petrasy's claim was in a UPI story widely reported at the time (e.g. *Washington Post*, February 18, 1973, "Pathet Lao Says No Truce, No American POWs").
— Kissinger's claim appears in article listed above.

Page 3n — General Walters' comment was made before the House Select Committee on Missing Persons in Southeast Asia (its report issued December 13, 1976, is listed in Note to Readers).

Page 4 — The Pathet Lao offer was reported in the *New York Times*, March 28, 1973, p. 3.
— Shields was quoted in UPI story, April 14, 1973. POW mothers, Mrs. Cressman and Mrs. Matejov, claim he said that the statements were forced on him.
— Nguyen Thanh Son's claims and the request that details be played down are in a Department of State telegram, as was the fact of cooperation. A copy is in the authors' files.
— Fifty POWs were discussed in Associated Press story, January 31, 1973.

Page 5 — Jerry Mooney, as mentioned, is the source of much information obtained by electronic tracing. The authors have his affidavits in their files.
— The lists with the names of men who were known to be captive, but were not listed as MIAs, have been handed over to investigators for the Senate Foreign Relations Committee.
— Much of the information about "Special Talents" and disabled prisoners was gathered during interviews with Jerry Mooney, former director of the Defense Intelligence Agency, General Eugene Tighe, and with active service officers in the U.S. armed forces and in the armed forces of non-communist governments in Southeast Asia who requested anonymity.

Page 6 — Families of POW/MIAs in Laos and Cambodia have supplied intelligence reports and documents in which the armed forces admit that some men were alive after shootdowns and that this

was not made known. The men were declared
dead. The families have supplied copies to the
authors.

— The pencilled names are dealt with in the text.
See notes to p. 51.

— Senate Foreign Relations Committee investigators, in response to reports from the families,
have asked for a copy of the classified documents
registered by the officials.

Page 7 — *Americans Missing in Southeast Asia*, the published proceedings of the House Select Committee on Missing persons, December 13, 1976, is
available. It is listed in Note to Readers.

— The Peace Agreement is a matter of public record.

Page 8 — President Nixon's letter to Prime Minister Pham
Van Dong of Vietnam, dated February 1, 1973,
was finally released May 19, 1977, by the Department of State.

Page 9 — Scores of refugees, to whom we have talked,
assert that the Vietnamese considered prisoners
as bargaining tools (e.g. *Brooklyn Park Post*, July
18, 1985, re. John Soukhindy). The Hanoi government, furthermore, made this clear to William
Stevenson during visits there.

— Ex-Marine Bobby Garwood, who escaped from
Vietnam in 1979, records the use of statements
by U.S. officials to demoralize prisoners. Col.
Nick Rowe and other specialists in escape-and-
invasion detailed these methods for the author.

— One intelligence chief was General Eugene
Tighe.

— "The Mortician" is treated in more detail later in
the text, pp. 172-173. His reports were confirmed
by General Eugene Tighe and members of the
Tighe commission, as well as by intelligence
reports.

Page 10 — The *60 Minutes* program is treated throughout
the first eight chapters in the text.

	— A copy of the White House publication is in the files of the American Defense Institute and the authors' files.
	— General Tighe's humiliation is chronicled in the text, pp. 221-223.
Page 11	— Information about MACV Studies and Observations Group is taken from a Pentagon textbook, relevant portions of which are in the possession of the authors.
	— Prisoner intelligence has been discussed in numerous congressional hearings, such as testimony by General Williams before the Subcommittee on Asian and Pacific Affairs, July 14, 1983.
	— The unit to rescue prisoners is discussed in the textbook mentioned above.
Page 12	— Allegations against Casey were made by a senior CIA officer with experience of intelligence operations since the Burma campaigns in World War II. They were repeated in news reports concerning the resignation of John Horton, one of the CIA's most experienced officers. He resigned after an argument in which, it was said, Casey asked him to change reports.
Page 14	— The office that the "federal government investigator" claimed to be with was the GAO, Office of Special Investigations. This was verified by several checks.

Chapter 1 – Traitor

Page 19	— A copy of the Davison/Eddings letter is in the authors' files.
	— *Soldier of Fortune,* POW/MIA Special "Bo Gritz: Hero or Huckster?" Spring 1983.
Page 21	— The information about Robert Garwood's court martial comes from transcripts of the court-martial proceedings. They were on loan to author Jensen-Stevenson at *60 Minutes* during the period she worked on the *60 Minutes* POW seg-

Page 22
ment. Records of official loan are in the authors' files.

— The presiding judge at Garwood's court martial was interviewed by the authors, who also interviewed other direct witnesses to the court martial. In addition, they relied on media reports of the time.

— See note to p. 120 re. Tuttle.

Page 26
— Records of interviews with Colonel Switzer and lie-detector expert Chris Gugas are in the authors' files.

Page 27
— See note to p. 69 re. Garwood.

Chapter 2 – "Roadblocks" in the Name of National Security

Page 40
— Henry Kissinger's concerns were diplomatic. This was sometimes forgotten by his military critics, judging the Vietnam War solely in military terms. As late as 7 May 1990, Kissinger wrote in the *International Herald Tribune* that the war, for a diplomat, was a matter of national prestige. Diplomacy, Kissinger wrote, required *"above all, a proper perception of forces. If these are correctly calculated, diplomacy can be successful."* In 1973, from Kissinger's point of view, it was vital to maintain the impression of American strength and resolution. Knowing how public support at home was declining, the diplomat expected that Communist Vietnam would strike at every point of vulnerability. The Paris peace agreement was the best that could be negotiated in the circumstances. The chance for an honorable withdrawal from Vietnam would vanish if Hanoi's leaders detected weaknesses such as an inexplicable concern for prisoners-of-war beyond those offered.

Page 41
— Copy of taped interview with Garwood in Vietnam just before his release is in authors' files.

Page 42
— On March 25, 1976, Walter Cronkite testified before the House Select Committee on Missing

Persons about Kissinger's correspondence with Hanoi. The committee had been holding hearings since March 12, 1976. See also note to p. 3n.

— Authors also consulted the testimony before the House Select Committee on Missing Persons, April 7, 1976, of Ms. Anita Lauve, former Foreign Service Officer in Vietnam, Consultant to the Rand Corporation, described by the Committee as one of the foremost experts on the French POW/MIA experience.

Page 45

— For a professional psychoanalytical analysis of the events described to the authors by Garwood, see the article "Coercive Persuasion: The Myth of Free Will" by psychologist Edna Hunter, *Air University Review* (undated). Hunter headed the POW Center for the Department of Defense from 1971 to 1978.

— Records of the interview with Colonel Switzer are in the authors' files.

— It was procedure to interview those released in 1973. This was confirmed by Edna Hunter, whose job was to do the interviews, and by many returned prisoners. For further note on Garwood see note to p. 69.

Page 46

— For discussion of behavior under coercion see article quoted above. The autors also have notes of an interview with the psychiatrist hired by Garwood's government defense.

— Garwood's defense lawyer later said that he had kept the photograph to use, in the event of conviction, to bargain for a better settlement.

Page 47

— State Department memos concerning Garwood prior to his escape are available in the Carter Memorial Library. The authors and Mark Waple have copies.

Page 48

— For Nixon letter see notes to p. 8.

— See note above for memos re. Garwood (p. 47).

— Commodore Brooks's statement from a report he

made to the Subcommittee on Asian and Pacific Affairs, U.S. House of Representatives, June 27, 1985. The proceedings are published.

Page 49 — Casey spoke freely to author Bill Stevenson because he knew him through his World War II friend, British Security Coordination director Sir William (Intrepid) Stephenson. Casey persuaded President Reagan to provide a plug for Stevenson's book *Intrepid's Last Case.*

Page 50 — Sergeant Cressman's draft letter outlining his dilemma, along with voluminous material collected by the Cressman family and their lawyer Dermot Foley after Peter Cressman was shot down February 4, 1973, are in the authors' files. This includes intelligence reports tracing Cressman's capture and imprisonment and a lengthy correspondence with government officials. Jerry Mooney also confirmed that Cressman and some of his crew-mates survived (affidavit from Mooney in files of Senate Foreign Relations Committee and with authors). See also Mooney affidavit in Appendix 3.

Page 51 — Information about family conversations with Shields and Hendon was passed on to the authors during a number of interviews.

— Jerry Mooney outlined standard procedure for reporting sightings immediately to officials. Confirmed by Senate investigators.

— Memo by Department of Defense dissenters was dealt with in notes to p. 6.

Page 52 — The evasive admission from government is in the Cressman file and is referred to in earlier note, p. 6.

Page 53 — Diane Van Renselaar has kept extensive files of correspondence with officials and government records. She and her lawyer found Larry Van Renselaar's name on government lists of prisoners.

— The claims about pension benefits being cut have come from numerous family members whose men took part in secret activities.

Page 54

— Many of these lists have once again been declassified and are now available from the National Archives Machine Readable Branch. Copies of others are still in the files of a number of POW activists. Those wishing to look them up would do well to have specific information about the prisoner or list they wish to track down, since there are numerous possible locations. The authors found the staff very helpful.

— The authors were told about Applegate's words being edited by a number of people who were witness to the original remarks. The report of the committee is listed in the Note to Readers, August 8, 1984. He had also raised the POW issue in Congress on February 23, 1984.

Page 55

— Records of the conversation with Shaheen are in the authors' files.

Page 56

— CBS researcher, Nellie Duncan, was present during many interviews with Billy Hendon. His intelligence work was mentioned in news reports. Hendon has turned over his records to the Senate Foreign Relations Committee.

— Larry O'Daniel, author of *Missing in Action: Trail of Deceit* (in bibliography), says an intelligence chief told him about the rescue plans. O'Daniel filed an affidavit to that effect with Mark Waple for the *Smith vs. The President* lawsuit.

Page 57

— President Reagan stated this position on signing a Resolution and Proclamation – POW-MIA Recognition Day, 1981 (June 12), reprinted in *Public Papers of the President*, p. 508.

Page 58

— The Measles Map is a classified document put together over many years by intelligence analysts. It was recently shown to about a hundred congressmen, some of whom confirmed its existence and contents.

Page 61   — Tighe based his assertions on the fact that, through all his years as DIA head, he had access to the best and most complete intelligence on POWs and made it a priority. Each morning he looked at a file of the latest prisoner intelligence. He stated his conviction on tape. A similar conviction about the accuracy of POW intelligence reports was voiced by General Williams, Tighe's successor at DIA, in a hearing before the Subcommittee on Asian and Pacific Affairs, July 14, 1983. (At the same hearing, General Williams referred to the Measles Map.)

— Fearing for their safety, Garwood never made his list of prisoners public, but in a later informal but highly professional debriefing, undertaken by General Tighe and lie-detector expert Chris Gugas, Garwood's material was judged to be accurate. Some of Garwood's claims were outlined in an article in the *Washington Times*, May 21, 1985.

Page 63   — Records of the conversation with the lawyer are in the files.

Chapter 3: Taking on the Government

Page 66   — Copies of the records of Badey's investigation are with the Foreign Relations Committee investigators – as are photographs.

Page 67   — Mrs. Foley provided the authors with a copy of her letter from President Reagan.

Page 68   — A copy of General Lam Van Phat's letter is in the files of Mark Waple.

Page 69   — A copy of the transcript of the interview with Garwood and the one-page DIA evaluation is in Mark Waple's files. Unsure and frightened by warnings of retribution if he talked about prisoners, Garwood spoke only of second-hand knowledge of their existence and denied having seen prisoners himself. He phrased his claims during the time of his court martial in terms of it being "general knowledge" that there were American prisoners, and said that he had overheard snatches of conversations amongst guards. It was not until 1984 that he spoke openly of personal knowledge of specific groups of men, and then he was careful to state that he would provide names only to the government.

Page 70   — Shields made similar statements to Billy Hendon.

Page 71   — A copy of Bill Bennett's letter to Solarz is in the authors' file as is a copy of the newspaper article from the *Dallas Times-Herald*, October 28, 1984. The parade, held on the eve of the Republican National Convention, was seen as a potential embarrassment to Reagan.

Page 73   — Stephen Solarz became known in subsequent years as the expert on U.S. foreign policy, especially in Asia. He was featured in a *Washington Post* column in May 1990 as "the world expert on Cambodia," and his frequent journeys to Southeast Asia won him considerable newspaper coverage.

Pages 75-8   — Copies of the file on Major Smith and Sergeant McIntire and their allegations are with their lawyer, Mark Waple, and with the Senate Foreign Relations Committee Investigators. The case *Smith et al. vs. Reagan et al.* (637 Federal Supplement 964) was eventually defeated in the Supreme Court. See text p. 397.

Page 76   — Major General Leuer denies all the allegations. See p. 174.

Pages 84-5   — Barnes's mission is treated later in this book and in Barnes's own book, *Bohica* (see bibliography).

Page 87   — Pentagon sources are confidential. *U.S. News and World Report*, November 3, 1986, and *Pentagon Warriors* by Steve Emerson cover the issue of special forces and mention ISA and the aborted rescue mission. The *Congressional Record*, May 28, 1987 (E2140-1) conveys the information about ISA, secret wars, and POW rescue mission that is discussed in the text.

Page 89   — Dorothy McDaniel made notes of the Childress
             telephone call. They are in the authors' files.
             Although Red McDaniel has spoken openly
             about this call on many public occasions,
             Childress has never denied the conversation.

Chapter 5: The Government Position

Page 96   — The Howard testimony is part of the *Smith vs. The
             President* lawsuit. It is in Mark Waple's files and
             was made available to the authors. It is also in the
             files of Senate Foreign Relations Committee
             investigators.

Page 98   — Smith's and McIntire's combat records are in
             Mark Waple's files.

Page 99   — A transcript of the Armitage interview is in the
             authors' files.

Page 102   — The "key supporter" phrase was applied to So-
             larz by Washington correspondent Tim Cornwall
             in an article in *The Nation*, a Bangkok newspaper,
             May 28, 1990. Solarz drew fire from the executive
             director of Vietnam Veterans of America in a
             debate hosted by ABC television news for his
             support of "shameful" U.S. policy in Cambodia.
             His support for the controversial Republican pol-
             icy in Cambodia is also described by Kenton
             Clymer in the April *Indochina Issues/90*. (See also
             note to p. 409.)

Page 106   — Videotape of Liam Atkins telling his story is in
             Christic Institute files.

Page 107   — Marian Shelton's information from a participant
             in the operation was made available to the
             authors during the writing of the book. Her
             records are now in Mark Waple's files. For a
             detailed article outlining the intelligence on
             Charles Shelton, see series of articles entitled
             "The Last POW: The Mystery of Air Force Col.
             Charles E. Shelton" in *Riverside Press Enterprise*,
             April 29, 1985; May 27, 1985; July 29, 1985. The

author of the articles, David Hendrix, was cooperating with a Senate investigation five years later.

Page 111 — Although David Hatcher did not have the formal title of Bureau Chief in Bangkok, Ed Joyce, the President of CBS News at the time, confirmed to the authors that, even though he was not formally Bureau Chief because there was no real bureau, Hatcher, naturally, with CBS's approval, billed himself as the bureau chief in going about his work.

Pages 113-119 — The entire Howard file is with Mark Waple, as is all material on Smith and McIntire. Mark Waple made files available.

Page 120 — My interview with Tuttle was arranged by Red McDaniel, who had received an official briefing on the subject (see text). Records are in the authors' files.

Pages 121-122— Authors have records of all interviews with Barnes. Barnes has repeated his claims in numerous speeches, in interviews, under "sodium amytal," and in his own book, *Bohica* (in bibliography). An additional interview on the subject of his off-line covert activities is in the files of the Christic Institute.

Page 124 — The proceedings of the Senate confirmation hearings are a matter of public record. Published as *Nomination of Henry A. Kissinger*, Hearings Before the Committee on Foreign Relations, United States Senate, Part 1, September 7, 10, 11, and 14, 1973.

Chapter 8: There but for the Grace of God...

Page 136 — The reactions of the Marine Corps lawyers were described to the authors by one of Garwood's attorneys.

Page 138 — A copy of the White House rebuttal of the "Dead or Alive" program on *60 Minutes* is in Capt. Red

McDaniel's files. At the time there were those in the POW community who requested and got copies. Since it was a government publication and was not classified, it should legally be available from the office that issued it – the Department of Defense.

Pages 139-141 — Le Boutillier made his allegations against Col. Childress to numerous witnesses. He also made the allegations during a videotaped interview with the Christian Broadcasting Network.

Page 143 — Air America's involvement in shipping drugs is widely rumored and is mentioned in published accounts, such as Alfred McCoy, *The Politics of Heroin in Southeast Asia* (see bibliography), p. 278. An interview with a former Royal Laotian Air Force officer who claims to have been a direct witness to these shipments is in the authors' files and in the files of Senate Foreign Relations Committee investigators. See also note to p. 149.

Chapter 9: Lies in Laos

Page 146 — Nixon's denial was reported in the newspapers of the day.

Page 148 — The analysis of the seizure of Site 85 is commonly called the CHECO Report. It has been reclassified.

Page 149 — The military role of the Ravens in the secret war in Laos is extensively covered in Christopher Robbins, *The Ravens: The Men Who Flew in America's Secret War in Laos* (in bibliography). Robbins does not mention freighting of opium by the Ravens. Air America, the CIA airline, however, is alleged, in Alfred McCoy's *Politics of Heroin in Southeast Asia*, to have freighted the drug for Vang Pao before the United States helped fund Vang Pao's own airline. See also note to p. 143. However, John Ranelagh, in *The Agency* (in bibliography), reminds the reader (p. 425n) that the Church Committee found no evidence that the CIA was actively involved in the drug trade.

Page 150   — Casino Man requested anonymity, but Col. Earl Hopper, Sr., former director of the National League of Families, chairman of the Live POW Committee, and head of Task Force Omega, confirmed that he had been a high-ranking officer in the CIA.

Page 151   — All documents concerning the harassment of Casino Man's friend and his staff are in Earl Hopper's files and with the Senate Foreign Relations Committee investigation.

Page 153   — Jerry Mooney confirmed to the authors the existence of a list of the names of some three hundred men missing in Laos.

Page 155   — The Canadian government source cannot be named. Interview is in file notes.

Page 156   — Ross Perot interviewed the witness to the White House meeting at length and passed the information on to the authors.

Pages 156-157— The meeting with Richard Allen was witnessed by seven veterans including Capt. Red McDaniel. John Brown passed the notes from that meeting on to the authors, and they were corroborated by other members of the group who participated.

Page 157   — Some intelligence experts have a marked bias towards technical intelligence. It is this bias LeGro was noting in Polgar.

Chapter 10: Telling Dirty Secrets

Page 160   — See earlier references to Jerry Mooney's material. He has made everything available to the authors and to the Senate Foreign Relations Committee investigators.

Page 162   — Jerry Mooney's affidavits for Mark Waple have been made available to many people, including the American Defense Institute.

Page 164   — Mark Waple kept a log of all his phone calls, with notes, in which this call is recorded.

Page 166   — Barnes's testimony before Murkowski's Veterans Affairs Committee, which began in January 1986, is on videotape. Red McDaniel has a copy of the tape. Barnes made the same allegations in countless speeches and in his book, *Bohica* (in bibliography).

Pages 168-169 — Shirah's information about possible classified information, which was recorded in the authors' notes, was passed on to the Senate Foreign Relations Committee investigators. They also confirmed Shirah's information directly with him.

Pages 170-171 — Billy Hendon told the authors the entire story of his mission to Hanoi, and it also appeared on the *20/20* program on POWs.

Page 172   — "The Mortician" is treated in the notes to page 9. In a letter dated July 27, 1984, John R. Oberst, of the POW/MIA Division of the Defense Intelligence Agency, said that the Mortician's evidence about live prisoners, which had been referred to in congressional testimony by former DIA Chief Gen. James A. Williams as "credible" or "accurate," had later been determined to be a "fabrication."

Page 173   — See notes for page 48 for source of Commodore Brooks's comments.

Page 174   — Leuer's positive assessments of Major Smith are in files of Mark Waple and the authors.

Pages 175-176 — The story of the stand-down of the Delta raid is also covered in Steven Emerson's book *Secret Warriors* (see bibliography).

Chapter 11: Complications and Conspiracies

Pages 179-180 — The Vietnamese comments to Hendon, Benjamin Gilman (Rep., N.Y.), Frank McCloskey (Dem., Ind.) and others about prisoners possibly being held in remote mountainous regions was reported in the press at the time. AP and UPI stories were carried, for example, in the Manchester, N.H., *Union Leader,* February 16, 1986 and the *Chicago Tribune,* February 20, 1986.

Pages 181-182— What the vets of MACV-SOG said about secret units matched what the authors had learned from portions of the Pentagon textbook mentioned in the notes to p. 11.

Pages 185-186— Much of this material on EATSCO appeared in the press at the time. Although the *Washington Post,* the *Wall Street Journal* and the wire services were on the trail of the story, the first report to mention EATSCO in print was a September 6, 1981, article in the *New York Times.* Wilson was first indicted on July 19, 1982. *60 Minutes* staffers spoke to E. Lawrence Barcella, Jr., the prosecutor in the Wilson case. The authors also have some of the original police reports in the Wilson case. Bud Fensterwald, one of Ed Wilson's Washington attorneys, has been asking for EATSCO documents under seal. Documents he has been able to obtain are available to the authors.

Page 186   — See notes to p. 66 re. Badey.

Pages 187-188— Testimony Shinkle gave to the House Subcommittee on Asian and Pacific Affairs (July 4, 1978) and his affidavit in the *Smith vs. The President* lawsuit both attest to his conviction that American military personnel are being held against their will in Southeast Asia.

Page 190   — Information about the satellite pictures was also brought out by representative Douglas Applegate on the congressional floor, August 4, 1984. It was edited for national security reasons, but there were many witnesses. It was confirmed to the authors by Applegate's staffer, Tim Secrest, and POW activist Mike Van Atta. The hearing was published as *Prisoners of War/Missing in Action in Southeast Asia.* (See Note to Readers.)

Page 194   — Taylor's notes record his conversation with the retired U.S. admiral.

Chapter 12: Prisoners and Politics

Page 195   — Information on Jerry Daniels and his death comes not only from primary interviews mentioned in the text, but also from the BBC files on the same matter. State Department and other communications are in the BBC's files.

Page 196   — The activities and failure of the Nugan Hand Bank were the subject of an Australian Royal Commission (*Royal Commission of Inquiry into the Activities of Nugan Hand Group*, 2 vols.). It is also mentioned in *The Chronology: The Documented Day-by-Day Account of the Secret Military Assistance to Iran and the Contras* (p. 25). There was also a series of articles by Jonathan Kwitny in the *Wall Street Journal* (April 24, 25, 26, 1982). The first article was entitled "Australian Mystery: The Collapse of Nugan Hand Banks Discloses Links with some High-Ranking American Military and Intelligence Officials."

Page 197   — See note above re. Nugan Hand.

                 — The transcripts of Rewald's trial (CIPA hearing), containing Judge Fong's statement, are not readily available.

Page 198   — David Taylor did a report for the BBC's News and Public Affairs Department on the credentials of Rewald's prosecutor. Notes on Taylor's conversations with the prosecutor are in the BBC offices.

                 — John F. Kelly made the BBRDW documents available to the authors.

Page 199   — A record of the Harris interview is among the many materials that David Taylor made available to the authors.

Page 200   — The family of James Ray made all their voluminous documentation available to the authors.

Page 201   — Murkowski's remark to the family was made privately when they approached him after the hearings. Ray's mother, father, and sister all confirmed this to the authors.

Page 202 — Kissinger's denial of prisoners in Cambodia was widely quoted in news accounts of the day (e.g. *Washington Post*, February 18, 1973).
— See reference to Vernon Walters in note to p. 3n.

Page 203 — The authors have records of Ashworth interview.

Page 204 — Vang Pao's status as a mercenary leader during the U.S. secret war in Laos is treated in other publications (e.g. Christopher Robbins, *The Ravens*; Alfred McCoy, *The Politics of Heroin in Southeast Asia*, both of which are cited in the bibliography). His role is confirmed by the commanders of armed forces in Thailand who fought in Laos.

Page 207 — Casino Man's friend turned the records of his harassment over to investigators for the Senate Foreign Relations Committee in 1990.

Page 208 — Oksenberg's memos are in the Carter Library. Copies are also in the files of Mark Waple.

Page 209 — A copy of the National Security Council 1979 memo is in the authors' files.

Chapter 13: Silencing the Critics

Page 212 — David Taylor has a record of the conversation with Panessa and Bonnyville.

Pages 214-218 — The BBC files on the circumstances surrounding Daniels' death include notes of primary interviews, and copies of State Department and other communications.

Page 215 — A copy of the Haig cable is in the authors' files.

Pages 217-218 — Patricia Penn was a colleague of William Stevenson, and spoke with him in Southeast Asia about the situation after travelling through Hmong territories in the early years of U.S. involvement. Her story was outlined in David Taylor's BBC records.

Page 220 — Mrs. Foley provided the authors with a copy of her letter from President Reagan.

Page 221   — General Tighe confirmed to the authors that his understanding was that the commission findings were to be made public. This was also the understanding of congressmen and commission members, such as Gen. Robinson Risner, Billy Hendon, and Bob Smith.

Page 222   — Caspar Weinberger's accusation was made in the presence of a number of witnesses, some of whom repeated it to General Tighe.

Page 224   — It is important to note that Tighe's official report, submitted to DIA, was classified and no part was ever released. Instead Tighe was asked to report on his commission's findings before the House Subcommittee on Asian and Pacific Affairs.

The congressional hearing report of that committee meeting, October 15, 1986 (Congressional Resolution 129), was entitled *Tighe Report on American POW's and MIA's*. Despite the title, General Tighe was asked to confine his remarks to ten minutes.

Brig. General Shufelt made his remarks about the "team" during this hearing (page 48 of the proceedings).

— During the period when transcripts of Tighe's remarks were kept in Solarz's office, they could be viewed only at the discretion of the office staff. Both Mark Waple and Mike Van Atta saw the transcripts in the office and Mark Waple recorded the contents by reading them into a tape recorder.

Page 225   — North's connecting of arms sales with hostages is in *The Chronology: The Documented Day-by-Day Account of the Secret Military Assistance to Iran and the Contras* (see bibliography), pp. 530-1.

— A copy of the official "Press Guidance" is in Red McDaniel's files and the files of Task Force Omega. Many POW activist groups keep copies of all government press releases that touch on the subject. It should also be available from the

National League of Families.

Pages 225-226— Perot's testimony is recorded in the Tighe Report, (pp. 40-48). See note to p. 224.

Page 227   — Laxalt's remarks were noted by John Brown and his group.

Page 228   — The Marsh/Weinberger communication was confirmed to the authors by a senior Pentagon source. It is also discussed in Steven Emerson's *Secret Warriors* (in bibliography), pp. 132-3.

Chapter 14: The Radical, the Billionaire, and the Green Beret

Page 231   — Glenn Robinette's testimony was described in news reports (e.g. *Washington Post*, June 24, 1987, and Reuters, June 29, 1987) and is in Danny Sheehan's files. An article in the *Washington Post*, June 29, 1987, reported that Contra funds were used to fight the Christic suit. According to the article, "More than $100,000 from Swiss Iran-contra bank accounts was spent for private detective work and legal fees in connection with a lawsuit filed against retired Air Force major general Richard V. Secord and other key members of Lt. Col. Oliver North's private network . . . the payments were justified because the suit threatened to 'knock out' the secret system former National Security Council aide North set up to supply arms to the contras during a two-year ban on official U.S. military aid to the rebels. . . . Secord hired Glenn A. Robinette to investigate the backgrounds of those behind the Christic lawsuit."

Page 233   — The final result of Kerry's concern was a Senate investigation and report entitled *Drugs, Law Enforcement and Foreign Policy: A Report of the Subcommittee on Terrorism, Narcotics and International Operations* (April 13, 1989). (House Crimes Subcommittee investigated the same allegations of drug and arms smuggling, and reported July 12, 1987.)

In mid-April of 1986, Senator Kerry met with Senate Foreign Relations Committee Chairman Richard Lugar to ask for an official investigation into the "private network" run from the White House by Oliver North. He also met with Senator Clairborne Pell, R.I. This meeting was confirmed by Jonathan Weiner, Chief Legal Counsel for Senator Kerry's staff, and his Chief of Staff, Dick McCall, to Danny Sheehan and reporter Brian Barger, who was then with Associated Press and is now Chief of CNN's investigative news unit. Kerry's call for an investigation appeared in news reports. Lugar was unresponsive and reported to the NSC that he found Kerry's charges groundless. Senator Pell promised Kerry that if Democrats won the next election he would help establish a subcommittee to investigate the matter. Kerry would later head a subcommittee investigating these charges.

Notes about Kerry's investigation and meetings, including an internal memo about the nature of the "private network" run out of the White House by Jonathan Weiner, are in the April 13, 1989, Senate Foreign Relations Committee Report, Appendix. In addition, Berkeley Professor Peter Dale Scott, a Fellow at the Center for International Development in Washington, D.C., wrote a critique of the Kerry official report, contrasting staff group notes with limited official statements.

Pages 233-234— The NSC statement mirrors the findings of the Tower Report, which cleared those implicated in the Iran/Contra affair and is based on statements made by Senator Lugar.

Page 234 — The Costa Rican report is in the files of the Christic Institute and was made available to the authors.

— The inside story on the charges against Kerry

were confirmed by a congressional staffer who was in a position to know. The story appeared in the *Washington Times,* June 13, 1986.

Page 238 — Glenn Robinette. See earlier note, p. 231.

— Col. Hopper was informed by the Air Force that his son had been killed in action. Col. Hopper frequently pointed out in letters to DIA officials that the Foreign Claims Settlement Commission, Department of Justice, September 24, 1982, stated that "Earl P. Hopper, Jr., survived the crash and was captured on January 10, 1968," and he found other records supporting this. The DIA circulated to POW groups and to Congressman Solarz a statement saying "there is no evidence Lt. Hopper was able to eject from his aircraft."

Col. Hopper himself had an extensive background in intelligence and staff work.

Page 239 — See previous notes on Mrs. Foley's letter.

Page 240 — A senior Pentagon source provided contents of the secret memo from Weinberger. It is also quoted in *Secret Warriors* by Steven Emerson.

— Transcripts of Rewald's trial (CIPA hearing), containing Judge Fong's statement, are not available to the public. See note p. 197.

— Transcript of Clarence E. Johnson's affidavit is in Appendix 4.

Page 241 — See note to p. 3 for Kissinger's dealings with the Laotians.

Page 242 — Barnes also repeated his assertions in his own book, *Bohica* (see bibliography). Many officials have stated categorically that the book cannot be relied upon and contains many false allegations. Experts in special operations have pointed out to the authors internal evidence that Barnes could not invent certain details.

— Our Pentagon source confirmed to us that security was tightened by Hanoi after the attempted raid.

Page 243   — Perot, with his Presidential mandate, had
                     security clearance.

Chapter 15: The Vanishing Cabbie

Page 250   — The stories we had heard of a failed 1982 mis-
                     sion alleged that it had been planned to go after
                     the same men who were identified in the "Fort
                     Apache" satellite photos.
                   — Excerpts from Reagan's letter to the National
                     League of Families are in the authors' files.
Page 251   — Casey's involvement in leaking the story of the
                     Tehran raid failure is a matter of record and
                     appeared in newspaper accounts.

Chapter 16: The Drug Lord

Page 256   — Gorman's memos are in the files of Senator
                     Kerry's Senate Subcommittee on Terrorism,
                     Narcotics and International Operations. Authors
                     have only the quotations from the open part of
                     the hearings. Report cited earlier in notes
                     to p. 233.
Page 257   — Gorman's memos were quoted before the Kerry
                     Committee. Final report is *Drugs, Law Enforce-
                     ment and Foreign Policy: Panama* (2 vols.). Wash-
                     ington: U.S. Government Printing Office, 1988.
                   — The Danny Sheehan lawsuit is described in the
                     text, pp. 257-8. The lawsuit *Avirgan vs. Hall et al.*
                     (86-1146 CIV-King; additional 87-1545-CIV-King)
                     was filed in May 1986. In June 1988 the judge
                     summarily dismissed the case and awarded the
                     defendants almost a million dollars in attorneys'
                     fees, saying there was no basis for the suit. An
                     appeal (88-5720, 11th Circuit Court of Appeal)
                     was immediately filed and the case is still before
                     the Court of Appeal.
Page 259   — Copies of Bo Gritz's affidavits were supplied by
                     his lawyer as part of the official court record. His
                     remark about King was made during an
                     interview.

— Khun Sa's claims were recorded by Gritz, who felt Khun Sa believed the claims.

Self-styled revolutionary "General" Khun Sa is not simply the major drug kingpin which he was portrayed as when he was indicted by the United States on ten drug-trafficking charges, December 20, 1989. (The indictment remained sealed until March 15, 1990, and was then reported. See *Washington Post*, Section A, March 16, 1990, and *U.S. News and World Report*, March 26, 1990). "The largest dope-pusher in the Golden Triangle," he was called by U.S. Attorney-General Richard Thornburgh. But at fifty-seven, Khun Sa is seen in the highlands of Burma as the toughest survivor of the many civil wars fought by hill tribes against the central government of Burma since 1948. As leader of a Shan State independence movement, Khun Sa has claimed he is only asking for rights promised during World War II when the British and Americans needed Shan and other hill tribe support in clandestine warfare against the Japanese. His territory adjoins northern Thailand and he claims his followers are financed by taxes he levies on smugglers of illicit drugs heading for the traditional clearing-house of Bangkok. In negotiations during June 1990 with the Burmese central government in Rangoon, he repeated his oft-heard offer (mentioned in the *U.S. News and World Report* article listed above) to stop the cultivation of opium if foreign governments help him substitute harmless cash crops or give financial aid. He argued that hill tribes could not be easily weaned from opium-growing, their only source of income for generations, where poppies flourish and little else grows. Thailand's chief of narcotics suppression, Police General Kovid Phupanich, stated in a 1990 government report that Khun Sa controlled 60 per cent of the

Golden Triangle's output and supplied 40 per cent of all heroin entering the U.S.A.

Others point to mixed motives and tangled loyalties in the Golden Triangle. Professor Alfred McCoy, author of *The Politics of Heroin in Southeast Asia* (details given in bibliography), was quoted in the June 1, 1990 issue of *Asiaweek* (published by Time-Warner) as saying, "The indictment of one man cannot alter things." A leading Thai narcotics expert told the authors in Thailand, "I could lead an attack on Khun Sa's headquarters and kill him tomorrow, but a thousand others would spring up in his place. We need to undertake a long term program like the Thailand royal projects by King Rama IX that avoids head on collisions with traditional lifestyles. Too many anti-drug campaigns are run by foreigners who think you can stop the growers overnight." Khun Sa's 1989 offer to Washington was to root out the poppies for U.S. $300 million, which makes him seemingly a profiteer. But Thai experts working to convert opium-growers in adjacent hills have estimated this may well be the cost of weaning Khun Sa's Shans off drugs.

Pages 259-260— See note pp. 395-397 re. Bo Gritz.

Page 260   — Lance Trimmer was held for some time for questioning. The authors spoke to Trimmer at length. His materials had not been returned until after he was released.

Pages 260-261— DIA correspondence on Gritz's attempt to look for Americans shows that he was in direct and formal contact with, and was encouraged by, DIA officials, who provided him with intelligence support.

Page 261   — Videotapes of Khun Sa's statements are in the authors' files. The validity of Khun Sa's allegations have been attacked on the grounds that, in the video, there appear to be legal papers outlining the same accusations that Khun Sa is making. Khun Sa could conceivably have taken his cue from such sources.

Page 262 — Khun Sa's position as a drug warlord is common knowledge. It is discussed in *Drugs, the U.S., and Khun Sa*, by Francis Belanger, which is in the bibliography. See also note to p. 259 above.

Page 263 — The four-volume report of the Australian Joint Task Force on Drug-Trafficking may be consulted in the library of the Australian embassy in Washington, D.C. The report of the Royal Commission is cited in the bibliography.

— Laos's stance is a matter of public record. The authors confirmed it with the U.S. public information office and with an official of the government of Laos based in Bangkok.

Pages 263-264— Khun Sa's reply was to send the Vitaly Levin piece mentioned on pp. 264-265.

Page 264 — The claim that the Canadian government had conveyed messages from its Beijing embassy concerning prisoners was made by a Canadian government source. The Canadian government officially denies it. There have been other suggestions that the Canadians have been involved in the issue at other times. A letter is on file in federal district court in Great Falls, Montana, which shows that the Canadian government agreed in 1985 to be a "receiving station" for a group of American POWs that was alleged to include a Canadian civilian. The letter is signed by Canadian External Affairs minister Joe Clark. It is also in the files of attorney Patricia Cotten, Great Falls, Montana. The story was told in the *Wall Street Journal* by reporter Bill Paul, January 21, 1987.

Chapter 17: Buried Lists

Pages 267-268— The lists described in the text are in Mike Van

Atta's files as well as in Red McDaniel's files. The aerial photos are in Van Atta's files.

Pages 268 — Tighe spoke before the Subcommittee on Asian and Pacific Affairs (see note to p. 224).

— The National League of Families' Press Guidance sheet should be available from the League. A complete record of press-guidance sheets is in the files of POW activist organizations Homecoming II and Task Force Omega, as well as in computerized files.

— Tighe spoke of Special Talents in an unbroadcast part of the *60 Minutes* interviews, and in other interviews with the authors.

— Armitage's denial of Tighe's assertions are from unbroadcast portions of interviews.

Page 269 — STs are cited in Mooney affidavit in Appendix 3 when he refers to prisoners who were MB, or "Moscow Bound."

Pages 272-275— The authors spoke with Sam and Bob over several days during a national meeting of POW activists at which they were all giving speeches. Sam and Bob's speech, during which they told their story, is on videotape in the files of the Forget-Me-Not association.

Page 274 — The NBC producer has related the same story to Senate staffers.

Chapter 18: The Business of Covert Ops

Page 276 — Admiral Stansfield Turner discusses this subject in his book, *Secrecy and Democracy* (in bibliography).

— The scandal about security at the U.S. embassy in Moscow created a national uproar and was widely reported in the press of the day (e.g. *New York Times*, April 8, 1987, and *Washington Post*, April 29, and May 7, 1987). It was later also the subject of an article in *Time* magazine, July 10, 1989.

Pages 278-282— A record of the conversation with Ed Wilson is in the authors' files. In addition, the authors had access to records of interviews Ed Wilson gave to Danny Sheehan of the Christic Institute.

— Ed Wilson's lawyer is continuing to try to get access to Wilson's court papers. He has already had some success.

Page 282   — CIA reform is covered in Stansfield Turner's own book, *Secrecy and Democracy*. (See bibliography.)

Pages 283-284— A copy of the section of the Pentagon study, which outlines special warfare units, is in the authors' files. The Pentagon text has been verified by a source with security clearance.

Page 284   — The testimony before Congress, May 12, 1975, was one of the very few times that Von Marbod gave any public accounting of his job.

Chapter 19: The Sleaze Factor

Page 285   — Information about Von Marbod's connection with the "40 Committee" was obtained through sources who worked with him at the time.

— The Presidential Executive Order was first issued by President Gerald Ford in 1974 and re-issued in a stronger form by President Jimmy Carter in 1977.

Pages 285-286— In his own memoirs, *Honorable Man* (see bibliography), pp. 270-2, Colby disputes the casualty figures and defends Phoenix, pointing out that over 85 per cent of the 20,000 casualties he testified to in 1971 were killed in combat.

The *Village Voice*, commenting in June 1990 on articles by Kathy Kadane the previous month in U.S. newspapers, including the *Spartanburg Herald-Journal*, concerning CIA activities in Southeast Asia during the Vietnam War, said former CIA Director William Colby "admitted to Kadane that his infamous Phoenix Program – a joint U.S.-Vietnamese effort set up in 1967 to 'neutralize' supporters of Ho Chi Minh's National Liberation Front and widely criticized for its human rights abuses – was modelled on the success of Suharto's bloody PKI purge." The PKI, the Indonesian Communist Party, was liquidated by President Suharto in 1965-6 (when Suharto was a military officer serving under President Sukarno) after the U.S. government allegedly supplied names of suspected communists and leftists. The *Washington Post* had estimated in 1966 that 500,000 were killed in the purge. According to a *Village Voice* article by Doug Ireland, "The CIA in 1968 put the figure at 250,000."

Page 286 — Von Marbod's resignation on December 1, 1981, is part of the public record. It was discussed in *Manhunt* by Peter Maas and cited in *The Chronology: The Documented Day-by-Day Account of the Secret Military Assistance to Iran and the Contras* (both in bibliography). The reference to narcolepsy is made in *Manhunt*, p. 235.

Page 287 — See Report of the Royal Commission into the Activities of the Nugan Hand (in the bibliography).

— The findings of the Pentagon inquiry were also confirmed by an internal Pentagon source.

— A Group of Task Force 157 members sued the Agency for retirement benefits when it was dissolved. This, for the first time, gave public acknowledgement that the secret organization was a real entity. Records are in the files of Washington attorney Bernard Fensterwald, III. See also note below.

— The fact that Inman passed Wilson's name to the FBI was confirmed by a confidential source. Inman's termination of Task Force 157 and his "firing" of Wilson is discussed in articles in *Geo*, vol.6 (May 1984), pp. 16, 18 and in *Playboy* vol. 29 (May 1982), pp. 100, 102-3.

Page 288   — Shackley's claim that his acquaintance with Wilson was merely social was repeated in *Manhunt* by Peter Maas (see bibliography), p. 8.
                    — The *New York Times*, June 14, 1981, published one of the earlier reports leaking the Wilson affair, but the name of EATSCO first appeared in a *Times* article, September 6, 1981. See note to pp. 185-186.

Pages 288-289— Secord's suspension and reinstatement were widely reported in the press. They were also mentioned in *The Chronology* (see bibliography), p. 13.

Page 290   — The authors made a request to the FBI to see the complaint that Admiral Inman filed.

Pages 290-291— John Brown and his group of veterans kept extensive records of their interviews. The authors also conducted individual interviews with Colonel LeGro, Tony Duke, and other members of the group.

Page 291   — Both former Congressman John Le Boutillier and John Brown told the authors about the confrontation with Schultz.

Page 292   — An anonymous refutation, denying a claim in a Christic Institute affidavit that Armitage had been in business with Aderholt, was sent to news and other organizations.

Page 293   — When the authors called DIA to ask about the allegations against Aderholt, they were informed that no such allegations were on record. They were told DIA knew nothing about the matter. The Air Force also said it had no record of charges. NSC officials refused to comment.

Page 294   — Earl Hopper's lists are available to the authors.
Page 295   — The FBI report is dated March 17, 1985.

Chapter 20: Getting "Bo"

Page 299   — The Christic Institute has files on Stephen Carr. These were backed up by the report of Senator

John Kerry's Subcommittee on Terrorism, Narcotics and International Operations, cited in note to p. 233. Notes of Kerry's interview conducted with the informant who worked loading covert planes with Carr are in the April 13 report by the Subcommittee, Appendix.

Pages 300-301— The authors made their own notes of conversations with Scott Barnes and David Taylor. In addition, David Taylor made his records available.

Pages 302-307— Dorothy McDaniel and the author both kept records of the conversations with Scott Barnes that occur over the following pages.

Pages 305-307— A record of "The Ear" conversation is in the authors' files and the files of the Christic Institute.

Page 308   — A record of the conversation with "True Man," who must remain anonymous, is in the authors' and Senate committee files.

Page 309   — An account of the near termination of ISA appears in Emerson, *Secret Warriors* (see bibliography), p. 81.

Page 310   — Adverse reports on ISA activities were reported in the media (e.g. article by Carlyle Murphy and Charles R. Babcock, *Washington Post* staff writers, in the *Washington Post National Weekly Edition*, December 16, 1985).

— Shinkle appeared before the congressional committee, July 4 weekend, 1978. See notes to pp. 187-188.

Pages 311-313— A record of the Gritz interview is in the authors' files.

Page 311   — Sir Colin Gubbins made his comment, for the record, directly to William Stevenson.

Pages 311-312— The authors have a copy of the letter on DIA stationery in their files. DIA has questioned the authenticity of the letter, and individual DIA officers say it has been proved a forgery.

Page 312 — Gritz's confidential submission to the President is available in the authors' files.

Pages 313-314— Charges against Gritz have been confirmed to the authors by his lawyer, Lanny Wade.

Page 314 — Gritz's record is in the authors' files. It is also in his attorney's files.

Chapter 21: Scott Barnes Tells His Story

Page 316 — For material from Barnes interview, see notes to pp. 302-307.

Page 317 — Complete tapes of the truth-drug interview are in Mark Waple's files. An edited version is in BBC files.

Pages 317-322— Barnes made all these claims about his mission in interviews with the authors. He also told the same story in his book, *Bohica*, and in numerous speeches and in television and radio interviews.

Page 322 — David Taylor's notes of his conversation with J.D. Bath were made available to the authors. Bath would not talk to the authors.

Pages 322-323— The authors have records of the interview with Dr. Matthew Meselson.

Page 323 — Formal records on the Robinson investigation were not made available to the authors, but records of conversations with Lt. Col. Flocke and the Fairfax County police sergeant are in authors' files.

Page 324 — The tape of Taylor's conversation with Panessa and Bonnyville is in the BBC files. Taylor checked the agents' credentials, as did Ross Perot and Jim Badey, to whom they also spoke.

Page 325 — Barnes made virtually the same calls to Taylor and to the authors, and the three often compared notes. Although Barnes recanted about seeing POWs in Laos, he would soon be telling the same story to POW activist groups. When his book, *Bohica*, was published with the same story, he again promoted it openly – but always with POW activist groups. Marian Shelton said she felt he could only feel unafraid when he was with people who believed him, trusted him, and would go out of their way to protect him – as most POW families did.

Page 330   — Sworn statements from USAF officers are in the authors' files. The chaplains of other denominations who served with Father Shelton voluntarily wrote unusually strong letters of support for him (which are also on file). They characterized him as a man who completely fulfilled the moral obligations of his calling.

Pages 331-332— Records of conversations with the technical sergeant and the electrical engineer are in the authors' files, as are those of the conversation with Col. James Millsap. Although Millsap was critical of Shelton for continuing to speak out on the POW issue, he did not question his moral probity.

Congressional committee investigators in 1990 reported that, while interviewing the electrical engineer, they were told the remarks had been misinterpreted. The same person had pleaded the protection of secrecy rules in refusing to discuss the report with author Jensen-Stevenson.

Pages 332-333— Ann Holland's documents include the letter from the senior U.S. Army officer.

Page 333   — Commander Hugh Taylor had access to a USAF report on the seizure of the site to which he drew the authors' attention.

Chapter 23: Perot Makes a Move

Page 338   — The comment to the congressmen was reported in the media. See earlier notes to pp. 179-180.

Page 346   — Some other delegates described the discussions during the mission.

— Nguyen Dy Dien's quote is in the *New York Times*.

Page 347   — The hearing is available as Proceedings of the

September 30, 1987, Hearing of the Subcommittee on Asian and Pacific Affairs of the Committee
on Foreign Affairs, House of Representatives,
100th Congress.

— Incorporation documents are in the authors' files.

Pages 347-348— Red McDaniel was attacked during a nationally
televised hearing. Videotapes of this proceeding
are in McDaniel's files. The record is on p. 36 of
the committee report cited in the note to p. 347
above.

Page 348 — Paul Mather, the head of JCRC, makes this reve-
lation in an internal document entitled *The MIA
Story in Southeast Asia*. A copy is in the files of the
authors and of the Senate Foreign Relations
Committee investigators.

— Vessey would also make several more trips to
Hanoi, one as late as January 1990. However, he
never again spoke publicly with the same determination about getting live men back that he had
used in our first conversation and/or in his July
1983 speech before the National League of Families. A transcript of the speech should be available from the National League of Families.

Chapter 24: Garwood Debriefed

Pages 351-359— A transcript of the debriefing of Garwood by
Tighe and Gugas is in the authors' files.

Page 357 — A copy of Van Phat's letter is in the authors' files.

Pages 357-358— The new agreement by which the United States
gave sanctuary to South Vietnamese prisoners
from "reform" camps was reported in the media
in the early spring of 1989 (e.g. *Washington Post*,
January 16 and 18, 1990, and *Washington Times*,
January 24, 1990). The authors were living in
Bangkok when the first group of South Vietnamese arrived there and moved on to the United
States. The actual program was announced in the
Department of Defense Bulletin, November 1989,
p. 63.

Pages 360-364— Records of the conversation with Casino Man are in the authors' files. Col. Earl Hopper has tape-recorded similar interviews.

Page 363   — Inman's remarks were reported in the press. They were also quoted in an article by James A. Natban, entitled "Dateline Australia: America's Foreign Watergate?" in *Foreign Policy*, Winter, 1982-1983.

Page 364   — Kayak's story is told in *The Ravens* by Christopher Robbins (see bibliography). It was repeated to the authors by James R. Shirah.

Chapter 25: Vietnam Revisited

Pages 366-367— The research for this chapter was also used as the basis for a series of newspaper articles.

Page 377   — The Nguyen Van Linh statement appeared in *Time* magazine, September 21, 1987.

Chapter 26: What the Government Always Knew

Page 378   — Records of the conversations with Bobby Garwood are in the authors' files.

Chapter 27: A Matter of Ethics

Page 387   — Information on Eagleburger's trips to Vietnam was received from a confidential State Department source.

Pages 389-390— After reports of Armitage's nomination for Deputy Secretary of State for Southeast Asian Affairs, Secretary of the Navy, and Secretary of the Army had appeared in the press, the White House announced the nomination had not been formally submitted to the Senate. The FBI had, however, done the background check that is part of a formal nomination. (A Pentagon spokesman said this had nothing to do with the nomination not going forward.) Armitage's resignation was reported in the *New York Times*, May 26, 1990, "Bush Selection as Secretary of the Army Withdraws to Avoid Grilling." In early 1990, Armitage was appointed by President Bush to head negotiations on the future of U.S. installations in the Philippines.

Page 391 — Letters said to be from American MIAs are in the authors' files as well as in Red McDaniel's files.

Pages 394-397— All the material relating to the *U.S. vs. James "Bo" Gritz* is in the files of Gritz's lawyer. In June 1990, Gritz reportedly faced a new federal grand jury investigation. A *Los Angeles Times* article (June 6, 1990) stated that W. Patrick Moriarty, a convicted political corrupter, paid Gritz $2,000 in connection with business trips that Gritz made to China, Singapore, and other areas of Asia. Gritz is quoted as saying the visits were legitimate business trips, during which he was to negotiate an oil interest that Moriarty had set up between China and Indonesia.

Pages 398-399— Records of Smith's material are in the files of Mark Waple.

Page 398 — Information about the top-secret unit in Bangkok is from confidential government sources in Thailand, where the authors were living at the time. See also the work-in-progress by Elsie Webber, author of *The Saving Rain*, published by Branden Inc., Boston, 1989, an excellent eyewitness account of Khmer Rouge atrocities. Webber had spent ten years working among Cambodian refugees when the authors spoke with her in 1990. She was then Executive Director of the Refugee Outreach Committee, and "as an American citizen found myself at odds with outdated U.S. policy on Cambodia."

Chapter 28: The Secret War

Pages 400-415— During 1989 and 1990, the authors lived in Thailand and interviewed many people who had direct involvement with these issues.

Page 402   — The 600-page internal document was made available to the authors, but is not generally accessible.

Page 404   — The authors interviewed Kukrit Pramoj.

Pages 405-406— The Bangkok columnist spoke to the authors and also wrote several columns with this theme.

Page 406   — According to John Brown and his group of vets, former National Security Advisor Richard Allen attributed this remark to Alexander Haig. See earlier note on the meeting of the vets with Allen, pp. 290-291.

              — The statistics are from the Thai National Security Council and the United Nations.

Page 408   — The fact that the Thai government is paying to get back Thai prisoners is general knowledge in Thailand.

Page 409   — The Stone/Colby article was published in the *Los Angeles Times*, and was reprinted in the *International Herald Tribune*, October 25, 1989. Another Stone article was reprinted in the *International Herald Tribune*, November 17, 1989. The White House continued to use financial and intelligence resources to fight the communists in Cambodia.

              An article entitled "American Assistance to the Cambodian Resistance Forces" by Kenton J. Clymer, Professor of History at the University of Texas, published in *Indochina Issues 90*, a publication put out by the Indochina Project of the Center for International Policy and the Vietnam Veterans of America Foundation, deals with the assistance to the Cambodian resistance forces and is a review of aid to them since 1982. The article states that Clymer had reviewed overt and covert aid to the Khmer Rouge and has covered all published congressional discussions, and they are outlined in the publication.

              In 1982, Assistant Secretary of State for East Asian and Pacific Affairs John D. Holdridge confirmed in testimony before the House Subcommittee on Asian and Pacific Affairs that for some time the United States had given moral and political support to the Cambodian resistance. Direct covert aid expanded significantly in 1982. An amendment to allow lethal aid passed comfortably in the House on July 9, 1985, although the *Far East Review* broke the story about covert aid in 1984.

Both the *Washington Post* and the *New York Times,* according to the article, quoted that at least $3.5 million had been stolen in connection with the distribution of U.S. covert assistance in Cambodia.

Page 411 — Copy of the Haig telex, praising Daniels after his death, is in the authors' files and the BBC files.

Pages 411-412 — As a correspondent based in Malaysia at the time, William Stevenson has first-hand knowledge of the events involving the British Special Air Service.

— Douglas Hurd's announcement was made in early November, 1989.

— Kissinger's declaration that he had been told there were no more prisoners in Cambodia is cited earlier. See notes to p. 3.

Page 414 — Khun Sa's indictment was widely reported in the media (e.g. *USA Today,* May 24, 1990, and the *Bangkok Post,* December 13, 1989). See also note to p. 259.

Postscript: *Plausible Deniability*

Pages 416-418 — The Smith and McIntire material is in the authors' files, as cited earlier. Classified material is in the files of Mark Waple and the Senate Foreign Relations Committee investigators.

The controversy continues. As this book was going to press, lawyers for Richard Armitage wrote to the authors, taking exception to articles written by William Stevenson, and stating in the most emphatic terms that Mr. Armitage has never engaged in any improper activities or had any improper connections with anyone in Southeast Asia. They included a letter to them from Jonathan Kwitny, who has investigated charges against Mr. Armitage and concluded that "there has not been one shred of reliable evidence that Mr. Armitage involved himself with drug-trafficking, money-laundering, or profiteering from his public offices . . . [or] had anything to do with Nugan Hand."

BIBLIOGRAPHY

Badey, James R. *Dragons and Tigers*. Loomis, California: Palmer Enterprises, 1988.

Bamrungsuk, Surachart. "United States Foreign Policy and Thai Military Rule, 1947-1977." Thesis, Cornell University, 1985. Published in Bangkok.

Barnes, Scott, with Melva Libb. *Bohica*. Canton, Ohio: Bohica Corporation, 1987.

Belanger, Francis. *Drugs, the U.S., and Khan Sa*. Bangkok: Editions Duang Kamol, 1989.

Brown, John M.G. *Rice Paddy Grunt: Unfading Memories of the Vietnam Generation*. Lake Bluff, Illinois: Regnery Books, 1986.

Chanda, Nayan. *Brother Enemy*. New York: Harcourt Brace, Jovanovich, 1986.

Colby, William Egan. *Honorable Men: My Life in the CIA*. New York: Simon and Schuster, 1978.

Cruikshank, Charles. *Special Operations Executive in the Far East: The Official History*. Oxford: The University Press, 1983.

Emerson, Steven. *Secret Warriors: Inside the Covert Military Operations of the Reagan Era*. New York: G.P. Putnam's Sons, 1988.

Groom, Winston, and Duncan Spencer. *Conversations with the Enemy*. New York: Penguin Books, 1983.

Herrington, Stuart A. *Peace with Honor?* Navato, California: Presidio Books, 1983.

Kerdphol, General Saiyud (Former Supreme Commander of Thai Armed Forces: Counter-Insurgency, 1965-1985). *The Struggle for Thailand*. Bangkok: S. Research Center, 1986.

Kwitny, Jonathan, *The Crimes of Patriots: A True Tale of Dope, Diety Money, and the CIA*. New York: Norton, 1987.

Lawyers' Committee for Human Rights. *Cambodia*. New York, 1987.

Maas, Peter. *Manhunt*. New York: Random House, 1986.

McCoy, Alfred W., with Cathleen B. Read and Leonard P. Adams, III. *The Politics of Heroin in Southeast Asia*. New York: Harper and Row, 1972.

McDaniel, Eugene B., with James Johnson. *Scars and Stripes: The True Story of One Man's Courage in Facing Death as a Vietnam POW*. (Reprint of *Before Honor*. Philadelphia and New York: A.J. Holman, 1975.)

The National Security Archive. *The Chronology: The Documented Day-by-Day Account of the Secret Military Assistance to Iran and the Contras*. New York: Warner Books, 1987.

O'Daniel, Larry J. *Missing in Action: Trail of Deceit*. New Rochelle, N.Y.: Arlington House, 1979.

Ranelagh, John. *The Agency: The Rise and Decline of the CIA*. New York: Simon and Schuster, 1986.

Robbins, Christopher. *The Ravens*. New York: Crown, 1987.

Rosenblum, Mort. *Back Home: A Foreign Correspondent Rediscovers America*. New York: Morrow, 1989.

Royal Commission of Inquiry into the Activities of the Nugan Hand Group – Final Reports. 2 vols. Canberra: Australian Government Publishing Service, 1985.

Shawcross, William. *Quality of Mercy: Cambodia, Holocaust, and Modern Conscience*. New York: Simon and Schuster, 1984.

———. *Sideshow: Kissinger, Nixon and the Destruction of Cambodia*. New York: Simon and Schuster, 1979.

Snepp, Frank. *Decent Interval*. New York: Vintage, 1978.

Stevenson, William. *The Yellow Wind*. Cambridge, Mass.: Riverside Press, 1951.

Stockdale, Jim, and Sybil Stockdale. *In Love and War*. New York: Harper and Row, 1984.

Summers, Harry G., Jr. *Vietnam Almanac*. New York and Oxford: Facts on File, 1985.

Tower, John, Edmund Muskie, and Brent Scowcroft. *The Tower Commission Report: The Full Text of the President's Special Review Board*. Introduction by R.W. Apple, Jr. A New York Times Special. New York: Bantam Books and Times Books, 1987.

Turner, Stansfield. *Secrecy and Democracy: The CIA in Transition*. Boston: Houghton Mifflin, 1985.

INDEX